BANK AND FINANCIAL MARKET EFFICIENCY: GLOBAL PERSPECTIVES

RESEARCH IN BANKING AND FINANCE

Series Editors: Iftekhar Hasan and William C. Hunter

RESEARCH IN BANKING AND FINANCE VOLUME 5

BANK AND FINANCIAL MARKET EFFICIENCY: GLOBAL PERSPECTIVES

EDITED BY

IFTEKHAR HASAN

Rensselaer Polytechnic Institute, USA

WILLIAM C. HUNTER

University of Connecticut, USA

2004

ELSEVIER

JAI

Amsterdam – Boston – Heidelberg – London – New York – Oxford – Paris
San Diego – San Francisco – Singapore – Sydney – Tokyo

ELSEVIER B.V.
Sara Burgerhartstraat 25
P.O. Box 211,
1000 AE Amsterdam
The Netherlands

ELSEVIER Inc.
525 B Street, Suite 1900
San Diego,
CA 92101-4495
USA

ELSEVIER Ltd
The Boulevard, Langford Lane Kidlington,
Oxford OX5 1GB
UK

ELSEVIER Ltd
84 Theobalds Road
London
WC1X 8RR
UK

First edition 2004

Library of Congress Cataloging in Publication Data
A catalog record is available from the Library of Congress.

British Library Cataloguing in Publication Data
A catalogue record is available from the British Library.

ISBN: 0-7623-1099-5
ISSN: 1567-7915 (Series)

♾ The paper used in this publication meets the requirements of ANSI/NISO Z39.48-1992 (Permanence of Paper). Printed in The Netherlands.

CONTENTS

LIST OF CONTRIBUTORS

Farhad Ameen	Department of Behavioral/Social Sciences, SUNY/Westchester Community College, New York, USA
Asokan Anandarajan	New Jersey Institute of Technology, Newark, USA
A. Sinan Cebenoyan	Department of Finance, Hofstra University, New York, USA
Fatma Cebenoyan	Department of Economics, Hunter College, City University of New York, USA
Sungho Choi	Lally School of Management and Technology, Rensselaer Polytechnic Institute, New York, USA
S. Young Chung	Hyundai Research Institute, S. Korea
Elizabeth S. Cooperman	University of Colorado at Denver, Colorado, USA
Omer Demirel	King Fahd University of Petroleum and Minerals
Gerald P. Dwyer, Jr.	Federal Reserve Bank of Atlanta, Atlanta, USA
Paul Evans	Economics Department, Ohio State University, Columbus Ohio, USA
Rifat Gorener	Lally School of Management and Technology, Rensselaer Polytechnic Institute, New York, USA
Gautam Goswami	Graduate School of Business, Fordham University, New York, USA
R. W. Hafer	Department of Economics and Finance, Southern Illinois University – Edwardsville, Illinois, USA
Tanweer Hasan	School of Finance and Financial Services, Roosevelt University, USA

David Hossain	Department of Accounting, California State University-Los Angeles, USA
Sung-Chang Jung	College of Business Administration, Chonnam National University, S. Korea
Wares Karim	Faculty of Commerce and Administration Victoria University of Wellington, New Zealand
Halil Kiymaz	Department of Finance, University of Houston – Clear Lake, Texas, USA
Mohamed Nurullah	Glasgow Caledonian University, Glasgow, UK
James P. Murtagh	Lally School of Management and Technology, Rensselaer Polytechnic Institute, New York, USA
John R. Norsworthy	Lally School of Management and Technology, Rensselaer Polytechnic Institute, New York, USA
Mahendra Raj	Aberdeen Business School, Robert Gordon University, Aberdeen, UK
Charles A. Register	Department of Economics, Florida Atlantic University, Florida, USA
Uygar Urganci	Nestle S.A.
Victor E. Vaugirard	University of Paris at Sorbonne, France

INTRODUCTION☆

This volume consists of three groups of papers. The first seeks to identify the determinants of *monetary and bank efficiency* and the key factors that contribute to successful monetary and banking operations. The contributions provide evidence on monetary and bank efficiency drawing on our rich historical experiences and as well as from forward looking perspectives. The second set of papers seeks to increase our understanding of the institutional factors that enhance or detract from the efficient manner in which markets work. These papers also examine the linkage between various macro economic variables and *market efficiency*. Taking market efficiency as a reasonable approximation to reality, the final group of papers provides insights into *stock valuation* and *optimum portfolio selection*.

MONETARY AND BANK EFFICIENCY

With respect to improving monetary and bank operating and productive efficiency, several papers in this volume present innovative analyses from both the historical and forward-looking perspectives. The paper by Paul Evans examines the efficiency issue from a historical and macro perspective. He examines the monetary collapse in the U.S. in the first half of the twentieth century and provides a solution that would have avoided the collapse and crisis. His findings clearly have policy implications for the conduct of monetary policy today. He concludes that changes in the level of demand deposits between 1922 and 1941 stemmed primarily from changes in Federal Reserve policy. Because the public treated demand deposits as a shock-absorbing buffer stock, changes in demand deposits produced changes in output without an intervening change in interest rates. His data suggests that if the Federal Reserve had increased reserves as rapidly from 1928 to 1933 as it had in the previous six years, and if it had acted as an effective lender of last resort, there would have been no monetary collapse.

Victor Vaughan examines international transmission of bank runs through informational channels using a third-generation model of financial crises. Bank short-term liabilities include loans granted by foreign creditors who have noisy

☆ The editors thank Xian Sun and Mingming Zhou for editorial assistance.

information about the liquidation costs of illiquid bank assets. A banking panic in a country induces lenders to downgrade early-liquidation yields in other countries, and thus, to bid lower prices to buy new debt. As a result, banks become more illiquid and are therefore more prone to self-fulfilling depositor's runs. Contagion intensity stems from the degree of correlation between yields across countries and the strength of the Bayesian reassessment of the premature-liquidation yield in the catalyst country.

The paper by Dwyer and Hafer examine the characteristics of banks that fail during episodes of banking panics. The authors provide insights into factors that contribute to bank failure by estimating the ex ante riskiness of a bank's portfolio. They examine the riskiness of portfolios relative to mean-variance frontiers and by examining leverage and notes relative to assets. The ex ante riskiness of a bank's portfolio is found to help predict which banks fail during a banking panic. The authors find that the ex ante variability of returns on a bank's portfolio consistently helps in predicting its fate. Furthermore, a bank's exposure to runs on notes is associated with a higher likelihood of failure and there is a clear association between a bank's mean return on its portfolio well before the on set of panics and the final outcomes. While the evidence in this paper is based on a fairly typical banking panic, the data examined is very unique relative to extant studies.

The paper by Cebenoyan, Cebenoyan, Cooperman, and Register examine the link between ownership structure and firm operating inefficiency, capital adequacy, risk, and return. The Bank for International Settlements is currently preparing the revised Basel Accord to improve the control of financial institution risk, including a focus on operational risk and the effect of corporate governance factors on risk. This paper examines the effect of ownership structure on operating inefficiency, as a proxy for operational risk, along with other risk and performance measures for U.S. thrifts operating in 1989–1994. The results suggest a very significant effect of ownership structure on thrift operating inefficiency and other performance and risk measures, implying that ownership structure should be an important regulatory concern. By using managerial cost inefficiency as a potential indicator of operational risk, the paper provides a link between ownership structure (as a corporate governance mechanism) and other risk and performance measures. In sum, the results of this article provide support for the proposition that corporate governance may and possibly should be made part of a regulatory framework.

Anandarajan and Hossain examine issues relating to bank performance in the Indian economy. Using a model developed by Ahmed, Takeda and Thomas, they find that during the time since Indian banks were allowed to participate in the stock market in 1994, bank managers have focused on earnings management to reduce perceptions of risk and maintain high stock prices. The findings indicate that reported earnings in the banking industry may not reflect the true economic reality underlying the numbers. The paper by Ameen also examines bank performance but concentrates on micro-credit banks in Bangladesh. His paper contributes by examining characteristics of loan defaulters – evaluating the significance of borrower's gender, opportunity cost of time, incentives, and ability in explaining variations in loan repayment rates in the Grameen Bank. A particularly significant result is that variations in opportunity costs have differing impacts on default rates between men and women. The main finding is that increases in a borrower's opportunity cost of time has a negative effect on repayment rates, and women have better repayment rates since they have lower opportunity costs of time. Ameen suggests that this may be because women have fewer economic opportunities in rural Bangladesh due to social and economic constraints. His finding that gender differences influence repayment should provide insight for banks to improve the quality of their performing assets.

While the afore-mentioned papers all take a historical perspective, Mohamed Nurullah takes a forward looking perspective. He examines the future of banks and predicts that banks will continue to engage in insurance activities. Because of the development of e-business, he concludes that banks in the future will no longer look like traditional banks. He predicts that banks will become "one-stop" shopping centers for all financial services and products. In essence, this paper analyzes developments over the past two decades and is set against the background of the broader structural changes that have taken place in national, regional and global banking markets. Five particularly important issues are reviewed: effects on different entry modes of banc assurance, risk and return effects of banks as well as insurance companies, the benefits of banc assurance with particular reference to economies of scale and economies of scope, shareholders wealth effects, and the effects on regulation and supervision.

MARKET EFFICIENCY

Regarding market efficiency, the paper by Tanweer Hasan and Wares Karim examines the issue from a macroeconomic angle looking at how government philosophy influences informational efficiency. On the other hand, the paper by Choi and Murtagh focus on how governmental intervention is impounded in stock prices. Goswami, Gung and Chung investigate whether macroeconomic variables that are related to stock prices in the United States also have a similar relationship in a vastly different cultural climate such as Korea.

Hasan and Karim investigate whether the removal of apartheid has had any impact on the state of informational efficiency of the South African equity market. The authors conduct their analysis by analyzing three sub periods – an apartheid period, a transition period, and a post-apartheid period. Overall, the results indicate that the state of informational efficiency in the South African equity market substantially improved during the transition and post-apartheid periods compared to the apartheid period. In their paper, Choi and Murtagh investigate market reaction to announcements of mergers and acquisitions (M&A) and the potential impact associated with government intervention (in the form of seal of approval) in the M&A process. They focus on five failed Korean banks in 1998. This paper does not find any value of the government seal of approval in South Korean failed bank mergers. In another study of efficiency in Korea, Goswami, Jung and Chung examine the short-run dynamics and the long term relationships between stock prices and six macroeconomic variables of the Korean economy using a vector error correction model. The results indicate that the long-term relationships between stock prices and the macroeconomic factors in Korea are similar to those found in the U.S. and Japan.

STOCK VALUATION AND PORTFOLIO SELECTION

With respect to the issue of stock valuation and portfolio selection, the paper by Raj sheds insight into the market for corporate control and discusses both the undervaluation of stocks and the criteria that potential buyers should consider. The paper analyses the relation between bidder returns and the acquisition of undervalued targets. Undervaluation is measured using valuation ratios, e.g. price-earnings and market-to-book ratios. The results show that bidding-firm stock returns are significantly positive in the period around the announcement of an acquisition of an undervalued firm. The paper also finds that the bid premium in these deals is lower than that in a control sample and that a relatively large number of bidders pay for the deal with their own shares. The study also sheds some light into the market for corporate control. The market is able to identify takeovers driven by the undervaluation phenomenon and accordingly impounds this information into the bidders' stock price. In the case of undervalued acquisitions, it is reported that the bidder may have a dominant position as evidenced by the greater use of share payments. Hence, it is in the interest of managements and shareholders to take account of these aspects in merger transactions.

Gorener, Demirel and Norsworthy provide a model for testing various investment strategies for portfolio selection and turnover, arbitrage, and risk management techniques. Their results suggest that their methods are sufficiently robust to justify their use in simulation tests when examining alternative investment portfolios. The final paper in this volume by Kiymaz and Urganci investigates the impact of foreign direct investment on Turkish stocks. The authors find the presence of a strong relationship between net foreign purchases of Turkish stocks and the Istanbul Stock Exchange Index returns. The evidence suggests that net foreign purchases influence industry portfolios differently. For example, in the case of three of the portfolios considered, a negative correlation is found between return and foreign purchases while the other remaining twelve portfolios exhibit a positive relationship between return and net foreign purchases.

In summary, the papers included in this volume exhibit both breath and depth and should be particularly interesting to investors, academicians and regulators.

Iftekar Hasan
William Curt Hunter
Editors

MONETARY COLLAPSE DURING THE GREAT DEPRESSION: DID THE STOCK OF MONEY FALL, OR WAS IT PUSHED?

Paul Evans

ABSTRACT

Demand deposits changed over the interwar period primarily because of Federal Reserve policy and because of changes in the incentives and opportunities facing banks and their loan customers. Because the public treated demand deposits as a shock-absorbing buffer stock, changes in demand deposits produced changes in output without an intervening change in interest rates. The empirical analysis suggests that no monetary collapse would have taken place if the Federal Reserve had increased reserves as rapidly from 1928 to 1933 as it had in the previous six years and if it had acted as an effective lender of last resort.

1. INTRODUCTION

There are two widely held views of why the U.S. stock of money collapsed between 1929 and 1933. In the first view, which Temin (1976) has taken, the money stock passively responded to money demand, which fell because falling autonomous spending forced output and the price level to fall. The collapse of the banking

Bank and Financial Market Efficiency: Global Perspectives
Research in Banking and Finance, Volume 5, 1–19

ISSN: 1567-7915/doi:10.1016/S1567-7915(04)05001-3

system was how the money stock fell; it would have fallen just as much even if the Federal Reserve had prevented the collapse of the banking system. In the second view, which Friedman and Schwartz (1963) have taken, the money stock fell because the Federal Reserve provided insufficient reserves to the banks and did not serve as an effective lender of last resort. The falling money stock forced output and the price level to fall so that money demand could eventually be equated to money supply.

This paper tests these views empirically, using monthly data that span the period 1922–1941. It finds little evidence that the demand deposit component of the money stock responded passively to demand. Rather, Federal Reserve policy and the behavior of banks and their loan customers apparently determined the stock of demand deposits, which the public treated as a buffer *a la* Starleaf (1970), Darby (1972), Carr and Darby (1981), Judd and Scadding (1981, 1982), Coats (1982), Judd (1983) and Laidler (1984). In addition, the paper finds that the 1929–1933 monetary collapse and the Great Depression would not have occurred, had the Federal Reserve increased reserves at a reasonable rate and acted as an effective lender of last resort.

The paper has the following structure. Section 2 lays out two simple models of how the stock of demand deposits is determined. They imply different correlations between demand deposits and other economic variables and are therefore potentially distinguishable using time-series techniques. Section 3 describes the data used in the analysis. Section 4 uses vector autoregressions fitted to these data to decide which of the models better explains the U.S. experience during the sample period 1922–1941. Section 5 then uses the fitted vector autoregressions to predict how demand deposits would have evolved between 1928 and 1933 if reserves had grown at the same rate they grew in the previous six years and if the Federal Reserve had served as an effective lender of last resort. Finally, Section 6 draws some conclusions.

2. MODELS OF DEMAND DEPOSITS

In this section, we lay out and discuss two very simple models of the short-run determination of the stock of demand deposits.[1] The first, which we term the conventional model,[2] assumes that the public always holds exactly the demand deposits it wants. The second, which we term the buffer-stock model, assumes that the public does not always hold the demand deposits it would want to hold, were it costless to adjust all of its asset stocks instantaneously. In other words, the public treats demand deposits as a buffer that absorbs some of the shocks it experiences. We show below that these models imply different short-run determinants for demand deposits and hence different explanations for the monetary collapse of the Great Depression.

2.1. The Conventional Model

Banks issue demand deposits that pay interest at the rate Z. They fix Z in the short run at the level Z* and then passively accept whatever demand deposits the public may choose to hold.[3] The supply of deposits is therefore infinitely elastic at

$$Z = Z^*. \tag{1}$$

The public holds demand deposits according to the equation

$$D^d = D(\underset{+}{Y}, \underset{+}{P}, \underset{-}{I}, \underset{+}{Z}, \underset{+}{UD}) \tag{2}$$

where Y is a vector of current and past outputs, P is a vector of current and past price levels, I is a vector of current and past open-market interest rates, UD is an error term, and the sign below each argument indicates the sign of D's derivative with respect to each entry of that argument. The form of (2) is completely conventional, having the properties that Laidler (1977) has shown characterized money-demand functions.

In equilibrium, the stocks of demand deposits supplied and demanded are equated, and each equals the observed demand-deposit stock D. Therefore, at each moment,

$$D = D(\underset{+}{Y}, \underset{+}{P}, \underset{-}{I}, \underset{+}{Z^*}, \underset{+}{UD}) \tag{3}$$

In this model, the stock of demand deposits depends solely on Y, P, I, Z and UD. Therefore, according to this model, demand deposits must have fallen over the period 1929–1933 because output, the price level and autonomous money demand fell during the period. The reason is that open-market interest rates also fell, thereby tending to raise demand deposits above the level that would otherwise have prevailed. In other words, Y, P, Z and UD must actually have contributed more that 100% to the fall. That many banks failed and that reserves also fell over the period is completely irrelevant for explaining the collapse in demand deposits.[4]

2.2. The Buffer-Stock Model[5]

The balance-sheet identity of the banks implies that one can describe how demand deposits evolve over time if one can describe how the other items on the balance sheet evolve. In this subsection, we lay out a simple model of the evolution of two stocks, reserves and "loans," which sum to the stock of demand deposits.

The loan stock as defined here is a composite asset that includes not only what is commonly called loans but also many other balance-sheet items. In adopting this definition, we are not merely simplifying the exposition but also assuming that one can indeed describe the composite asset without explaining its components separately.

The legal restrictions imposed on banks induce a demand for reserves of the form[6]

$$R^d = F(\underset{-}{MCF}, \underset{+}{D}, \underset{+}{RR}, \underset{+}{UR}), \tag{4}$$

where MCF is the marginal cost of funds to the banks, RR is the legal reserve ratio imposed on banks and UR is an error term. The reserve stock demanded falls as MCF rises because MCF is the marginal cost of obtaining funds to hold as reserves. In addition, the reserve ratio is high enough to impose a binding constraint on bank behavior.

In equilibrium, the reserve stock demanded equals the reserve stock supplied, and each equals the observed stock R so that F(MCR, D, RR, UR) = R. Solving this equation for MCF yields an equation of the form

$$MCF = C(\underset{-}{R}, \underset{+}{D}, \underset{+}{RR}, \underset{+}{UR}). \tag{5}$$

Banks face a marginal cost MCF of obtaining funds to lend, a marginal cost MCI of intermediation, and a marginal cost MCD of default risk. Competition drives banks to lend on terms that yield MCF + MCI + MCD. This total exceeds the explicit lending rate of the banks by the shadow costs incurred by loan customers in complying with the collateral, equity and quantitative restrictions that banks impose in order to mitigate moral hazard and adverse selection.[7] For this reason, one cannot readily measure MCF + MCI + MCD.

Loan customers borrow more, the lower MCF + MCI + MCD is. Furthermore, the more profitable the projects available to the loan customers appear to be, the more they want to borrow and the lower the banks will estimate MCD to be. We therefore assume that the stock of loans outstanding takes the form[8]

$$L = L(\underset{-}{MCF + MCI}, \underset{+}{X}, \underset{+}{UL}), \tag{6}$$

where UL is an error term and X is a vector of observable variables that are systematically related to how profitable the projects will be. For example, X could include as entries current and past outputs and price levels. Note that MCD, which is a function of X, is absorbed into the function L(•).

In formulating (6), we have implicitly assumed that loans and open-market securities are imperfect substitutes. This assumption makes the loan stock determinant and allows MCF + MCI to differ from the yield on riskless open-market securities. For this reason, monetary policy (MCF), internal bank cost conditions (MCI), and bank and loan-customer expectations (X) can affect the loan stock without necessarily affecting open-market interest rates.[9]

The balance-sheet identity together with Eqs (5) and (6) imply that

$$\mathrm{D} = \mathrm{R} + \mathrm{L}(\mathrm{C}(\mathrm{R}, \mathrm{D}, \mathrm{RR}, \mathrm{UR}), \mathrm{X}, \mathrm{UL}).$$

Solving this equation for D then yields an equation of the form

$$\mathrm{D} = \mathrm{H}(\underset{+}{\mathrm{R}}, \underset{-}{\mathrm{RR}}, \underset{-}{\mathrm{MCI}}, \underset{+}{\mathrm{X}}, \underset{-}{\mathrm{UR}}, \underset{+}{\mathrm{UL}}). \tag{7}$$

According to Eq. (7), the demand deposit stock depends on variables that affect the reserve-holding and lending behavior of the banks and the borrowing behavior of their loan customers, including Federal Reserve policy. Monetary policy can therefore produce collapsing demand deposits without necessarily raising open-market interest rates. It is not obvious, then, that stock of demand deposits fell primarily because of the declining economy.

2.3. The Transmission Mechanism and Dynamics

In the conventional model, the public is always holding the demand deposits it wants to hold. Furthermore, there are numerous financial markets subject to no important frictions. Interest rates are therefore the only quantitatively important linkages between the financial sector and the real sector.[10] To be specific, aggregate demand takes the form

$$\mathrm{A} = \mathrm{A}(\mathrm{Y}, \mathrm{P}, \mathrm{I}, \mathrm{UA}), \tag{8}$$

where UA is an error term.

In the buffer-stock model, the public is willing in the short run to hold a wide range of stock of demand deposits without any actions that would force quantitatively important changes in open-market interest rates.[11] Consequently, the stock of demand deposits is determined at each instant by Federal Reserve policy, by bank reserve-holding and lending behavior, and by loan-customer borrowing behavior. Therefore, at each instant, there is generally either an excess demand or an excess supply of demand deposits, where we define the demand for demand deposits to be the average stock that the public would want to hold over a long period of time, given the prevailing output, price level, open-market interest rate, stochastic environment, etc. Maximizing agents then condition other decisions on these (positive or negative) excess supplies, which are essentially predetermined to each agent at each instant. One would therefore expect aggregate demand to depend not only on Y, P, I and UA as in (8) above, but also on ESD, the excess supply of demand deposits[12] defined by

$$\mathrm{ESD} = \mathrm{D} - \mathrm{D(Y, P, I, Z, UD)}.$$

Our formulation of the buffer-stock model also suggests that many interest rates relevant to spending decisions are not observable in open markets. For example, open-market interest rates may not accurately measure MCF, the influence of monetary policy on banks, or MCF + MCI, the marginal cost of (riskless) borrowing from the banks. Therefore, to the extent that the stock of demand deposits proxies for MCF + MCI, aggregate demand will seem to depend on D as well as Y, P and I.

Dynamics are difficult to model, especially if one takes proper account of the Lucas critique. For this reason, we adopt the simplest dynamic specification possible:

$$y_{t+1} - y_t = k(A_t - y_t) \tag{9}$$

where y is current output, t is an index of time and k is a positive constant. According to Eq. (9), producers raise production by an amount proportional to the excess of aggregate demand over production. Equation (9) combined with the conventional model implies that output depends on past values of Y, P and I. In contrast, output will also appear to depend on past values of D if Eq. (9) is combined with the aggregate demand formulation suggested by the buffer-stock model. In that formulation, aggregate demand is increasing in the excess supply of demand deposits and decreasing in the marginal cost of funds to the banks and the marginal cost of bank intermediation.

2.4. *Testable Implications of the Two Models*

The conventional model – Eq. (3) – implies that, if one takes proper account of current and past outputs, price levels and open-market interest rates, demand deposits are not correlated with such variables as the marginal cost of intermediation, the legal reserve ratio and the reserve stock unless the error term UD is correlated with these variables. Even though UD may well be correlated with the marginal cost of intermediation and the reserve stock, it is unlikely to be correlated with the legal reserve ratio. The reason is that the Federal Reserve probably did not change this administered policy variable in response to UD. Therefore, if one should find strong correlations with the "supply-side" variables and much weaker correlations with the "demand side" variables, one can reject the conventional model.

The conventional model also implies that there should be no correlation between current output and past demand deposits, conditional on past open-market interest rates, outputs and price levels.

In contrast, the buffer-stock model – Eq. (7) – implies that the marginal cost of intermediation, the reserve stock and the legal reserve ratio should be correlated with demand deposits. Moreover, this model permits current output to be strongly correlated with past demand deposits even conditional on past outputs, price levels and interest rates.

In the next two sections, we discuss the data that we use for distinguishing between the two models and then examine the correlations among these data.

3. THE DATA[13]

The data used in the empirical analysis span the period 1921–1941 and are monthly. The variable that we wish to explain is Friedman and Schwartz's (1970) measure of demand deposits. We consider two groups of explanatory variables. The first consists of the Federal Reserve's industrial production index, the Conference Board's cost of living index and the 4–6 month commercial paper rate. They proxy for what the conventional model suggests are the most important determinants of demand deposits: output, the price level and the interest rate on open-market securities. The second group includes the legal reserve ratio of central reserve city banks, Friedman and Schwartz's (1963) measure of reserves, a measure of the failure rate of commercial banks,[14] and the price of gold. Except for the last variable, they proxy for what the buffer stock model suggests are important determinants of demand deposits. Specifically, the first two proxy for R and RR; and the failure rate proxies for MCI, the marginal cost of intermediation. Banks assess, monitor and police loans and acquire and service deposits. The marginal cost at which they can carry out these activities depends on the amount of expertise that they can bring to these activities and on the quality of the relationships that they have built up with loan and deposit customers. Panics and bank runs partly destroy the productivity of expertise and customer relationships, thereby raising the marginal cost of intermediation.[15] For this reason, the bank failure rate proxies for MCI. Unfortunately, it may also proxy for Z, the expected yield on demand deposits. The higher the failure rate is, the lower Z is and hence the less attractive demand deposits are. Therefore, a negative relationship between the bank failure rate and demand deposits does not unambiguously distinguish between the conventional model and the buffer-stock model.

Neither model suggests that the dollar price of gold is an important determinant of demand deposits. We have included it solely because it powerfully influenced industrial production and the cost of living.[16] The government administered the legal reserve ratio and the price of gold, keeping them constant for appreciable periods of time and changing them when and as it pleased. These policy variables may have responded with lags to stochastic economic variables (for example, to the stocks of bank reserves and gold). Nevertheless, to simplify my empirical analysis, we have treated them as if they are exogenous nonstochastic variables.

4. EMPIRICAL FINDINGS[17]

If demand deposits are a buffer stock, and if the marginal cost of funds to the banks and the marginal cost of borrowing from the banks are as difficult to measure as we think they are, one cannot successfully estimate either the structure of the financial sector or the linkages of that sector to the real sector. One must therefore use some other technique.

We use vector autoregressions to investigate the issues raised in Sections 1 and 2. This technique enables some structural conclusions to be drawn even though we have estimated no explicitly structural equations.[18] Although a structural model would permit much more informative conclusions, those that we do draw directly address the issues under consideration. We fitted the system of vector autoregressions to six stochastic variables and two exogenous nonstochastic variables. The six stochastic variables are the failure rate (FR), the commercial paper rate (CPR), the logarithm of the industrial production index (LIP), the logarithm of the cost of living index (LCOL), the logarithm of reserves (LR), and the logarithm of demand deposits (LDD). The two nonstochastic variables are the legal reserve ratio (RR), and the logarithm of the price of gold (LPG). In addition, each vector autoregression includes a constant term, a dummy variable for the bank holiday in March 1933,[19] eleven seasonal dummy variables,[20] and a time trend. The sample period over which we fitted the vector autoregression is January 1922 to December 1941, a period including 240 observations.[21] The vector autoregressions that we report in this paper include 8 lagged values of the 6 stochastic variables; the current value of RR; the current and 2 lagged values of LPG; a constant term; a time trend; and 12 dummy variables – for a total 82 right-hand side variables. We arrived at this form for the vector autoregressions after considerable experimentation. To be specific, we found that some of the regressions lose significant explanatory power with shorter lag lengths and none gain significant explanatory power with longer lag lengths. In any case, all lag lengths longer than three give similar results. Additional lagged values of RR and LPG contributed no significant explanatory power to the system of vector autoregressions.

Table 1. Marginal Significance Level for Excluding Each Variable from Each Vector Autoregression.

Independent Variables	Dependent Variables					
	FR	CPR	LIP	LCOL	LR	LDD
FR	0.38	0.00	0.00	0.15	0.00	0.03
CPR	0.00	0.00	0.00	0.10	0.07	0.92
LIP	0.53	0.19	0.00	0.01	0.34	0.13
LCOL	0.11	0.73	0.04	0.00	0.25	0.25
LR	0.84	0.97	0.14	0.47	0.00	0.01
LDD	0.43	0.84	0.00	0.11	0.11	0.00
RR	0.18	0.69	0.28	0.32	0.66	0.00
LPG	0.16	0.67	0.00	0.00	0.00	0.04

Because 82 is a large number and because there are 6 vector autoregressions, it is not sensible to provide a full description of our results. We therefore provide only the marginal significance levels of the F statistics for excluding each variable from each vector autoregression and some discussion of the individual coefficients.

Table 1, which provides the marginal significance levels for excluding the row variable from the column vector autoregression, has two important implications. First, past values of industrial production, the cost of living and especially the commercial paper rate have little explanatory power for current demand deposits.[22] In contrast, the legal reserve ratio, past failure rates and past reserves have highly significant effects on current demand deposits. To conclude, then, the variables that the buffer-stock model suggests are important are in fact important, but the variables that the conventional model suggests are important are not.

Second, industrial production is highly significantly associated with past demand deposits.[23] This association is inconsistent with the conventional model. Examining the individual coefficients from the LDD and the LIP regressions reinforces the evidence against the conventional model and for the buffer-stock model. In the regression for LDD, only one of the twenty-four estimated coefficients on CPR, LIP and LCOL is statistically significant at the 0.05 level and only COL's coefficient sum is significant.[24] On the other hand, many of the coefficients on FR, LR and RR are significant as are the coefficient sums −4.29 (1.84), 0.106 (0.026) and −0.00292 (0.00077). The signs of these sums seem to be consistent with the buffer-stock model. In the regression for LIP, LDD lagged one month enters with the highly significant coefficient 0.355 (0.145), which is again highly significant. The positive sum for LDD's coefficients is much more consistent with the buffer-stock model in which demand deposits proxy for the excess supply of demand deposits and for the marginal cost of borrowing from the banks than with the conventional model in which observable open-market interest rates are the only important linkage between the financial sector and the real sector.

The conventional model does not unambiguously rule out an association between past reserves and current demand deposits. The reason is that past reserves can be correlated with the error term UD in the demand function for demand deposits. For example, UD can be serially correlated and its past realizations might have influenced the reserves then held by banks. What the model does rule out is any correlation with an exogenous variable like the legal reserve ratio. Given past values of the commercial paper rate, industrial production and the cost of living, this variable should not affect demand deposits.

A negative association between past failure rates and current demand deposits is also consistent with the conventional model because Z is decreasing in the expected failure rate. If, however, the only important linkage between the financial sector and the real sector is through open-market interest rates – a proposition that is part of the conventional view – current industrial production should not be correlated with past failure rates, given past values of industrial production, the cost of living and the commercial paper rate. In fact, there is a highly significant negative association. To the extent that the failure rate as well as the stock of demand deposits proxies for the marginal cost of borrowing from the banks, this finding is consistent with the buffer-stock model.

Table 2 reports the contemporaneous correlations of the residuals from the regressions for FR, CPR, LIP, LCOL, LR and LDD. The correlations of the LDD residuals with the CPR, LIP and LCOL residuals support the conventional model. They have the right signs, and two are highly significant. The buffer-stock model, however, is at least as consistent with the correlations in Table 2. The LDD residuals are highly correlated with the FR and LR residuals, and the signs of these correlations are those predicted by the buffer-stock model. Furthermore, the correlation with the LR residuals is substantially larger than those with the CPR, LIP and LCOL residuals. Finally, if X, the vector of observable variables

Table 2. Contemporaneous Correlation Matrix of the Residuals.

	CPR	LIP	LCOL	LR	LDD
FR	0.248**	0.156*	−0.075	−0.002	−0.169**
CPR		0.050	0.029	−0.188**	−0.169**
LIP			0.096	0.107	0.232**
LCOL				−0.037	0.117
LR					0.438**

*Statistically significant at the 0.05 level.

**Statistically significant at the 0.01 level.

Table 3. Variance Decompositions of LDD at Various Lead Times.

Lead Time in Months	% of Variance Due to Innovations in					
	FR	CPR	LIP	LCOL	LR	LDD
1	3	2	5	1	16	73
2	3	2	9	1	16	69
3	4	1	12	2	16	65
4	6	2	14	1	14	63
5	8	2	14	1	14	31
6	9	2	13	2	15	59
9	13	1	12	4	17	53
12	15	2	12	5	20	46
18	18	8	11	6	26	31
24	19	15	10	7	28	21
36	21	21	9	7	30	12
48	21	22	8	7	30	12

systematically related to profitability, includes Y, P and I, the evidence adduced above for the conventional model is also consistent with the buffer-stock model.

Table 3 presents some variance decompositions for LDD. The last six columns of the table report the percent of LDD's forecast variance due to the innovations in each of the six stochastic variables in the vector autoregressions that we have fitted. The lead times for these forecasts appear in the first column. In calculating this decomposition, the ordering of the variables is important because the variables ordered before a particular variable receive all the credit for its correlations with them. In other words, they are considered to be exogenous vis-à-vis this variable. We impose the ordering (FR, CPR, LIP, LCOL, LR, LDD). We have ordered FR first because banks fail in a given month primarily because of reverses suffered over a considerable period prior to that month. Consequently, the contemporaneous correlations between the failure rate and other variables should primarily reflect the effects of the failure rate on these variables over the one-month sampling interval. CPR comes next because the *Federal Reserve Bulletins* published during the sample period strongly suggest that the Federal Reserve tried to stabilize short-term, open-market interest rates for periods lasting at least a month.[25] This policy made CPR approximately exogenous vis-à-vis the other variables in the model. LIP and LCOL come next so that these variables can affect LDD as much as possible. The commercial paper rate and the industrial production index are monthly averages, and the cost of living was measured near the middle of each month. In contrast, reserves and demand deposits are end-of-month data. It is therefore reasonable to order LR and LDD after CPR, LIP and LCOL. Finally, ordering LR before LDD gives LR as much scope as possible to affect LDD.

Table 4. Alternative Variance Decompositions of LDD.

Lead Times in Months	% of Variance Due to Innovations in[a]	
	LDD	LR
1	89	0
2	85	0
3	81	0
4	77	0
5	75	0
6	74	0
9	69	1
12	63	3
18	48	8
24	37	13
36	21	20
48	16	25

[a] Only the columns for LDD and LR appear in this table. The other columns would simply duplicate those of Table 3.

The figures in Table 3 provide further evidence against the conventional model and for the buffer-stock model. The innovations to variables that are important in the conventional model (CPR, LIP and LCOL) never contribute as much to LDD's forecast variance as the innovations to the variables that are important in the buffer-stock model (LF and LR). For example, at long leads, the latter innovations

Table 5. Variance Decompositions of LIP at Several Lead Times.

Lead Time in Months	% of Variance Due to Innovations in					
	FR	CPR	LIP	LCOL	LR	LDD
1	2	1	97	0	0	0
2	2	2	94	0	0	1
3	2	2	92	0	0	4
4	3	2	86	0	0	8
5	3	3	79	1	0	14
6	4	4	71	1	1	19
9	7	8	53	2	2	28
12	9	12	43	2	3	31
18	10	18	35	2	6	29
24	12	21	29	3	11	24
36	15	22	23	5	17	18
48	17	23	19	6	19	16

contribute 52% of LDD's forecast variance while the former contribute only 37%. Moreover, the dominance is even greater at short lags.

Table 4 show that these conclusions are only somewhat weakened if LR is ordered after LDD, thereby minimizing its importance. Although LR's innovations uniformly contribute less to the forecast variance of LDD, they still contribute much at long leads.

Table 5 provides perhaps the strongest evidence against the conventional model and for the buffer-stock model. It show that past innovations in LF, LR and LDD can contribute as much as half of LIP's forecast variance. This fact is inconsistent with the conventional model, but perfectly consistent with the buffer-stock model.

5. AN EXPLANATION OF THE 1929–1933 MONETARY COLLAPSE

The empirical evidence of the previous section supports the buffer-stock model and gives one reason to think: (a) that open-market interest rates during the interwar period proxy poorly for the marginal cost of funds to the banks and for the marginal cost of borrowing from the banks; (b) that reserves and demand deposits proxy well for these variables; (c) that demand deposits can be in excess demand or supply in a meaningful sense; and (d) that aggregate demand is strongly related to the marginal cost of borrowing from the banks and/or the excess supply of demand deposits. If propositions (a)–(d) are valid, one can reasonably argue that a tight monetary policy combined with the failure of the Federal Reserve to serve as an effective lender of last resort acted as the push that led to monetary collapse during the Great Depression. This collapse in turn exacerbated the contraction in economic activity.

The first step in the argument is to show that the marginal cost of funds to the banks could well have remained high even though the commercial paper rate was drifting downward. Figure 1 provides the evidence for this assertion. The solid-line plots the actual path for reserves from January 1928 to March 1933, and the dashed line plots the path that reserves would have followed, had they grown each month at their average growth rate over the previous six years. The gap between the two widens fairly steadily.

According to Eq. (4), a likely way for this widening gap to have occurred is for MCF to have remained high, or even to have risen, over much of the period. In other words, a tight monetary policy produced the widening reserve gap. The second step is to claim that the bank runs sharply raised the marginal cost of intermediation. Combined with the high MCF, the high MCI spelled sharply reduced loans and a sharply increased marginal cost of borrowing from the banks. The former led demand deposits to collapse, and the latter depressed aggregate demand.

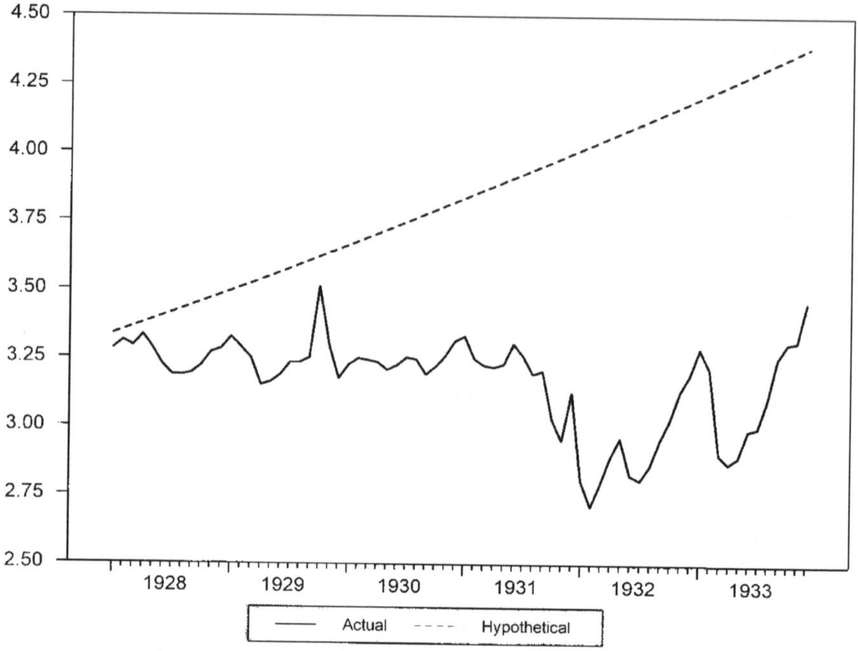

Fig. 1. Actual and Hypothetical Reserves.

The third step is to claim that the collapse in demand deposits generated excess demand for demand deposits, contributing further impetus to the fall in aggregate demand.

The fourth step is to note that depressed aggregate demand implied low profitability, less bank lending, less demand deposits, and still more downward pressure on aggregate demand.

The final step is to use the vector autoregressions discussed in the previous section to simulate what would have happened to demand deposits, had monetary policy as measured by reserves been no tighter than it was from December 1921 to December 1927[26] and had the Federal Reserve served as an effective lender of last resort, preventing the bank failure rate from exceeding its peak value before the bank runs. In this simulation, we assume that the vector autoregression describing CPR, LIP, LCOL and LDD and the innovations to these variables would not have changed appreciably, had this different monetary policy been pursued. We further assume that the ordering (FR, CPR, LIP, LCOL, LR, LDD) is appropriate. Because these assumptions are strong – especially the former one[27] – one should regard the simulations simply as evidence that the above explanation of the monetary

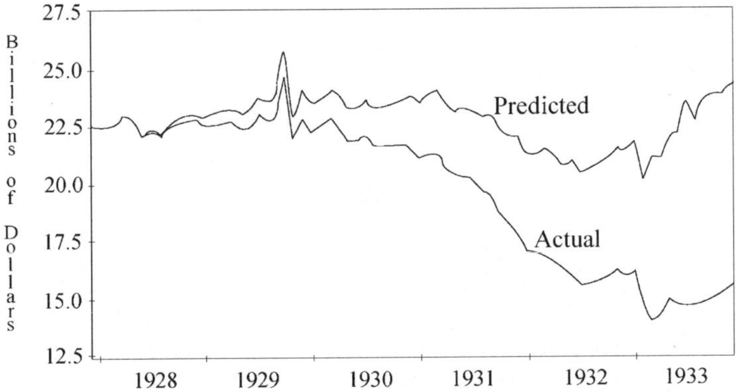

Fig. 2. Actual and Predicted Demand Deposits.

collapse is consistent with the data rather than as a claim that demand deposits would indeed have evolved as simulated. Figure 2 plots the actual and simulated paths of demand deposits over the period between January 1928 and March 1933. Clearly, demand deposits do not collapse along the simulated path as they do along the actual path. Therefore, tightness of monetary policy and the bank runs could well have precipitated monetary collapse during the Great Depression.

Note that, even with reserve growth at its average 1922–1927 rate and with an effective lender of last resort, demand deposits would apparently have stagnated between March 1930 and March 1931 and would then have drifted downward over the next two years. The reason is that this monetary policy would only have ameliorated the 1930–1933 contraction, not prevented it. Falling output and prices would still have depressed bank lending. To have prevented the Great Depression would apparently have required an active policy: e.g. injection reserves after the stock-market crash and devaluing with Britain between September and December 1931.[28]

6. CONCLUSIONS

This paper finds that changes in demand deposits between 1922 and 1941 stemmed primarily from changes in Federal Reserve policy and in the incentives and opportunities facing banks and their loan customers. Demand deposits responded weakly to changes in the incentives and opportunities facing the holders of demand deposits. The public treated demand deposits as a shock-absorbing buffer stock. Since the public was willing in a meaningful sense to be off its demand function for demand deposits, changes in demand deposits produced changes in output without first affecting open-market interest rates. Finally, the data suggest that, if the Federal Reserve had increased reserves as rapidly from 1928 to 1933 as it had in the previous six years and if it had acted as an effective lender of last resort, there would have been no monetary collapse.

NOTES

1. We assume throughout the theoretical analysis that the Federal Reserve supplies currency completely passively so that the currency stock always equals currency demand. With this assumption, we can abstract from currency. In the empirical sections, we also focus on demand deposits. The reason is that the monetary collapse of 1929–1933 was really a collapse of the demand deposit component of the money stock. Currency increased over the period. We have, however, obtained results similar to those reported in Sections 4 and 5 using in place of demand deposits each of the following: M1, total bank deposits and M2.
2. We call this model conventional because it is a simplified version of widely used macroeconomic models; e.g. the Federal Reserve Board's monthly money-market model. The conventional model has not always been widely enough used to deserve that appellation, however. Tobin (1963) once called it the "new view."
3. The analysis would apply equally well if the deposit interest rate were subject to a binding ceiling set by the government.
4. Of course, the bank failures and the fall in reserves could indirectly have affected D through Y, P, I or Z.
5. The model of this section is similar to Hetzel's (1982).
6. See Wallace (1982) for a demonstration that legal restrictions are the sine qua non for a positive, downward-sloping demand for the government's non-interest-bearing monetary liabilities.
7. Jaffee and Russell (1976) and Stiglitz and Weiss (1981) have emphasized that quantitative restrictions on loan contracts are important when information is imperfect.
8. If loan customers can borrow from securities markets as well as from the banks but do not regard the two forms of borrowing as perfect substitutes, the open-market interest rate will appear as an additional argument in L(•). For simplicity, we rule out this possibility.
9. See Brunner and Meltzer (1976) for further discussion of this issue.
10. See Tobin (1969) for some examples of such a model.
11. Judd (1983, pp. 39–41) and Laidler (1984) have justified this assumption. Kanniainen (1984) has provided a theoretical rationale for it.
12. See Judd and Scadding (1981) and Laidler (1984) for an extended discussion of this assumption.
13. These data are available from the author upon request.
14. The Federal Reserve has compiled monthly data on the average deposit level of suspended banks for each month between January 1921 and December 1936 and for each year between 1937 and 1941. (See the September 1937 and subsequent issues of the Federal Reserve Bulletin.) For the period January 1921 to December 1936, the failure rate is just the deposits in suspended banks for the given month divided by Friedman and Schwartz's measure of total commercial bank deposits in the previous month. Since monthly data are not available after December 1936, we calculated the failure rates for each month after that date

by dividing the average level of deposits in suspended banks for the entire year by deposits for the month prior to the observation month. Because the failure rate was essentially zero after 1936, interpolating in this manner is unlikely to have seriously affected my estimates.

15. Bernanke (1983) provides a more complete discussion of this issue.

16. For evidence, see Evans (1996) and Table 1.

17. See Sims (1980a) and Gordon and King (1982) for discussions of the techniques used in this section. See also Cooley and LeRoy (1983) for a critique of these techniques.

18. Of course, to obtain these conclusions, we must impose identifying restrictions. We believe that the ones we impose are more credible than those we should have to impose in order to estimate an explicitly structural model.

19. We include this dummy variable because the bank holiday severely distorted many of the series in March 1933.

20. Even though each series is supposedly nonseasonal or seasonally adjusted, many of the seasonal dummy variables were statistically significant at the 0.05 level.

21. FR is not available prior to January 1921. Allowing initial values for the regressions used up enough 1921 observations to make January 1922 the most attractive starting date. The terminal date occurs just before the mobilization for the World War II.

22. Sims (1980b), Gordon and Wilcox (1981) and Schwartz (1981) have obtained similar results for the M1 money stock.

23. Sims (1980b) and Gordon and Wilcox (1981) have obtained similar results for the M1 money stock.

24. The sum is 0.196 (0.074). Here as well as in the text, the figure in parentheses is the standard error.

25. Over the sample period, the *Bulletin* devoted much attention to monitoring and reporting "money-market conditions" and often credited the Federal Reserve for them. In contrast, no one in the Federal Reserve System even bothered to calculate and report monetary aggregates like M1 and M2. The column labeled CPR in Table 1 provides some quantitative evidence that the Federal Reserve prevented open-market interest rates from responding much to market forces over appreciable periods of time. Except for the failure rate, past values of the stochastic variables, which measure market forces, had no statistically significant effects on the commercial paper rate.

26. To be specific, we had reserves grow each month by 0.389556%. Of course, a constant growth rate for reserves is inconsistent in the long run with maintaining a fixed price of gold. Therefore, the government would eventually have had to devalue or revalue. We assume that this day of reckoning would have come well after 1933. This assumption may not be as unreasonable as it seems since the rest of the gold-standard (nascent dollar-standard) world would probably not have deflated or inflated much relative to the U.S.

27. See Lucas (1976) for a demonstration that changing policy regime can drastically alter vector autoregressions.

28. One simulation suggests that overlaying the policy described in the text with a one-time, permanent, 10% increase in reserves during November 1929 and with a devaluation between September and December 1931 matching Britain's would have converted the Great Depression into a mild recession ending in December 1930. Over the period between September 1929 and March 1933 when industrial production actually fell an average of 22% a year, the simulation indicates that industrial production would instead have grown 7% a year. Demand deposits would fairly consistently have grown 4.4% a year over the same period, thereby permitting this expansion to have occurred.

REFERENCES

Bernanke, B. S. (1983). Nonmonetary effects of the financial crisis in the propagation of the great depression. *American Economic Review*, *73*(June), 257–276.

Brunner, K., & Meltzer, A. H. (1976). An aggregative theory for a closed economy. In: J. Stein (Ed.), *Monetarism* (pp. 66–103). Amsterdam: North Holland.

Carr, J., & Darby, M. R. (1981). The role of money supply shocks in the short-run demand for money. *Journal of Monetary Economics*, *8*(September), 183–200.

Coats, W. W. (1982). Modeling the short-run demand for money with exogenous supply. *Economic Inquiry*, *20*(April), 222–239.

Cooley, T. F., & LeRoy, S. F. (1983). *A theoretical macroeconomics: A critique*. University of California, Santa Barbara (March).

Darby, M. R. (1972). The allocation of transitory income among consumers' assets. *American Economic Review*, *62*(December), 743–760.

Evans, P. (1996). An econometric analysis of the causes of the great depressions in the U.S. *Managerial Finance* (in press).

Friedman, M., & Schwartz, A. J. (1963). *Monetary history of the United States, 1876–1960*. Princeton, NJ: Princeton University Press for NBER.

Friedman, M., & Schwartz, A. J. (1970). *Monetary statistics of the United States*. New York: Columbia University Press for NBER.

Gordon, R. J., & King, S. (1982). The output cost of disinflation in traditional and vector autoregressive models. *Brookings Papers on Economic Activity*, *1*, 205–244.

Gordon, R. J., & Wilcox, J. A. (1981). Monetarist interpretations of the great depressions: An evaluation and critique. In: K. Brunner (Ed.), *The Great Depression Revisited* (pp. 49–107). Boston: Martinus Nijhoff.

Hetzel, R. L. (1982). The October 1979 regime of monetary control and the behavior of the money supply in 1980. *Journal of Money, Credit, and Banking*, *14*(May), 234–251.

Jaffee, D., & Russell, T. (1976). Imperfect information and credit rationing. *Quarterly Journal of Economics*, *90*(November), 651–666.

Judd, J. P. (1983). Deregulated deposit rates and monetary policy. *Federal Reserve Bank of San Francisco Economic Review* (Fall), 27–44.

Judd, J. P., & Scadding, J. L. (1981). Liability management, bank loans, and deposit 'market' disequilibrium. *Federal Reserve Bank of San Francisco Economic Review* (Summer), 21–44.

Judd, J. P., & Scadding, J. L. (1982). Dynamic adjustment in the demand for money: Tests of alternative hypotheses. *Federal Reserve Bank of San Francisco Economic Review* (Fall), 19–30.

Kanniainen, V. (1984). *On the shock-absorption view of money: International evidence from the 1960's and 1970's*. Research Department, Bank of Finland.

Laidler, D. E. W. (1977). *The demand for money: Theories and evidence*. Philadelphia: Harper & Row.

Laidler, D. E. W. (1984). The buffer stock notion in monetary economics. *Economic Journal* (March), 17–34.

Lucas, R. E., Jr. (1976). Econometric policy evaluation: A critique. *Carnegie-Rochester Conference Series on Public Policy*, *1*, 19–46.

Schwartz, A. J. (1981). Understanding 1929–1933. In: K. Brunner (Ed.), *The Great Depression Revisited* (pp. 5–48). Boston: Martinus Nijhoff.

Sims, C. A. (1980a). Macroeconomics and reality. *Econometrica*, *48*(January), I-48.

Sims, C. A. (1980b). Comparison of interwar and postwar business cycles: Monetarism reconsidered. *American Economic Review*, *70*(May), 250–257.

Starleaf, D. R. (1970). The specification of money demand/money supply models which involve the use of distributed lags. *Journal of Finance* (September), 743–760.

Stiglitz, J. E., & Weiss, A. (1981). Rationing in markets with imperfect information. *American Economic Review*, *71*(June), 393–410.

Temin, P. (1976). *Did monetary forces cause the great depression?* New York: Norton.

Tobin, J. (1963). Commercial banks as creators of 'money'. In: D. Carson (Ed.), *Banking and Monetary Studies* (pp. 408–419). Homewood, IL: Irwin.

Tobin, J. (1969). A general equilibrium approach to monetary theory. *Journal of Money, Credit and Banking*, *1*(February), 15–29.

Wallace, N. (1982). A legal restrictions theory of the demand for 'money' and the role of monetary policy. *Federal Reserve Bank of Minneapolis Quarterly Review* (Winter), 1–7.

INFORMATION AND INTERNATIONAL SPREAD OF BANKING PANICS

Victor E. Vaugirard

ABSTRACT

This paper features pure contagion of financial crises across countries, in a model where bank panics are equilibrium outcomes as a result of an asset-liability maturity mismatch. Banks' short-term liabilities include loans granted by foreign investors who have imperfect information about liquidation costs of assets. A bank failure in a country induces lenders to downgrade early-liquidation yields in other countries, and thus to bid lower prices to buy new debt. Banks become more illiquid and are therefore more prone to self-fulfilling depositors' runs. The severity of contagion sharpens with a higher degree of correlation between yields across countries and a greater strength of the Bayesian reassessment of the early-liquidation yield in the catalyst country.

1. INTRODUCTION

"Crises like company." Financial contagion is not a new phenomenon. In fact, the development of international trade and financial links has been closely accompanied by the cross-country spread of financial crises. In recent times however, the magnitude of crisis spillovers has intensified, and the real effects of spillovers on economies have tended to be sharper. In particular, the severity of the Asian flu and the Russian virus in 1997–1998 has renewed the interest for

Bank and Financial Market Efficiency: Global Perspectives
Research in Banking and Finance, Volume 5, 21–46

ISSN: 1567-7915/doi:10.1016/S1567-7915(04)05002-5

the study of contagion and entails a deeper understanding of how a crisis might internationally spread.

Close trade or financial links within regions or common external economic factors are channels of "real contagion." Important as these conduits generally are, Masson (1999) and others have argued that these linkages were weak in the contagion of the Tequila crisis from Mexico to Argentina and Brazil in 1994–1995, the contemporaneous crises in several East-Asian countries in 1997–1998, and the ripple effects of the Russian default in August 1998 on many emerging markets. This makes the case for "pure contagion," that is, the spread of crises unrelated to effective shifts in macroeconomic fundamentals.

Most models of pure contagion display an information channel. In an incomplete information environment, a crisis in one country may lead to "shifts in market sentiment," or may lead to changes in the interpretation given to existing information. Change in the risk tolerance of investors (Kumar & Persaud, 2002) or loss of confidence underlie the former. Information reassessment can materialize in various forms: herd behavior – on the grounds of asymmetric costly information and/or size heterogeneity; or informational cascades – based on the combination of asymmetric information and sequential decisions; or a reappraisal of economic fundamentals; or an alteration in the device that enables players to coordinate on a particular equilibrium when several arise. Incidentally, this last form could illustrate a shift in market sentiment as well. The "wake-up call" hypothesis of Goldstein (1998) also is ambivalent. It means that a financial crisis in a country, possibly interpreted as an indicator of equally severe problems in others that are perceived as being in a similar macroeconomic position, may lead to a reassessment of the desirability of investing in those countries. This is why we stopped short of strongly contrasting shifts in market sentiment and reinterpretation of existing information.

Most existing models of informational contagion feature financial markets and are based on asymmetric information. Calvo (1999) presents a model of capital markets populated by informed and uninformed investors. The uninformed try to extract information from informed investors' trades. This opens up the possibility that, if informed investors are forced to sell emerging market securities, say, to meet margin calls, then uninformed investors may misread this action as signaling low returns in emerging markets. Kodres and Pritsker (2002) emphasize optimal portfolio rebalancing as a channel. When portfolio reallocation occurs in markets with information asymmetries, the resulting price movements are exaggerated because the order flow is misconstrued as being information-based.

At this point, we have made the case for informational contagion and referred to such models in which financial assets play a key role. Nevertheless, recent episodes of financial fragility went far beyond mere falls of securities prices, and therefore, it is of interest to build a model of informational contagion in line with the new theoretical foundations of crises.

The literature on financial crises has trended in new directions in the aftermath of the crises in East and Southeast Asia of 1997–1998. These crises have led to a questioning of anterior models that basically viewed crises as retribution for governments that have mismanaged the economy, or as the consequences of lack of credibility. Most of the economies at stake, as a matter of fact, enjoyed government surpluses and increasing foreign exchange reserves, in contrast with the suggestions of first-generation models (Flood & Garber, 1984; Krugman, 1979), and also enjoyed low unemployment and booming exports, unlike what second-generation models (Obstfeld, 1994) would imply. Accordingly, a third generation of models of financial crises has emerged, whose common denominator is the key role assigned to financial structure fragility and financial institutions. Two strings of this literature, displaying multiple equilibria, can be affiliated with Krugman (1999), Caballero and Krishnamurthy (2001) and Aghion, Bacchetta and Banerjee (2001, 2003), on the one hand, and Chang and Velasco (2000, 2001), on the other hand. The former line of works develops the so-called balance sheet approach, that is, credit-constrained firms with a high proportion of debt denominated in foreign currency, while the latter highlights bank runs concomitant to stops of capital inflows due to an internationally illiquid banking sector. Our starting point will be the framework of Chang and Velasco (2001).

While recent literature has provided theoretical foundations for either contagion or self-fulfilling crises, models in which both co-exist have barely been studied. For instance, Masson (1999) sketches the possibility of informational contagion in a second-generation model of balance-of-payments crisis, yet he stops short of specifying how a crisis in a given country entails shifts in expectations that may ignite a crisis in another country. Indeed, the key sticking point in attempting to display pure contagion in models of financial crises with multiple equilibria is that mechanisms for jumps between those equilibria are usually not articulated. Therefore, those models cannot capture a contagious effect in which a crisis in one country (i.e. a particular outcome among multiple equilibrium outcomes) affects the likelihood of a crisis in another one. It is not a catch 22 though.

A first way out is to make the most of the equilibrium selection technique pioneered by Carlsson and van Damme (1993), and implemented by Morris and Shin (1998) in a framework of speculative attacks, which makes it possible to rule out multiple equilibria, self-fulfilling prophecies notwithstanding, and relate aggregate outcomes to observable variables. A key feature of the "global games" paradigm is incomplete information about relevant economic variables. Such a vintage point generates a failure of common knowledge of the fundamentals, and therefore agents' beliefs and actions cannot be perfectly coordinated. In other words, the implicit assumption of most models with multiple equilibria no longer holds. For instance, Dasgupta (2003) studies the spread of panics between banks related by capital connections. Goldstein and Pauzner (2003) examine contagion of reversals of investment portfolios as a consequence of wealth effects for investors. Vaugirard (2004) substantiates the propagation of capital flow reversals based on changes in the interpretation given to existing information.

A second approach is to keep working with multiple equilibria while being capable of identifying a particular channel amidst the various possible aforementioned. We follow along this second line and we now specify the problem position. We mean to single out reassessment of fundamentals as a vector of informational contagion of crises. This broadly boils down to featuring a Bayesian update of economic variables, while ruling out twists in coordination of beliefs. Highlighting the former entails that we be able to determine probability of crises and to relate this probability to the distribution of fundamentals, in a context of multiple equilibria. Hence, crises must stem from the combination of realized values of economic variables and self-fulfilling expectations, as opposed to expectational shifts alone. In turn, this combination is the outcome of strategic interactions between players. We must therefore structure a strategic game sufficiently elaborated, so that players face non-trivial strategic decisions, and at the same time, amenable enough to allow for computation of probabilities. This is our challenge.

To have a clear-cut picture of how our paper contrasts with the existing literature on contagious bank failures, the reader must keep in mind two points. First, we mean to highlight international transmission of bank runs through an informational conduit. Second, these bank failures must be concomitant to sudden reversals of international capital flows and/or to falls in asset prices. Indeed, we are interested in providing theoretical foundations for the propagation of recent turmoil in the emerging markets for which these facets of financial fragility have been simultaneously observed. In this respect, merely exhibiting theoretical mechanisms for cross-country correlated banking crises misses the point; international clustering of bank failures must be displayed along with other types of financial fragility.

That being said, diverse models of contagious bank failures written so far, while not explicitly meant for multi-economy issues, could straightforwardly be adapted to international spreads by merely thinking of the corresponding banks as being located in different countries. In so doing, however, one would simply derive bank runs that are correlated across countries, which is insufficient as stated above. Yet, one such work is worth mentioning here, since we will refer to it in the body of the paper. Chen (1999) displays contagion through an informational channel. He introduces asymmetric information regarding the value of bank assets among depositors in the model of Diamond and Dybvig (1983). Therefore, a first-come-first-served rule in bank withdrawals creates information externalities forcing depositors to respond prematurely to noisy information such as failures of other banks. This paves the way for the information-cascades story we previously underscored as a possible explanation for contagion. However, bank creditors – other than depositors – being irrelevant in Chen, a multi-country interpretation of his model does not yield an additional type of fragility.

On the other hand, Garber and Grilli (1989) do exhibit contagious bank runs along with falls in asset prices. Yet, the spread takes place through financial links. Upon the materialization of a bank run in a country, a foreign banking system buys its assets, say, long-term securities, at a bargain price, thus creating a wealth effect for the representative agent of the foreign country. It follows that foreign consumers may decide to consume beyond initially expected. Since foreign banks lack sufficient liquidity to meet the implied withdrawals, the apparently favorable opportunity available to the foreign country may actually turn out to lead to a run on the foreign banking system. Nevertheless, this model featuring no foreign creditors cannot account for sudden reversals of short-term international capital flows, and therefore does not lie in the category of third-generation crisis models.

A paper related to ours is in fact a model of informational contagion of sovereign debt default, not of bank runs. Chang and Majnoni (2002) study contagion in a model in which financial crises occur due to the combination of weak fundamentals and adverse self-fulfilling expectations of international investors. A debt default in one country, while possibly triggered by purely expectational shifts, may infect other countries, as it leads investors to rationally update their beliefs about fundamentals of the latter, and therefore, to require a higher return for allowing those governments to rollover their outstanding debt; which consequently raises the likelihood of a strategic default. Thus, their model and ours have in common a Bayesian update of beliefs regarding suitable variables as the vector of contagion. That said, our paper features bank debt rollover while theirs is about public debt service. Consequently, equilibrium outcomes in their model stem from the interaction of a government strategic decision of default and foreign lenders' expectations regarding being repaid. In contrast, our model includes no such strategic decision of default, since banks possibly fail because of purely expectational depositors' runs. What may appear innocuous actually entails our being much more careful when defining and deriving equilibrium outcomes.

To the best of our knowledge, no papers feature informational contagion in a third-generation model of financial crises, and this contribution is intended to fill part of this gap. In our paper, self-fulfilling domestic depositors' runs are equilibrium outcomes because of a maturity mismatch between banks' liabilities and assets. Those liabilities include loans granted by foreign creditors who have imperfect information about early-liquidation yields of illiquid assets. After observing a crisis in a country, lenders downgrade those yields in other countries, and therefore bid lower prices to buy new debt issued by their banks. As a result, those banks become more illiquid and are therefore more prone to runs. The vulnerability to contagion and its intensity sharpen with a higher degree of correlation between yields across countries and with a greater strength of the Bayesian reassessment of the early-liquidation yield in the catalyst country.

The paper proceeds as follows. In Section 2, we capitalize on the third-generation model of financial crises of Chang and Velasco (2001), that is, an open-economy extension of the bank run model of Diamond and Dybvig (1983). Yet, our respective focuses of attention are set in different directions. While they are interested in proving that banks may rationally choose to put themselves in a position of illiquidity, thus running the risk of self-fulfilling runs, we mean to highlight how foreign creditors' expectations regarding being repaid are affected by, and in turn, impinge on the likelihood of home depositors' runs. As a result, we concentrate on a stage of debt rollover, and thus take a demand deposit system as given. Importantly, we also introduce an informational edge of home depositors over foreign creditors regarding liquidation costs of assets, which is a credible story in most emerging markets. In this respect, we model the early-liquidation yield of the illiquid technology as a Bernouilli random variable.

In Section 3, we first show that bank runs stem from the combination of the realized value of the premature-liquidation yield, which conditions the liquidity position of the representative bank, self-fulfilling domestic depositors' adverse expectations and self-validating foreign creditors' beliefs regarding being repaid. Second, we prove that multiple equilibria can arise and, if so, we introduce a sunspots variable to coordinate creditors' expectations. Finally, we compute the probability of bank runs. The important conclusion of this section is that the odds of depositors' runs increase with the subjective appraisal by creditors of the chance that the short-term yield takes its low value.

In Section 4, we prove that bank runs in a country may propagate to another country via an informational channel, as foreign creditors reassess early-liquidation yields. The rationale underlying this international transmission can be disentangled as follows. First, the materialization of a bank run in a country induces international lenders to downgrade the early-liquidation yield of the illiquid technology in that country. Indeed, since the likelihood of bank runs is increasing in the prior probability of the early-liquidation yield taking its low value, then, upon occurrence of a run, the posterior probability that the yield takes its low value rises, on the grounds of Bayes' rule. Second, that downgrade in the catalyst country in turn implies a downgrade in the other country, provided their short-term yields are positively correlated. And third, that reappraisal in the other country consequently entails bank runs being more likely in that country, using again the important result of the previous section.

Section 5 emphasizes that both the degree of correlation between yields across countries and the strength of the Bayesian reassessment of the early-liquidation yield in the catalyst country play a crucial role in the vulnerability to contagion as well as its intensity.

Section 6 summarizes the central findings, and discusses some suggestions for future research.

2. MODEL

In this section, banks are described as maturity transformers that take liquid deposits and borrow foreign funds, and invest part of the proceeds in illiquid assets. This results in a maturity mismatch between their liabilities and their assets, therefore creating the possibility of self-fulfilling bank runs.

Our starting point is an open-economy extension by Chang and Velasco (2001) of the bank run model of Diamond and Dybvig (1983). We will however depart from Chang and Velasco's model, hereafter referred to as the "benchmark model," in several ways. First and more importantly, our respective focuses of attention are set in different directions. While they are interested in proving that banks may rationally choose to put themselves in a position of illiquidity, therefore running the risk of self-fulfilling runs, we mean to shed light on how foreign creditors' expectations regarding being repaid are affected by, and in turn, impinge on the likelihood of home depositors' runs. As a result, while they must first derive optimal (complete) allocations, we concentrate on a stage of debt rollover by the bank, and thus take an allocation as given, merely imposing that some compatibility conditions be satisfied. Second, and consistently with our different focus of attention, whereas our framework features foreign creditors' rational-expectations decision regarding what price to charge for allowing the bank to rollover its outstanding debt, the benchmark model merely considers either mechanical full rollover or no rollover at all. Consequently, our model captures a strategic interaction between domestic depositors, on the one hand, and foreign creditors, on the other hand, while the benchmark model merely displays a coordination game among depositors. In this respect, we take a stance close to a variant of the benchmark model by Chang and Velasco (2000). Third, we introduce an informational edge of home depositors over foreign creditors regarding liquidation costs of assets. That information asymmetry, along with the strategic interplay, enables us to obtain an extensive set of equilibria in the resulting game, which may yield multiple equilibria, eventually. And then, we will extend the model to a two-economy framework, in the section of contagion.

2.1. Setup

In this subsection, we lay down the main traits of the benchmark model. As in Diamond and Dybvig (1983), a combination of preferences and investment technologies is such that depositors are better off by forming a "bank" rather than acting in isolation.

A small open economy is populated by a large number of ex ante identical agents. There are three periods indexed by $t = 0, 1, 2$, and only one good, which is freely traded in the world market and can be consumed and invested. The price of consumption in the world market is fixed and normalized at one unit of foreign currency (a "dollar"). Home agents can borrow only from identical foreign lenders. These creditors are assumed risk-neutral – which is consistent with the small size of the economy, and can freely borrow or lend in a world capital market where interest rates are zero. Hence, foreign creditors will lend to domestic agents if and only if they are (credibly) promised an expected net return of zero. Also, domestic agents can invest as much as they want in this world capital market.

The country enjoys access to a long-term technology whose yield per dollar invested at $t = 0$ is $R > 1$ dollars at $t = 2$, and $r < 1$ dollars at $t = 1$. In other words, an investment is productive if held for two periods, but illiquid. While there is no uncertainty about R, r is a random variable whose distribution as well as the corresponding information structure will be made precise in the next subsection.

Each domestic agent may be forced to consume early depending on her "type," which she discovers at $t = 1$. With probability λ she is "impatient" and derives utility only from Period-1 consumption, while with probability $(1 - \lambda)$ she is "patient" and derives utility only from Period-2 consumption. Type realizations are independently and identically distributed (i.i.d.) across agents. In addition, the realization of each agent's type is private information to that agent. Incidentally, the long-term yield R and the proportion λ of impatient consumers being assumed constant, there is no aggregate uncertainty in this model, unlike Allen and Gale's (1998).

In this setup, it can be proved that risk-averse domestic agents may profit from pooling their resources and acting collectively rather than in isolation. Accordingly, it is assumed that they form a coalition, called a "bank." Indeed, this bank perfectly forecasts its liquidity needs at Period 1, as a result of the law of large numbers, and thus will not plan to liquidate prematurely part of the long-term asset, since this is costly. On the other hand, individuals cannot accurately forecast their liquidity needs, since they do not know their type until Period 1, and may therefore plan to liquidate their long-term assets early, thus costly, if they turn out to be impatient. To reinforce this incentive to act collectively, we could possibly argue that a coalition has a comparative advantage in investing in projects due to size indivisibilities.

2.2. *Debt Rollover and Information Structure*

In this subsection, we focus on the step of debt rollover by the bank, and we depart from the benchmark model in that we introduce asymmetric information between depositors and creditors regarding the early-liquidation yield of the illiquid asset.

The representative bank designs demand deposits. These contracts stipulate that, in Period 0, each agent must surrender to the bank her endowment and her capacity to borrow abroad, in return for the right to withdraw, at her discretion, either x units of consumption in Period 1 or y in Period 2. The bank borrows abroad an amount f in Period 0, with a part d of this debt maturing in Period 1, referred to as the short-term debt hereafter, and thus $f - d$ maturing in Period 2. The bank uses the proceeds of its borrowing, f, along with the endowment surrendered by home agents, e, to invest an amount k in the long-term illiquid technology and to invest an amount b in the world capital market. This means that the bank buys b dollars of the world liquid asset as international reserves.

At this point, we take an allocation as given, as elaborated upon introducing this section. Chang and Velasco (2000, 2001) derive optimal complete allocations and prove that banks may be prone to crises. They may rationally choose to put themselves in a position of illiquidity, thus taking the risk of self-fulfilling runs, if the cost of doing so is more than offset by the expected payoff of the long-term technology. In contrast, we mean to highlight how creditors' expectations regarding being repaid are affected by, and in turn condition the likelihood of depositors' runs. Therefore, acknowledging that it has already been vindicated that deposit contracts may comprise run equilibrium outcomes, we take an allocation as given, merely imposing that some compatibility conditions be satisfied. Incidentally, Garber and Grilli (1989) and Chen (1999) take a similar stance. Besides, our focus being the step of the bank's debt rollover, we must set d exogenously, as contrasted with an amount of ongoing debt previously determined within an optimal allocation. In the same vein, we want to keep room to maneuver for x and d so as to later exhibit several types of equilibrium. In addition, from a practical standpoint, it is dubious that demand deposit systems are determined with optimizing programs, solvency ratios notwithstanding. Not only do new management teams inherit situations, in all countries, but also, and particularly in emerging markets, such contracts more likely stem from domestic political conditions or the amount of funds available in international markets, not to mention the extent of crony capitalism.

We now concentrate on Period 1, with the short-term debt maturing. The representative bank attempts to roll it over by selling to foreign creditors claims to d dollars, payable in Period 2, in a competitive auction. These foreign creditors have an opportunity cost of funds of zero within Periods 1 and 2, and thus, being rational and risk-neutral, will buy the new debt issue if and only if its price, denoted by S, is equal to their subjective probability that the debt will be honored. The auction proceeds, $X = Sd$, are immediately transferred to the bank, which simultaneously pays out its maturing debt amounting to d. Hence, the net outflow attached to the debt operation in Period 1 is $(1 - S)d$.

Assumption 1. Domestic depositors have an informational edge over foreign creditors regarding early-liquidation yields. More precisely, the true value of r becomes known to home agents at Period 1, upon deciding on whether or not to run on the bank. On the other hand, foreign lenders only know its prior distribution, when about to make the decision regarding buying the new debt issue. For the sake of simplicity, we assume that this distribution is a Bernouilli random variable, taking a low value r_L, with probability $q \in [0, 1]$, or a high value r_H, with probability $(1 - q)$, which satisfy $r_L < r_H < 1$.

This informational edge is a credible story in emerging markets. Liquidation costs depend on each country's strength of bankruptcy laws as well as their enforcement, which implies that home depositors have a clear informational advantage, since information acquisition is costly for foreign lenders. This bias is further increased if we account for the fact that domestic agents may even take actions that affect these costs and for the opacity that surrounds cronyism. Foreigners are therefore unlikely to truly know the liquidation values until there actually is a run. By the same token, early-liquidation yields are likely to be correlated across emerging markets. We will return to that last point in the section on contagion.

Assumption 2. The withdrawal limits x and y of the deposit contract satisfy the conditions:

$$\lambda x \leq b, \tag{1}$$

$$(1 - \lambda)y + f \leq Rk, \tag{2}$$

and

$$x \leq y. \tag{3}$$

Condition (1) is a Period-1 feasibility constraint stating that the values of x and b chosen by the bank must be such that its Period-1 liquidities cover the expected withdrawals for consumption of the impatient. It is meant to ensure that an equilibrium without runs always exists. This inequality yet warrants two comments. First, the bank implicitly acknowledges that it will not liquidate prematurely the illiquid asset. Second, the bank implicitly expects the outstanding short-term debt d to be fully rolled over. This means that the bank disregards the possibility of depositors' runs when setting the value of x. Nonetheless, the probability of bank runs is strictly positive in the models of Chang and Velasco (2000, 2001) as pointed out above, which implies that stating Condition (1) in that form entails assuming away rational expectations for the bank, i.e. at a collective level. In other words, we assume that the exogenous event (sunspot) that could trigger a bank run in Period 1 is completely unexpected as of Period 0, which rules out, strictly speaking, rational expectations. In so doing, we follow along the lines of Garber and Grilli (1989) and Chang and Velasco (2001). It is noteworthy that Chang and Velasco (2000) relate deriving a continuum of optimal allocations (vs. unique solution) to disregarding the possibility of bank runs. This is fully consistent with our model that intends to keep some margin in setting x and d, as already pointed out. What is more, we will later constrain the probability of adverse sunspots to be low, which further improves the suitability of our framework.

Condition (2) is a Period-2 feasibility constraint. In particular, it ensures that foreign creditors are fully reimbursed the amount extended in Period 1, provided the bank does not go bankrupt in the meantime.

Condition (3) is an incentive-compatibility constraint relative to patient agents. If a patient depositor claims impatience, she obtains x in Period 1. The best she can do is then to deposit that amount in the world market, and hence get back and consume x in Period 2. On the other hand, by not misrepresenting her type, she is entitled to withdraw y in Period 2. Condition (3) is thus a truth-telling incentive that the bank must respect since agents' types are private information to them. However, whether or not patient agents will behave accordingly will depend on their expectations about being in fact served in Period 2, to which we turn next.

3. EQUILIBRIA

In this section, we first show that bank runs stem from the combination of the realized value of the early-liquidation yield, which conditions the liquidity position of the representative bank, self-fulfilling domestic depositors' adverse expectations, and self-validating foreign creditors' beliefs regarding being repaid. Second, we prove that multiple equilibria can arise and, if so, we introduce a sunspots variable to coordinate creditors' expectations. Finally, we compute the probability of bank runs and highlight that their likelihood increases with the subjective appraisal by creditors of the chance that the short-term yield takes a low value. In our model, informational contagion of crises is rooted in that last result.

We refer to the introduction of Section 2 for a perspective on how our modifications of the benchmark model allow to reach an extensive set of equilibria. What is more, while these amendments may appear innocuous, they actually entail that we be careful about specifying equilibrium outcomes.

3.1. Timing

In this subsection, we expound the timing of withdrawals and debt rollover in order to properly define depositors' and creditors' decision problems.

Domestic depositors learn their type in Period 1, and face the strategic decision on whether or not to withdraw according to their true type. Simultaneously, foreign creditors must decide what price to bid for the new debt issued by the bank, and this, according to their prior assessment of the early-liquidation yield. To make these decision problems well defined, we make an additional assumption on the demand deposit system. The bank attends to the requests of depositors on a first-come-first-served basis. This assumption is essential in that it provides late consumers an incentive to misrepresent their type if they fear a bank failure, which paves the way for bank runs. On the other hand, if late consumers behave according to their true type, the bank will not fail according to Condition (1), and they will be better off due to Condition (3). It follows that depositors face indeed a non-trivial strategic decision.

Hence, depositors visit the bank in random order at Period 1. Upon their respective arrival to the bank, each depositor may withdraw x on demand. To service withdrawals and short-term debt repayment, the bank first uses its world liquid asset b and attempts to roll over its maturing debt d, and then liquidates part of the long-term asset if necessary. Besides, the auction among creditors concerning the debt rollover was described in the previous section.

3.2. Definitions

This subsection is devoted to properly defining equilibrium outcomes and to highlighting that international lenders' beliefs – regarding the chance of being repaid if they enable the bank to extend its short-term debt – interact with home depositors' self-fulfilling expectations, to magnify the odds of depositors' runs, eventually.

An equilibrium is a description of the strategies of depositors and creditors and of aggregate outcomes such that: the aggregate outcomes are implied by those strategies; and each depositor or creditor strategy is optimal for her, given the aggregate outcomes. We stress that the strategic game in which those actors are involved can further be disentangled into two sub-games. The first one is a strategic interaction between the group of home depositors, on the one hand, and the group of foreign creditors, on the other hand. The second one is a coordination game among domestic depositors upon deciding whether or not to run. Moreover, foreign lenders would have to coordinate their behavior so as to select an equilibrium should several arise.

Let us first note that the game has an "honest equilibrium" in which each depositor withdrawal decision matches her true type and creditors allow for the full rollover of the short-term debt. This stems from the bank's solvency conditions and the incentive compatibility clause stated in Assumption 2. Hence, we concentrate on equilibria comprising bank run outcomes.

Definition 1. The bank is illiquid if its potential short-term liabilities exceed the liquidation value of its assets. Formally:

$$x + (1 - S)d > rk + b, \tag{4}$$

where r is the realized value of the early-liquidation yield. We remind that S is the price bid by lenders for the new debt issue, and that it is equal to their subjective probability that the debt will be honored.

Incidentally, we use in (4), "r" for an *ex post* value, as for the random variable. This is meant to keep notation at a minimum, and hopefully not misleading, since we will use r_{H} or r_{L} in the sequel.

Now, a bank run equilibrium exists if and only if the bank is illiquid. Indeed, suppose Condition (4) is satisfied. If all depositors attempt to withdraw their deposits in Period 1, this collective behavior turns out to be individually optimal since it forces the bank to fail before meeting all the claims made on it. The converse holds true due to the truth-telling condition (3): If (4) is not satisfied, then depositors cannot force the bank to go bankrupt; therefore, patient consumers who run get x instead of $y \geq x$, which means that running is not individually optimal.

Assumption 3. Depositors base their decision to run on the realization of sunspots and the bank's liquidity position. More specifically, there is a publicly-observed random variable that takes the value 1 with probability $p \in [0, 1]$ or 0 with probability $1 - p$. While this variable does not affect the fundamentals of the economy, depositors condition their behavior on its realization, that is, it acts as a coordination device: A bank run takes place if and only if the bank is illiquid and the realization of the sunspot variable is 1.

We first emphasize the depositors' decision process, and then point out several implications of this assumption. Home depositors base their decision on whether or not to run on two cumulative factors. First, they assess the liquidity position of the representative bank. Second, conditionally on the bank being illiquid, they coordinate their expectations, thus their behavior, by means of a mechanism, extraneous to economic fundamentals. Yet, it is noteworthy that the former actually involves a third factor: the appraisal by depositors of the return required by foreign creditors to enable the bank to roll over its outstanding debt. This assessment in turn entails that domestic depositors have to account for the fact that liquidation costs of the long-term asset are uncertain to foreign agents. In other words, though knowing the true values of those costs upon making a decision regarding early withdrawal, late consumers must take account of their randomness to foreigners.

Assumption 3 warrants further comments. First, Condition (4) being satisfied, both runs and no-runs are possible equilibrium outcomes. In other words, a run is never a sure outcome. Second, foreign creditors' behavior conditions the likelihood of runs, in the sense that Condition (4) is more stringent than its counterpart with full rollover (i.e. $S = 1$). Actually, the behavior of creditors may, by itself, cause a depositors' run: It may be the case that (4) holds with $S < 1$ and does not hold with $S = 1$. Third, if there is a run, creditors who would have accepted to buy the new debt, would be repaid nothing in Period 2, since the bank goes bankrupt. Points 2 and 3 taken together imply that, not only is it rational for creditors not to enable the bank to rollover its debt if they fear a depositors' run, but also, this fear may be self-fulfilling. Fourth, lenders are repaid if and only if there are no runs. Indeed, they are fully reimbursed if depositors do not run, as ensured by Condition (2) (the bank then does not fail in Period 1 by virtue of Provision (1), and thus, Condition (2) applies), while they are paid nothing back if depositors run in Period 1 (Point 3 above). It follows that rational risk-neutral foreign creditors, who bid the price of the new debt to the probability of being paid back, offer $S = 1 - g$, where g is the ex ante probability of bank runs.

We are now equipped to determine equilibrium outcomes.

3.3. Equilibrium Types and Multiple Equilibria

For clarity, we label as an "equilibrium type," an equilibrium defined in association with the early-liquidation yield. We first display equilibrium types that can arise according to the parameters of the demand deposit system, and then prove that two types of equilibrium can simultaneously arise.

Equilibria can be of three types depending on the deposit contract set by the bank. First, a run equilibrium is a possible outcome irrespectively of the realization of r. This means that Condition (4) holds for r_{H} (*a fortiori* for r_{L}). Therefore, the probability of a run is p (probability of adverse sunspot for depositors). International creditors acknowledge this, and accordingly bid $S = (1 - p)$ (see Point 4 in comments of Assumption 3), which amounts to a debt rollover of pd. This means that a necessary and sufficient condition (NSC) for there be a run equilibrium irrespectively of the realization of r is:

$$x > x_S = r_{\mathrm{H}}k + b - pd. \tag{5}$$

Second, a run equilibrium is a possible outcome if and only if the early-liquidation yield takes its low value. This means that Condition (4) holds for r_{L} and does not hold for r_{H}. It follows that the probability of a run is pq – where q is the probability of r being equal to r_{L} – and that creditors bid $S = (1 - pq)$, which boils down to a debt extension of pqd. As a result, a NSC for there be a run equilibrium only if $r = r_{\mathrm{L}}$ is:

$$x_1 = r_{\mathrm{H}}k + b - pqd > x > x_0 = r_{\mathrm{L}}k + b - pqd. \tag{6}$$

Third and last, a run equilibrium is not a possible outcome irrespectively of the realization of r. This means that Condition (4) never holds. The probability of a run being zero, rational creditors bid $S = 1$, that is, there is full rollover of the debt. Consequently, a NSC for this type of equilibrium is:

$$x < x_N = r_{\mathrm{L}}k + b. \tag{7}$$

Now, there are several possibilities for the respective positions of x_0, x_1, x_N, and x_S. The only inequalities that hold are: $x_0 < x_1, x_S < x_1$, and $x_0 < x_N$; and taking account of all cases would be tedious. Fortunately, it turns out that there is only one remaining case: $x_0 < x_N < x_S < x_1$, if restricting the analysis to low values of p. Indeed, it suffices to observe that, for $p = 0$, $x_S = r_{\mathrm{H}}k + b$, thus, is superior to x_N; and therefore, it follows by continuity that this inequality still holds for p low enough. Then, we make use of the previous three inequalities to obtain the only remaining possibility. We assume in the sequel that p is sufficiently low so as to be in this case. Incidentally, we refer to our discussion following Assumption 2 regarding the suitability of restricting to a low p.

At this point, we have showed that there are three types of equilibrium, and we now claim that two types can simultaneously stand. In other words, there may be multiple equilibria. More specifically, only one type of equilibrium can arise in the three following situations for the withdrawal limit: $x < x_0$ (run equilibrium outcome never possible), $x > x_1$ (run always possible), and $x \in [x_N, x_S]$ (run possible if and only if $r = r_{\mathrm{L}}$). On the other hand, two types of equilibrium coexist in the two following situations: $x \in [x_0, x_N]$ (both outcomes "never run" and "run if and only if $r = r_{\mathrm{L}}$" can arise), and $x \in [x_S, x_1]$ (both outcomes "run always possible" and "run possible if and only if $r = r_{\mathrm{L}}$" are possible). Incidentally, we previously underscored that the representative bank is prone to runs, which means that the situation $x < x_0$ can be assumed away without loss of generality.

3.4. Equilibrium Selection and Probability of Bank Runs

In this subsection, we first introduce sunspots specific to creditors, and then compute the ex ante probability of bank runs. This eventually enables us to emphasize that this probability increases with the chance that the early-liquidation yield takes a low value, which opens the door for informational contagion.

We saw that x can be such that two types of equilibrium arise. If so, we need a mechanism to coordinate foreign creditors' expectations. We assume that there is an equiprobable random variable that allows them to select a particular equilibrium. This sunspots variable has no effects on economic fundamentals and is independent of that one defined for domestic depositors. We take weights of $\frac{1}{2}$ for the sake of simplicity.

Once this coordination device is specified, the model determines the ex ante probability of bank run equilibrium outcomes. To illustrate, suppose that x lie in $[x_S, x_1]$. With probability $\frac{1}{2}$, the equilibrium type is "run equilibrium outcome possible irrespectively of realization of r," and then, the probability of a run equilibrium outcome is p; and with probability $\frac{1}{2}$, the equilibrium type is "run equilibrium outcome possible if and only if $r = r_L$," and then, the probability of a run is pq. It follows that the probability of a bank run is $\frac{1}{2}\,p(1+q)$, in the case $x \in [x_S, x_1]$. Likewise, the probability of a bank run in the case $x \in [x_0, x_N]$ is $\frac{1}{2}\,pq$. Also, in the case $x > x_1 (x \in [x_N, x_S]$, respectively), the probability of a bank run is p (pq, respectively).

In a nutshell, there are four configurations. Two of them display one equilibrium type; a run equilibrium outcome exists in either configuration, yet conditionally on the realization of r; and then, whether or not a run does materialize depends on sunspots for home depositors. Two other configurations feature two types of equilibrium each; in either configuration, the selection between the two equilibrium types is based on sunspots for foreign creditors; in either configuration and for either equilibrium picked, a run equilibrium outcome exists; and then, whether or not a run actually takes place depends on sunspots for home depositors.

The important conclusion of this subsection is that the probability of bank runs increases with q, the prior subjective probability that the early-liquidation yield of the illiquid asset is low. The underlying rationale is that the more likely a low yield, the lower the price bid by foreign creditors to buy the new debt issue, hence the more likely the bank in an illiquid position for any given demand deposit parameters. Actually, this holds except for the case $x > x_1$ (i.e. withdrawal limit x set high), in which the probability of a run is already the highest possible ($= p$), making a rise in q irrelevant.

Eventually, bank runs stem from the combination of the realized value of the early-liquidation yield, which conditions the liquidity position of the representative bank, self-fulfilling domestic depositors' adverse expectations and self-validating foreign creditors' beliefs regarding being repaid. Those creditors' beliefs are themselves linked to their assessment of the early-liquidation yield of the illiquid asset. So far, we have likened this subjective assessment to the prior distribution, and have not thought of what may affect this appraisal. A crisis in another country may have this role, as we turn to next.

4. CONTAGION

In this section, we prove that bank runs in a country may propagate to other countries through an informational channel, as international creditors reassess early-liquidation yields.

The rationale underlying this international transmission can be disentangled as follows. First, the materialization of a bank run in a country induces international lenders to downgrade the early-liquidation yield of the illiquid technology in that country. Indeed, the likelihood of bank runs were showed to be increasing in the prior probability of the early-liquidation yield taking its low value; therefore, upon occurrence of a run, the posterior probability that the early-liquidation yield takes its low value rises, on the grounds of Bayes' rule. Second, that downgrade in the catalyst country in turn implies a rise in the subjective probability that the early-liquidation yield takes its low value in another country, provided these yields are positively correlated across countries. And third, that rise in probability in the other country consequently entails bank runs being more likely in that country, using again the important result of the previous section.

We laid down in the introduction various possible explanations for informational contagion in the framework of multiple equilibria. We have already ruled out some of them by construction: Herd behavior, since foreign creditors have the same information and the same size; Informational cascades, since they act simultaneously; Shifts in risk aversion, since creditors are risk-neutral. In the remainder of this section, we first assume away alterations in the coordination device of expectations as a possible culprit for the spread of crises, and then, we formally prove that informational contagion arises from reappraisal of early-liquidation yields by international lenders. Along the way, we highlight that cross-country correlation of yields is necessary to ignite this engine of contagion.

4.1. Two-Country Model

We extend the preceding framework to two economies. We specify the distributional relation between the liquidation costs of their technologies, and we pay attention to the sequential coordination of international lenders' expectations.

We consider two small open economies, say, A and B, during two consecutive periods. Country A is the economy examined in the previous section, and we re-label its parameters with Superscript A, while using Superscript B in the other country. The two countries have the same fundamental structure. The analysis in Country B is analogous to A, except for the crucial fact that international lenders know whether or not a bank run has occurred in A when about to make a decision re buying the new debt issued by the representative bank in B. We mean to prove that a financial crisis in A may impinge on the likelihood of a run in B due to this additional information. We first lay down two important assumptions.

Assumption 4. Early-liquidation yields of illiquid assets are positively correlated across countries.

This assumption is essential to informational contagion. Groups of countries in emerging markets display clear-cut similarities relevant for liquidation values: the strength of bankruptcy laws, the extent of their enforcement, the fact that domestic agents may even take actions that affect these costs, or the opacity that surrounds crony capitalism. This homogeneity entails early-liquidation yields being correlated across these countries. Besides, together with that information acquisition is costly, not only does it also imply that home agents have an informational edge over foreign creditors regarding these early-liquidation yields, as was previously stated, but also that foreigners are likely to reappraise liquidation values should a run materialize in any of those countries.

Assumption 5. Sunspots variables concerning creditors are independently and identically distributed across time and countries. This not only means that, when multiple equilibria exist, the manner an equilibrium is selected in B is the same as in A, but also, and more importantly, that the coordination mechanism in B is independent of what occurred in A.

This assumption clears up the ambiguity underscored in the introduction. We rule out alterations in the coordination device of foreign creditors' expectations following a run in A. It follows that the sole remaining vector of informational contagion is here the reassessment of liquidation yields, which we formally prove next.

4.2. Informational Contagion

International creditors condition their behavior at the debt auction of Country-B's representative bank, not on the unconditional probabilities of B's premature-liquidation yield, but on such probabilities conditional on whether there was a crisis in A. This opens the door for contagion.

Theorem 1. There is informational contagion from Country A to Country B, that is to say, a bank run in Country A increases the likelihood of a bank run in Country B, and this infection is solely based on a Bayesian update of international creditors' beliefs about early-liquidation yields.

We refer to the introduction of this section for the underlying rationale.

Proof: We showed in the previous section that the likelihood of bank runs increases with q, the foreign creditors subjective probability of the early-liquidation yield taking its low value. It therefore suffices to prove that this subjective assessment regarding B-technology increases if a crisis materializes in Country A, to obtain the theorem. Specifically, we must check that:

$$P(r^{\mathrm{B}} = r_{\mathrm{L}}^{\mathrm{B}} | C^{\mathrm{A}}) \geq P(r^{\mathrm{B}} = r_{\mathrm{L}}^{\mathrm{B}}), \tag{8}$$

where the LHS member stands for the probability of r^{B} being low, conditional on a crisis in Country A.

While the economic intuition behind (8) is clear-cut and was sketched after Assumption 4, formally proving it involves coping with the different configurations displayed in Section 3. This will lead to some tedious but necessary computations.

We start with the two simple configurations where only one type of equilibrium exists in Country A. One of them is $x^{\mathrm{A}} > x_1^{\mathrm{A}}$, i.e. a bank run in A is always possible, irrespectively of the realization of r^{A}. In this case, a crisis in A means that the sunspots variable for A-depositors takes the unfavorable value, say, $D^{\mathrm{A}} = D_{\mathrm{U}}^{\mathrm{A}}$. We thus obtain:

$$P(r^{\mathrm{B}} = r_{\mathrm{L}}^{\mathrm{B}} | C^{\mathrm{A}}) = P(r^{\mathrm{B}} = r_{\mathrm{L}}^{\mathrm{B}} | D^{\mathrm{A}} = D_{\mathrm{U}}^{\mathrm{A}}) = P(r^{\mathrm{B}} = r_{\mathrm{L}}^{\mathrm{B}}), \tag{9}$$

where the second equality follows from the assumption that sunspots variables do not affect economic fundamentals. Thus, in this case, (8) actually is an equality. The intuition for this was somehow sketched when commenting on the probability of bank runs in the end of the preceding section. Indeed, in the case $x^{\mathrm{A}} > x_1^{\mathrm{A}}$ (i.e. withdrawal limit x^{A} set high), the probability of a run in A is already the highest possible ($= p$), which sterilizes the effect on the likelihood of a run in A of a rise in the probability of the early-liquidation yield taking its low value. Thus, the materialization of a run in A does not change the (posterior) appraisal of the early-liquidation yield in Country A, thus in Country B either.

In the three other cases, Inequality (8) holds strictly as we now show. The other configuration with one type of equilibrium is $x_N^A < x^A < x_S^A$, i.e. a run in A is possible if and only if $r^A = r_L^A$. In this case, a crisis occurs in A if $r^A = r_L^A$ and the sunspots variable for A-depositors takes the unfavorable value, $D^A = D_U^A$. We thus obtain:

$$P(r^B = r_L^B | C^A) = P(r^B = r_L^B | (r^A = r_L^A) \cap (D^A = D_U^A))$$
$$= P(r^B = r_L^B | r^A = r_L^A) > P(r^B = r_L^B), \quad (10)$$

where the second equality again follows from the assumption that sunspots variables do not affect economic fundamentals, and the strict inequality follows from the positive correlation between r^A and r^B. Thus, in this case, we have proved that Inequality (8) holds strictly.

We now consider a configuration with two types of equilibrium possible: $x_S^A < x^A < x_1^A$. The first type is "run in A is possible irrespectively of value of r^A"; the second type is "run in A is possible if and only if $r^A = r_L^A$." The selection between the two types is based on the sunspots variable F^A for foreign creditors, which takes two values, F_1^A or F_2^A, each with probability $\frac{1}{2}$. C^A can thus be disentangled as:

$$C^A \equiv \{(F^A = F_1^A) \cap (D^A = D_U^A)\} \bar{u} \{(F^A = F_2^A) \cap (r^A = r_L^A) \cap (D^A = D_U^A)\}, \quad (11)$$

where the symbol $\bar{u}$ designates the union of two disjoint sets. It follows that:

$$P(r^B = r_L^B | C^A) = \frac{P(r^B = r_L^B \cap C^A)}{P(C^A)}$$
$$= \frac{P((r^B = r_L^B) \cap (F^A = F_1^A) \cap (D^A = D_U^A)) + P((r^B = r_L^B) \cap (F^A = F_2^A) \cap (r^A = r_L^A) \cap (D^A = D_U^A))}{P(C^A)}$$
$$= \frac{P(r^B = r_L^B)P(F^A = F_1^A)P(D^A = D_U^A) + P((r^B = r_L^B) \cap (r^A = r_L^A))P(F^A = F_2^A)P(D^A = D_U^A)}{P(C^A)}$$
$$= \frac{P(r^B = r_L^B)P(F^A = F_1^A)P(D^A = D_U^A) + P((r^B = r_L^B)|(r^A = r_L^A))P(r^A = r_L^A)P(F^A = F_2^A)P(D^A = D_U^A)}{P(C^A)}, \quad (12)$$

where we use again that sunspots do not affect economic variables, together with that depositors and creditors sunspots variables are independent. Further, making use again of: $P(r^B = r_L^B | (r^A = r_L^A) > P(r^B = r_L^B)$, due to the positive correlation between r^{A} and r^{B}, (12) yields:

$$P(r^{\mathrm{B}} = r_{\mathrm{L}}^{\mathrm{B}}|C^{\mathrm{A}}) > \frac{P(r^{\mathrm{B}} = r_{\mathrm{L}}^{\mathrm{B}})P(F^{\mathrm{A}} = F_1^{\mathrm{A}})P(D^{\mathrm{A}} = D_{\mathrm{U}}^{\mathrm{A}}) + P(r^{\mathrm{B}} = r_{\mathrm{L}}^{\mathrm{B}})P(r^{\mathrm{A}} = r_{\mathrm{L}}^{\mathrm{A}})P(F^{\mathrm{A}} = F_2^{\mathrm{A}})P(D^{\mathrm{A}} = D_{\mathrm{U}}^{\mathrm{A}})}{P(C^{\mathrm{A}})}. \tag{13}$$

Putting $P(r^{\mathrm{B}} = r_{\mathrm{L}}^{\mathrm{B}})$ in factor in the RHS of (13), we obtain Inequality (8), strictly.

Last, deriving (8) for the other configuration with two possible types of equilibrium: $x_0^{\mathrm{A}} < x^{\mathrm{A}} < x_N^{\mathrm{A}}$, is straightforward. Indeed, since C^{A} then boils down to $\{(F^{\mathrm{A}} = F_1^{\mathrm{A}}) \cap (r^{\mathrm{A}} = r_{\mathrm{L}}^{\mathrm{A}}) \cap (D^{\mathrm{A}} = D_{\mathrm{U}}^{\mathrm{A}})\}$, it follows that: $P(r^{\mathrm{B}} = r_{\mathrm{L}}^{\mathrm{B}}|C^{\mathrm{A}}) = P(r^{\mathrm{B}} = r_{\mathrm{L}}^{\mathrm{B}}|r^{\mathrm{A}} = r_{\mathrm{L}}^{\mathrm{A}}) > P(r^{\mathrm{B}} = r_{\mathrm{L}}^{\mathrm{B}})$.

To sum it up, we have showed that, $P(r^{\mathrm{B}} = r_{\mathrm{L}}^{\mathrm{B}}|C^{\mathrm{A}}) > P(r^{\mathrm{B}} = r_{\mathrm{L}}^{\mathrm{B}})$, in all configurations, except for configuration "$x^{\mathrm{A}} > x_1^{\mathrm{A}}$," where it is an equality. This completes the proof of Theorem 1. □

We have proved that bank runs in a country may propagate to other countries, as international creditors reassess early-liquidation yields. At this point, we concede however that the use of Bayes' rule to update beliefs *within the catalyst country* is not apparent. It is actually mingled with other quantities above. To illustrate, take the configuration leading to (10). We have $C^{\mathrm{A}} \equiv (r^{\mathrm{A}} = r_{\mathrm{L}}^{\mathrm{A}}) \cap (D^{\mathrm{A}} = D_{\mathrm{U}}^{\mathrm{A}})$, thus, $P(r^{\mathrm{A}} = r_{\mathrm{L}}^{\mathrm{A}}|C^{\mathrm{A}}) = 1$. Consequently, this Bayesian update is somewhat hidden when proving (10). The next section is somehow intended to sort this out.

5. DISCUSSION

In this section, we show that both the degree of correlation between yields across countries and the strength of the Bayesian reassessment of the early-liquidation yield in the country in which the crisis originates play a crucial role in the vulnerability to contagion as well as its intensity.

Proposition 1. The intensity of contagion satisfies the relation:

$$P(r^{\mathrm{B}} = r_{\mathrm{L}}^{\mathrm{B}}|C^{\mathrm{A}}) - P(r^{\mathrm{B}} = r_{\mathrm{L}}^{\mathrm{B}}) = \frac{[P(r^{\mathrm{B}} = r_{\mathrm{L}}^{\mathrm{B}}|r^{\mathrm{A}} = r_{\mathrm{L}}^{\mathrm{A}}) - P(r^{\mathrm{B}} = r_{\mathrm{L}}^{\mathrm{B}})] \times [P(r^{\mathrm{A}} = r_{\mathrm{L}}^{\mathrm{A}}|C^{\mathrm{A}}) - P(r^{\mathrm{A}} = r_{\mathrm{L}}^{\mathrm{A}})]}{1 - P(r^{\mathrm{A}} = r_{\mathrm{L}}^{\mathrm{A}})}, \tag{14}$$

where the LHS is our definition and measure of intensity (or size) of contagion.

We first comment on Proposition 1 before proving it. It displays how the dependence between the yields, measured by the first factor of the RHS of (14), and the extent of the beliefs update about the yield in the catalyst country, as reflected by the second factor of the RHS, combine to entail contagion down the road. We purposely do not use the word "reinforce" as will be clear right on. Formula (14) has several important implications. First, it shows that a statistical positive relation between the yields is necessary for vulnerability to contagion, in a two-country model. This can be contrasted with the findings of Goldstein and Pauzner (2003) who exhibit contagion through wealth effects, while assuming away cross-country correlation between economic fundamentals. Second, it shows that a Bayesian update of the early-liquidation yield *in the catalyst country* is also necessary to activate contagion. To put it another way, dependence between yields, while necessary, is not sufficient to make a country vulnerable to contagion. Third, the intensity of contagion increases with the extent of the Bayesian update in the catalyst country. Points 2 and 3 respond to the point raised upon concluding the previous section. Besides, after the computations made in the following proof, we will be capable of ranking configurations according to the size of contagion.

Proof of Proposition 1: We first prove (14) in Configuration 3, where:

$$C^{\mathrm{A}} \equiv \{(F^{\mathrm{A}} = F_1^{\mathrm{A}}) \cap (D^{\mathrm{A}} = D_{\mathrm{U}}^{\mathrm{A}})\}\bar{u}\{(F^{\mathrm{A}} = F_2^{\mathrm{A}}) \cap (r^{\mathrm{A}} = r_{\mathrm{L}}^{\mathrm{A}}) \cap (D^{\mathrm{A}} = D_{\mathrm{U}}^{\mathrm{A}})\},$$

and then we will show that (14) applies in a basic fashion in other configurations.

To do so, we capitalize on Equality (12). Likewise, we have:

$$P(r^{\mathrm{A}} = r_{\mathrm{L}}^{\mathrm{A}}|C^{\mathrm{A}}) = \frac{P(r^{\mathrm{A}}=r_{\mathrm{L}}^{\mathrm{A}})P(F^{\mathrm{A}}=F_1^{\mathrm{A}})P(D^{\mathrm{A}}=D_{\mathrm{U}}^{\mathrm{A}}) + P(r^{\mathrm{A}}=r_{\mathrm{L}}^{\mathrm{A}})P(F^{\mathrm{A}}=F_2^{\mathrm{A}})P(D^{\mathrm{A}}=D_{\mathrm{U}}^{\mathrm{A}})}{P(C^{\mathrm{A}})}. \tag{15}$$

Now, (12) can be rewritten:

$$P(r^{\mathrm{B}} = r_{\mathrm{L}}^{\mathrm{B}}|C^{\mathrm{A}}) - P(r^{\mathrm{B}} = r_{\mathrm{L}}^{\mathrm{B}}) = \frac{[P((r^{\mathrm{B}} = r_{\mathrm{L}}^{\mathrm{B}})|(r^{\mathrm{A}} = r_{\mathrm{L}}^{\mathrm{A}})) - P(r^{\mathrm{B}} = r_{\mathrm{L}}^{\mathrm{B}})] \times [P(r^{\mathrm{A}} = r_{\mathrm{L}}^{\mathrm{A}})P(F^{\mathrm{A}} = F_2^{\mathrm{A}})P(D^{\mathrm{A}} = D_{\mathrm{U}}^{\mathrm{A}})]}{P(C^{\mathrm{A}})}, \tag{16}$$

and similarly, (15) can be rewritten:

$$P(r^{\mathrm{A}} = r_{\mathrm{L}}^{\mathrm{A}}|C^{\mathrm{A}}) - P(r^{\mathrm{A}} = r_{\mathrm{L}}^{\mathrm{A}}) = \frac{[1 - P(r^{\mathrm{A}} = r_{\mathrm{L}}^{\mathrm{A}})] \times [P(r^{\mathrm{A}} = r_{\mathrm{L}}^{\mathrm{A}})P(F^{\mathrm{A}} = F_2^{\mathrm{A}})P(D^{\mathrm{A}} = D_{\mathrm{U}}^{\mathrm{A}})]}{P(C^{\mathrm{A}})}. \tag{17}$$

Combining (16) and (17) yields (14).

In the other configurations, (14) still holds, while shrinking though. In Configuration 1, where $C^A \equiv (D^A = D^A_U)$, we have: $P(r^A = r^A_L|C^A) = P(r^A = r^A_L)$, which, together with (9), imply that the LHS and RHS in (14) are each equal to 0. Thus, (14) holds.

In Configuration 2, where $C^A \equiv (r^A = r^A_L) \cap (D^A = D^A_U)$, we have: $P(r^A = r^A_L|C^A) = 1$. It follows that (14) boils down to $P(r^B = r^B_L|C^A) = P(r^B = r^B_L|r^A = r^A_L)$, which is the equality leading to (10), thus, (14) is again true.

Last, in Configuration 4, where $C^A \equiv \{(F^A = F^A_1) \cap (r^A = r^A_L) \cap (D^A = D^A_U)\}$, we have again: $P(r^A = r^A_L|C^A) = 1$, and the argument is the same as above. This concludes the proof of Proposition 1. □

We see that the intensity of contagion is the sharpest possible for Configurations 2 and 4. Its size is:

$$P(r^B = r^B_L|C^A) - P(r^B = r^B_L) = [P(r^B = r^B_L|r^A = r^A_L) - P(r^B = r^B_L)], \quad (18)$$

which reflects that the statistical relation is fully at work. The rationale is that, in either case, the materialization of a crisis reveals that $(r^A = r^A_L)$, unequivocally.

On the other hand, there is no contagion in Configuration 1. Indeed, a run being possible irrespectively of the realization of r^A, the occurrence of a run conveys no information on the early-liquidation yield in Country A, thus, neither in B.

Now, in Configuration 3, the size of contagion is lesser than (18), holding for cases 2 and 4. The reason is that the materialization of a run in A conveys only noisy information regarding r^A. Indeed, it is consistent with both "run possible irrespectively of realization of r^A" and "run possible if and only if $r^A = r^A_L$." Therefore, the statistical relation between the yields is somehow dampened by this uncertainty. We can further compute the size of contagion in this case:

$$P(r^A = r^A_L|C^A) = \frac{P(C^A|r^A = r^A_L)P(r^A = r^A_L)}{P(C^A)} = \frac{2q^A}{1+q^A}, \quad (19)$$

where we use: $P(C^A) = \frac{1}{2}p(1 + q^A)$, as computed in Section 3.4. Relation (14) then writes:

$$P(r^B = r^B_L|C^A) - P(r^B = r^B_L) = [P(r^B = r^B_L|r^A = r^A_L) - P(r^B = r^B_L)]q^A. \quad (20)$$

To encapsulate, both the statistical dependence of the yields and the extent of the downgrade in the catalyst country play a crucial role in the vulnerability to contagion and its intensity.

To conclude this section, it is worth noting that the previous two-economy model can be straightforwardly extended to more countries. The only amendment is that the Bayesian updating process of beliefs about the early-liquidation yield in a third country, say C, entails conditioning beliefs on the outcomes in both Countries A and B. And so on, when accounting for more countries.

6. CONCLUSION

This paper featured international contagion of bank runs in a third-generation model of financial crises through an informational channel. To do so, we capitalized on a model of financial crises by Chang and Velasco (2001), while focusing on debt rollover and taking a demand deposit system as given. We departed from that model by taking account of foreign creditors' expectations regarding being repaid and by introducing an informational edge of home depositors over foreign creditors regarding liquidation costs of assets. We then extended the resulting model to a two-country framework.

Our main findings have been the following. First, the probability of bank crisis increases with the subjective appraisal by foreign creditors of the chance that the early-liquidation yield takes a low value. Second, bank panics in a country may propagate to other countries, as foreign creditors reassess early-liquidation yields. Indeed, lenders bid lower prices to buy new debt issued by banks in those countries, which entails that those banks become more illiquid and are therefore more prone to runs. Third, both the degree of correlation between yields across countries and the strength of the Bayesian reassessment of the early-liquidation yield in the catalyst country play a crucial role in the vulnerability to contagion as well as its intensity.

While opening the door for the spread of bank runs and concomitant sudden reversals of capital flows, the model developed in this paper is not, strictly speaking, a model of contagion of twin crises, since it does not incorporate a monetary sector. A possible follow-up is thus to allow for the simultaneous spread of currency crises by bringing in a monetary sector. A second possible extension is paving the way for simultaneous drops in securities prices. Indeed, as pointed out in the introduction, collapses of asset values have often been observed in recent crises. Introducing collateralized borrowing in the model may be a step in the right direction. Another idea for a related paper is highlighting informational contagion in second-generation models of crises with an equilibrium selection mechanism *à la* Carlsson and van Damme (1993).

REFERENCES

Aghion, P., Bacchetta, P., & Banerjee, A. (2001). Currency crises and monetary policy in an economy with credit constraints. *European Economic Review*, *45*, 1121–1150.

Aghion, P., Bacchetta P., & Banerjee, A. (2003). A balance sheet approach to currency crises. *Journal of Economic Theory* (forthcoming).

Allen, F., & Gale, D. M. (1998). Optimal financial crises. *The Journal of Finance*, *53*, 1245–1284.

Caballero, R., & Krishnamurthy, A. (2001). International and domestic collateral constraints in a model of emerging market crises. *Journal of Monetary Economics*, *48*, 513–548.

Calvo, G. A. (1999). Contagion in emerging markets: When Wall Street is a carrier. Working Paper, University of Maryland. http://www.bsos.umd.edu/econ/ciecrp.htm.

Carlsson, H., & van Damme, E. (1993). Global games and equilibrium selection. *Econometrica*, *61*, 989–1018.

Chang, R., & Majnoni, G. (2002). Fundamentals, beliefs, and financial contagion. *European Economic Review*, *46*, 801–808.

Chang, R., & Velasco, A. (2000). Banks, debt maturity and financial crises. *Journal of International Economics*, *51*, 169–194.

Chang, R., & Velasco, A. (2001). A model of financial crises in emerging markets. *Quarterly Journal of Economics*, *116*, 489–517.

Chen, Y. (1999). Banking panics: The role of the first-come, first-served rule and information externalities. *Journal of Political Economy*, *107*, 946–968.

Dasgupta, A. (2003). Financial contagion through capital connections: A model of the origin and spread of bank panics. Working Paper, Yale University. http://fmg2.lse.ac.uk/~amil/research.html.

Diamond, D. W., & Dybvig, P. H. (1983). Bank runs, deposit insurance, and liquidity. *Journal of Political Economy*, *91*, 401–419.

Flood, R. P., & Garber, P. M. (1984). Collapsing exchange-rate regimes. *Journal of International Economics*, *17*, 1–13.

Garber, P. M., & Grilli, V. U. (1989). Bank runs in open economies and the international transmission of panics. *Journal of International Economics*, *27*, 165–175.

Goldstein, I., & Pauzner, P. (2003). Contagion of self-fulfilling financial crises due to diversification of investment portfolios. Working Paper, Tel Aviv University. http://www.tau.ac.il/~pauzner.

Goldstein, M. (1998). The Asian financial crises: Causes, cures and systemic implications. In: *Policy Analyses in International Economics* (Vol. 55). Washington, DC: Institute for International Economics.

Kodres, L. E., & Pritsker, M. (2002). A rational expectations model of financial contagion. *The Journal of Finance*, *57*, 769–799.

Krugman, P. R. (1979). A model of balance-of-payments crisis. *Journal of Money, Credit, and Banking*, *11*, 311–325.

Krugman, P. R. (1999). Balance sheets, the transfer problem and financial crises. In: *International Finance and Financial Crises: Essays in Honor of Robert P. Flood Jr.* Washington, DC: International Monetary Fund.

Kumar, M. S., & Persaud, A. (2002). Pure contagion and investors' shifting risk appetite: Analytical issues and empirical evidence. *International Finance*, *5*, 401–436.

Masson, P. R. (1999). Contagion: Macroeconomic models with multiple equilibria. *Journal of International Money and Finance*, *18*, 587–602.

Morris, S., & Shin, H. S. (1998). Unique equilibrium in a model of self-fulfilling currency attacks. *American Economic Review*, *88*, 587–597.

Obstfeld, M. (1994). The logic of currency crises. *Cahiers Économiques et Monétaires*, *43*, 189–213.

Vaugirard, V. E. (2004). Informational contagion of sudden stops in a global games framework. *Open Economies Review*, *15*, 169–192.

BANK FAILURES IN BANKING PANICS: RISKY BANKS OR ROAD KILL?

Gerald P. Dwyer Jr. and R. W. Hafer

ABSTRACT

Are banks that fail in banking panics the riskiest ones prior to the panics? The free banking era in the United States provides useful data to examine this question because the assets held by the banks were traded on the New York Stock Exchange. We estimate the ex ante riskiness of a bank's portfolio by examining the portfolio relative to mean-variance frontiers and by examining its leverage and notes relative to assets. The ex ante riskiness of a bank's portfolio helps to predict which banks fail in a banking panic.

1. INTRODUCTION

Are banks that fail in banking panics the riskiest ones or are they just in the wrong place at the wrong time, in short "road kill?" Many discussions of banking panics and banking crises suggest that the riskiest banks are the ones most likely to fail. There is no doubt that the banks that fail are in a panic are those most susceptible to the problems at the time. Are these banks the ones that appear before the panic to be the most susceptible to problems? This question acquires some importance because banks are using value at risk to measure their riskiness, and banking regulators are encouraging banks to do so (Altman & Saunders, 2001). Correctly measured, it is hard to imagine a world in which reducing an individual bank's riskiness does not reduce its probability of failing (e.g. Kolari et al., 2002; Wheelock & Wilson, 1995). It is not obvious, though, that reducing an individual bank's ex

Bank and Financial Market Efficiency: Global Perspectives
Research in Banking and Finance, Volume 5, 47–70

ISSN: 1567-7915/doi:10.1016/S1567-7915(04)05003-7

ante riskiness is likely to reduce its probability of failing in a banking panic or financial crisis.

In this paper, we examine whether a bank's ex ante riskiness is a reliable guide to its fate in a banking panic. In general, it is extremely difficult to tell whether the banks that appeared riskiest before the event were the ones that failed in banking panics such as at the start of the 1930s Great Depression. There is substantial evidence that banking panics are associated with events that have negative effects on the value of banks' assets as opposed to being sunspot phenomena (Gorton, 1988; Gorton & Winton, 2002; Hasan & Dwyer, 1994; Rolnick & Weber, 1984). Banks' ex post exposures to the actual events invariably are clear after the fact, whether the events are banking panics in the 1800s, the Depression in the 1930s, the Texas oil bust in the 1980s, or the Asian financial crisis in the 1990s. Deposit flows in the Great Depression are consistent with at least some depositors being able to predict in 1929 and later years which banks were more likely to fail (Calomiris & Mason, 1997; Saunders & Wilson, 1996), but riskier banks from the standpoint of 1928 may or may not have been those that appeared most likely to fail in later years (Gorton & Winton, 2002). Banks generally hold nonmarketable assets and these assets' riskiness is not entirely apparent from banks' balance sheets at the time even if it is apparent now from information available to researchers today. Further clouding the evidence on the ex ante riskiness of banks, government authorities exercised substantial discretion concerning individual banks' fates.

Because of these problems with recent episodes, we use data from banking panics in 1860 to examine the importance of ex ante riskiness for banks' fates in a panic. There were runs on state banking systems in this period, which makes it possible to use these data to examine banks' fates in these panics (Bodenhorn, 2003; Hasan & Dwyer, 1994). Available evidence indicates that the single most important predictor of which banks failed during these runs are their ex post losses on bond portfolios (Dwyer & Hasan, 2003; Economopoulos, 1990; Hasan & Dwyer, 1994). These banks' primary activity was issuing banknotes that were used as currency by the public with bonds held as required backing for the banknotes. Hence, these bond portfolios were not an ancillary part of a bank's business that happened to turn out badly; these portfolios were an integral part of the banks' business. The ex ante riskiness of these bonds can be estimated from market prices of the bonds in trades on the New York Stock Exchange (Dwyer, Hafer & Weber, 1999). These market prices before the panics makes it possible for us to use standard financial tools to estimate banks' ex ante riskiness in an important part of their business.[1]

Before presenting the empirical analysis, we briefly describe free banking in the United States. These free banks were not laissez faire banks; there were substantial legal restrictions on how banks operated.[2] These banks were called *free banks* because there was no discretionary restriction of entry into banking, a business that revolved around issuing notes used as currency. These free banking systems were an innovation compared to the pre-existing chartered banking in which a bank had to be granted an individual legislative charter to operate. Runs on banking systems occurred in various states in 1854, 1857 and 1860, but the paucity of data for 1854 makes the 1854 runs unlikely to be informative and the relatively few failures in 1857 make the 1857 panic useless by itself for comparing failed banks with other banks. As a result, we focus on panics at the onset of the Civil War in 1860 in which selected state banking systems had many free banks failing.

In our empirical analysis, we estimate the riskiness of banks' bond portfolios relative to the mean variance frontiers and find substantial support for the proposition that this measure of their portfolio's ex ante riskiness is informative for predicting their fates. Banks' leverage and exposures to runs on notes also help to predict their fates.

2. FREE BANKING

Free banking in the United States began in 1837 when Michigan passed the first free banking law and ended in the 1860s when the federal government created the national banking system. This era in U.S. banking history has received a great deal of attention, partly to examine whether these relatively unregulated banks engaged in widespread fraud and partly to examine the implications of more recent banking regulation.

Because the federal government did not charter banks, all banks in the free banking period were state banks. Bank entry in states with free banking laws was not subject to discretionary control and was easier than in states that did not have free banking laws (Economopoulos & O'Neill, 1995). In a free banking state, a bank could be opened and issue banknotes after satisfying specific, legislative requirements. These requirements included meeting minimum bank capital requirements and providing collateral for banknotes issued.

The aggregate balance sheets in Table 1 for free banks in Illinois, Indiana and Wisconsin illustrate the free banks' activities. Bonds and loans are over seventy percent of total assets, with the percentage of assets that are state bonds varying substantially, from 61% in Illinois to 36% in Indiana and 28% in Wisconsin. Notes and deposits are approximately 60% of total liabilities, with the percentage of liabilities that are notes also varying substantially, from 57% in Illinois to 28% in Indiana and 25% in Wisconsin. Equity capital is a substantial source of funding for the free banks: 35% of liabilities in Illinois; 42% in Indiana; and 40% in Wisconsin. In these as in other free banking states, liabilities primarily

Table 1. Balance Sheets of Free Banks in Illinois, Indiana, and Wisconsin (Thousands of Dollars).

Aggregates with Summary Common Categories	Illinois (October 1, 1860)		Indiana (January 7, 1861)		Wisconsin (January 7, 1861)	
	Dollars	Fraction	Dollars	Fraction	Dollars	Fraction
Assets						
Bonds	11,921	0.613	1,298	0.355	4,656	0.279
Loans	2,485	0.128	1,480	0.405	8,051	0.483
Notes of other banks	287	0.015	134	0.037	1,163	0.070
Cash and other cash items, due from banks and brokers	3,576	0.184	292	0.080	871	0.052
Specie	506	0.026	195	0.053	371	0.022
Real estate	518	0.027	70	0.019	364	0.022
Other accounts	145	0.007	189	0.052	1,199	0.072
Total assets	19,438		3,658		16,676	
Liabilities						
Notes in circulation	11,011	0.566	1,036	0.283	4,233	0.254
Deposits	808	0.042	782	0.214	4,081	0.245
Due to others	486	0.025	77	0.021	1,634	0.098
Other accounts	381	0.020	213	0.058	0	0.000
Capital	6,751	0.347	1,550	0.424	6,732	0.404
Total liabilities	19,437		3,658		16,681	

Notes: Data are from individual banks' balance sheets. We have used common titles for categories with slightly different titles in the originals and have combined related items to make the states' balance sheets comparable. Assets and liabilities do not add to exact equality in the originals.

Sources: The data are from U.S. Congress (1861). The states and the respective pages are: Illinois, pp. 222–227; Indiana, pp. 231–232; Wisconsin, pp. 256–277.

are banknotes and equity capital. In this period, notes issued by banks are the predominant form of currency in the United States with no government-provided currency in existence.

The holdings of bonds and issuance of notes are related: state laws of the period required free banks to hold bonds as backing for their notes. Table 2 summarizes the free banking laws concerning banknotes and bonds, here illustrated by the laws in Illinois, Indiana and Wisconsin as of 1861. These free banking laws required that the banks hold bonds, with the banks having substantial latitude about exactly which bonds to hold. Hence, the attitude of a bank's owner toward risk could be reflected in the particular bonds held by a bank. The laws in all three states imposed substantial penalties on a bank for not redeeming its notes on demand, up to forfeiture of the bank's charter. The laws in many states also required that a bank keep collateral related to the value of the notes after the notes were issued. Failure to maintain sufficient backing in the bond account in Illinois and Wisconsin

Table 2. Major Provisions of the Free Banking Lawsà Illinois, Indiana and Wisconsin at Start of 1861.

Restriction	Illinois	Indiana	Wisconsin
Backing for banknotes			
Eligible bonds	U.S. and states paying full interest	U.S., Indiana and states paying interest semi-annually or more frequently	U.S. and states paying full interest. Also secured Wisconsin railroad bonds with 7% coupon, but not more than half of a bank's total bond deposit
Value of bonds used to determine notes issues	Ninety percent of the last 6 months average price. Fifty percent if coupon less than 6%. Not more than par value or market value at time of deposit	Ten elevenths of value. Shall be, or made equal to, 6% coupon bonds. Not more than par value or market value at time of deposit	The average of the last 6 months price. Shall be, or be made equal to, 6% coupon bonds. Not more than par value or market value at time of deposit
Other limits on notes issued	None	Total note issue for all free banks not more than $6 million	Total note issue not to exceed subscribed capital
Bond account deficient when	Bonds lessened in value or insufficient as security	Bonds have depreciated in value by 5% or issuer fails to pay interest	Market value of bonds for 60 days less than value at which deposited
Grace period to make up deficiency	Reasonable time (in practice before 1861, 40 days)	None specified	30 days
At end of grace period	Bank closed	Nothing	Bank closed
Bank size			
Minimum size	Minimum subscribed and paid-in capital of $50,000	At least $50,000 in bonds deposited	Minimum subscribed capital of $25,000
Maximum size	None	Total note issue not to exceed $200,000	$500,000
Stockholders' liability	Double subscribed capital	Double subscribed capital	Double subscribed capital plus bond for value of one-quarter of notes issued
Liability after sale or transfer of stock	6 months	1 year	6 months
Protested notes			
Grace period to redeem	10 days	None	10 days
At end of grace period	Bank closed	Bank closed	Bank closed
Penalty paid to holder of protested notes	12% per year	10% per year	5% damages

Sources: Illinois (1851–1861), Indiana (1851–1861), and Wisconsin (1852–1861).

resulted in forfeiture of the bank's charter, a provision which was enforced. There was no such provision in Indiana.

Many free banks failed. Research on free banking has focused on whether free banks that failed were primarily due to owners operating unsound banks sometimes called "wildcat banks" – or to exogenous events. The general conclusion from the research is that banks generally were operated in a way that was consistent with the banks continuing operations absent some negative exogenous event (Bodenhorn, 2003; Economopoulos, 1988; Rolnick & Weber, 1984). A related argument about free banking is a claim that banks would locate in remote areas "where the wildcats roam," thereby raising the cost of redeeming banknotes and of acquiring information about the banks. Dwyer (1996) examines this colorful view of banks' choices of locations and finds evidence inconsistent with it after some experience with free banking.

The importance of exogenous events for explaining free banks' failures has received a great deal of attention. For example, Rolnick and Weber (1983, 1984), Economopoulos (1988, 1990), Hasan and Dwyer (1994) and Dwyer and Hasan (2003) examine the effects on free banks of the decline in southern bond prices at the onset of the Civil War. All of these authors find that holdings of southern bonds and losses on those bonds are important determinants of whether free banks remained open or ceased operations.

Hasan and Dwyer (1994) and Dwyer and Hasan (2003) examine whether there were runs on the banking systems and conclude that such runs did occur, contrary to some prior suggestions. Dwyer and Hasan find that the much higher failure rate in Illinois than in Wisconsin in 1861 is partly explained by a suspension of payments in Wisconsin and not in Illinois. This suspension also reduced noteholders' losses in Wisconsin. Dwyer and Hasan's evidence also indicates that the ex post decreases in the value of the banks' bond portfolios and their leverage are important for explaining both which banks closed and noteholders' losses in those banks.

3. THE RISKINESS OF BANKS' PORTFOLIOS

These ex post losses on southern bonds at the start of the Civil War do not imply that portfolios with substantial amounts of these bonds were riskier ex ante. Bond prices and constructed portfolios provide evidence concerning the riskiness of the bonds in banks' portfolios.

We concentrate on the runs on Illinois' and Wisconsin's banking systems at the start of Civil War, in which many banks failed. We also include data from Indiana, which had fewer bank failures, as a contrast. There also were runs

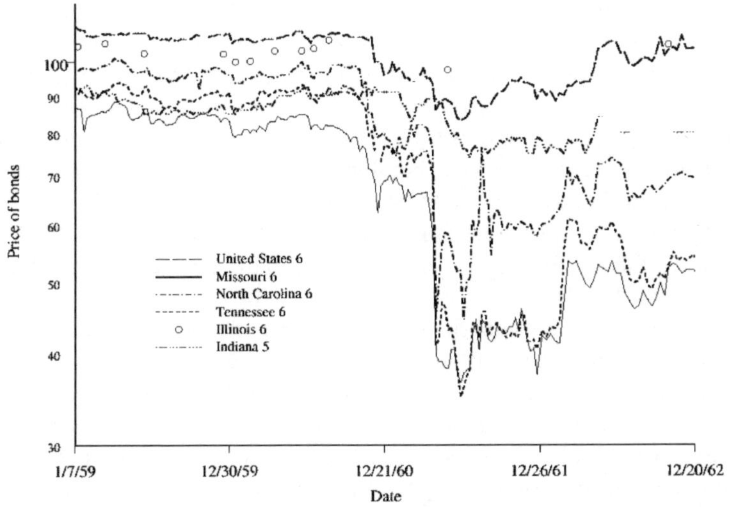

Fig. 1. Prices of Bonds (January 7, 1859 to December 20, 1862).

on free banking systems in 1854 in Indiana and 1857 in New York. For 1854, there is little of the weekly data on bond prices that we use to estimate efficient portfolios of bonds (Dwyer, Hafer & Weber, 1999). In 1857, relatively few banks failed.

3.1. Bond Prices

Figure 1 shows weekly data on bond prices from 1859 through 1862 for northern, border state and southern bonds from Dwyer, Hafer and Weber (1999). The figure includes the prices of state government bonds that account for at least 10% of banks' portfolios in Illinois, Indiana or Wisconsin in October 1860. Bonds issued by Illinois and Indiana are more than ten percent of the banks' bond holdings in those states respectively, but these bonds are relatively unimportant in other states. United States bonds are included in the figure for comparison with the state bonds; these bonds were not held by any banks in Indiana and Wisconsin and they are less than ten percent of Illinois banks' aggregate portfolio.

The onset of the Civil War is evident in Fig. 1. There are large decreases in the prices of southern bonds after Lincoln's nomination in May 1860 and precipitous decreases with the beginning of open warfare in April 1861. While the prices of southern and border state bonds fall at the start of the Civil War, the prices of U.S. and northern bonds do not fall nearly as much.

The decreases in southern bond prices are an important contributor to the closure of 44% of the banks in Wisconsin and over 87% of the banks in Illinois during a period when two of the 20 banks in Indiana closed.[3] Almost two-thirds of the bonds held by Illinois and Wisconsin banks are the southern and border state bonds that so clearly reflect the onset of the Civil War. Only 35% of the bonds held by Indiana banks are southern bonds, but this does not reflect greater diversification: over 60% of the bonds held by Indiana banks are Indiana bonds. The price of Indiana bonds has a substantial fall, from about 90% of par in early 1861 to 70% of par later in the year, but this is small relative to the price decreases of southern and border state bonds.

Ex post, a portfolio of southern bonds was risky in the sense that there were large losses on those bonds. The criticism that free banks were risky because they held risky portfolios is long-standing (Dowrie, 1913; Hammond, 1957; Krueger, 1933).

Ex ante, a portfolio of southern bonds may or may not have been particularly risky. Greater riskiness of southern and border state bonds even before Lincoln was nominated in May 1860 is suggested by these bonds' lower prices in Fig. 1. Southern and border state bonds generally have the same 6% coupon as northern and U.S. bonds. Absent knowledge of any other differences, greater default risk could explain these lower prices. There is no other apparent evidence of greater risk, though, and the risk of a portfolio of bonds is a function of the covariance of the returns, not just the volatility of individual bond's returns or the probability of individual defaults.

Efficient portfolios of the bonds held by the banks and the riskiness of the banks' actual portfolios can provide more systematic evidence on the riskiness of these bond portfolios. The underlying bond data are weekly returns. The banks' actual portfolios included small amounts of many securities, and data are not available for all of these securities. For example, six banks in Wisconsin have relatively small holdings of Michigan bonds, for which we have no prices. We estimate the riskiness of actual portfolios and the efficient portfolios using prices for securities that are widely held by the banks. These are prices of bonds issued by the United States government and the states of California, Georgia, Indiana, Kentucky, Louisiana, Missouri, North Carolina, Ohio, Pennsylvania, Tennessee and Virginia. We have no reason to think that the omission of other bonds biases our results one way or the other. The omitted bonds tend to be northern bonds, but they are likely to be less liquid precisely because they are not traded often enough to create a useful record. Overall, we think that it is better to omit the bonds on which we have no data than to make speculative assumptions about the first and second moments of their returns.

Figure 2 shows efficient frontiers estimated for dates chosen to highlight major events. These frontiers show the minimum variance given the rate of return, with

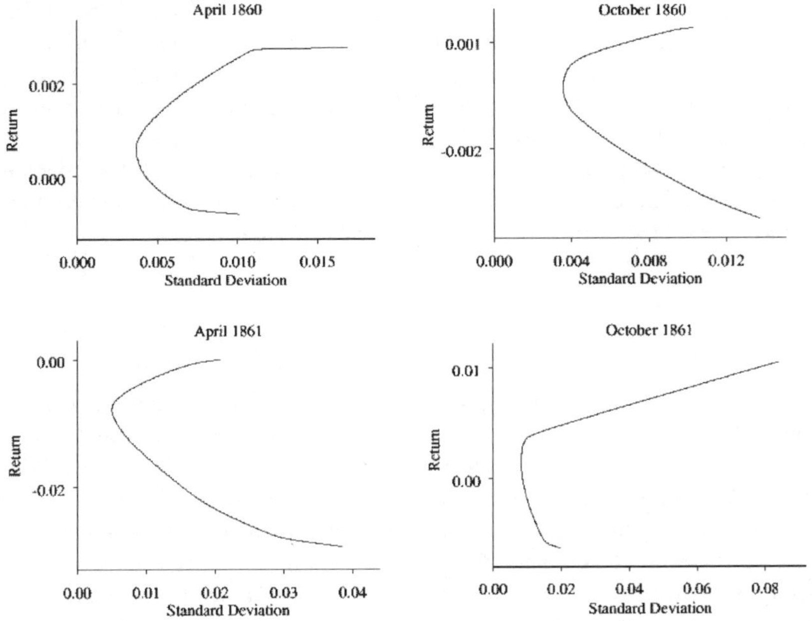

Fig. 2. Efficient Frontiers.

the returns ranging from the lowest to the highest. We estimate efficient frontiers for: April 1860, just prior to Lincoln's nomination; October 1860, just prior to Lincoln's election; April 1861, the start of the hostilities; and October 1861, when the war is in progress. Each of these frontiers uses the most recent 26 weeks of data through the end of the month to estimate the means and standard deviations of the portfolios.[4]

The frontiers in Fig. 2 have rough parabolic shapes. The implication that a risk-return frontier must be parabolic relies on unrestricted weights of various securities, and the frontiers in Fig. 2 are estimated subject to the restriction that bond holdings be nonnegative. We impose this restriction because a portfolio that is short some bonds is not consistent with the laws of this period or with the portfolio being held as backing for notes. We also do not include a risk-free asset because very few banks held the risk-free asset – gold or silver that paid zero interest – backing for their notes.[5]

The estimated frontiers reflect the dramatically worsening situation in terms of both the portfolios' returns and standard deviations. By April 1861, none of the bonds has a positive return for the prior 26 weeks.[6] The returns for the next half year, from April 1861 to October 1861, range up to 1.05% per week, but these high returns are accompanied by high standard deviations. The standard deviation of the minimum-standard-deviation portfolio is a good summary measure of the volatility of returns. The minimum standard deviations are 0.37% per week in April 1860 and 0.36% per week in October 1860. The minimum standard deviation in April 1861 increases almost 40% to 0.50% per week. The minimum standard deviation in the six months from April 1861 to October 1861 is higher yet: 0.83% per week. While this standard deviation indicates continuing substantial turmoil after the fall in bond prices, at least the prices of most bonds are increasing.

3.2. The Riskiness of Banks' Portfolios

Figure 3 shows the fates of banks with different portfolios combined with the efficient frontier for April 1860. The left-hand panel shows banks that remained open or closed, and the right-hand panel shows banks that failed.[7] We define a bank as *closing* if the bank ceased operating and noteholders were paid in full. We combine data on banks that close with those that remain open because noteholders suffer no losses in closed banks.[8] We define a bank as *failing* if the bank ceased operating and noteholders were paid less than the face value of their notes from the bank's bond account.[9] The data plotted are the weekly mean returns and standard deviations in April 1860 for banks in Illinois, Indiana and Wisconsin that existed

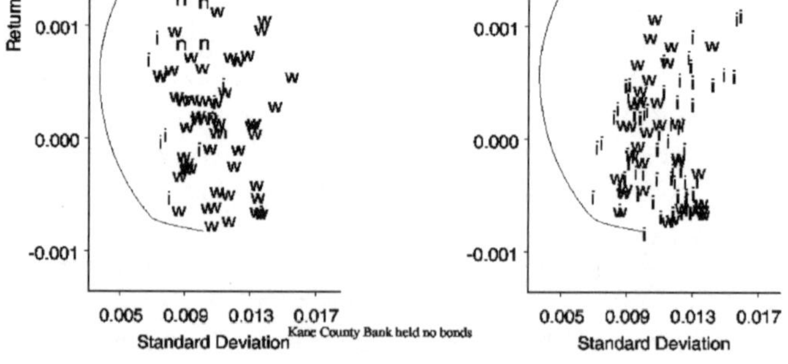

Fig. 3. Banks' Fates and Their Portfolios.

in October. The estimates do not substantially reflect the banks' relative ability to estimate the risk and implications of war because October 1860 precedes Lincoln's election and the dramatic drop in bond prices. The symbols in Fig. 3 are letters indicating the state in which a bank is located. The letter *i* indicates a bank in Illinois, the letter *n* indicates a bank in Indiana and the letter *w* indicates a bank in Wisconsin.[10]

The striking contrast visible in Fig. 3 is the higher returns for banks that closed or remained open compared to banks that failed. For a given standard deviation, the banks that failed have noticeably lower returns. This is especially striking because these average returns are for November 1859 through April 1860, well before the election leading to the Civil War. It is not apparent that the banks which failed were the riskiest ex ante in terms of raw standard deviations. On the other hand, it is clear that the banks with lower returns for a given standard deviation were more likely to fail. That said, the banks in both sides of the figure are clustered around low returns, presumably at least partly due to deviations of ex post returns from expected returns. The banks in Indiana appear to have higher returns than the other banks, with many of the Indiana banks in the upper half of the area enclosed by the frontier.

Figure 4 examines the riskiness of banks that failed compared to the riskiness of other banks in a different way. The ex ante standard deviation of the return on a bank's portfolios is one possible way to examine the bank's likelihood of failure. Leverage is another measure of risk, which can be measured in a variety of

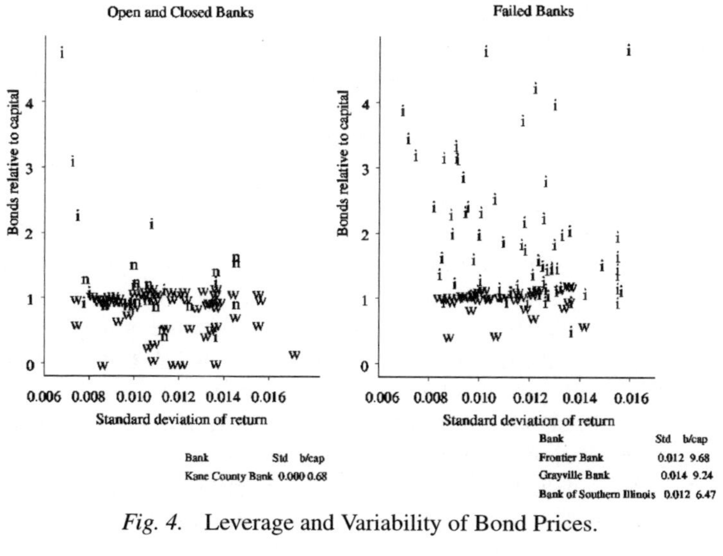

Fig. 4. Leverage and Variability of Bond Prices.

ways. In Fig. 4, we measure leverage by the ratio of bonds to capital because this measure of leverage reflects the risk borne by stockholders for a given standard deviation of returns. Figure 4 is similar to Fig. 3, with the open and closed banks in the left panel and the failed banks in the right panel and the same symbols for the observations. Figure 4 shows that banks which stayed open or closed have a low ratio of bonds to capital, a low standard deviation, or both. Many banks that failed have similar ratios of bonds to capital and standard deviations as banks that did not fail, but a fair number of banks that failed in Illinois have relatively high ratios of bonds to capital and high standard deviations. Figure 4 also shows that banks in Illinois have far higher ratios of bonds to capital than banks in Indiana and Wisconsin. The average ratio of bonds to capital is 2.22 in Illinois, 1.12 in Indiana and 0.92 in Wisconsin. The lower ratio of bonds to capital in Wisconsin than in the other two states is explained by the legal restriction in Wisconsin limiting notes issued by banks to no more than their equity capital. There is no similar explanation for the contrast between Indiana and Illinois though. Combinations of high leverage and high portfolio risk appear to be associated with failure, although the relative importance of the two is not discernable from the figure alone.

4. THE PREDICTABILITY OF BANK FAILURES CONDITIONAL ON EX ANTE RISKINESS

In this section, we report our statistical analysis of the relationship between banks' and the ex ante riskiness of their bond portfolios and their leverage. We estimate the probability of failure using a maximum likelihood estimator to estimate the relationship between a bank's riskiness and its fate. The equation for the probability of a bank remaining open is a standard probit with an underlying normal distribution of the unobservable variable, the present value of the bank's earnings.

The measures of ex ante risk that we use are related to a bank's bond portfolio and leverage. The leverage that matters to owners of a bank is the ratio of bonds to equity capital. The lower this ratio, the more the losses that can be absorbed by stockholders before a bank has a negative book value of capital. As an additional measure of risk, our statistical analysis includes the exposure of a bank to a run on its notes, measured by the ratio of notes to assets. Because we know that there was a run on banknotes in 1861, this measure of exposure to a run on notes may be an ex post measure of risk and not an ex ante measure, which means that caution is required in interpreting it as a measure of ex ante risk.

In our statistical analysis, we use the returns on banks' portfolios for the 26 weeks ending in May 1860. These data from late 1859 and early 1860 are prior to Lincoln's nomination and are unlikely to reflect the full effects of Lincoln's nomination, his election, the secession of southern states and the subsequent outbreak of war. They may partly reflect anticipation of those events. We measure the riskiness of the banks' portfolios using both the mean weekly return and the weekly return's standard deviation. Figure 3 also suggests that deviations from the efficient frontier may be important, possibly due to managerial inefficiency, an argument related to that Wheelock and Wilson (1995). We measure a bank's deviation from the frontier by the horizontal, vertical and Euclidian distances from the frontier.

Some additional variables are from the banks' balance sheets. The balance sheet data are from balance sheets in October 1860 for banks in Illinois and Indiana and in January 1861 for banks in Wisconsin.

These measures of ex ante risk are not the only variables that are likely to be important for determining a bank's present value. Additional variables included in the statistical analysis are: a dummy variable equal to one for a bank in Indiana and Wisconsin and zero for a bank in Illinois; a bank's age; the population density of the county in which a bank is located; and the bank's assets. We include a dummy variable equal to one for banks in Indiana and Wisconsin and zero for Illinois, a grouping consistent with the characteristics of the banks and the regulatory environment.[11] The balance sheets of banks in Illinois have smaller deposits and loans compared to banks in Indiana and Wisconsin. In addition, Illinois closed banks when a bank's bond account was deficient or someone protested the bank's notes, but Wisconsin had an effective suspension of payments (Dwyer & Hasan, 2003). Indiana never closed banks solely because of deficient bond accounts. We include the bank's age in the equations as a dummy variable equal to zero unless a bank is one year old or less in October 1861 in Illinois and Indiana or in January 1862 in Wisconsin. This measure of age is consistent with Gorton's (1996) evidence on the riskiness of new banks. Population density is included because low population density may be associated with remote locations and wildcat banking. Finally, we include the asset size of each bank, which may be associated with sunk costs in building the bank's reputation or other factors. It is possible that larger banks are more likely to stay open than smaller banks, although there is no strong theoretical reason to expect any particular relationship.

4.1. Portfolio Riskiness

Table 3 presents the results of estimating these equations including all variables other than deviations from the banks' efficient portfolio frontiers. Several variables are transformed by logarithms because the equation's fit is better

Table 3. Banks Remaining Open and Closing Compared to Banks Failing Illinois, Indiana and Wisconsin 1861.

Right-Hand-Side Variables	All Variables		Return Deleted	
	Coefficient Std. Dev.	Marginal Effect *p*-Value	Coefficient Std. Dev.	Marginal Effect *p*-Value
Intercept	−0.471		−2.544	
	3.397	0.890	3.172	0.667
Dummy variable for	1.286	0.409	1.555	0.479
Indiana and	0.362	$<10^{-3}$	0.343	$<10^{-3}$
Wisconsin				
Standard deviation of	−171.022	−51.264	−151.982	−45.150
bonds' return	52.612	0.001	51.842	0.003
Mean return on bonds	472.162	141.531		
	158.795	0.003		
Logarithm of	1.333	0.399	1.239	0.368
bonds/capital	0.396	$<10^{-3}$	0.382	0.001
Logarithm of	−2.242	−0.672	−2.163	−0.642
notes/assets	0.0451	$<10^{-3}$	0.437	$<10^{-3}$
Dummy variable for age	−0.120	−0.041	−0.079	−0.027
not more than 1 year	0.304	0.692	0.292	0.786
Population density	−0.507	−0.152	−1.871	−0.556
	1.900	0.789	1.857	0.313
Logarithm of assets	−0.108	−0.032	0.062	0.018
	0.281	0.700	0.260	0.811
Maximized value of log likelihood	77.919		−82.682	
Number of observations	199		199	
Chi-square likelihood ratio test statistic	106.818		97.290	
Degrees of freedom	8		7	
p-Value	$<10^{-3}$		$<10^{-3}$	

when logarithmic transformations of the variables are used. The table reports the estimated coefficients and their standard errors. The table also presents the *p*-values of likelihood ratio tests of the hypothesis that each coefficient is zero and the marginal effects of a change in each variable. The marginal effects of continuous variables are the partial derivatives of the estimated equation evaluated at the means of the right-hand-side variables.[12] The marginal effects of dummy variables are the changes in the probability associated with a change in the dummy variable from zero to one. The table also includes the likelihood ratio statistic to test whether all coefficients other than the intercept are zero.

The control variables' estimated coefficients in Table 3 that are statistically significant generally have the anticipated signs. The surprising result is the positive sign of the ratio of bonds to capital.[13] This estimate may reflect the endogeneity of this particular variable, with higher present-value banks holding more bonds relative to capital. This positive coefficient also can be interpreted as indicating that Wisconsin's restriction on note issuance relative to capital reduced the banks' present values.

These coefficient estimates in Table 3 provide substantial support for the informativeness of a bank's ex ante riskiness. A bank's ex ante riskiness is measured by the standard deviation of the portfolio's return, the mean return, the bank's leverage and its exposure to a run on notes. Both the standard deviation and the mean return are statistically significant; they also are jointly significant. In addition, higher notes relative to assets clearly increases the probability of failure, with this coefficient also having a p-value less than 0.1%.

The positive estimated coefficient of the mean return on bonds, which is the opposite of what would be expected if a higher return is associated with more risk and a lower probability of continuing in business, suggests a problem. This positive coefficient is more consistent with the mean return being a measure of a bank's ex post losses. The correlation between the mean return on the bond portfolio for the 26 weeks ending in April 1860 and an ex post measure of loss per dollar of notes is −0.526.[14] This negative correlation suggests that the mean return partly reflects later losses but is hardly sufficient to be sure.

This interpretation of the mean return also is consistent with the lower return in April 1860 for banks that failed compared to banks that did not fail, a comparison evident in Fig. 3. In this figure, this appears as vertical deviations from the efficient frontier. These deviations from the efficient frontier may be due to unexpected decreases in the prices of bonds, decreases that continued into 1861 and resulted in the demise of many banks; they also may simply reflect inefficiency of many insufficiently diversified banks.

In any case, our conclusion about the importance of ex ante risk is not dependent on the mean return on bonds. The second estimated equation in Table 3 shows that the risk variables continue to be important when the mean return is excluded from the estimated equation. There is practically no effect on the other estimated coefficients. The standard deviation of returns still helps to predict whether a bank remains open and the Chi-square test statistic for the standard deviation's coefficients being zero has a p-value of 0.3%. Notes relative to assets continue to be informative and consistent with higher values indicating higher risk. A bank's leverage appears to be informative, although this does not reflect risk directly: the coefficient on leverage is positive, an anomalous coefficient from the point of view of higher ratios of bonds to capital indicating higher risk.

The association between a bank's standard deviation and its fate is the clearest evidence that the ex ante riskiness of a bank's bond portfolio helps to predict whether a bank fails. The importance of exposure to a run on notes bolsters the result for the standard deviation, but the interpretation of its importance hinges on a judgement about the ex ante risk of a run on notes. The mean return on portfolios is quite statistically significant, but its interpretation is not obvious. In the next section, we explore the association between a bank's mean return, its fate and the possibility that lower mean returns are associated with ex ante inefficiency of banks' portfolios.

4.2. Portfolio Inefficiency

Figure 3 suggests that deviations from the efficient frontier may be important for predicting which banks fail. The two panels of Table 4 present test statistics for examining the importance of those deviations. The first panel shows test statistics for horizontal and vertical deviations from the efficient frontier. We interpret these statistics as providing little support for the importance of inefficient portfolios, overall being consistent with the proposition that the mean return largely is important because it is a proxy for ex post losses. Vertical deviations associated with lower mean returns are statistically significant but horizontal deviations are not. The vertical deviations are more directly affected by unexpected decreases in bond prices than are the insignificant horizontal deviations. Further evidence that the mean return is a proxy for the ex post loss is provided by the change in the p-value for the mean return when the vertical deviation is added to the equation:

Table 4. Test Statistics for Alternative Hypotheses.

Hypothesis	Chi-Square Test Statistic	Degrees of Freedom	p-Value
Equations with horizontal and vertical deviations from frontier added			
No vertical deviation	9.155	1	0.002
No horizontal deviation	0.258	1	0.612
No horizontal deviation and no vertical deviation	9.399	2	0.009
No vertical deviation conditional on no horizontal deviation	9.141	1	0.003
No horizontal deviation conditional on no vertical deviation	0.244	1	0.622
No standard deviation	4.391	1	0.036
Equations with Euclidian Distance from frontier added			
No Euclidian deviation	0.088	1	0.767
No standard deviation	2.936	1	0.087

the mean return's p-value changes from a statistically significant 0.3% to a very insignificant 55.8%.

The bottom panel of Table 4 shows tests based on using Euclidian distance to measure deviations from the frontier. The Euclidian distance is the minimum distance to the frontier from the bank's mean return and standard deviation. This measure of distance has a p-value of 76.7%, nowhere near statistically significant at usual significance levels. This measure provides no support for the importance of the deviations from the frontier, although this measure of distance reflects the vertical deviation in addition to the horizontal deviation. Overall, we conclude that there is little evidence that deviations from the frontier are important, although there is some additional evidence that the coefficient of the mean return partly reflects ex post losses.

5. CONCLUSION

Greater ex ante riskiness helps to predict a bank's fate, at least in this banking panic. The ex ante variability of returns on a bank's portfolio consistently helps predict its fate. While the importance of the standard deviation is the strongest evidence for the importance of ex ante risk, this is not the only evidence. We find that a bank's exposure to runs on notes is associated with a higher likelihood of failure. There is a clear association between a bank's mean return on its portfolio well before the panics and the final outcomes, but this is clouded by the correlation of the mean return and the later ex post loss.

The evidence in this paper is based on one episode, but it is a fairly typical banking panic with atypical data available. An exogenous event occurred that raised questions about the ability of the banks to honor their obligations and a run on the banks ensued. We find that riskier banks were more likely to fail. In this panic, measures of risk based on typical, everyday events are informative about outcomes associated with an atypical event – a banking panic.

We conclude that predicting the fate of a bank in a banking panic may be like predicting the fate of a person crossing the road. Generally it's a car that you don't see that hits you, but you are less likely to get hit if you cross more prudently.

NOTES

1. The notes issued by free banks were traded at less than par value at locations distant from the banks. There is virtually no useful information from the discount rates on these notes for our analysis because notes of continuing banks in a state generally were discounted at the same rate (Gorton, 1996, 1999).

2. Bodenhorn (2003) provides a thorough overview of state banking before the Civil War, including free banking. Selgin and White (1994) summarize the literature on laissez faire banking and discuss its relationship to the literature on historical banking systems.

3. One of these two banks – the Boone County Bank – was a new bank whose owners issued fraudulent currency.

4. These frontiers are more informative than alternatives which we examined based on only 13 weeks of returns or as many as 52 weeks of returns.

5. The only United States government securities for which prices are available are long-term bonds. These long-term bonds are included in the portfolios.

6. While it might be desirable to examine the weights of individual securities, standard estimation procedures estimate the weights imprecisely relative to the frontier (Best & Grauer, 1991; Britten-Jones, 1999).

7. In Illinois, a bank is counted as closed or failing if there is no balance sheet information in the October 1861 report or it is reported to be ceasing operations in that report. In Indiana, a bank is counted as closed or failing if it is reported to be ceasing operations in the January 1862 report for the fiscal year ending October 1861. In Wisconsin, a bank is counted as closed or failing if there is not balance sheet information in the January 1862 report or it is reported to be ceasing operations in that report.

8. Fourteen of the ninety banks in the left panel of Fig. 3 closed, and the bank with the highest return in that figure is one that closed.

9. The analysis in this figure reflects only information on what noteholders were paid by the state banking regulator. Noteholders may have received more payments, because banks had other assets and stockholders were liable for up to twice the book value of capital in the bank. Information on such payments is relatively difficult to acquire though because it is likely to be available only in the courthouses of the counties in which banks were located if the information exists at all.

10. The portfolios' mean returns and standard deviations are computed using banks' holdings in October 1860 because the earliest prior data are from late 1859, which is likely to be too far before the fall in bond process early to be representative of the banks' actual portfolio.

11. A statistical analysis with a separate dummy variable for Indiana is not particularly informative because no banks closed in Indiana and left adequate data available. A statistical analysis similar to that in the paper for Illinois and Wisconsin without Indiana in the final set of data produces similar results and the same conclusions.

12. Losses relative to capital are measured in dollars per dollar. Population density is measured as persons per acre. The average mean return in 0.000220 per week with a standard deviation across banks of 0.000779 per week. The average standard deviation of the portfolios is 0.011254 per week with a standard deviation across banks of 0.002348.

13. Dwyer and Hasan (2003) report a similar finding.

14. The correlation of the loss per dollar of notes and the standard deviation of the portfolio's return in 0.19, smaller in magnitude.

ACKNOWLEDGMENTS

Federal Reserve Bank of Atlanta, Research Department, 1000 Peachtree, Atlanta, GA 30309, USA; e-mail gdwyer@dwyerecon.com; phone 404-498-7095; fax

404-498-8810; Department of Economics and Finance, Southern Illinois University – Edwardsville Alumni Hall, Edwardsville, Illinois 62026, USA; e-mail rhafer@siue.edu; phone (618) 650-2747; fax (618) 650-3047. Earlier versions of this paper were presented at the FDIC, the Universidad de Malaga, the Universidad Carlos III de Madrid, Texas Tech University, Tilburg University, and the Tor Vergata Financial Conference. We thank the seminar participants, Scott Hein, and Larry Wall for comments that substantially improved the paper. Research assistance from Shalini Patel and Daniel Waggoner is appreciated. The views expressed here are the authors' and not necessarily those of the Federal Reserve Bank of Atlanta or the Federal Reserve System. Any errors are the authors' responsibility.

REFERENCES

Altman, E. I., & Saunders, A. (2001). An analysis and critique of the BIS proposal on capital adequacy and ratings. *Journal of Banking and Finance*, *25*(January), 25–46.

Best, M. J., & Grauer, R. R. (1991). On the sensitivity of mean-variance-efficient portfolios to changes in asset means: Some analytical and computational results. *Review of Financial Studies*, *4*(2), 315–342.

Bodenhorn, H. (2003). *State banking in early America*. Oxford: Oxford University Press.

Britten-Jones, M. (1999). The sampling error in estimates of mean-variance efficient portfolio weights. *Journal of Finance*, *54*(April), 655–671.

Calomiris, C. W., & Mason, J. R. (1997). Contagion and bank failures during the great depression: The June 1932 Chicago banking panic. *American Economic Review*, *87*(December), 863–883.

Dowrie, G. W. (1913). *The development of banking in Illinois, 1817–1863*. Vol. 11, No. 4 of the series, University of Illinois Studies in the Social Sciences. Urbana: University of Illinois.

Dwyer, G. P., Jr. (1996). Wildcat banking, banking panics and free banking in the United States. *Federal Reserve Bank of Atlanta Economic Review*, *81*(December), 1–20.

Dwyer, G. P., Jr., Hafer, R. W., & Weber, W. E. (1999). Weekly U.S. and state bond prices. *Historical Methods*, *32*(Winter), 37–42.

Dwyer, G. P., Jr., & Hasan, I. (2003). *Suspensions of payments, bank failures and the nonbank publics losses*. Unpublished paper, Federal Reserve Bank of Atlanta.

Economopoulos, A. J. (1988). Illinois free banking experience. *Journal of Money, Credit and Banking*, *20*(May), 249–264.

Economopoulos, A. J. (1990). Free bank failures in New York and Wisconsin: A portfolio analysis. *Explorations in Economic History*, *27*(October), 421–441.

Economopoulos, A. J., & O'Neill, H. (1995). Bank entry during the antebellum period. *Journal of Money, Credit and Banking*, *27*(November), 1071–1085.

Gorton, G. (1988). Banking panics and business cycles. *Oxford Economic Papers*, *40*, 751–781.

Gorton, G. (1996). Reputation formation in early bank note markets. *Journal of Political Economy*, *104*(April), 346–397.

Gorton, G. (1999). Pricing free bank notes. *Journal of Monetary Economics*, *44*(August), 33–64.

Gorton, G., & Winton, A. (2002). Financial intermediation. Working Paper.

Hammond, B. (1957). *Banks and politics in America from the revolution to the Civil War*. Princeton: Princeton University Press.
Hasan, I., & Dwyer, G. P., Jr. (1994). Bank runs in the free banking period. *Journal of Money, Credit and Banking*, *26*(May), 271–288.
Illinois (1851–1861). *Laws of Illinois*.
Indiana (1851–1861). *Laws of the state of Indiana*.
Kolari, J., Glennon, D., Shin, H., & Caputo, M. (2002). Predicting large U.S. commercial bank failures. *Journal of Economics and Business* (July–August), 361–387.
Krueger, L. (1933). *History of commercial banking in Wisconsin*. Madison: University of Wisconsin.
Rolnick, A. J., & Weber, W. E. (1983). New evidence on the free banking era. *American Economic Review*, *73*(December), 1080–1091.
Rolnick, A. J., & Weber, W. E. (1984). The causes of free bank failures. *Journal of Monetary Economics*, *14*(October), 269–291.
Saunders, A., & Wilson, B. (1996). Contagious bank runs: Evidence from the 1929–1933 period. *Journal of Financial Intermediation*, *4*(October), 409–423.
Selgin, G. A., & White, L. H. (1994). How would the invisible hand handle money? *Journal of Economic Literature*, *32*(December), 1718–1749.
U.S. Congress (1861). House Executive Document 77, 36th Congress, 2nd Session.
Wheelock, D. C., & Wilson, P. W. (1995). Explaining bank failures: Deposit insurance, regulation, and efficiency. *Review of Economics and Statistics*, *77*(November), 689–700.
Wisconsin (1852–1861). *Laws of Wisconsin*.

DATA APPENDIX

This appendix indicates the sources of data not already given in the text of the paper.

Indiana

Banks and Their Fates

The sources are: Auditor of State, Indiana (1858, pp. 31–43; 1860, pp. 36–47; 1862a, pp. 335–348; and 1862b, pp. 285–306). We include a bank in our statistical analysis if it reports balance sheet information for October 1860. We conclude that the bank closed if it does not report balance sheet information for October 1861 or is reported to be closing.

Bond Holdings and Other Balance Sheet Data

The holdings of bonds for October 31, 1860 are from Auditor of State, Indiana (1860, pp. 36–47). The data on the each bank's notes, capital and assets are from the same source.

Counties in Which Banks Are Located

The counties in which banks are located are determined from the reports by the Auditor of State and the U.S. Census. The reports by the Auditor of State list the towns in which the banks are located if it is not part of the name (Auditor of State, Indiana (1860, pp. 36–47). The 1860 Census (U.S. Department of the Interior, 1864, State of Indiana, Table No. 3, Population of Cities and Towns, pp. 113–128) gives the county in which many communities are located. In cases in which the community is not included in the 1860 Census, we also use the 1850 Census (U.S. Department of the Interior, 1854, Population of such Cities [etc.] in the United States, pp. 339–393) and the 1870 Census (U.S. Department of the Interior, 1872, Table III State of Indiana, pp. 122–131).

Population

The populations of counties in Indiana are from the 1860 Census (U.S. Department of Interior, 1864, State of Indiana, Table No. 2, Population by Color and Condition, pp. 111–113).

Illinois

Banks and Their Fates

The sources are: U.S. Congress (1859, pp. 290–293; 1861, pp. 214–248; and 1863, pp. 160–164); *Annual Reports of Bank Commissioners of the State of Illinois*; Economopoulos (1988).

Bond Holdings

Data on individual banks' holdings of individual bonds are not available from published sources. The data on individual bank's holdings of bonds are from unpublished data collected by Andrew Economopoulos. He estimates the stocks by following the deposits and withdrawals of bonds over time. There is a nontrivial difference between the aggregate data on holdings of each bond by all banks for October 1860 (U.S. Congress, 1861, p. 290) and the total of Economopoulos's estimates for that date. Economopoulos's estimates of each bank's deposit are quite different than the amounts on reports submitted to the Bank Commissioner and, without an adjustment, these estimates imply quite unlikely ratios of bonds to other assets for individual banks. We estimate the bonds held by each bank by applying Economopoulos's estimate of the fraction of each bank's bonds held in the various bonds with the Bank Commissioner's data on each bank's total holdings of bonds in October 1860.

Other Balance Sheet Data
The data on each bank's notes, capital and assets for October 31, 1860 are from U.S. Congress (1861, pp. 214–248).

Counties in Which Banks Are Located
The counties in which banks are located are determined from reports by the Bank Commissioner, the U.S. Census and banknote reporters. The *Report of Bank Commissioners of the State of Illinois*, January 11, 1861 published in the U.S. Congress (1861, pp. 214–229) gives the community in which banks are located if the community's name is not part of the bank's name. The counties in which banks are located are determined from reports to the Bank Commissioner, the U.S. Census and banknote reporters. The *Report of Bank Commissioners of the State of Illinois*, January 11, 1861 published in the U.S. Congress (1861, pp. 214–229) gives the community in which banks are located if the community's name is not part of the bank's name. The 1860 Census (U.S. Department of the Interior, 1864, State of Illinois, Table No. 3, Population of Cities and Towns, pp. 533–543) gives the county in which many communities are located. In cases in which the community is not included in the 1860 Census, we use the county given in one or more banknote reporters. Unfortunately, the counties in which several banks are located still are unresolved by this procedure. The main reason is that the Census Office did not receive information on subdivisions of several relatively large counties with several banks. As a result, we use the similar information from the 1870 Census (U.S. Department of the Interior, 1872, Table III, Population of Civil Divisions less than Counties, State of Illinois pp. 108–121) to determine the county for these banks.

This procedure determines the counties for all banks except the Bank of Southern Illinois in Bolton, Illinois. The comparable table in the 1880 Census (U.S. Department of the Interior, 1883, Population of Civil Divisions less than Counties, Table III, Illinois, pp. 145–147) provides the county for some unincorporated towns and Bolton is included. On the other hand, Dowrie (1913, p. 149) indicates that, in 1857, Bolton is a town in Williamson County with one family. We do not know if the bank moved after the 1857 amendment to Illinois' free banking law required that a bank be in a town or village with at least 200 people, and if it did move, where. We put the Bank of Southern Illinois in Williamson County.

Population
The populations of counties in Illinois are from the 1860 Census (U.S. Department of the Interior, 1864, State of Illinois, Table No. 2, Population by Color and Condition, pp. 86–87).

Wisconsin

Banks and Their Fates

The sources are: U.S. Congress (1857; 1861, pp. 249–255; and 1863, pp. 200–209); and Rolnick and Weber (1982; Appendix, 1983). The data on the number of banks are based on an unpublished worksheet, based on the state reports in the House Executive Documents, provided by Arthur Rolnick and Warren Weber.

Bond Holdings and Other Balance Sheet Data

The distribution of each bank's bond holdings and the data on each bank's notes, capital and assets are from the *Annual Report of the Bank Comptroller of the State of Wisconsin* fiscal year ending September 30, 1860 published in the U.S. Congress (1861, pp. 249–255, 278–302).

Counties in Which Banks Are Located

The counties in which banks are located are determined from reports to the Comptroller, the U.S. Census and banknote reporters. The *Annual Report of the Bank Comptroller of the State of Wisconsin* for the fiscal year ending September 30, 1860 published in the U.S. Congress (1861, pp. 249–255, 278–302) gives the community in which banks are located if the community is not part of the bank's name. The 1860 Census (U.S. Department of the Interior, 1864, State of Wisconsin, Table No. 3, Population of Cities and Towns, pp. 533–543) gives the county in which a community is located. In cases in which the community is not included in the 1860 Census, we use the county given in one or more banknote reporters. This procedure determines the county in which all but two banks are located. We assume that the community of New London in 1860 is located in Waupaca county in 1860, as is the current town with that name. We also assume that the community of North Pepin in 1860 is north of Pepin in Pepin county.

Population

The populations in counties in Wisconsin are from the 1860 Census (U.S. Department of the Interior, 1864, State of Wisconsin, Table No. 2, Population by Color and Condition, p. 532).

DATA APPENDIX REFERENCES

Auditor of State, Indiana (1858). *Annual Report of the Auditor of State of the State of Indiana . . . for the fiscal year ending October 31, 1858*. Indianapolis: State of Indiana.

Auditor of State, Indiana (1860). *Annual Report of the Auditor of State of the State of Indiana . . . for the fiscal year ending October 31, 1860*. Indianapolis: State of Indiana.
Auditor of State, Indiana (1862a). *Annual Report of the Auditor of State of the State of Indiana . . . for the fiscal year ending October 31, 1861*. Indianapolis: State of Indiana.
Auditor of State, Indiana (1862b). *Annual Report of the Auditor of State of the State of Indiana . . . for the fiscal year ending October 31, 1862*. Indianapolis: State of Indiana.
Annual Reports of Bank Commissioners of the State of Illinois, Seventeen to Twenty-second General Assembly of Illinois. 1851–1861. Springfield, Bailhache and Baker, Lanphier and Walker.
Hodges' Journal of Finance and Bank Reporter, June 9, 1860, January 1861 (Vol. 12, No. 1), June 26, 1861 and January 15, 1862.
Inventory of the Articles of the State Banking Department of Wisconsin (1942). The Wisconsin Historical Records Survey Project, Madison, Wisconsin.
Rolnick, A. J., & Weber, W. E. (1982). A theory of free bank failures: Tests and implications. *Staff Report* 79. Federal Reserve Bank of Minneapolis (April).
Thompson's Bank Note and Commercial Reporter, January 14, 1860.
U.S. Comptroller of the Currency (1876). Annual Report.
U.S. Congress (1853). House Executive Document 66, 32nd Congress, 2nd Session.
U.S. Congress (1854). House Executive Document 102, 33rd Congress, 1st Session.
U.S. Congress (1855). House Executive Document 82, 33rd Congress, 2nd Session.
U.S. Congress (1856). House Executive Document 102, 34th Congress, 1st Session.
U.S. Congress (1857). House Executive Document 87, 34th Congress, 3rd Session.
U.S. Congress (1858). House Executive Document 107, 35th Congress, 1st Session.
U.S. Congress (1859). House Executive Document 112, 35th Congress, 2nd Session.
U.S. Congress (1860). House Executive Document 49, 36th Congress, 1st Session.
U.S. Congress (1861a). House Executive Document 77, 36th Congress, 2nd Session.
U.S. Congress (1861b). House Executive Document 25, 37th Congress, 2nd Session.
U.S. Congress (1863). House Executive Document 20, 38th Congress, 1st Session.
U.S. Department of the Interior (1854). *Statistical View of the United States*. Washington: A. O. P. Nicholson, Public Printer.
U.S. Department of the Interior (1864). *Population of the United States in 1860*. Washington: Government Printing Office.
U.S. Department of the Interior (1872). *The Statistics of the Population of the United States*. Ninth Census, Volume I. Washington: Government Printing Office.
U.S. Department of the Interior (1883). *Statistics of the Population of the United States at the Tenth Census*. Washington: Government Printing Office, 1883.

OWNERSHIP STRUCTURE, OPERATING INEFFICIENCY AND REGULATORY REFORM: AN ANALYSIS OF U.S. THRIFTS

Fatma Cebenoyan, A. Sinan Cebenoyan, Elizabeth S. Cooperman and Charles A. Register

ABSTRACT

The Bank for International Settlements is currently preparing the revised Basel Accord to improve the control of financial institution risk, including a focus on operational risk and the effect of corporate governance factors on risk. This paper examines the effect of ownership structure on operating inefficiency, as a proxy for operational risk, along with other risk and performance measures for U.S. thrifts operating in 1989–1994. We find a very significant effect of ownership structure on thrift operating inefficiency and other performance and risk measures, suggesting that ownership structure should be an important regulatory concern.

1. INTRODUCTION

In the aftermath of the Savings and Loans crisis of the 1980s, incentive structures that lead to better alignment of owner-manager objectives, and better management

Bank and Financial Market Efficiency: Global Perspectives
Research in Banking and Finance, Volume 5, 71–88

ISSN: 1567-7915/doi:10.1016/S1567-7915(04)05004-9

of depository institutions, have been widely debated (Barth, 1991, among others; Kane, 1989). Regulators have been concerned about the links between corporate governance and proper risk management, and whether corporate governance structure will mitigate risks in banking.[1] An effective corporate governance structure involves better alignment of owner-manager conflicts through ownership structure and market discipline. It remains to be seen if and at what ownership level the alignment of the agent-owner interests coincides with regulatory objectives for prudent risk-taking by managers, as well as enhancement of financial institution performance.

On a parallel track, regulators across the globe have been trying to develop ways to contain risk in the banking system through enhanced capital requirements including additional explicit capital requirements for operational risk under the New Basel Capital Accord (Basel II). Under the new accord *operational risk* includes "the risk of direct or indirect loss resulting from inadequate or failed internal processes, people and systems..."[2] Currently, however, only broad measures for the extent of operational risk, such as total assets for traditional lending operations, have been suggested, and the Basel Committee on Banking Supervision has asked for comments on better ways to measure operating risk.[3]

In this paper, we propose controllable managerial inefficiency as a proxy measure for the internal operating risk of traditional depository institutions. Using this proxy, we examine the relationship between ownership structure and firm inefficiency, along with other performance and risk measures. Considerable research for traditional depository institutions has focused on cost-inefficiency as a measure of depository institution operating risk. Studies find a high correlation between cost-inefficiency and aspects of bank operating risk including earnings volatility, non-performing loans, and the likelihood of failure.[4] For uniformity and simplicity, we use a sample of large, stock-chartered thrifts to examine the relationships between both managerial and institutional investor ownership and operating risk, as proxied by cost inefficiency, as well as other risk and performance measures.

Our empirical results show a non-linear relationship between managerial ownership and operational risk and capital adequacy measures. Increased managerial ownership appears to reduce cost inefficiency and increase capital ratios only at relatively high levels. Interestingly, institutional ownership (outsiders) has an insignificant effect on inefficiency, possibly suggesting that the lack of transparency for bank operations may inhibit effective discipline by outside owners. In contrast, institutional investor ownership has a significant, positive effect on other, more transparent, risk and performance measures. Taken together, the results suggest that managerial stock ownership may serve as an effective mechanism to reduce managerial agency costs for thrifts, and improve firms' capital, and operating risk but only if managers control a relatively large share of the firm's stock. Similarly, institutional investor ownership can be an effective corporate control device, but apparently only for the more observable attributes, such as capital adequacy, and return on assets.

In the remaining paper, Section 2 provides a brief overview of previous studies examining the relation between ownership and firm performance. Section 3 presents the empirical models and data used in the study. Section 4 contains the results, and Section 5 provides conclusions.

2. OVERVIEW OF RELEVANT RESEARCH

As improvements in firm efficiency, capital adequacy, return on assets (ROA), and risk/performance rankings of firms would unambiguously be desirable for market participants as well as regulators, we focus on literature that helps us establish the link between these measures and ownership structure. Of the studies that directly offer evidence on the relation between managerial stock ownership and bank inefficiency, Pi and Timme (1993) consider the effect of CEO ownership structure on the cost inefficiency of a sample of very large bank holding companies (BHCs) during the late 1980s. They find superior performance for banks with relatively high CEO managerial ownership, but only when the CEO is not also the chairman of the board. Pi and Timme, note however, that banks in their sample had a very low average CEO ownership. Berger and Mester (1997) examine the correlation between managerial ownership and inefficiency, as a minor portion of a larger study of BHCs operating in 1990–1995. Based on their particular sample of large BHCs, they do not find managerial stock ownership to be a significant determinant. A recent study by DeYoung, Spong and Sullivan (2001) examines the relation between ownership and managerial inefficiency for a random sample of small, closely-held U.S. banks in the Tenth Federal Reserve District from 1991 to 1994. They find for smaller, more closely held banks that as managerial stock ownership rises, inefficiency falls. However, at higher levels of ownership inefficiency rises. Hence, depending on the nature of the sample, very small or very large banks, the few studies examining ownership and inefficiency have had mixed results.

A second group of studies focus more on the relation between managerial stock ownership and market risk measures in the 1980s and early 1990s. Studies examining publicly-traded bank holding companies (BHCs) and thrifts generally find a positive, linear relationship between manager ownership and market risk in the 1980s, but a negative significant relationship in the 1990s (Anderson & Fraser, 2000; Chen, Steiner & Whyte, 1998; Knopf & Teall, 1996; Saunders, Strock & Travlos, 1990). When charter value is controlled for, greater risk-taking appears to be predominantly associated with lower charter value institutions that are manager-owned (see Brewer & Saidenberg, 1996, for thrifts; Demsetz, Saidenberg & Strahan, 1997, for banks).

A third category of studies uses accounting risk measures to avoid potential selection bias problems of omitting firms that are privately held when market-risk measures are used. Cebenoyan, Cooperman and Register (1999) examining thrift samples and non-linearity in ownership find evidence of greater risk-taking by low-charter value, manager-owned thrifts in the 1980s, similar to other studies using market data. However, in the 1990s, they find evidence of greater risk-taking by higher charter value, manager-owned thrifts. Sullivan and Spong (1998, 1999) find similar results for a sample of closely held banks, with higher risk at higher ownership levels. Gorton and Rosen (1995), however, examining a large sample of banks in the 1980s find superior (lower risk, higher return) loan portfolio for banks, with ownership of 40% or higher, and entrenchment effects at lower ownership levels. Institutional investor ownership does not have a significant effect on loan portfolio choice. Somewhat consistent with Gorton and Rosen's results, Byrd, Fraser, Lee and Williams (2000) find a lower probability of failure for manager-owned thrifts in the 1980s. Hence, studies generally support a significant effect of ownership on bank/thrift risk-taking behavior, but whether this effect is salutary or harmful to the firm is less clear.

The Bank for International Settlements and regulators in general are concerned about the safety of the banking firm as well as the banking system. To this effect they have imposed measures that extract a price on higher risk holdings in the form of higher required capital levels. Recently faced with criticism of the Basel Accord of 1988, a major revision of banking regulations is underway. To better control the risks of the banking firm, capital adequacy requirements are coupled with effective supervision, and market discipline (the three pillars). Accommodations have also been proposed to better recognize, measure, and mitigate operational risk. From this perspective, the empirical literature in banking has yet to develop good measures of operational risk. The BIS encourages the development of new techniques to measure, monitor and mitigate operational risk for different types of financial institutions, suggesting currently very broad proxies for the extent of a firm's risk, such as total assets for traditional lending operations and income for investment bank/securities operations,[5] noting that this is currently very much a work-in-progress.

Over the past decade, bank researchers developed better measures of financial institution efficiency, focusing particularly on measuring inefficiency in bank operations based on stochastic cost and/or profit frontiers. The concept of cost-inefficiency may prove to be a valuable proxy for "the risk of loss resulting from inadequate or failed internal processes, people, and systems" for traditional lending institutions. The stochastic inefficiency concept identifies the performance gap, stemming from managerial choices (which may reflect "inadequate or failed internal processes, people, and systems"), between a specific firm and the estimated best-practice frontier of its peers. Berger and Humphrey (1997) note that cost-inefficiency can be used by regulators concerned about limiting systemic risk, with researchers finding significant relationships between inefficiency measures and several different aspects of operational risk, including problem loans, negative cash flow, poor management quality, and the likelihood of bank/thrift closure or failure (see Berger & Humphrey, 1992; Cebenoyan, Cooperman & Register, 1993; Hermalin & Wallace, 1994, among others). Studies by Barr, Seiford and Siems (1994) for banks and Kramer (1997) for insurance companies also find cost-inefficiency to be a significant factor in predicting firm failure. In a similar vein, DeYoung (1998) finds a strong positive correlation between efficiency and management quality, as proxied by bank CAMEL ratings, and Berger and DeYoung (1997) find cost efficiency to Granger-cause reductions in problem loans, with a rise in cost inefficiency often followed by a rise in non-performing loans. Berger and Mester (1997) find a similar relationship between problem loans and bank cost inefficiency, suggesting that banks that are poor at managing operations are poor at risk management as well. They also find inefficiency to be correlated with the volatility of return on assets.

Based on the strong relationship observed in previous studies between cost-inefficiency and operating risk characteristics, in this paper we use cost inefficiency as a proxy for managerial internal short-comings to capture the potential operational risk of traditional lending institutions. We also add to the previous literature by examining the relations between both managerial and institutional investor ownership structure on firm inefficiency, as well as other risk and performance measures. The data and empirical methods, including how cost inefficiency measures are estimated, are discussed in the following section.

3. DATA AND METHODOLOGY

3.1. Data

We collect financial ratios and external risk/performance rating measures (PEER rankings) from *Sheshunoff's S&L Quarterly* for each year, 1989–1994, published by Sheshunoff Information Services, Inc., Austin, Texas. Income and balance sheet data come from the annual balance sheet and income statements on Office of Thrift Supervision call reports for U.S. stock-chartered thrifts on the *Thomson Thrift Analysis and Forecasting CD* for 1989–1994. Our ownership and market to book data is from *The SNL Quarterly Thrift Digest*, 1990–1995 (SNL Securities, Charlottesville, Virginia). Manager and director ownership are based on 13D, 13G, and F11 filings to the SEC, FDIC, or OTS by individuals currently holding more than 5% of a firm's common stock, supplemented by the beneficial ownership information disclosed in proxy filings. Institutional ownership data are compiled from 13F filings.[6] Unemployment rates are from various issues of the U. S. Bureau of the Census, *Statistical Abstract of the U.S.*, Washington, DC.

To avoid any bias associated with three-year limitations placed on managerial ownership for thrifts converting to stock ownership after 1980,[7] our sample encompasses the period 1989–1994 for all thrifts with complete data. The sample begins in 1989, a year of restored regulatory oversight under FIRREA. The sample ends in 1994, because of the large number of sample thrifts that merged with other thrifts and banks from 1995 on. Mirroring the consolidation of the entire thrift industry, over 55% of sample thrifts were taken over after 1994. Given these restrictions, our sample includes 81 thrifts operating for the six continuous years, encompassing 486 observations. These thrifts in our sample as large stock-chartered thrifts controlled about 22% of total U.S. thrift assets for the period we examine.

3.2. *Estimation for Cost Inefficiency Measures*

As noted earlier, the economic performance measure we employ to proxy for operational risk is cost inefficiency.[8] Cost inefficiency provides a measure of how much a particular firm's cost deviates from the best practice firm's minimum cost for the same output under the same conditions. This information is derived from a cost function that evaluates the firm's variable costs in terms of variable outputs, variable input prices, fixed inputs, random error and inefficiency. It can be stated as:

$$C = f(\mathrm{y}, \mathrm{w}, z, u_{\mathrm{c}}, v_{\mathrm{c}}) \tag{1}$$

where C equals variable costs, y, vector of variable outputs, w, a vector of prices of variable inputs, and z are quantities of any fixed inputs included to account for their effects on variable costs, since they may be substitutable or complementary with variable inputs. The terms u and v are, respectively, inefficiency and random-error terms. To estimate the error term in Eq. (1) and in turn calculate each firm's cost inefficiency index u, we estimate the following popular multiproduct translog cost specification (suppressing individual thrift subscripts), where j represents the different variable outputs and k, the different variable inputs:

$$\ln C = \alpha + \sum_{j=1}^{5}\beta_j \ln \mathrm{y}_j + \sum_{k=1}^{2}\gamma_k \ln \mathrm{w}_k + \frac{1}{2}\sum_{j=1}^{5}\sum_{l=1}^{5}\beta_{jl}\ln \mathrm{y}_j \ln \mathrm{y}_l + \frac{1}{2}\sum_{k=1}^{2}\sum_{l=1}^{2}\gamma_{kl}\ln \mathrm{w}_k \ln \mathrm{w}_l + \sum_{j=1}^{5}\sum_{k=1}^{2}\delta_{jk}\ln \mathrm{y}_j \ln \mathrm{w}_k + \sum_{k=1}^{2}\ln z_k + \ln u + \ln v \tag{2}$$

As pointed out by previous studies, the translog function provides consistent inefficiency rankings relative to other functional forms. It also has the advantage of simplicity.[9]

Following the arguments of Sealey and Lindley (1977), we use a financial intermediation approach to specify thrift inputs and outputs in the cost function. This method assumes thrifts use physical capital, deposits, other borrowings and labor as inputs to produce earning assets. In this estimation, five outputs are used: (1) 1–4 family mortgage loans and mortgage-backed securities; (2) multifamily and non-residential mortgage loans; (3) non-mortgage loans including consumer and commercial loans and lease financing; (4) cash and other security investments including U.S. government and agency securities, municipals, and other securities; and (5) construction and land loans, and real estate and service-corporation investment. The prices of two variable inputs, w_k, are used: (1) labor and (2) deposits and other borrowings. We measure the price of labor as total expenditures on employees divided by the number of full-time equivalent employees at the end of the year. The price of deposits is total interest expense divided by total deposits and other borrowings. We further impose the usual linear homogeneity in input price restrictions in estimation. Two fixed input quantities, z, are also included: the dollar value of physical capital (premises and other fixed assets) and the dollar value of financial equity capital.[10] The managerial choice of the levels of these variables directly impacts the firm's distance from the efficient frontier as measured by CINEFF, the firm's cost inefficiency score. The following section describes the cross-sectional models using CINEFF and other alternative risk/performance variables as the dependent variable.

3.3. Primary Cross-Sectional Models

To establish the effect of ownership structure on regulatory-desirable firm attributes, cross-sectional regressions of the following form are estimated:

$$\begin{aligned}\text{PERF, RISK}_i = {} & \beta_0 + \beta_1\,\text{INSIDE}_i + \beta_2\,\text{INSIDESQ}_i + \beta_3\,\text{OUTSIDE}_i \\ & + \beta_4\,\text{LOGSIZE}_i + \beta_5\,\text{UNEMP}_i + \beta_6\,\text{MKBK}_i \\ & + \beta_7\,\text{YEAR}_i + \varepsilon_i \qquad (3)\end{aligned}$$

where PERF, RISK = alternative performance and risk measures, INSIDE = the percentage of equity held by managers and directors, INSIDESQ = the square of INSIDE, (used if non-linearity is implied), OUTSIDE = the percentage of equity held by institutional directors, LOGSIZE = the log of asset size of a thrift, UNEMP = a control variable for regional economic factors, MKBK = market to book value of equity, as a proxy for thrift charter value, YEAR = a set of 5, year-specific dummies, with 1989 as the reference, and $\varepsilon =$ a random error term.

For alternative risk and performance measures, we use: CINEFF, a firm's cost inefficiency score as a proxy for operational risk; CAPRATIO (equity to assets) for capital adequacy; PEER (Sheshunoff risk ranking) for overall risk, and ROA (return on assets) as a measure of a firm's financial performance. PEER is a risk-performance measure developed by Sheshunoff Information Services based on capital, asset quality, earnings, and liquidity, where similar size firms are ranked from 1 (highest risk) to 99 (lowest risk). The Sheshunoff rankings are similar to unpublished regulatory CAMEL rankings, excluding the management factor.[11]

For independent variables, in addition to INSIDE and INSIDESQ,[12] for the effects of managerial ownership, OUTSIDE is included to control for effects of institutional ownership, as a device for better corporate governance. McConnell and Servaes (1990) and other studies find institutional investor ownership to have a significant effect on firm performance.

To control for size, regional economic conditions, and charter value that previous studies find at times to affect thrift's performance (Anderson & Fraser, 2000; Brewer & Saidenberg, 1996; Cebenoyan, Cooperman & Register, 1993; Demirguc-Kunt, 1989), we include LOGSIZE, UNEMP and MKBK. LOGSIZE is the log of asset size in millions. UNEMP is the unemployment rate for the thrift's home state. MKBK is a proxy for thrift charter value, measured as the ratio of a firm's market to book value of equity for individual thrifts for each year, as used in other studies as a proxy for bank charter value including Galloway, Lee and Roden (1997). Buser, Chen and Kane (1981), Marcus (1984) and Keeley (1990) point out that banks with higher charter values will avoid excessive risk-taking to protect against closure and loss of a valuable charter and reputation capital. Brewer and Saidenberg (1996) and Anderson and Fraser (2000), among other studies, find charter value to be negatively related to firm or market risk measures. Berger and Mester (1997) and other studies, find asset size to be significantly related to firm efficiency. Studies also find thrifts in states suffering economic distress tend to have relatively higher inefficiency scores.

Finally, we include a set of five, year-specific dummies (YEAR) that capture trends in performance affecting all firms within the period relative to performance in 1989. Should performance benefits exist for the restructuring, adaptation of new technology, or renewed regulatory vigor that all thrifts have experienced during the period, we would expect them to be reflected in these dummies. Based on the work of Stiroh (1997) which showed thrift cost efficiency to improve in the mid-1990s, we do anticipate finding thrift performance improving across the six years studied.

4. EMPIRICAL RESULTS

4.1. Descriptive Statistics

Table 1 reports descriptive statistics for variables used in the primary cross-sectional regression models. The mean cost inefficiency score for the sample, CINEFF, is 11.2%, indicating that the average thrift produces its outputs at a cost that is about 11% greater than necessary. This figure is within the observed ranges of existing cost efficiency studies of depository institutions (see Berger & Humphrey, 1997). The inefficiency score at this stage should be interpreted for operational risk purposes as the cost inefficiency ranking of the firm relative to its peers, with a higher score indicating greater managerial cost inefficiency. The mean for INSIDE is about 18%, and that for OUTSIDE about 17%, somewhat higher than the means observed by Gorton and Rosen (1995) for the sample of banks they observed in the 1980s. Gorton and Rosen had a mean of 15.25% for insider holdings and 7.87% for outsider holdings for the banks they examined. The mean for the market-to-book ratio, MKBK, is 0.84. Prior to 1991, thrifts had very low market to book ratios but with improved profitability in the 1990s, these ratios averaged greater than one during the later part of the sample period. UNEMP, the average state unemployment rate was about 6% over the period. The mean asset size, SIZE, is $2 billion, with firms ranging from $68 million to $39.7 billion.

Table 1. Descriptive Statistics for Cross-Sectional Analysis Variables ($N = 486$).

Symbol	Mean	Std	Min	Max
CINEFF	0.112	0.063	0.021	0.559
INSIDE	17.958%	13.924%	0.260%	72.700%
OUTSIDE	16.922%	18.756%	0.000%	91.100%
SIZE	2,079.408	5,353.498	68.645	39,697.36
UNEMP	6.145%	1.485%	2.200%	11.300%
MKBK	0.838	0.403	0.083	2.207
ROA	0.528%	0.997%	−6.330%	2.930%
PEER	54.395	26.924	0.000	99.000
CAPRATIO	7.296%	3.061%	0.295%	21.327%

Notes: This table provides the descriptive statistics for the 1989–1994 sample. CINEFF is thrift's cost inefficiency score. INSIDE is the percentage of stock held by officers and directors. OUTSIDE is the percentage of stock held by institutional investors. SIZE is the asset size in millions. UNEMP is the state unemployment rate. MKBK is the market to book value of equity. ROA is net income to assets. PEER is a Sheshunoff safety ranking from 0 to 99. CAPRATIO is tangible equity to assets.

The mean ROA is 0.53% over the period with a wide range from −6.33 to 2.93%. The average for CAPRATIO (equity to assets) is about 7.30% ranging from about 0.30 to 21%. This wide range reflects the generally improving capital ratios over the period, as well as the thrift industry's naturally wide range of capitalization. The average for PEER is 54. PEER ranges from 0 to 99, with higher values indicating more favorable rankings.

4.2. Cross-Sectional Results

Regression results, throughout the paper, use White's (1980) consistent variance-covariance estimation procedure to adjust for heteroscedasticity. Table 2 presents the regression results using inefficiency, capital ratio, peer rankings, and ROA as the dependent variables. The significant Wald chi-squares indicate relatively good fits for all the models.

For the CINEFF model, where CINEFF is a firm's inefficiency score, the coefficient on INSIDE is significant and positive, while the coefficient on INSIDESQ is significant and negative. These outcomes suggest that as managerial ownership rises initially, so does cost inefficiency as a proxy for operational risk. Above a threshold of about 33%, however, further increases in managerial ownership are associated with falling cost inefficiency.[13] Higher managerial ownership leads to greater cost inefficiency up to the turning point of 33%. After the turning point of 33% ownership, rising ownership results in lower cost inefficiency. OUTSIDE is not significantly related to cost inefficiency, possibly as a result of the often-cited information asymmetries in the industry (Gorton & Rosen, 1995; Ross, 1989; Zeckhauser & Pound, 1990). Perhaps because of information asymmetries, institutional investors appear to have little monitoring ability and control over thrifts' operational risk, as proxied by cost inefficiency, providing little evidence of market discipline from this perspective. This result lends support to regulatory efforts that aim to establish market discipline through greater transparency.

Interestingly, the dummy variables for the different years strongly support the contention that the thrift industry, on average, significantly improved its cost inefficiency performance during the period. Specifically, the coefficients on the year-dummies are negative and increase in size, and become significantly negative in 1992 through 1994 (years 4–6). This is clearly a hopeful sign for an industry that performed so poorly during the 1980s. The coefficient on LOGSIZE is significant and positive indicating greater cost inefficiency for larger thrifts, in contrast to Berger and Mester's (1997) finding of no relationship for their sample of banks in the 1990s. This may indicate that larger banks seem to have higher operational inefficiency, or may be better able to tolerate greater inefficiency. The

Table 2. Cross-Sectional Regression Results on Cost Inefficiency (CINEFF), Capital Ratio (CAPRATIO), Sheshunoff Risk Ranking (PEER), and Return on Assets (ROA) for Thrift Sample 1989–1994 (*t*-Statistics in Parentheses Below Coefficients).

	CINEFF	CAPRATIO	PEER	ROA
Constant	0.02547	15.4140	80.4700	0.00960
	(1.250)	(14.590***)	(10.720***)	(4.191***)
INSIDE	0.00265	−0.05909	0.1396	0.00007
	(3.644***)	(−2.201**)	(1.828*)	(2.515***)
INSIDESQ	−0.00004	0.00072		
	(−3.625***)	(1.925*)		
OUTSIDE	0.00005	0.06614	0.7560	0.00014
	(0.206)	(6.005***)	(8.784***)	(4.201***)
LOGSIZE	0.00631	−1.6443	−6.8363	−0.00243
	(1.883*)	(−10.830***)	(−6.201***)	(−5.492***)
UNEMP	0.00322	0.0931	−1.2833	−0.00020
	(1.702*)	(1.164)	(−1.760*)	(−0.696)
MKBK	0.01225	1.8092	31.0040	0.01060
	(1.241)	(4.592***)	(8.639***)	(6.797***)
YEAR2	−0.00368	0.0066	−3.0770	−0.00120
	(−0.368)	(0.016)	(−0.980)	(−0.843)
YEAR3	−0.00895	−0.1772	−11.0170	0.00070
	(−0.864)	(−0.388)	(−3.180***)	(0.487)
YEAR4	−0.02047	−0.2284	−25.7300	0.00156
	(−1.996*)	(−0.433)	(−6.226***)	(1.175)
YEAR5	−0.02534	0.3630	−27.5780	0.00048
	(−2.294**)	(0.737)	(−6.671***)	(0.272)
YEAR6	−0.0321	0.1273	−23.6180	−0.00053
	(−2.785***)	(0.258)	(−6.535***)	(−0.421)
Turning point INSIDE	33.125%	41.035%	None	None
Wald chi square	27.226***	169.076***	282.808***	112.252***
Number of observations	486	486	486	486

Notes: INSIDE is the percentage of stock held by officers and directors. INSIDESQ is the square of INSIDE. OUTSIDE is the percentage of stock held by institutional investors. LOGSIZE is the log of the assets in millions. UNEMP is the state unemployment rate. MKBK is the market to book value of equity. YEAR2–6 are year dummy variables. Wald Chi Square is a test of whether the independent variables are jointly different from zero.

*Significant at 0.10 level.

**Significant at 0.05 level.

***Significant at 0.01 level.

coefficient on UNEMP is also significant and positive, consistent with Cebenoyan, Cooperman and Register's (1993) finding of greater inefficiency for thrifts in economically-distressed states.[14]

The next column of Table 2 shows the regression results for CAPRATIO. For this regression, the coefficient on INSIDE is significant and negative, and the coefficient on INSIDESQ is significant and positive. The turning point on the CAPRATIO for INSIDE is about 41%, a result completely in keeping with the turning point on bank risk-taking identified by Gorton and Rosen (1995). At low levels of managerial ownership, capital ratios fall, but at levels of ownership above about 41%, capital ratios rise with managerial ownership. These results imply that capital adequacy is enhanced through managerial stockholdings, just like operational risk, but only once relatively high levels of inside ownership are reached. In contrast to the results on cost inefficiency/operational risk, here, OUTSIDE is significant and positive, supporting market discipline exercised by institutional investors. As with other researchers (Demsetz, Saidenberg & Strahan, 1997) we find the coefficient on LOGSIZE significant and negative indicating lower capital ratios for larger thrifts. Consistent with previous studies that find a negative relation between charter value and bank risk-taking (Brewer & Saidenberg, 1996; Demsetz, Saidenberg & Strahan, 1997), the coefficient on MKBK is significant and positive, indicating higher capital ratios for thrifts with higher charter values.

For the PEER regression, which gives us a measure of the overall financial health of the firm in a CAMEL-like evaluation, from 1 (low) to 99 (high), we find results that strongly support the notion that high inside and outside ownership improve the ranking of the firm. Lagrange multiplier tests indicated that the relation between managerial ownership and PEER was linear, so INSIDESQ is excluded as an independent variable. As managerial stock ownership rises, regardless of its level, PEER rises. For OUTSIDE, the coefficient is also positive and highly significant, with a positive linear relationship. As institutional investor ownership rises, PEER rankings rise. YEAR dummy variables are significant and negative for years 3–6. This may suggest greater thrift risk-taking, reflected in lower PEER ratings over time, as the economy improved over the 1990s, as suggested recently by some regulators during the period. UNEMP was significant and negative for the PEER regression, indicating greater risk for thrifts in areas that were more economically distressed.

As most regulatory action and assessments are based on accounting indicators of firm performance, and as a robustness test of our results, we also included ROA as a dependent variable in our model. Except for the year dummies, the results are very similar to the PEER model results. Lagrange multiplier tests indicate a positive linear relationship between managerial ownership and ROA. That is, as managerial ownership rises throughout its range, accounting financial performance improves. The result on ROA is similar to that observed by Cebenoyan,

Cooperman and Register (1999) using a different sample of thrifts in the early 1990s. The coefficient on OUTSIDE is significant and positive, indicating superior performance for thrifts with greater institutional investor ownership as well. For other control variables, the coefficient on LOGSIZE is significant and negative. As thrifts got larger over this period, ROA generally falls. The coefficient on MKBK is significant and positive indicating superior performance for higher charter value thrifts. The time dummy variables are insignificant.

Taken together, the models support the notion that aligning the interests of managers and outside owners can prove beneficial in terms of reducing operational risk and improving capital adequacy, and the overall performance of the firm. With this said, for the operational inefficiency and capital risk measures, beneficial effects apparently require a significant managerial stock ownership level. Prior to this level of managerial stockholdings, entrenchment appears with increases in managerial holdings leading to sub-optimal firm performance. The empirical results are consistent with those of Gorton and Rosen's (1995) findings of greater value maximizing behavior, for banks with high levels of ownership of about 40% or higher in the 1980s. Gorton and Rosen suggest that lower levels of managerial ownership allow managers the power to engage in expense preference behavior and imprudent risk taking, while high levels encourage managers to act prudently to enhance firm value.

Institutional investor ownership appears to have a beneficial effect on capital risk, overall risk, and return on assets at any level, but has little effect on operational risk. This result is also consistent with Gorton and Rosen's (1995) finding of institutional investor ownership having no effect on loan portfolio choice. Our results similarly find institutional investors to have little effect on internal firm cost inefficiency or operational risk, but to have a positive effect on external performance measures.

5. SUMMARY AND CONCLUSIONS

This paper examines links between ownership structure and firm operating inefficiency, capital adequacy, risk, and return. As such, it also provides implications for the effects of managerial and institutional investor ownership on regulatory concerns, as the Bank for International Settlements is currently proposing to improve the control of credit, market, and operational risk within the Basel Accord. The paper uses managerial cost inefficiency as a potential indicator of operational risk, and provides results that link ownership structure as a corporate governance mechanism to operational inefficiency and other risk and performance measures.

Analyzing a sample of thrifts over the six-year period 1989–1994, the empirical results suggest that managerial stock ownership generally can be effective in aligning the interests of managers, owners, and regulators for improved performance and reduced operational risk, but only once a relatively high threshold of managerial ownership is reached. As managers come to hold more than one-third of the firm's outstanding shares, cost inefficiency, our proxy for operational risk, is reduced. The same cannot be said for institutional investors, perhaps due to their inability to pierce the opaqueness of thrifts. This suggests an inability on the part of institutional investors to effectively monitor and discipline much of thrift's internal operations. Hence, our results support the need for increasing transparency and better disclosures for bank operations, and financial indicators. For capital adequacy, we observe similar implications: only at higher levels (41%) of insider stake do we observe a positive relationship. This time though, and not surprisingly, we do see institutional investors' holdings being significantly related to higher capital ratios, since capital ratios are easier to observe than operational inefficiency. The results are further confirmed in regressions of firm CAMEL-like rankings, and ROA. Both indicators are positively related to inside and outside ownership levels.

Taken together, these results provide support for the proposition that corporate governance may and possibly should be made part of a regulatory framework. However, it must be pointed out that well-known agency conflicts may only diminish at relatively high levels of insider holdings. Although our results may not apply to other financial services firms, given our sample of relatively homogeneous thrifts, the results seem to clearly establish a link between corporate governance and firm performance and risk. One implication that may be generalized is that market discipline can play a role through external institutional investor monitoring when firm risk and performance attributes can be easily observed. The paper also offers cost inefficiency as a possible proxy for the establishment of relative operational risk levels. Operational risk is related to the way management chooses to put together the inputs that lead to the production of its outputs.

On a caveat, additional research is needed, particularly for the banking industry to confirm these results and to examine other incentive systems that are used to align managers with external stockholders, including other forms of performance-based compensation arrangements. Finally, the results should not be assumed to necessarily hold for non-financial firms. These issues are beyond the scope of this paper and are left for future research.

NOTES

1. See http://www.fdic.gov/deposit/deposits/international/guidance/guidance/moralhazard.pdf. FDIC Chairman Donald E. Powell, for instance, recently tied the

collapses of Enron and World Com (clear indicators of operational risk) to poor corporate governance practices, see http://www.fdic.gov/news/news/press/2003/pr1903.html.

2. http://www.bis.org/publ/bcbsca02.pdf and http://www.bis.org/publ/bcbsca07.pdf.

3. See Basel Committee on Banking Supervision Consultative Document, Operational Risk, January 2001, p. 7.

4. See Berger and Humphrey (1997) for a detailed discussion of these links. Berger, Hancock and Humphrey (1993), also point out that more efficient banks may take fewer risks to protect their more profitable franchises.

5. Basel Committee on Banking Supervision. *Consultative Document Operational Risk*, January 2001.

6. Since data on large non-institutional block-holders were not included in the data collected for outside ownership by SNL Securities, OUTSIDE excludes other large block-holders. Most other papers use 5% block-holders. Consequently, our measure may under-estimate the effect of large external shareholders on managerial operating inefficiencies.

7. After 1980, regulations for conversions prevented an alignment of the interests of managers and stockholders for a three-year period by incorporating an anti-takeover rule in which any beneficial ownership by an individual could be no more than 10% for any class of equity security for three years following conversion. Limits were also placed on the amount of stock that could be offered during this period: (1) to 5% for any person or identified group; and (2) to 15–25% for all officers and directors (see Cordell, MacDonald & Wohar, 1993).

8. See Aigner, Lovell and Schmidt (1977), Meeusen and Broeck (1977) and Jondrow et al. (1982) for a description of this methodology. For more recent applications, see Berger and Mester (1997) and Rogers (1998).

9. For greater precision in calculating efficiency scores, Berger and Mester (1997) suggest the use of a Fourier-flexible function form, which is less restrictive than a translog cost function. However, the translog form is easier to use, and for ranking decisions, studies demonstrate that it provides similar rankings as other forms (see LeCompte & Smith, 1990; Mester, 1987; and Cebenoyan, Cooperman, Register & Hudgins, 1993, for a discussion, applications of the translog form).

10. See Rogers (1998) and Berger and Mester (1997) for a detailed description of the methodology, which this section heavily draws from. The input and output measures are similar to those used by Cebenoyan, Cooperman and Register (1993). Results of the frontier estimations and descriptive statistics of the variables entering the model are available from the authors upon request.

11. See *Sheshunoff S&L Quarterly: Ratings and Analysis* for a more detailed description of these ratings. This analysis is published by Sheshunoff Information Services.

12. To determine whether a model should include INSIDESQ, we use Lagrange multiplier tests (see Ramanathan, 1992, p. 313).

13. The turning point is calculated by solving for the unknown managerial ownership level at which the full effect is equal to zero.

14. We also performed tests for other turning points on ownership using piecewise dummy variables (0–5%, 5–20%, 25–30%, >30%), as well as an alternative $INSIDE^3$ variable. Other than the >30% ownership dummy variable, these dummy variables and the $INSIDE^3$ variable were insignificant. In addition, we tested for outliers by removing individual firms with high levels of ownership from the sample. The results were similar with the exclusion of these firms.

ACKNOWLEDGMENTS

The authors are grateful to Robert DeYoung, Steven Todd and participants at research seminars at the University of Colorado-Denver and Colorado State University, and Financial Management Association and Midwest Finance Association meetings for helpful comments on previous versions of this paper. Elizabeth Cooperman thanks The Business School at the University of Colorado-Denver for a summer research grant to help collect part of the data for this study.

REFERENCES

Aigner, D. J., Lovell, C. A., & Schmidt, P. (1977). Formulation and estimation of stochastic frontier production function models. *Journal of Econometrics*, *6*, 21–37.

Anderson, R. C., & Fraser, D. R. (2000). Corporate control, bank risk taking, and the health of the banking industry. *Journal of Banking and Finance*, *24*, 1383–1398.

Barr, R., Seiford, L., & Siems, T. (1994). Forecasting bank failure: A non-parametric approach. *Recherches Economiques de Louvain*, *60*, 411–429.

Barth, J. R. (1991). *The great savings and loan debacle*. Washington, DC: American Enterprise Institute.

Berger, A. N., & DeYoung, R. (1997). Problem loans and cost efficiency in commercial banks. *Journal of Banking and Finance*, *21*, 849–870.

Berger, A. N., Hancock, D., & Humphrey, D. B. (1993). Banking efficiency derived from the profit function. *Journal of Banking and Finance*, *17*, 317–347.

Berger, A. N., & Humphrey, D. B. (1992). Measurement and efficiency issues in commercial banking. In: Z. Griliches (Ed.), *Measurement Issues in the Service Sectors* (pp. 245–279). National Bureau of Economic Research, Chicago: University of Chicago Press.

Berger, A. N., & Humphrey, D. B. (1997). Efficiency of financial institutions: International survey and directions for future research. *European Journal of Operational Research*, *98*, 175–212.

Berger, A. N., & Mester, L. J. (1997). Inside the black box: What explains differences in the efficiencies of financial institutions? *Journal of Banking and Finance*, *21*, 895–947.

Brewer, E., & Saidenberg, M. R. (1996). Franchise value, ownership structure and risk at savings institutions. Federal Reserve Bank of New York, Working Paper.

Buser, S. A., Chen, A. H., & Kane, E. J. (1981). Federal deposit insurance, regulatory policy, and optimal bank capital. *Journal of Finance*, *36*, 51–60.

Byrd, J. W., Fraser, D. R., Lee, S. D., & Williams, T. (2000). Deregulation, natural selection, and governance structure: Evidence from the savings and loan crisis. Working Paper, Texas A&M University.

Cebenoyan, A. S., Cooperman, E. S., & Register, C. A. (1993). Firm efficiency and the regulatory closure of S&Ls: An empirical investigation. *Review of Economic and Statistics*, *3*, 540–545.

Cebenoyan, A. S., Cooperman, E. S., & Register, C. A. (1999). Ownership structure, charter value, and risk-taking behavior for thrifts. *Financial Management*, *28*, 5–27.

Cebenoyan, A. S., Cooperman, E. S., Register, C. A., & Hudgins, S. C. (1993). The relative efficiency of stock vs. mutual S&Ls: A stochastic cost frontier approach. *Journal of Financial Services Research*, *7*, 151–170.

Chen, C. R., Steiner, T. L., & Whyte, A. M. (1998). Risk-taking behavior and management ownership in depository institutions. *Journal of Financial Research*, *21*, 1–16.

Cordell, L. R., MacDonald, G. D., & Wohar, M. E. (1993). Corporate ownership and the thrift crisis. *Journal of Law and Economics*, *36*, 719–756.

Demirguc-Kunt, A. (1989). Deposit-institution failures: A review of the literature. *Federal Reserve Bank of Cleveland Economic Review*, 2–18.

Demsetz, R., Saidenberg, M., & Strahan, P. (1997). Agency problems and risk taking at banks. Federal Reserve Bank of New York, Working Paper.

DeYoung, R. (1998). X-inefficiency and management quality in commerical banks. *Journal of Financial Services Research*, *13*, 5–22.

DeYoung, R., Spong, K., & Sullivan, R. J. (2001). Managerial shareholding and the performance of closely held firms: The case of commercial banks. *Journal of Banking and Finance*, *25*, 1209–1243.

Galloway, T. M., Lee, W. B., & Roden, D. M. (1997). Bank's changing incentives and opportunities for risk taking. *Journal of Banking and Finance*, *21*, 509–527.

Gorton, G., & Rosen, R. (1995). Corporate control, portfolio choice, and the decline of banking. *Journal of Finance*, *50*, 1377–1420.

Hermalin, B. E., & Wallace, N. E. (1994). The determinants of efficiency and solvency in savings and loans. *Rand Journal of Economics*, *25*, 361–381.

Jondrow, J., Lovell, C. A. K., Materov, I. S., & Schmidt, P. (1982). On estimation of technical inefficiency in the stochastic frontier production function model. *Journal of Econometrics*, *19*, 233–328.

Kane, E. J. (1989). *The S&L insurance mess: How did it happen?* Washington, DC: Urban Institute Press.

Keeley, M. C. (1990). Deposit insurance, risk, and market power in banking. *American Economic Review*, *80*, 1183–1200.

Knopf, J. D., & Teall, J. L. (1996). Risk-taking behavior in the U.S. thrift industry: Ownership structure and regulatory changes. *Journal of Banking and Finance*, *26*, 1329–1350.

Kramer, B. (1997). N.E.W.S.: A model for the evaluation of non-life insurance companies. *European Journal of Operational Research*, *98*, 420–431.

LeCompte, R. L., & Smith, S. D. (1990). Changes in the cost of intermediation: The case of savings and loans. *Journal of Finance*, *45*, 1337–1346.

Marcus, A. J. (1984). Deregulation and bank financial policy. *Journal of Banking and Finance*, *8*, 557–565.

McConnell, J. J., & Servaes, H. (1990). Additional evidence on equity ownership and corporate value. *Journal of Financial Economics*, *27*, 595–612.

Meeusen, W., & Broeck, J. (1977). Efficiency estimation from Cobb-Douglas production function with composed error. *International Economic Review*, *18*, 435–444.

Mester, L. J. (1987). A multiproduct cost study of savings and loans. *Journal of Finance*, *42*, 423–445.

Pi, L., & Timme, S. G. (1993). Corporate control and bank efficiency. *Journal of Bankingand Finance*, *17*, 515–530.

Ramanathan, R. (1992). *Introductory econometrics with applications* (2nd ed., pp. 313–316). New York, NY: Harcourt Brace Jovanovich College Publishers.

Rogers, K. E. (1998). Nontraditional activities and the efficiency of U.S. commercial banks. *Journal of Banking and Finance*, *22*, 467–482.

Ross, S. A. (1989). Institutional markets, financial markets, and financial innovation. *Journal of Finance*, *44*, 541–556.

Saunders, A., Strock, E., & Travlos, N. G. (1990). Ownership structure, deregulation, and bank risk taking. *Journal of Finance*, *45*, 643–654.

Sealey, C. W., Jr., & Lindley, J. T. (1977). Inputs, outputs, and the theory of production and cost at depository financial institutions. *Journal of Finance*, *32*, 1251–1266.

Stiroh, K. J. (1997). The evolution of an industry: U.S. thrifts in the 1990s. *Journal of Banking and Finance*, *21*, 1375–1394.

Sullivan, R. J., & Spong, K. R. (1998). How does ownership structure and manager wealth influence risk? A look at ownership structure, manager wealth, and risk in commercial banks. *Financial Industry Perspectives*, 15–40.

Sullivan, R. J., & Spong, K. (1999). Ownership structure, manager wealth and risk in commercial banks. Working Paper, Federal Reserve Bank of Kansas City.

White, H. (1980). A heteroskedasticity consistent covariance matrix estimator and a direct test for heteroskedasticity. *Econometrica*, 817–838.

Zeckhauser, R. J., & Pound, J. (1990). *Are large shareholders effective monitors? An investigation of share ownership and corporate performance, in asymmetric information, corporate finance, and investment* (pp. 149–180). R. G. Hubbard (Ed.). University of Chicago Press.

MANAGEMENT OF EARNINGS BY FINANCIAL INSTITUTIONS IN THE INDIAN SUBCONTINENT

Asokan Anandarajan and David Hossain

ABSTRACT

This study examines earnings management by financial institutions in India. In particular we examine the extent to which loan loss provisions are used as a tool to manage earnings. While much research has been done on this issue internationally, there is a paucity of research focusing on banks in the Indian subcontinent. In this research we replicate methodology used by Ahmed, Takeda and Thomas (1998). Indian banks are unique in that about 80% are state owned. Indian state owned banks are characterized by a large proportion of non-performing assets (socialist laws force them to lend 40% of their portfolios to rural areas where chance of default are as high as 70%), poor productivity (only one-tenth that of the U.S.), high costs (due to the necessity to provide "patronage jobs"), and low probabilities of bankruptcy (since the government bails out those in financial distress). In this environment, new legislation enacted in 1994 enabled banks to issue shares and tap the capital market. As an added measure managers can now own shares in their banks. We test if, in this unique environment, managers engage in earnings and capital management. The results indicate that overall banks do engage in earnings management and capital management. Further, earnings management is more pronounced for those banks participating in the stock market.

Bank and Financial Market Efficiency: Global Perspectives
Research in Banking and Finance, Volume 5, 89–108

ISSN: 1567-7915/doi:10.1016/S1567-7915(04)05005-0

However, we found no evidence that banks use loan loss provisions to signal future intentions.

1. INTRODUCTION

Much research in academic journals has focused on earnings management by financial institutions. The issue of earnings management by financial institutions is important. It is important to regulators and investors since they have to know to what extent reported earnings are "managed." If earnings are managed to a large extent, then it may not be possible to discern risk. While financial institutions can use many tools to manage earnings, the literature has largely focused on the use of loan loss provisions (LLPs) as a tool for earnings management. The focus has been on loan loss provisions because this is one of the few tools over which banks have greater latitude for discretion. In general, banks are supposed to anticipate future losses and the LLP is a reflection of their anticipation. These losses obviously cannot be anticipated with certainty. Hence, banks have a great deal of discretion in setting this target. While it is expected that managers set LLPs based on anticipated losses, as they are supposed to do, in reality prior research indicates that banks use LLPs for avoiding minimum capital adequacy requirements (referred to as capital management), to manage earnings to reduce volatility and hence, ensure stable stock prices (referred to as earnings management) and to send signals to investors (referred to as signaling). In particular, LLPs have been linked to earnings management when bank managers' compensation is linked to reported earnings (De Chow & Skinner, 2000; Montgomery, 1998; Turner & Godwin, 1999). This situation is exacerbated when managers have stock options in their banks. This provides further impetus to manage earnings since there is an incentive to keep stock prices high for the purpose of maximizing compensation.

Research has focused on the role of LLPs in earnings management (refer Ahmed, Takeda & Thomas, 1998; Beatty, Chamberlain & S. Magliolo, 1995; Greenwalt & Sinkey, 1988 among others). Other researchers have focused on the role of LLPs in capital management (refer Beatty, Chamberlain & Magliolo, 1995; Collins, Shackelford & Wahlen, 1995; Kim & Kross, 1998; Moyer, 1990; among others). Finally, researchers have examined the use of LLPs as a tool for signaling information to investors in the stock market (refer Liu & Ryan, 1995; Wahlen, 1994 among others). While research in this area has been done extensively in the United States, emerging research has also examined the use of LLPs in other environments focusing on European countries (Anandarajan, Hasan & Lozano-Vivas, 2003). However, there is a paucity of similar research using data from the Indian subcontinent. The purpose of this study is to reduce this gap by examining the role of loan loss provisions (LLP) in earnings management, managing capital adequacy ratios, and as a tool for signaling in India. In this study we replicate the research of Ahmed, Takeda and Thomas (1998) who examined the role of loan loss provisions in capital management, earnings management, and as a tool for signaling in the U.S. banking industry. We use the same methodology but test different hypothesis appropriate to India.

This article is organized as follows. In the next section we review pertinent research on LLPs. In the following section we provide the theoretical underpinnings of our hypotheses followed by a brief review of the Indian banking industry. We then provide a description of the data and model specifications and discuss the variables used in this study. Finally, we discuss the empirical results and then state our conclusions.

2. LITERATURE REVIEW

The research in this area can be broadly broken into three main areas: studies that examined the association of LLPs to capital management, studies that examined the association of LLPs with earnings management and, finally, studies that examined the use of LLPs as a signaling device. These will now be considered individually.

2.1. Studies Examining the Association of LLPs with Capital Management

Studies in this area can be dichotomized into two categories, namely, research that examined the association of LLPs to capital management prior to capital adequacy regulation enacted in the United States in 1989 and studies that examined the association of LLPs to capital management in the post capital adequacy regime. The first published research in this field was by Moyer (1990). Moyer found a significant association between LLPs and capital management. Moyer concluded that banks in financial distress increased LLPs to increase the numerator of the capital adequacy ratio in order to avoid the costs of violation.

The main criticism of the Moyer research was that the study did not include nor consider other measures that could be used for enhancing the capital ratio. (For example, loan write offs.) Moyer also did not consider the interdependence of these other factors. Beatty, Chamberlain and Magliolo (1995) developed a methodology that enabled examination when these decisions are made simultaneously. Having established a superior methodology, Beatty et al. corroborated the findings of Moyer, namely, that there was a significant association between LLPs and capital management. However, the results are not in consensus. Collins et al. (1995) conducted a similar study using similar methodology and hypotheses and concluded that there was no significant association between LLPs and capital management. More recent research also found no significant association between LLPs and capital management (Ahmed, Takeda & Thomas, 1998; Kim & Kross, 1998).

2.2. Studies Examining the Relationship Between LLPs and Earnings Management

The studies in this area are considerably more than studies that tested the association of LLPs with capital management. We shall focus only on some of the studies pertinent to this research. Studies that used data prior to the 1989 capital adequacy regulation will be considered first. In an early study, Scheiner (1981) concluded that commercial banks did not use LLPs to smooth reported income. Even though he found an association, he attributed the association to higher business failures rather than a concerted effort by managers to manipulate earnings. Ma (1988), on the other hand, concluded that LLPs and loan charge-offs were jointly used smooth earnings. Subsequent studies all came to similar conclusions, namely, that LLPs were positively associated with earnings management (Beaver & Engel, 1996; Beaver et al., 1989; Collins et al., 1995; Liu & Ryan, 1995; Liu et al., 1997; Scholes et al., 1990).

Studies using data after the 1989 capital adequacy regulation era is limited to a well-executed paper by Ahmed et al. (1998). The authors did not find strong evidence of earnings management via loan loss provisions after the new capital adequacy regulation came into effect. Hence, in summary, the results indicate that prior to the new capital adequacy regulation there was strong evidence of earnings management while in the period after the association appears to have weakened.

2.3. LLP as a Mechanism to Signal Private Information About Future Earnings

The signaling hypothesis was initially expounded by Beaver et al. (1989). They stated that investors would perceive an increase in LLP as positive and indicative of prudent and conservative management (refer also Beaver & Engel, 1996; Wahlen, 1994). However, the evidence with respect to the signaling hypothesis is not wholly proven. In a more recent study Liu et al. (1997) provided further evidence to corroborate the signaling hypothesis. However Ahmed et al. (1998) did not find evidence to support the hypothesis. The general summary is that, while the preponderance of studies concludes the possibility that LLPs are used as a signaling device, the evidence is mixed.

3. THE INDIAN BANKING SYSTEM

3.1. Overview

The modern banking system in India started with the establishment of General Bank of India in 1786. In the mid-nineteenth century the East India Company established the Bank of Bengal in 1809, the Bank of Bombay in 1840 and the Bank of Madras in 1843. These were initially independent units and were referred to as the Presidency banks. Subsequently, these three banks were amalgamated and became known as the Imperial Bank of India. After independence the Imperial Bank of India (which till then functioned as a private bank) was nationalized under the State Bank of India Act of 1955 and became known as the State Bank of India. Nationalization was a major theme during the period after independence due to the socialist philosophy adopted by the first prime minister, Jawaharlal Nehru. In 1969 his daughter Indira Gandhi, then premier, continued this process by nationalizing 14 major banks. Indian banks are unique in many respects. Prior to 1991 all banks were state owned. In 1991 when the government opened banking to private banks (ICICA bank and Bank of America are examples), the public sector has dropped by 20%. However, state owned banks still controls approximately 80% of the country's banking assets. The key chronological events of banks in India are shown in Table 1.

Currently, the combined affiliation of the 37 listed government affiliated banks is \$13.75 billion. The dominance of these banks in the Indian economy can be characterized by the fact that the 147 publicly traded information technology companies combined account for \$13.68 billion in assets (Business Week, June 23, 2003). Of these states owned banks, the State Bank of India is the country's largest with \$83 billion in assets. The New Delhi based Oriental Bank of Commerce is at the other end of the scale with \$7.5 billion in assets.

3.1.1. General and Unique Characteristics of the Indian Banking Environment

The Indian government has a tradition of using state owned banks to rescue failing institutions or to funnel money to favored projects which has little chance of paying off the loan. Further, a study by McKinsey and Co., consultants finds that the productivity of Indian banks are only one-tenth of the productivity of U.S. banks (Business Week, June 10, 2002). In general India's banking system is so dysfunctional that it is slowing the economy. Non-performing assets, poor

Table 1. Chronology of Banks in India: Key Events in the Period 1950–2003.

Date	Key Event
1949	The Reserve Bank of India (RBI) is nationalized and made a central bank by an act of parliament
1956	Nationalization continues. All Life Insurance Companies now nationalized
1969	Nationalization completed. Fourteen major banks nationalized by Mrs Indira Gandhi. Now all banks are state owned.
1992	Dual exchange rate system is instituted under liberalized rate. Now exchange rate moves from managed floated regime to a market determined one. Expected to provide boost to export industry
1992	RBI introduces a Risk-Assets-Ratio for banks as a capital adequacy measure
1993	RBI introduces Risk-Assets-Ratio for banks as a capital adequacy measure
1993	Guidelines for setting up private sector banks are issued
1993	Process of convertability is started and rupee is made convertible on current account. Expected to provide a stimulus to business and hence should provide an impetus to banks as well
1994	UTI becomes the first private bank to start operations
1994	RBI issued guidelines on prudential norms. Banks should achieve minimum capital adequacy ratio is set at 6% on their risk weighted assets and off balance sheet exposures; to be maintained by March 31, 1995
1994	Amendment to Banking Companies Act. Enabled all state owned banks to tap the capital market. The nationalized banks can now strengthen their capital base by issuing stock
1994	Full convertibility taken by making the rupee convertible on the current account
1994	Oriental Bank of Commerce becomes the first state owned bank to raise a significant amount of money by issuing stock in the stock market (Rs 387.2 crore)
2003	New law enacted by parliament. Enables banks to sue customers when they default on payments to obtain payment. Stock prices of state owned banks surge. State owned bank capitalization now greater than info tech companies capitalization

productivity and inability to raise capital from the stock market characterize Indian banks. The reasons are not purely inefficient management on the part of the banks. Kumar (2001) notes that socialist laws that force them to lend at least 40% of their portfolios to rural areas (where probability of loan default hovers between 67 and 70%) have hobbled Indian banks. Further, the poor performance can also be attributed to "patronage jobs" provided by the government to the well connected. Indian banks are required to spend close to 18% of their income on labor. This compares poorly because, as Kumar notes, the global average is around 7–9%.

Further, the Indian government, unlike those of Japan and China, which have been trying to tackle the problem of bad loans for a decade, has not confronted its banking problems. The government routinely bails out banks that are in the deepest trouble. To illustrate, in February 2002, the Industrial Development Bank

Table 2. NPA (Non-Performing Assets of Indian Banks).

Year	Gross NPA (in Crore Rupees)	Gross NPA as Percentage of Loans
1993	39,253	23.2
1994	41,041	24.8
1995	38,385	19.5
1996	41,661	18
1997	47,300	15.7
1998	50,815	14.4
1999	58,722	14.7
2000	53,066	13
2001	56,608	13

Note: These indicate the high nature of non-performing loans that are a unique characteristic of Indian Banks. Compare with an average of 1.5% for banks in the United States and Europe. The positive note is that the amounts are decreasing and should continue to decrease especially after the implementation of the new laws that give more teeth to banks to sue defaulters for money owed.

asked for and obtained $458 million to bail itself out of financial difficulty. In August 2002, the Indian government organized a bailout comprising $215 million for the Industrial Finance Corporation of India. This phenomenon has resulted in state owned banks having higher credit ratings than the Indian government itself because the market is confident that the government will bail out banks in financial distress and hence bankruptcy is not possible regardless of financial predicament.

In the 1990s Indian banks were characterized by very high non-performing loans. During this period the overall average estimated bad debt was $23 million according to Business Week. This is more than 20% of their portfolios. This compares very poorly with their counterparts in the United States and Europe which have an average bad debt ratio of 1.5%. In this respect, the only country in the world that comes close to India is Japan with 15% ratio of non-performing loans. Table 2 shows the figures for non-performing loans over a ten year period. As can be evidenced from Table 2 there is an improvement over the last ten years with non-performing loans reducing from 23 to 13%.

Kumar (2001) notes that more than half of the non-performing loans are owed by companies that are financially sound. It is not that they cannot pay, they chose not to. As an illustration, the New Delhi based Oriental Bank of Commerce has $7.5 billion in assets, its outstanding loans are $1 billion but it has $200 million in bad debts (Business Week, June 2003).

3.1.2. Current Environmental Changes and its Impact on Indian Banks

In the last few years, under the government of Prime Minister Vajpayee, India has deregulated and delicensed many sectors of the economy. Foreign exchange regulations have been liberalized and the value of the Indian currency has now been left to the dynamics of market forces. Exporters have been encouraged by incentives while reduced tariffs and duties have wooed foreign investors and industrialists. In 1994 an amendment to the Banking Companies Act of 1970 enabled state owned banks to enter and seek funding from the stock market. This additional source of funding enabled state owned banks to strengthen their capital base especially as the law allowed them to seek as much as 49% of their capital base from the stock market.

In 2003 the Government of India initiated new law that enabled state owned banks to prosecute those who defaulted on loans. This sent a strong signal to the stock market that cash flows from state owned banks would increase significantly. The net result was an increase in a rally and surge in stock prices of India's majority state owned banks. Business week reports that this surge has resulted in the market capitalization of state owned banks exceeding that of the Indian information technology sector.

3.1.3. Minimum Capital Adequacy Regulation in India

In April 1992 the Reserve Bank of India (RBI) introduced a risk assets ratio measure for banks as a capital adequacy measure. On June 13, 1994, RBI introduced further guidelines on prudential norms. The banks' minimum capital adequacy ratio (based on the 1992 act, subsequently amended by the 1994 act) had to be 6% on their risk weighted assets and off balance sheet exposures. A time period till March 1995 was given for banks to attain this ratio. In this ratio, loan reserves constitute a component of the numerator.

4. HYPOTHESES

The hypotheses are based on two premises. First, since Indian banks, including state owned, now depend on the stock market for a significant portion of their funding, there is an incentive to manage earnings to convey a signal of earnings stability. Signals conveying information that companies are stable, should in turn positively influence stock prices.

Indian managers are now given stocks in their institutions. Based on this background of Indian banks, we submit that banks may manage capital using loan loss provisions since the new regulation came into effect. We posit that commercial banks will have a greater incentive to manipulate capital and earnings using loan loss reserves relative to other institutions. Further, commercial banks having shares in the stock market will have a greater incentive to manipulate relative to commercial banks not participating in the stock market since they are now responsible to investors. A further motivation can be induced by the fact that senior managers may now have stock options thus increasing the impetus to engage in some form of earnings management. Based on this, our hypothesis is stated as follows:

H1a. The higher the cost of violating capital constraints, the more likely it is that banks will manage capital via loan loss provisions.

H1b. Commercial banks will have a greater incentive to manipulate capital via loan loss provisions than other financial intermediaries.

H1c. Commercial banks active in the stock market will have a greater incentive to manipulate capital via loan loss provisions than other commercial banks not enlisted in the capital market.

H2a. Overall, loan loss provisions will be positively associated with earnings.

H2b. The relation between loan loss provisions and earnings (before loan loss provisions) will be more positive for commercial banks relative to other financial intermediaries.

H2c. The relation between loan loss provisions and earnings (before loan loss provision) will be more positive for commercial banks active in the stock market than for those commercial banks that do not participate in the stock market.

Finally, as in prior studies, we generate a hypothesis to test if LLPs are used as a tool for signaling management intentions to the stock market for those Indian banks that participate in the stock market. Hence the final hypothesis is stated as follows:

H3. Loan loss provisions are positively related to one-year ahead changes in earnings (before loan loss provisions) for those commercial banks that participate in the stock market.

5. DATA AND MODEL SPECIFICATIONS

5.1. Sample

Our sample covers the period 1994–2001. We use 1994 as a starting point because that is when the government enacted capital adequacy regulation (see Table 1 for chronology of key events). We had a total of 72 commercial banks, 18 credit institutions and 17 cooperative banks in our original sample. After deleting those for which data was incomplete, our final sample comprised 60 commercial banks, 8 credit institutions, and 8 cooperative banks. Of these, 37 commercial banks and 8 credit institutions actively seek funds in the Indian stock exchange.

Table 3. Indian Financial Intermediates.

Years	Commercial Banks	Other Banks (Credit Institutions)	Other Banks (Cooperatives)
Number of institutions			
1994–2001	72	18	17
Number of institutions with complete data			
1994–2001	60	8	8
Number of institutions involved in the capital market with complete data			
	37	9	0
Number of observations with complete data			
	475	60	55
Percentage share of industry assets			
1994–2001	61%	18%	21%
Mean and (standard deviation) of key variables across samples			
Loan loss provisions (000)			
1994–2001	38,435 (1,818)	32,683 (973)	22,371 (432)
Loan loss provision to total loan			
1994–2001	1.672 (0.695)	1.215 (0.481)	0.952 (0.376)
Actual loan losses (000)			
1994–2001	32,501 (1,073)	26,952 (753)	20,083 (842)
Actual loan losses tot total assets			
1994–2001	1.126 (1.01)	0.968 (0.636)	0.710 (0.487)

The commercial banks account for 61% of industry assets while credit institutions account for 18% and cooperative banks account for 21%. In Table 3 we also provide information about the loan loss provisions of those banks in our sample.

Table 4 provides a descriptive statistics of the variables used in this study.

5.2. Methodology

The following regression model was used to examine how LLPs are used in earnings management and capital management.

$$\begin{aligned}\text{LLP} = {} & a_0 + a_1\Delta\text{LLOSS} + a_2\Delta\text{GDP} + a_3\text{CAP} + a_4\text{EBT} + a_5\text{CDUM} \\ & + a_6\text{SDUM} + a_7\text{LASSETS} + a_8\text{CFEER} + a_9\text{CDUM} \times \text{CAP} \\ & + a_{10}\text{CDUM} \times \text{EBT} + \text{SDUM} \times \text{CAP} + \text{SDUM} \times \text{EBT}\end{aligned}$$

Table 4. Descriptive Statistics.

	Commercial Banks		Other Types of Banks (Cooperatives and Credit Institutions)	
	Mean	Standard Deviation	Mean	Standard Deviation
Loan loss provisions to loans (LLP)	1.672***	0.695	1.168	0.504
Loan losses to assets (LLA)	1.126***	1.014	0.843	0.541
Change in loan losses (ΔLLA)	1.981**	0.425	1.427	0.856
Change in GDP (ΔGDP)	2.091	1.763	2.018	1.421
Capital to minimum required capital (EBT)	2.963*	1.416	2.856	2.431
Stock returns (SRETURN)	5.322**	1.245	7.083	3.972
Book value of equity to assets (BVETA)	7.362*	2.083	6.991	3.016
Return on assets (ROA)	1.471**	0.964	1.719	1.020
Commission and fees to assets (CFEER)	0.574*	0.392	0.658	0.507
Total assets (000)	678,275**	209,012	1,376,005	1,028,234
Number of observation	475		115	

Note: ***, **, * significantly different at the $p = 0.01, 0.05, 0.10$ levels respectively. Regulatory Capital requirement is not applicable for sub-sample of the non-commercial banks sample given they are involved in investment banking activities.

where,

LLP = Loan loss provision to loans outstanding
ΔLLOSS = Change in loan losses
ΔGDP = Percentage change in gross domestic product
CAP = Ratio of actual regulatory capital (primary or Tier 1 capital) before loan loss reserves to the minimum required regulatory capital
EBT = Earnings before taxes and loan loss provision/average Total assets
CDUM = Dummy variable (1 = commercial banks; 0 = Other banks)
SDUM = Dummy variable (1 = commercial banks active in stock Market; 0 = banks not enlisted in the stock market)
LASSETS = Log of total assets
CFEER = Commission and fee income to total assets
CDUM × CAP = Interaction of type of financial intermediaries (commercial Banks vs. other types of banks) with ratio of regulatory capital

CDUM × EBT = Interaction of type of financial intermediaries (commercial Banks vs. other types of banks) with earnings before LLP
SDUM × CAP = Interaction of type of commercial bank (commercial bank In stock market relative to banks not in the stock market) With ratio of regulatory capital and type of regime
SDUM × EBT = Interaction of type of commercial bank (commercial bank in stock market relative to banks not in the stock market) with earnings before LLP

In the above regression ΔLLOSS and ΔGDP are internal and external indicators of the level of risk faced by a bank. Increase in loan losses would necessitate that the bank increases its loan loss provisions to take account of the additional risk. Similarly ΔGDP is used as a surrogate for economic activity. Decrease in percentage change in GDP indicates a slump in the economy that may accentuate the risk of loan default for banks.

The organizational form dummy variable (CDUM) takes on the value of 1 if the banking institution is a commercial bank and 0 if it is other. The organizational form dummy variable (SDUM) takes on the value of 1 if the banking institution is a commercial bank participating in the stock market and 0 if not. Commercial banks participating in the stock market have direct monitoring or profit making pressure from stockholders (owners). Therefore, their managers may have a greater incentive to manipulate income.

The log of total assets is another control variable that measures the size of the bank. In general, larger banks may have higher levels of business and may be expected to have higher loan loss provisions than smaller banks. CFEER is commission and fee income as a proportion of total assets. A higher income in this category indicates an interest in non-depository banking activities and thus relatively less dependency on traditional lending activities. It is plausible that these institutions are more active in allocating appropriate loan loss reserve estimates in order to provide an image of a "safer financial institution" providing multiple services for clients. One may argue the contrary stating that, given most of the traditional income for depository institutions come from deposits and lending activities, commissions and fees may represent an aggressive and non-traditional mode of banking activity. Banks involved in such non-depository activity and strategy may have experienced higher credit risk and thus may allocate inflated amounts to the loan loss provision for the purpose of off setting risks associated with an anticipated uncertain future.

CDUM × CAP indicates the interaction of type of financial intermediary with ratio of regulatory capital. If commercial banks have a greater propensity to manipulate the capital adequacy ratio we would expect the coefficient of the interaction to be positive. CDUM × EBT indicates the interaction of type of financial intermediary (commercial banks vs. others) with earnings before loan loss provisions. If commercial banks engage in earnings management relative to others we would expect the coefficient of this interaction term to be positive. SDUM × CAP indicates the interaction of type of commercial banks (commercial banks in stock market relative to banks not in stock market) with ratio of regulatory capital. If commercial banks in stock market have a greater propensity to manipulate ratios, then we would expect the coefficient of the interaction to be positive. Finally, SDUM × EBT indicates the interaction of commercial banks (commercial banks in stock market relative to banks not in the stock market) with earnings before loan loss provisions. If commercial banks engage in earnings management, we would expect this ratio to be significant and positive.

6. EMPIRICAL RESULTS

The regression results are shown in Table 5. We report a multiple number of regressions that incorporate different independent variables.

Table 5. Determining Factors of LLP OLS Regressions (t-Statistics in Parenthesis).

	1	2	3	4
Intercept	0.025 (2.04)**	0.0376 (2.94)***	0.026 (3.05)***	0.028 (3.46)***
ΔLLOSS	0.131 (2.91)***	0.159 (3.04)***	0.164 (2.99)***	0.137 (3.17)***
ΔGDP	0.010 (1.80)*	0.011 (1.71)*	0.013 (1.60)	0.021 (1.56)
CAP	−0.039 (2.49)**	−0.048 (2.42)**	−0.198 (2.83)**	−0.205 (2.80)**
EBT	0.010 (3.22)***	0.018 (3.07)***	0.029 (2.99)***	0.006 (2.28)**
CDUM	−0.009 (1.75)*	−0.008 (1.62)	–	–
SDUM	–	–	−0.021 (2.57)**	−0.020 (2.66)**
LASSETS	0.002 (1.09)	0.004 (1.28)	0.007 (1.36)	0.006 (1.45)
CFEER	−0.098 (2.76)**	−0.114 (2.82)**	−0.163 (2.73)**	−0.143 (2.69)**
CDUM × CAP	–	−0.229 (2.05)**	–	–
CDUM × EBT	–	0.009 (2.70)**	–	–
SDUM × CAP	–		–	−0.222 (3.29)***
SDUM × EBT	–		–	0.258 (3.79)***
Adjusted R^2	0.3265	0.3409	0.3891	0.4004
F-Statistics	100.57***	105.18***	108.04***	111.07***
Number of observations	590	590	368	368

Note: ***, **, * significantly different at the $p = 0.01, 0.05, 0.10$ levels respectively.

The first regression model does not include the interaction variables. The second model has, in addition, the CDUM × CAP and CDUM × EBT interaction variables while the third model specifically tests results for commercial banks in the stock market (variable designated as SDUM. The model statistics in estimate 1 reveals that the basic model (reported in column 1) explains almost 33% of the model with marginal increase to 34 and 39% by including interaction variables. In all estimates, the R^2 and F-statistics show strong model statistics.

The results in the first model indicate that, overall, loan loss experience, economic activity, the level of the capital adequacy ratio, and level of earnings, and non-traditional banking activity all significantly influence the level of LLPs. The change in actual loan loss is positively associated with LLP levels. Similarly, the variable ΔGDP is positively associated with LLPs indicating that the specific nature of Indian economy influences provisions for loan losses as can be expected. Interestingly both capital and earnings are significantly associated with LLP (significant at the 5 and 1% levels respectively). The negative sign of the CAP ratio indicates that, overall, the lower the capital ratio (i.e. the closer it moves to the minimum required capital), the higher the loan loss provision. This is consistent with the findings of Moyer (1990) and Beatty et al. (1995) that loan loss provisions are used as a mechanism to increase loan loss reserves. This finding supports hypothesis H1a that Indian banking institutions manage capital using loan loss provisions. Similarly, earnings are significantly and positively associated with LLP. This is also in accordance with earnings management theory discussed in the literature review section. This finding supports hypothesis H2a that states loan loss provisions will be used to manipulate earnings, hence implying a positive relationship. The sign of the coefficient indicates that, as earnings decline, loan loss provisions are reduced in order to manage earnings. Thus, it would appear that overall, for the whole sample, when interactions are not taken into account, both earnings management and capital management did occur.

The CFEER coefficient indicates that banks with greater non-traditional banking activities are less likely to have higher loan loss provisions in their books. These findings are consistent with the theory in the published literature.

The second regression model in column 2 of Table 5 incorporates two interactions, namely, CDUM × CAP and CDUM × EBT. As shown in Table 5, the relationship in the first model still holds true. The coefficient of the CDUM × CAP interaction variable in model 2 is negative and significant at p-value 0.01 level. This indicates that commercial banks use loan loss provisions to manage capital in order to avoid violation of minimum capital requirements relative to other financial intermediaries. This finding supports hypothesis H1b. The coefficient of the SDUM × CAP interaction variable (in model 4) is negative and significant.

This finding supports hypothesis H1c which states that commercial banks active in the stock market have an incentive to manipulate capital via loan loss provisions than other commercial banks not listed on the stock market. This corroborates the theory that these banks (which are responsible to investors and whose stock prices may be adversely affected), will have a greater incentive to manipulate loan loss provisions to avoid violating capital adequacy regulation. The coefficient of the interaction term CDUM × EBT is significant and positive (refer model 2). This indicates that commercial banks overall use loan loss provisions to manipulate earnings which supports hypothesis H2b. The coefficient of the SDUM × CAP interaction variable is significant (refer model 4) and negative, this indicates that commercial banks active in the stock market have a greater incentive to manipulate capital relative to commercial banks that do not participate in the stock market. This supports hypothesis H1c. Similarly, the coefficient of the SDUM × EBT interaction variable is positive and significant at the p-value 0.05 level (refer model 4). This indicates that commercial banks in India which participate in the stock market are more aggressive in earnings management using loan loss provisions relative to commercial banks that do not participate in the stock market. This finding supports our hypothesis H2c.

In Table 5 we examine earnings management and capital management behavior of banks via loan loss provisions. In Table 6 we examine whether loan loss

Table 6. Tests of the Signaling Hypothesis (t-Statistics in Parenthesis).

	Dependent Variable LLP		Dependent Variable $\Delta EBTPMVE_{(t+1)}$	
	1	2	3	4
Intercept	0.048 (1.06)	0.030 (1.35)	0.022 (3.67)***	0.037 (3.76)***
ΔLLOSS	0.129 (5.91)***	0.166 (6.50)***	–	–
ΔGDP	0.006 (1.28)	0.007 (1.37)	–	–
CAP	−0.073 (1.76)*	−0.059 (1.84)	–	–
EBT	0.029 (2.97)***	0.027 (2.95)***	–	–
CDUM	−0.016 (1.80)*		−0.026 (1.73)*	–
SDUM	–	−0.035 (2.75)**	–	−0.029 (2.45)**
ΔEBTP (1 year ahead)	−0.027 (3.44)**	−0.030 (3.69)**	–	–
ΔEBTPMVE	–	–	−0.019 (2.68)**	−0.021 (2.04)**
ULLPMVE	–	–	−0.402 (2.77)**	−0.402 (3.55)**
Adjusted R^2	0.2187	0.1619	0.1586	0.1434
F-Statistics	77.05	33.09	28.53	20.63
Number of observations	504	322	504	322

provisions are used as a tool for signaling future earnings (i.e. the signaling theory) to test hypothesis H3.The regression model employed was:

$$\mathrm{LLP} = a_0 + a_1\Delta\mathrm{LLOSS} + a_2\Delta\mathrm{GDP} + a_3\mathrm{CAP} + a_4\mathrm{EBT} + a_5\mathrm{CDUM} + a_6\mathrm{SDUM} + a_7\Delta\mathrm{EBTP} + a_8\mathrm{EBTPMVE} + a_9\mathrm{ULLPMVE}$$

where

ΔEBTP = One year ahead change in earnings

$\Delta\mathrm{EBTPMVE}_{(t+1)}$ = Future (one year ahead) change in earnings before provisions and taxes (divided by market value of equity at the beginning of that year)

CAP = Ratio of actual regulatory capital before loan loss reserves to the minimum required regulatory capital

ΔEBTPMVE = Change in earnings before provisions and taxes (divided by market value of equity at the beginning of the year)

ULLPMVE = Unexpected loan loss provision measured by the residuals from a regression of loan loss provisions (deflated by beginning of year market value of equity) on expected change in non-performing loans, beginning of year loan loss allowance, beginning of year non-performing loans, and three loan composition variables all deflated by beginning of year market value of equity. The expected change in non-performing loans is the predicted value in regression of change in non-performing loans and the 3 loan composition variables all deflated by beginning of year market value of equity.

(all other variables as defined earlier)

In this model we examine whether loan loss provisions are related to future earnings changes after controlling for economic determinants of loan loss provisions using regressions similar to those in Table 5 augmented by the change in one-year ahead earnings before taxes and loan loss provisions. If signaling of this type is an important determinant of loan loss provisions, then we should observe a positive relation between the one-year ahead change in earnings and loan loss provisions as reported in Wahlen (1994) and others. This is because signaling theory postulates that increase in LLPs are used to signal good news about future earnings changes.

The first regression in Table 6 presents the results of the augmented regression. The coefficient of the one-year ahead change in earnings is negative and significantly different from zero at the 1% level. The sign of the coefficient and its significance is not consistent with the signaling hypotheses. The results are not consistent with the findings reported in Wahlen (1994) who concluded that the signaling hypothesis was valid. The results here are, however, consistent with the findings of Ahmed et al. (1998) who did not find evidence of the signaling hypothesis in the United States. The second regression is identical to the first regression in Table 5 except that we incorporate two control variables, namely, SDUM (a dummy variable representing commercial bank type, 1 if commercial bank participated in the stock exchange; 0 otherwise). The coefficient of this variable was significant. Overall, the coefficient of the one-year ahead change in earnings was still negative and significantly different from zero at the 1% level. Thus, we do not find evidence to support the signaling hypothesis.

To further understand this phenomena we reexamined the signaling hypothesis using Wahlen's (1994) model that was also used by Ahmed et al. The regressions are shown in columns 3 and 4 of Table 5. In these models we only used commercial banks for which consistent stock market return data was available.

The model examined in column 3 is as follows:

$$\Delta \text{EBTPMVE}_{(t+1)} = a_0 + a_1\text{CDUM} + a_2\Delta\text{EBTPMVE} + a_3\text{ULLPMVE}$$

where

$\Delta \text{EBTPMVE}_{(t+1)}$ = Future (one year ahead) change in earnings before provisions and taxes (divided by market value of equity at the beginning of that year)

ΔEBTPMVE = Change in earnings before provisions and taxes (divided by market value of equity at the beginning of the year)

ULLPMVE = Unexpected loan loss provision measured by the residuals from a regression of loan loss provisions (deflated by beginning of year market value of equity) on expected change in non-performing loans, beginning of year loan loss allowance, beginning of year non-performing loans, and five loan composition variables all deflated by beginning of year market value of equity. The expected change in non-performing loans is the predicted value in regression of change in non-performing loans and the 5 loan composition variables all deflated by beginning of year market value of equity.

The models in columns 3 and 4 presents tests of signaling using the valuation approach used in Beaver and Engel (1994) and Ahmed et al. (1998). Regressions were run using the Wahlen and Ahmed et al.'s model for discretionary LLP provision and empirical specifications. Columns 3 and 4 of Table 6 presents the results of the models. The model presented in Table 6 is a similar regression to that of column 3 but including SDUM (commercial banks participating in stock exchange) rather than CDUM (all commercial banks). In essence, the results in both indicate that the relation between future earnings changes and the discretionary component of the loan loss provision remain negative and significantly different from zero at the 5% level. This is not consistent with the signaling hypothesis, which would postulate a positive relationship. These results are, however, consistent with Ahmed et al. who also found no evidence for signaling theory in their sample of U.S. banks.

7. CONCLUSIONS

Much research has examined earnings and capital management of banks in an international arena with specific reference to the use of tools such as loan loss provisions among others. It is generally agreed that LLPs are a popular mechanism used by banks for avoiding minimum capital adequacy regulation and earnings management. The bulk of the research has focused on banks in the United States and Europe. This is the first study to examine earnings management in the Indian subcontinent. The Indian subcontinent is a unique environment to study earnings management and capital management because it is characterized by requirements to serve customers who have a reputation for defaulting thus generating a high level of bad loans. Further, until recently the legal system was not conducive to banks using the courts to obtain payment. In summary, Indian banks are unique in that about 80% are state owned. Indian state owned banks are characterized by a large proportion of non-performing assets (socialist laws force them to lend 40% of their portfolios to rural areas where chance of default are as high as 70%); poor productivity (only one-tenth that of the U.S.); high costs (due to the necessity to provide "patronage jobs"); and low probabilities of bankruptcy (since the government bails them out). Further, it is only in the last decade that banks were allowed to issue to stock to finance their activities. In this environment, we test if managers engage in earnings management, capital management and to a lesser extent use LLPs for signaling future intentions. In this respect the objective of this study is to provide information on the accuracy of reported financial statement numbers.

Our results indicate that, overall, LLPs were used as a tool for avoiding capital adequacy regulation. Similarly, overall, LLPs were used as a tool for earnings management after controlling for the high level of bad debts. This intuitively makes sense. The findings indicate that commercial banks participating in the stock market pursue earnings management strategies relative to commercial banks not participating in the capital market. This is not surprising since there is an incentive to manage earnings to convey to investors a signal of stability. Finally, similar to the U.S., we did not find evidence that Indian banks used LLPs as a tool to signal their intentions about future earnings. The overall conclusion is that earnings management occurs and it is more pronounced for banks that participate in the stock market. Thus it is difficult to discern risk, and regulators and potential investors may have to place reliance on factors other than financial statement numbers alone in their evaluations.

REFERENCES

Ahmed, A. S., Takeda, C., & Thomas, S. (1998). Bank loan loss provisions: A reexamination of capital management, earnings management and signaling effects. *Journal of Accounting and Economics*, *28*, 1–25.

Anandarajan, A., Hasan, I., & Lozano-Vivas (2003). Loan loss provisions, earnings management and capital management: The experience of Spanish banks. *Advances in International Accounting*, *16*, 43–62.

Anonymous (2002). Will India's banks be crushed by bad loans? *Business Week* (June 10).

Anonymous (2003). Now the banks have teeth. *Business Week* (June 23).

Beatty, A., Chamberlain, S., & Magliolo, J. (1995). Managing financial reports of commercial banks: The influence of taxes, regulatory capital, and earnings. *Journal of Accounting Research*, *33*(2), 231–262.

Beaver, W., & Engel, E. (1996). Discretionary behavior with respect to allowances for loan losses and the behavior of security prices. *Journal of Accounting and Economics*, *22*(1–3), 177–206.

Beaver, W., Eger, C., Ryan, S., & Wolfson, M. (1989). Financial reporting and the structure of bank share prices. *Journal of Accounting Research*, *27*, 157–178.

Collins, J., Shackelford, D., & Wahlen, J. (1995). Bank differences in the coordination of regulatory capital, earnings and taxes. *Journal of Accounting Research*, *33*, 263–292.

De Chow, P. M., & Skinner, D. J. (2000). Earnings management: reconciling the views of accounting, academics, practitioners, and regulators. *Accounting Horizons*, *14*(2), 235–250.

Greenwalt, M., & Sinkey, J., Jr. (1988). Bank loan loss provisions and the income smoothing hypothesis: An empirical analysis, 1976–1984. *Journal of Financial Services Research*, *1*, 301–318.

Kim, M., & Kross, W. (1998). The impact of the 1989 change in bank capital standards on loan loss provisions and loan write-offs. *Journal of Accounting and Economics*, *25*(1), 69–100.

Kumar, H. (2001). Talent stakeout at India's state banks. *Business Week* (May 4).

Liu, C., & Ryan, S. (1995). The effect of bank loan portfolio composition on the market reaction to and anticipation of loan loss provisions. *Journal of Accounting Research*, *33*(1), 77–94.

Liu, C., Ryan, S., & Wahlen, J. (1997). Differential valuation implications of loan loss provisions across banks and fiscal agents. *The Accounting Review*, *72*(1), 133–146.

Ma, C. K. (1988). Loan loss reserve and income smoothing: The experience in the U.S. banking industry. *Journal of Business Finance and Accounting*, *15*(4), 487–497.

Montgomery, L. (1998). Recent developments affecting depository institutions. *FDIC Banking Review*, *11*(4), 26–34.

Moyer, S. E. (1990). Capital adequacy ratio regulations and accounting choices in commercial banks. *Journal of Accounting and Economics*, *13*(July), 123–154.

Scheiner, J. H. (1981). Income smoothing: An analysis in the banking industry. *Journal of Bank Research*, *12*, 1919–1923.

Scholes, M., Wilson, G. P., & Wolfson, M. (1990). Tax planning, regulatory capital planning, and financial reporting strategy for commercial banks. *Review of Financial Studies*, *3*, 625–650.

Turner, L. E., & Godwin, J. H. (1999). Auditing, earnings management and international accounting issues at the Securities and Exchange Commission. *Accounting Horizons*, *13*(3), 281–298.

Wahlen, J. (1994). The nature of information in commercial bank loan loss disclosures. *The Accounting Review*, *69*(3), 455–478.

LOAN REPAYMENT IN THE GRAMEEN BANK: THE IMPORTANCE OF BORROWER OPPORTUNITY COST AND GENDER

Farhad Ameen

ABSTRACT

This paper evaluates the significance of borrower gender, opportunity cost of time, ability, incentives, and monitoring by bank staff, on variations in loan repayment rates in the Grameen Bank. An increase in the opportunity cost of a borrower's time is found to have a negative effect on repayment, and variations in opportunity costs have different impacts on the repayment performance of men and women. The results suggest that the success of the Grameen Bank rests partly on its time-intensive procedures for borrowers that screen out those with high opportunity costs. The findings may also explain the higher repayment rates of women who typically face a lower opportunity cost of time in rural Bangladesh.

1. INTRODUCTION

It is by now widely accepted that the phenomenal success of the Grameen Bank's microcredit program can be explained by the very innovative institutional set-up used by the bank. The Grameen Bank's unique group lending scheme

Bank and Financial Market Efficiency: Global Perspectives
Research in Banking and Finance, Volume 5, 109–136

ISSN: 1567-7915/doi:10.1016/S1567-7915(04)05006-2

has been widely adopted by other microcredit institutions with much success. Its dramatically low default rate has prompted the adoption of dozens of similar credit programs around the world.[1] While much is known about the importance of the various facets of the bank's institutional set-up, we have yet to understand fully the reasons for the success of the design of the group lending program. Explanations about the bank's success range from rigorous economic analysis of incentive structures in group lending, to anecdotal explanations suggesting that "group solidarity" plays a major role in its success.

While several analytical models have analyzed the role of peer monitoring (see Armendariz de Aghion, 1999; Stiglitz, 1990; Varian, 1990), imperfect information in rural credit markets (Hoff & Stiglitz, 1990) and the incentives fostered by group lending (Bernasek, 1991; Besley & Coate, 1995), few empirical studies have explored the implications of these models. The empirical work has largely concentrated on other aspects of the program. For example, several studies have analyzed the effectiveness of the bank's credit program in reducing the poverty level and improving living standards of its borrowers (Hossain, 1986, 1988; Khandker, 1993). Others have assessed the impact of the loan program on borrower households. For example, Pitt and Khandker (1998) have found that the Grameen Bank's microcredit program has a larger impact on the behavior of poor households when women are the loan recipients instead of men. There have been some examinations of the extent of implicit subsidies involved in operating the bank, with a view to evaluating its financial and economic viability for sustained development in future and replicability in other countries (Khandker, Khalily & Khan, 1993, 1994, 1995; Yaron, 1992).

On the other hand, relatively few studies have empirically investigated the various theoretical models of the incentive structure created by the bank – that is, the use of self-selected groups, group lending, staggered loan disbursement, repeat loans, etc. – to enhance loan recovery. As such, we have not been able to isolate the relative importance of group lending in achieving high repayment rates, compared to other socio-economic factors and factors relating to borrower characteristics and gender.[2] Notably, Paxton, Graham and Thraen (2000) have drawn some conclusions on the design of group lending programs based on an empirical investigation of a Grameen-style program operating in Burkina Faso.

In this paper, I use data collected at the branch level of the Grameen Bank in Bangladesh to determine if the variation in repayment rates across branches can be explained by some of the theoretical conjectures in the literature. In particular, I wish to evaluate the relative importance of several socio-economic factors and certain incentive structures in their impact on the repayment rate. This is especially important in the light of evidence from certain other credit programs (notably the Badan Kredit Kecamatan[3] in Indonesia) that have managed to attain high repayment rates without using group lending, but by targeting borrowers similar to the Grameen Bank clientele (mostly poor, landless women). I also examine whether the higher repayment rates of women borrowers can be explained by other factors correlated to gender.

The main finding is that an increase in the opportunity cost of a borrower's time results in a negative effect on loan repayment, and that variations in opportunity costs have different impacts on the repayment performance of men and women. The results suggest that the success of the Grameen Bank rests partly on its time-intensive procedures for borrowers that screen out those with high opportunity costs, explaining the higher repayment rates of women who typically face a lower opportunity cost of time in rural Bangladesh.

This paper is divided into six sections. Section 2 discusses the various hypotheses to be tested. Section 3 is a brief description of the Grameen Bank branch-level data and the different variables available for use in the data set. Section 4 presents the empirical model to be tested and explains the methodology used. Some descriptive statistics are also presented in this section. The results of the regressions are presented in Section 5. I conclude in Section 6 with a discussion of the implications of the results and the limitations of this analysis.

2. THE HYPOTHESES TO BE EVALUATED

The Grameen Bank's worldwide fame rests squarely on one fact – that it has consistently maintained a repayment rate of over 95%, while lending to some of the poorest people in the world who have no physical collateral to offer against their loans. Remarkably, against all predicted odds, the repayment rate has stayed at this level even with continuous expansion of membership and coverage.[4]

Many have tried to explain the success of the bank as an exceptional case, dependent largely on the managerial abilities and charisma of its founder and managing director, Dr. Muhammad Yunus. It is difficult, however, to ignore the fact that other credit programs replicated along the same lines as the Grameen Bank, in different parts of the world, have met with similar success, maintaining exceptionally low default rates.[5] Common to all these different credit programs is the Grameen Bank's highly structured loan delivery and recovery mechanism. This includes very stringent screening to exclude all but the neediest landless villagers (mostly women) from its clientele.

The rules governing loan delivery and recovery, which have evolved over time, are strictly enforced by the bank staff. Exceptions are rarely made, suggesting that the myriad of rules and procedures may have played a role in achieving the high repayment rates. Loan rules and procedures include initial training sessions, self-selected group formations, staggered loan disbursement, weekly meetings, weekly repayments, repeat loans, savings, insurance contributions, and educational, hygienic, environmental and social obligations.[6] Indeed, in offering advice for replication of the Grameen Bank, Yunus[7] points out the importance of the rules in enforcing loan repayment and the central importance of the repayment rate in the Grameen Bank's operations:

> The branch manager should not change any rules of procedure without clear permission from the person responsible to do so. This is necessary because it is always found that the branch managers and bank workers try to solve their problems by bending rules and procedures. Unless somebody tough oversees their activities, soon all the rules and procedures will be replaced by temporary rules and procedures.
>
> In replicating Grameen Bank one must remember right from the beginning that if the recovery is not near 100%, no matter how good it looks, it is not Grameen Bank. All the strength of the Grameen Bank comes from its recovery performance. It is not merely the money which is reflected through the recovery rate, it is also the discipline which speaks loud and clear through the rate.

Some of the rules govern borrower behavior, while others concern the size and type of loans that are given. Borrower behavior is regulated even before potential applicants are approved. In order to be eligible to be a borrower, a potential member must undergo observation and training including seven days of continuous instruction to become conversant with the bank's rules and regulations. A potential borrower must participate in all training programs prior to being given a loan. Furthermore, borrowers must attend weekly meetings held in the presence of bank staff during the period the loan is being used. In other words, borrowers must attend 52 weekly meetings a year. It is not enough that a borrower repays her loan. She must be physically present at the meetings to repay her own installments. In addition to weekly meetings, special meetings may be called in order to discuss various group matters. Occasional "motivational" meetings are also arranged by the bank staff when members of groups face difficulties in making their loan payments.

Strict rules also govern the size and type of loans and repayment procedure. Each borrower is given a loan amount within a narrowly prescribed range. This range varies depending on the number of years a group has been in existence. Exceptions are not made to accommodate borrowers with abilities to absorb loans of different sizes. Collective, technology or house-building loans are never given to first time borrowers and are usually advanced only after a group has been in existence for several years, with all members performing satisfactorily in terms of their loan utilization and repayment. Borrowers are not allowed to repay loans early in order to get the next loan.[8] Loans are disbursed in a staggered fashion, so that everyone in a group does not receive a loan at the same time. Repeat loans are not advanced to any member of a group until all borrowers have repaid their previous loans.

Why are these group meetings, long training sessions, rules concerning type, size and timing of loans, so important to the Grameen Bank? In this paper I consider the conjecture that these institutional features, requirements and rules, play important roles in enhancing the bank's loan repayment rate by helping to screen potential borrowers (weeding out those with high opportunity costs of time), monitoring behavior and providing the "right" incentives for repayment. I investigate the significance of some of these institutional features in their effect on the repayment rate by evaluating data from a sample of Grameen Bank branches. Before moving onto an evaluation of the data, a discussion of these hypotheses is appropriate as discussed below.

2.1. Gender and Loan Repayment

The Grameen Bank has substantially increased its lending to women. In 1985, 65% of Grameen Bank borrowers were women. By September 2002, this number had increased to 95%. Three main reasons are put forward for the increase. First, women are the poorest of the poor and since the bank's objective is the socio-economic emancipation of the poorest, it follows that the bulk of the bank's clientele are women. Second, the Grameen Bank has reportedly found that the welfare of the borrower's family, and especially that of the children, is increased to a greater extent if the income from loan-financed projects is controlled by women rather than by their husbands. (Also see Pitt & Khandker, 1998.) Finally, there is evidence that women's groups have higher repayment rates than men's groups.[9] A look at the repayment performance of men and women in all existing Grameen Bank branches in 1990 and 1991 shows higher loan repayment rates for women. In 1990 with 781 branches in existence, the repayment rate for loans to women was 97% while the rate for men was 83%. The repayment rates for 1991, when the number of branches had increased to 915, was 95% for women and 77% for men. The difference in repayment rates justifies increased lending to women not just on social grounds but on economic grounds as well (that is, women have proved to be more creditworthy).

I use the data collected from the sample of Grameen Bank branches to test whether repayment rates are significantly higher for loans made to women compared to those made to men. Higher repayment rates for women may also be explained by other factors correlated with gender. If a statistically significant difference is found in loan repayment rates of men and women, a rigorous analysis of the causes of this difference is warranted.

2.2. *Borrower Incentives and Loan Repayment*

How do the incentives created by the institutional features of the Grameen Bank affect the repayment rate on loans? I explore the relationship between loan repayment and borrower incentives with respect to two particular features, the number of loans a borrower has received and the average size of a loan.

2.2.1. *First-Time Borrowers*

The Grameen Bank has continually expanded its operations and attracted new borrowers. At the same time, older borrowers who have maintained proper repayment records have received repeat loans of increasing size. Many borrowers over the years have successfully used loans to improve their standard of living and generate better business opportunities for themselves. As borrowers "mature," their dependence on Grameen Bank loans decrease in importance. Is there not, then, an increasing incentive for borrowers to default on their loans as the number of rounds increases?

One of Grameen Bank's stipulations (which appears not to be strictly enforced) is that borrowers who are able to increase their wealth and assets to a level above the maximum cut-off point to be considered "functionally landless,"[10] must be phased out of the program. Presumably, this rule would create adverse incentives (for repayment) for a borrower as he approaches the end of his borrowing cycles. In the last round of loans, a borrower would have no economic incentive to repay his loan.

Some evidence (Hossain, 1988) suggests that in fact repayment rates tend to drop off for older groups, which are the groups with decreasing proportions of first-time borrowers. The introduction of new types of loans, such as house-building and technology loans, to long time borrowers, may help explain why repayment rates have not fallen off further over time. The new loans for longer term projects, and with presumably higher returns, may have decreased the incentive for borrowers to default even after several rounds of loans.

A look at Grameen Bank's "program-level" data (that is, aggregates of all existing branches) between 1985 and 1991 shows that branches with more than 30% first-time borrowers have an average repayment rate of 96%, while branches with less than 25% first-time borrowers have an average repayment rate of 93%. I use the available branch-level data to evaluate whether the proportion of new (first-time) borrowers significantly impacts loan repayment rates.

2.2.2. *Average Loan Size*

It is widely believed that one of the main reasons that the Grameen Bank's credit program is able to achieve a high repayment rate is that its borrowers receive loans that are very small. Given the inability of assetless borrowers to secure loans from commercial banks, the borrowers have few alternatives in obtaining credit – mainly moneylenders in the village and credit programs like those of the Grameen Bank. Since the interest rates on Grameen Bank loans are significantly lower than the rates charged by moneylenders, and since the bank guarantees repeat loans on repayment of a previous loan, little incentive exists to default. This is because the value of the small current loan is outweighed by the present value of returns from the expected future stream of loans. This line of reasoning, in keeping with game theoretic analysis, would suggest that the incentive to willfully default can be reduced by keeping the loan size small.

Larger loan sizes may also decrease the ability to repay loans. As Armendariz de Aghion (1999) argues, bigger loans may involve proportionately higher monitoring effort by group members, which may not be feasible. Thus, by keeping loan sizes small, the Grameen Bank not only reduces the incentive to willfully default but may also be enabling successful utilization of loans by keeping monitoring requirements by the borrowing group at a level that is feasible for the group.

The program-level data for all branches between 1985 and 1991 shows an average repayment rate of 95% for branches with average loan sizes of less than Taka 7,500 and a rate of 93% for branches with average loans of more than Taka 11,000. I use the branch-level Grameen Bank data to test whether loan repayment rates decline significantly as average loan sizes increase.

2.3. Monitoring and Loan Repayment

It is widely known that in addition to any peer monitoring that might exist among members of a Grameen Bank borrowers' group, bank staff spend considerable time and effort in supervising and monitoring borrowers. Bank workers are required to conduct weekly center meetings. They also take an active part in borrowers' project selection and regularly check-up on the progress of their projects. They are partially responsible for helping borrowers who have difficulties in making repayments.[11]

The economic literature (as opposed to the institutional and sociological literature) on the Grameen Bank has thus far placed little emphasis on the importance of the bank staff's supervisory role in achieving high repayment rates. It has been widely assumed that the high repayment rates can be explained largely by peer monitoring. In a recent study, Jain (1996) suggests that:

> ... the credit policies of the bank do not constitute a sufficient explanation for the bank's success, and that its acclaimed policy of replacing individual collateral with group guarantee is in fact not practiced. The paper presents an alternate explanation for the success of the Grameen Bank ... it explains how Grameen Bank has been able to overcome typical problems of implementing development programs, *by sustaining good performance from its large workforce* (italics mine) (p. 2).

Anecdotal evidence collected by the author from a field trip to the Konokdia branch of the Grameen Bank, as well as interviews conducted with bank staff at both that branch and the head office seem to suggest that bank staff may indeed be instrumental in inducing the high repayment rates. How the bank is able to elicit this high level of effort from the staff is in itself a subject of study.

The program-level data shows that between 1985 and 1991, branches with less than 4 borrowers' centers per employee had an average repayment rate of 96%, while those with more than 4 centers per employee had a rate of 93%. I use the data to test for significant differences in repayment rates between branches, arising from the difference in the number of borrowers that each employee must supervise. The assumption here is that bank employees are able to devote more time and effort to monitoring each borrower if they have a smaller "case load." Therefore, branches where employees have higher "case loads" would experience lower repayment rates.

2.4. Opportunity Cost of Time, Ability, and Loan Repayment

Several additional variables are used to test the significance of the conjecture that loan repayment is strongly linked to the opportunity cost of time of the borrowers. I test the hypothesis that the loan repayment rate decreases as the opportunity cost of time (of the borrowers) increases.

The Grameen Bank's objective is to provide credit to the poorest of the poor in Bangladesh, especially to women. Unlike many other credit programs, including many organized and subsidized by the government, the Grameen Bank has scrupulously maintained its insistence on borrowers going through time consuming training, weekly meetings and other group activities. This has been the case regardless of the need for training (in bank affairs) and weekly attendance at meetings in order to repay loan installments. Attendance is required at every meeting by every borrower of a group, even if she is not currently a loan recipient. It is said that these activities promote group discipline and solidarity. It may well be the case, though, that these activities also play a role in weeding out those potential borrowers who are better off and have a high opportunity cost of time. The high cost of borrowing (in terms of time spent in required group and other activities), combined with the generally small loans and low income activities for which the loans are given, may ensure that only the poorest have the incentive to join the borrowing groups.[12]

By screening out those with the higher opportunity costs and attracting those with only the lowest opportunity costs of time, the Grameen bank may also be ensuring a high repayment rate on its loans. Borrowers with the lowest opportunity cost of time have the incentive to undertake the most effort in ensuring the success of their projects, since they have few other alternatives. By repaying loans fully on time, further new loans are ensured. Although a borrower's "ability" is likely to be positively correlated with opportunity cost, other features such as staggered disbursement and repeat loans might help to mitigate the adverse effects of selecting low opportunity cost (and low ability) borrowers. Staggering loan disbursement and giving repeated loans induces a higher level of effort, perhaps offsetting the effect of lower "ability."

In addition to the survey of the Grameen Bank branches, the data set contains socio-economic, geographic and infrastructure-related information about the regions where these branches are located. Several variables in the data set (such as distance to district headquarters, density of electrification, etc.) also have a bearing on the opportunity cost of time of people in the area. These variables are indicators of economic development (assumed to be positively correlated with opportunity cost) and therefore serve as a proxy for the opportunity cost of time of borrowers in each branch. I use the variables to determine the significance of the opportunity cost of time in its impact on loan repayment.

2.4.1. Distance to Greater District Headquarters

In general, in Bangladesh, distance from the headquarters of a district also has implications for commerce, employment opportunities, etc. As one moves further away from district headquarters, the quality of services, such as roads, postal service, health and schooling facilities, decline. Opportunities for banking, marketing, and commerce also decrease. Although distances may not be very great in absolute terms, the absence of paved roads and the preponderance of rivers make travel and transaction costs high.[13] Thus, in many ways, as one gets further away from district headquarters, one is less able to avail oneself of income earning opportunities. This includes employment opportunities as well as potential trading opportunities in larger markets.

Therefore, as one gets further away from district headquarters, the opportunity cost of time of potential Grameen Bank members decreases. This can be expected to make these borrowers better credit risks, since they have an incentive to devote more time and effort to projects financed by the Grameen Bank, given their lack of alternative opportunities. I test the hypothesis that branches located at greater distances from their respective district headquarters have significantly higher repayment rates.

2.4.2. Density of Electrification

The density of village electrification raises the opportunity cost of time of potential borrowers. The presence of electricity greatly increases the employment opportunities for those in a village, making possible the operation of many small-scale rural off-farm "industrial" enterprises such as mechanized paddy husking, use of power looms, etc. Thus, the presence of electricity in a village often creates employment for the landless, who work part time as farm hands on others' land. The expanded employment opportunities increases the opportunity cost of time. As potential borrowers in villages with electricity may have incentives to devote less time and effort on their Grameen Bank projects, I test the hypothesis that increasing electrification of villages significantly lowers repayment rates.

2.4.3. Density of Krishi Banks (Government Agricultural Banks)

The government's network of Krishi[14] banks are used to channel credit to the agricultural sector in Bangladesh. While the Krishi banks do target small and large farmers, most potential Grameen Bank borrowers would not qualify for loans from the Krishi bank, since they are for the most part landless, and Krishi banks require land or other assets as collateral. However, increased lending by the Krishi bank to farmers in a region leads to increased investment in farming and other agricultural activities and therefore an increase in the demand for farm labor. Many potential Grameen Bank members work part time as farm laborers.

Presumably, then, an increase in the financing of agricultural activities by the Krishi banks would increase the employment opportunities of potential Grameen Bank borrowers, thus increasing their opportunity cost of time. Therefore, I hypothesize that the repayment rate on Grameen Bank loans decreases as the density of Krishi banks in the region increases.

2.4.4. School Density

Access to schooling can increase a potential borrower's ability as well as her opportunity cost of time. Two countervailing effects exist. While education increases a borrower's alternatives to the Grameen Bank (enabling potential borrowers to use a wider range of available opportunities), it can also make her more successful in utilizing Grameen Bank loans.

Using the density of primary and secondary schools as a proxy for ability and experience, I test the data to determine the effect of changes in the density of primary and secondary schools in a region on loan repayment rates.

3. THE DATA

The data used in this paper was collected in a series of surveys of a random sample of Grameen Bank branches, by the World Bank and the Bangladesh Institute of

Development Studies. The data collected are year-end aggregates for each branch. A Grameen Bank branch is the smallest administrative unit of the bank and typically lends to borrowers in several neighboring villages.

This panel data set spans the period 1985–1991 and consists of information on 140 branches. All of the branches were surveyed annually. As new branches were added over the years, the number of branches surveyed increases each year. The data set includes information on loans disbursed, recovered, outstanding and overdue, organized by type of loans (i.e. type of activity for which the loan was disbursed).[15] Information also exists on the number of borrowers, groups and centers as well as the gender of the borrowers, and the borrowing round of the borrowers (i.e. whether first, second or third time borrower and so on). The data set also contains information on the employees of a branch as well as balance sheet items pertaining to a branch's expenditure, income, assets and liabilities. In addition, information on the branch's location (identified by thana[16] and district) and year of establishment, is included.

In addition to the branch-level Grameen Bank data, certain regional thana-level socio-economic, geographic, and infrastructure-related data were collected during the survey, from various secondary sources. This data set contains thana-level information for the areas where the branches are located, for 225 thanas. The geographic information includes the distance of a certain thana from its district headquarters and infrastructural information such as the density of villages electrified in the area. The socio-economic data includes the density of primary and secondary schools and the density of Krishi banks in the area.

After merging the two data sets (the Grameen Bank branch data and the socio-economic data), observations from 122 branches were retained. The sample includes 23 branches in 1985, 27 in 1986, 44 in 1987, 73 in 1988, 94 in 1989, 120 in 1990 and 122 in 1991. This includes 10% of the existing branches in 1985 and 1986, over 11% in 1987, over 14% of the branches in 1988 and 1989, over 15% in 1990, and 13% of the branches in 1991.

4. THE EMPIRICAL MODEL

The empirical model used to test the hypotheses is as follows:

$$\begin{aligned} \mathrm{RR}_{it} = {} & \alpha_i + \beta_1 \mathrm{FLOANPRO}_{it} + \beta_2 \mathrm{BORPRO1}_{it} + \beta_3 \mathrm{EMPBOR}_{it} + \beta_4 \mathrm{AVGL}_{it} \\ & + \beta_5 \mathrm{DISTDHQ}_{it} + \beta_6 \mathrm{ELECDEN}_{it} + \beta_7 \mathrm{KRBNKDEN}_{it} + \beta_8 \mathrm{SCHDEN}_{it} \\ & + \beta_9 \mathrm{LOGAGE} + \varepsilon_{it} \end{aligned}$$

where,

RR	= Repayment rate on loans in a given year.
FLOANPRO	= Proportion of loans disbursed to female borrowers in the preceding year.
BORPRO1	= First-time borrowers as a proportion of total number of borrowers in the branch, in the preceding year.
EMPBOR	= Number of bank employees per borrower, in the preceding year.
AVGL	= Average loan size in the preceding year.
DISTDHQ	= Distance to greater district headquarters.
ELECDEN	= Villages electrified per square kilometer in the preceding year.
KRBNKDEN	= Density of Krishi banks in the preceding year.
SCHDEN	= Primary and Secondary schools per square kilometer in the preceding year.
LOGAGE	= Log of the age of the branch.
i	= The ith Grameen Bank branch ($i = 1, \ldots, 122$).
t	= The tth year ($t = 1985, \ldots, 1991$).

Lagged values of all the explanatory variables (except for distance to district headquarters which is time invariant, and the age of the branch) are used. The Grameen Bank considers loans to be overdue only if they remain unpaid a year after disbursement. It is not possible to determine exactly when the overdue loans were disbursed. As an approximation I use the lagged values (i.e. from the preceding year) of the explanatory variables since they are likely to be highly correlated with the actual values of the variables when the overdue loans were disbursed.

Using the model described above, I also test for differences in the impact of the explanatory variables on the repayment rates of males and females (RRM and RRF). To do this, I separate the repayment rates and other variables for men and women by branch and year, and then stack them together. Creating a dummy variable for gender, I then create a nested equation with separate coefficients of each variable for men and women and can test whether the male and female estimated coefficients are significantly different from each other.

The branch level data set does not contain information on individual borrowers. All variables are aggregates for each branch surveyed. However, since the number of borrowers per branch is known, the data set yields information on averages per borrower for the branch. The information is broken down by borrower gender, allowing for a comparison of the loan repayment performance of male and female borrowers.

4.1. A Description of the Variables

The loan default rate is calculated by taking the amount of loans overdue as a percentage of outstanding loans for a given year. Subtracting the default rate from one yields the repayment rate, RR. The female and male repayment rates (RRF and RRM, respectively) are determined by using the same variables, overdue and outstanding loans, for each gender.

FLOANPRO is the proportion of total loans disbursed by a branch that went to female borrowers, in the preceding year. Using data from 1990 and 1991, the two years with the largest number of branches observed, I study the relationship between the proportion of loans to women and the repayment rate. The average loan repayment rate is generally higher for branches that have a higher percentage of loans to women.

BORPRO1 is the number of first-time borrowers in a given branch, expressed as a proportion of the total number of borrowers in that branch, in the preceding year. Branches with a greater proportion of first-time borrowers also had higher repayment rates, on average. However, one should use caution when interpreting this information since branches with a greater proportion of first-time borrowers are also relatively newer branches. Newer branches may have other reasons for better loan repayment performance, such as more extensive supervision and monitoring by bank staff, in the early stages of the establishment of a branch.

The average loan size, AVGL, is determined by dividing the total amount of loans disbursed in the preceding year, by the number of borrowers. The corresponding variables for female and male borrowers are AVGLF and AVGLM, respectively. On average, repayment rates appear to be higher with smaller loans, although the rates are high for some of the larger loan ranges. Also, female repayment rates appear to be higher than male rates for a given loan size. The decline in average repayment rates with larger loans may be linked to difficulties in managing loans of large sizes (Armendariz de Aghion, 1999), or a greater incentive to default as future loans from Grameen Bank become less attractive, compared to alternative opportunities generated by the borrowers' enhanced income and business capabilities.

EMPBOR is the number of bank employees per borrower of a branch, in the preceding year. Each bank assistant (branch-level field staff) is responsible for the supervision of several centers. A center is composed of five or six groups (or an average of about 25–30 borrowers). It is assumed that as a staff member's load of borrowers increases, he is less able to properly monitor and supervise each borrower. Thus, the EMPBOR variable is used as a proxy to capture the intensity with which a bank employee can monitor borrowers under his supervision. Repayment rates appear to increase with greater number of employees per borrower, although the rates do not vary widely.

Several geographic, socio-economic and infrastructure-related variables are used in the empirical model. DISTDHQ is the distance from the thana where a Grameen Bank branch is located to the greater district headquarters. The average repayment rate is higher for more remote branches. Branches located at a distance of more than 100 kilometers from their district headquarters have an almost perfect repayment rate.

The number of electrified villages per square kilometer of the thana in the preceding year is the variable ELECDEN. A majority of branches are located in regions with less than 0.2 villages electrified per square kilometer. The variation in repayment rates is not very great.

KRBNKDEN measures the preceding year's density of Krishi banks in the region where a Grameen Bank branch is located. Krishi (which, literally means agricultural, in Bengali) banks are government owned banks which channel loans specifically for rural agricultural projects. There appears to be little variation in repayment rates as the density of Krishi banks vary, although the rate comes closer to 100% as the density increases.

SCHDEN is the density of primary and secondary schools per square kilometer in the region. Repayment rates appear to increase as school densities increase, and come closer to 100% as the density approaches one school per square kilometer. The bulk of the branches are located in regions which have 0.3–0.9 schools per square kilometer.

As for the age of the branches, average repayment rates appear to decline markedly for older branches in 1991. Branches more than six years old have repayment rates under 90%.

Given the nature of the panel data, several different regressions were performed to examine the relationship between the variation in repayment rates across Grameen Bank branches and the aforementioned variables. I begin with *OLS* regressions on cross-sections for 1990 and 1991 (the two years for which a large number of observations are available). I then pool together observations from 1985 through 1991 and run an *OLS* regression on the pooled data. In order to control for branch-specific heterogeneity, I also perform *fixed effects* (FE) and *random effects* (RE) regressions. Finally, I perform regressions on the repayment rates of males and females. The two are nested in the same model to allow for comparisons of possible differences in the effect of the explanatory variables on repayment rates for males and females.

5. RESULTS

Table 1 provides summary statistics for all the independent and dependent variables used in the regressions. Table 2 gives the coefficients for the correlation

Table 1. Summary Statistics.

Variable	*N*	Mean	Std. Dev.	Minimum	Maximum
RR	503	0.98	0.066	0.51	1.00
RRF	503	0.98	0.070	0.31	1.00
RRM	196	0.94	0.148	0.12	1.00
FLOANPRO	371	0.93	0.144	0.04	1.00
BORPRO1	371	0.53	0.363	0.00	1.00
AVGL	371	5.418	5.26	0.259	40.014
AVGLF	371	5.834	8.25	0.247	79.381
AVGLM	135	10.634	14.62	0.370	91.824
EMPBOR	371	0.0116	0.012	0.0033	0.086
DISTDHQ	370	57.08	44.89	0.00	193.00
ELECDEN	370	0.126	0.195	0	0.946
KRBKDEN	368	0.008	0.006	0	0.026
SCHDEN	370	0.472	0.180	0.077	0.95
AGE	503	3.37	2.036	1.00	12.00

Note: RR, RRF, RRM, FLOANPRO and BORPRO1 are expressed as proportions. AVGL, AVGLF and AVGLM are in thousands of Takas. DISTDHQ is in km. ELECDEN, KRBKDEN and SCHDEN are densities expressed per square km.

between the variables. The summary statistics in Table 1 show that average repayment rate for females is slightly higher (98%, compared to 94% for males). On average, women received 93% of all loans. More than half the total number of borrowers are first-time borrowers. The average size of loans to males is significantly higher than loans to females (Taka 5,834 for females and Taka 10,634 for males). The average number of years that a branch had been in existence is 3.37 years.

5.1. Overall Repayment Rates

Table 3 presents the results for the regressions on the overall repayment rates. This includes results of the *cross-sectional OLS* regressions as well as the *OLS* regression on the *pooled* data (covering branches surveyed from 1985 to 1991). A possibility of misleading results exists due to the existence of unobserved branch-specific variables that are correlated with explanatory variables. For example, it is likely that the influence of management and organization at the branch-level on the repayment performance of borrowers, varies across branches. In order to control for this possibility of heterogeneity arising from unobserved variables, I also perform *fixed effects* (FE) and *random effects* (RE) regressions and compare the results with those from the *OLS* regressions.

Table 2. Correlation Coefficients.

Variables	RR	FLOANPRO	BORPROI	AVGL	EMPBOR	DISTDHQ	ELECDEN	KRBNKDEN	SCHDEN
RR	–	0.20	0.24	−0.13	0.11	0.15	−0.002	−0.11	0.18
FLOANPRO	0.20	–	0.30	−0.23	0.13	0.26	−0.09	0.25	−0.15
BORPRO1	0.24	0.30	–	−0.49	0.27	0.35	0.20	0.17	−0.19
AVGL	−0.13	−0.23	−0.49	–	−0.12	−0.30	−0.13	−0.33	0.22
EMPBOR	0.11	0.13	0.27	−0.12	–	0.05	0.20	0.05	−0.09
DISTDHQ	0.15	0.26	0.35	−0.30	0.05	–	0.02	0.36	−0.47
ELECDEN	−0.002	−0.09	0.20	−0.13	0.20	0.02	–	0.02	0.29
KRBNKDEN	−0.11	0.25	0.17	−0.33	0.05	0.37	0.02	–	−0.27
SCHDEN	0.18	−0.15	−0.19	0.22	−0.09	−0.47	0.29	−0.27	–
AGE	−0.35	−0.32	−0.64	0.56	−0.06	−0.24	−0.16	−0.27	0.04

Table 3. Regression Results Dependent Variable: Loan Repayment Rate (RR).

Variable	OLS (1990)	OLS (1991)	OLS (Pooled)	Fixed Effects	Random Effects
Proportion of loans to women	0.13 (1.95)	0.12 (1.86)	0.12 (3.95)	0.09 (1.37)	0.12 (3.95)
Proportion of first-time borrowers	0.01 (0.29)	0.028 (0.71)	−0.0002 (−0.016)	−0.004 (−0.22)	−0.0002 (−0.016)
Average loan size	0.0014 (0.672)	−0.0003 (−0.147)	−0.0003 (−0.37)	−0.0005 (−0.36)	−0.0003 (−0.37)
No. of bank employees per borrower	0.047 (0.06)	−2.05 (−1.527)	−0.59 (−1.86)	−0.956 (−2.39)	−0.59 (−1.86)
Distance from district headquarters	0.0002 (1.31)	0.0003 (2.003)	0.0002 (2.44)	Dropped	0.0002 (2.44)
Density of villages electrified	0.0005 (0.012)	−0.009 (−0.22)	−0.03 (−1.47)	−0.014 (−0.12)	−0.03 (−1.47)
Density of Krishi banks	−2.615 (−2.062)	−2.38 (−1.71)	−1.85 (−3.04)	3.54 (1.17)	−1.85 (−3.04)
Density of primary and secondary schools	0.09 (1.77)	0.14 (2.62)	0.09 (3.90)	−1.13 (−1.73)	0.09 (3.9)
Log of age of branch	−0.47 (−1.32)	−0.06 (−2.07)	−0.06 (−3.6)	−0.063 (−2.19)	−0.55 (−3.6)
Constant	0.86 (8.54)	0.88 (9.52)	0.90 (20.76)	–	–
F-Value	2.84	5.02	12.38	2.10	111.38 (Chi−sq.)
R^2	0.24	0.30	0.24	0.53	0.24
Adjusted R^2	0.15	0.24	0.22	0.28	–
No. of observations	92	115	368	368	368

Note: The numbers in parentheses are *t*-statistics except for the random effects model, for which they are asymptotic *z*-statistics.

5.1.1. Proportion of Loans to Females

The *proportion of loans to females* appears to have a positive effect on repayment rates in both years (significant at 5.5 and 6.5% for 1990 and 1991 respectively in the cross-sectional regression). Both the FE and RE regressions also show a positive relationship. However, in the FE regression the result is not statistically significant.

5.1.2. Incentive Variables (First-Time Borrowers, Average Loan Size)

For both years, the incentive variables – *proportion of first-time borrowers* and the *average loan size* – do not appear to have statistically significant effects on the repayment rate in any of the regressions.

5.1.3. Monitoring

The *employee-borrower ratio* does not appear to significantly affect repayment rates in the cross-sectional regression, although the effect is negative for 1991 and for the pooled data, counter to the expected positive effect. As in the pooled OLS regression, there appears to be a statistically significant but (unexpectedly) negative effect in both FE and RE regressions.

5.1.4. Opportunity Cost (Distance from District Headquarters; Electricity, School and Krishi Bank Densities) and Ability (School Density) Variables

Distance from district headquarters has the expected positive effect in the *OLS* regressions for both years but is significant only for 1991. This variable is dropped from the FE regression because it is time invariant. In the RE regression, however, it has a statistically significant positive effect on repayment, as expected. The *density of electrification* does not appear to have a statistically significant effect in either year in any of the regressions. Increased *density of Krishi banks* appears to have a statistically significant negative effect on repayment rates, as expected, in 1990 and 1991 (at 9%) and in the RE regression. Increased *density of schools* has statistically significant positive effects in both years, although for 1990 the significance level is 8%. The same result holds for the pooled OLS and the RE regression. In the FE regression, however, the effect is negative, although not significant at 5%.

Age of the branch appears to have a statistically significant negative effect for 1991. For 1990, the effect is negative but not statistically significant. Both the FE and RE models show significant negative effects.

5.2. Analysis of Results, Overall Repayment Rates

Both the cross-sectional and pooled data appear to support the hypotheses regarding the effect of opportunity cost and ability in explaining the variation in repayment rates. Except for the density of electrification, the other variables used to represent opportunity cost – distance from district headquarters, the density of Krishi banks – show the expected impact. The density of schooling has a significant positive effect supporting the conjecture that increased ability resulting from increased access to schools outweighs the negative effect arising from increased opportunity cost as a result of more schools.

The results also suggest that the average loan size and number of loans received do not play a significant role in explaining variations in the repayment rate, discounting the hypothesis about incentive effects of these variables.

The negative effect of the age of a branch may have several interpretations. One possible explanation is that newer branches are under pressure to demonstrate effectiveness and perform more intensive monitoring in the early stages, thereby achieving a better repayment rate. (Although it would be tempting to assume that the lower number of borrowers in newer branches allows for more intensive monitoring, the results thus far point to an insignificant or negative effect of higher employee-borrower ratios, on repayment.) It is possible that branches recruit the "best" borrowers initially and later move to more marginal borrowers.

The FE and RE regression results, on the whole, appear to support the results of the *OLS* regressions. The "opportunity cost" variables (distance from district headquarters and density of Krishi banks) appear significant in their effect on repayment rates while the "incentive" variables (proportion of first-time borrowers and average loan size) have statistically insignificant effects in all the regressions. For several variables, the RE regression yields statistically significant results where the FE model does not.[17]

5.3. Comparison of Male and Female Repayment Rates

In order to compare the possibly different impacts that the explanatory variables might have on men and women, regressions are run on male and female repayment rates (RRM and RRF, respectively). The two, however, are nested together in one model and so a gender dummy variable is used to estimate coefficients for males and females separately. I also test to determine if the coefficients for each variable are significantly different for men and women. The results are presented in Table 4.

Three of the regressions (OLS on the pooled data, FE and RE) show a statistically significant positive effect of the *proportion of loans to women* on the repayment rate for both men and women.

The cross-sectional regression for 1991, as well as the FE regressions show that the proportion of *first-time borrowers* has a statistically significant effect on the repayment rates of men, but not of women. This result, in keeping with the discussion on borrower "incentives," suggests that the incentive effects on men are

Table 4. Regression Results
Dependent Variable: Female and Male Loan Repayment Rates (RRF and RRM).

Variables	OLS (1990)	OLS (1991)	OLS (Pooled)	Fixed Effects	Random Effects
Gender dummy (1 = women; 0 = men)	−0.26 (−0.8)	−0.16 (−0.74)	0.0028 (0.024)	−0.0128 (−0.107)	0.0028 (0.024)
Proportion of loans to women					
Female coefficient	0.137 (1.31)	0.104 (1.40)	0.108 (2.53)	0.04 (0.54)	0.109 (2.53)
Male coefficient	0.014 (0.11)	0.09 (0.76)	0.116 (2.06)	0.06 (0.70)	0.116 (2.056)
Proportion of first-time borrowers					
Female coefficient	0.012 (0.23)	0.028 (0.59)	−0.06 (−0.25)	−0.013 (−0.48)**	−0.0057 (−0.249)
Male coefficient	0.009 (0.05)	0.164 (1.93)	0.06 (1.17)	0.08 (1.55)	0.056 (1.167)
Average loan size					
Female coefficient	0.00006 (0.046)	−0.0018 (−1.33)	−0.0005 (−0.70)	−0.0009 (−1.026)	−0.0005 (−0.70)
Male coefficient	0.0018 (1.065)	0.0002 (0.22)	0.0006 (0.89)	−0.0003 (−0.486)	0.0005 (0.887)
No. of bank employees per borrower					
Female coefficient	0.124 (0.104)*	−1.87 (−1.14)	−0.634 (−1.40)	−0.98 (−1.82)	−0.634 (−1.40)
Male coefficient	19.73 (2.78)	−4.40 (−0.53)	3.83 (1.03)	−3.08 (−0.74)	3.826 (1.032)
Distance from district headquarters					
Female coefficient	0.0002 (0.86)	0.0003 (1.445)**	0.0002 (1.736)**	Dropped	0.0002 (1.736)**
Male coefficient	0.0009 (1.684)	0.0011 (2.82)	0.0006 (2.85)		0.0006 (2.85)
Density of villages electrified					
Female coefficient	−0.004 (−0.065)	−0.214 (−0.45)	−0.025 (−0.85)*	0.06 (0.40)	−0.024 (−0.85)*
Male coefficient	0.205 (0.98)	−0.76 (−0.91)	−0.15 (−2.85)	−0.001 (−0.008)	−0.15 (−2.85)
Density of Krishi banks					
Female coefficient	−2.54 (−1.32)*	−2.49 (−1.49)*	−1.96 (−2.26)*	5.65 (1.38)**	−1.96 (−2.26)*
Male coefficient	−29.75 (−5.91)	−14.62 (−3.89)	−8.58 (−4.57)	1.70 (0.37)	−8.58 (−4.57)

Density of primary & secondary schools					
Female coefficient	0.099 (1.304)	0.144 (2.32)*	0.093 (2.74)**	−0.455 (−0.638)	0.09 (2.74)**
Male coefficient	0.039 (0.32)	0.383 (4.00)	0.209 (4.04)	−0.40 (−0.56)	0.21 (4.04)
Log of age of branch					
Female coefficient	−0.328 (−0.69)	−0.048 (−1.32)*	−0.06 (−2.86)	−0.09 (−2.66)	−0.06 (−2.86)
Male coefficient	−0.14 (−1.30)	−0.21 (−3.40)	−0.12 (−3.41)	−0.125 (−2.64)	−0.12 (−3.41)
Constant	1.10 (3.95)	1.05 (5.46)	0.926 (9.52)	–	–
F-Value	4.10	5.33	8.42	2.60	160.05 (Chi−sq.)
R^2	0.43	0.42	0.25	0.50	0.25
Adjusted R^2	0.32	0.36	0.22	0.30	–
No. of observations	125	157	504	504	504

Note: The numbers in parentheses are *t*-statistics except for random effects model, for which they are asymptotic *z*-statistics.

*Male and Female coefficients are statistically significantly different at 5%.

**Male and Female coefficients are statistically significantly different at 10%.

different from those facing women. Men receive larger loans on average, and also have more alternative economic opportunities if they default and therefore may also have more incentive to default after several rounds of loans. The *average loan size* did not appear to significantly impact repayment rates for men or women.

The *proportion of employees to borrowers* appeared to have a significant effect only for men in 1990.

The *distance from district headquarters* appears to have a statistically significant positive effect for men in both 1990 (at 10%) and 1991, and for both men and women (at 9%) in the pooled OLS and RE regressions. The *density of electrification* has a statistically significant negative effect on men in both the pooled OLS and RE regressions. The *density of Krishi banks* has a statistically significant negative effect on men in both years and on men and women in the pooled OLS and RE regressions. The *density of schools* appears to have a statistically significant positive effect for both men and women in the pooled OLS and RE regressions.

The *age of the branch* has a statistically significant negative effect for both men and women in the pooled OLS, FE and RE regressions, although it is significant only for males in 1991.

5.4. Joint Test on Male and Female Coefficients

Joint test on the coefficients show that the opportunity cost (of time) variables (distance from district headquarters, density of Krishi banks, density of electrification and density of schools) have a significantly different effect on men and women. The coefficient for the *distance from district headquarters* is statistically significant (at 10%) for the pooled OLS and RE regressions as well as for 1991. The coefficient for *density of electrification* is statistically significant for both the pooled OLS and RE regressions. The coefficient for the *density of Krishi banks* appears to be statistically significantly different for men and women in both years of the cross-sectional regression, the pooled OLS as well as the RE regressions. The coefficients for the *density of schools* are also statistically significantly different for men and women in the RE and the pooled OLS (at 6%) regressions.[18]

5.5. Analysis of Results, Female and Male Repayment Rates

The results support the contention that *opportunity cost* has significant impacts on repayment rates, and that men and women are affected differently by variations in their opportunity cost. The differences, I suggest, arise from the greater social and economic constraints on women, compared to men, in terms of their mobility and employment opportunities in rural Bangladesh. Thus, for example, the distance from district headquarters has a greater impact on men and less on women whose mobility may be constrained regardless of the distance. Similarly, the density of Krishi banks has a greater impact on men since they tend to be the primary recipients of Krishi bank loans. The presence of electrification likewise raises the opportunity cost of men (who have more economic opportunities) to a greater extent. Thus, these variables have a greater impact on the opportunity cost of time of men, compared to their effect on women. Social and economic constraints prevent women from taking advantage of the presence of potential economic alternatives to Grameen Bank projects. The effect of the increase in electrification and presence of Krishi banks, and increased proximity to district headquarters is thus less detrimental to women's repayment rates compared to the effect on men's.

The results also suggest that both men and women are positively affected by an increase in the density of schools. This result is consistent with the regression results on the overall repayment rate, suggesting that the positive effect of increased *ability* due to increased availability of schools more than compensates for the negative effect of increased opportunity cost.

The regression results also suggest that the average loan size or the proportion of first-time borrowers do not have a significant effect on repayment, implying that the hypotheses about borrower *incentives* are misplaced. However, economic theory makes a strong case for the incentive argument. It is likely that the variables available in the data set used do not adequately evaluate the effects of incentives on repayment, suggesting the need for appropriate data to evaluate the incentive effects of group lending.

I tested the conjecture that loan repayment rates increase as intensity of supervision (or *monitoring*) by the branch-level staff of the bank increases. The intensity of supervision was assumed to be directly related to the number of employees per borrower. The regressions, with the exception of the nested model, do not support this assumed relationship. Moreover, the sign on most of the estimates of EMPBOR is negative, contrary to expectation. This result is puzzling. One explanation for the possible negative link implied by the estimates might be related to the fact that branches where EMPBOR is large are also relatively new branches. The management of newer branches may not have the benefit of information that can be acquired only with time.[19] It is possible that the increase in the intensity of supervision due to the smaller "case-loads" is more than outweighed by the lack of adequate information about the borrowers and the villages. However, this explanation is contradicted by the results that consistently show a negative relationship between the age of a branch and its repayment performance. Unfortunately, the data set provides no direct way of measuring the intensity of supervision or monitoring by the bank employees. It is assumed that intensity must decline if employees oversee more borrowers, although monitoring intensity may well be endogenously determined and not directly related to the number of borrowers supervised by each employee.

This study has certain inherent weaknesses. Due to the nature of the data used (aggregate branch-wise information for Grameen Bank loans and borrowers, and thana-level aggregates for socio-economic factors) individual borrower performance could not be evaluated. All conclusions are drawn from average values of the variables. Also, the study has relied on several proxy variables. The rather low measures of fit (R^2 and adjusted R^2) of the regressions may be indicative of problems in the selection of proxy variables.

6. CONCLUSION

The regressions performed (*OLS*, *fixed effects* and *random effects*) examine the relationship between the variation in repayment rates across Grameen Bank branches and several variables relating to borrower gender, opportunity cost, incentives, ability, and monitoring by bank staff. The results throw light on theoretical issues raised in the literature on group-based microcredit, and pose some new questions.

6.1. The Role of Gender and Opportunity Cost

The data reveal a statistically significant positive relationship between the proportion of loans to women and the loan repayment rate. Does gender, then, have a role to play in loan repayment performance, and if so, what is the source of the difference in male and female repayment rates?

Estimates from the regressions suggest that the opportunity cost of time for borrowers may be significant in explaining the variation in repayment rates. The results do not reject the hypothesis that an increase in the opportunity cost of a borrower's time has a negative effect on repayment for both men and women. Additionally, the regressions support the hypothesis that the higher loan repayment rate for women is linked to the differences in opportunity cost of time for males and females. Therefore, the success of the Grameen Bank results partly from limited alternative economic opportunities facing borrowers. Fewer alternatives ensure that borrowers invest the appropriate amount of effort and care in their Grameen Bank projects.

The regression results are particularly significant in suggesting that opportunity costs have different impacts on men and women. Women in rural Bangladesh face greater constraints in the labor market and are effectively excluded from many kinds of employment opportunities accessible to men. In addition, women earn lower wages on average, bear a disproportionate share of domestic responsibilities and have more limited mobility than men. It follows that women benefit less from increased opportunities engendered by economic and infrastructure development and, therefore, their repayment performance suffers less from the availability of economic alternatives.

6.1.1. Screening

The results therefore suggest that the extensive time commitment required of borrowers is a mechanism for screening out those with high opportunity costs of time. The intensive training sessions and weekly meetings perform this screening function. While these sessions ostensibly educate borrowers on financial and social matters, inculcate discipline and build group solidarity, they may also impose a considerable cost (in terms of lost time) on borrowers.

This analysis raises important issues. Hitherto it has been assumed that group lending and borrower's gender are crucial to the success of the Grameen Bank. I suggest that the opportunity cost of time for borrowers plays a key role in loan repayment, and that differences in performances of men and women may be explained by differences in opportunity cost. Further study is required to isolate the extent to which opportunity cost is instrumental in determining repayment behavior, and to explore other factors that may explain differences in repayment rates of men and women. This analysis has been limited by the nature of the data used (branch-level aggregate data). A thorough-going analysis of the significance of gender and opportunity cost in loan repayment requires data on individual borrower characteristics as well as data that captures peer monitoring and peer support in groups.

This paper has evaluated the significance of borrower gender, opportunity cost of time, ability, incentives, and monitoring by bank staff, on variations in loan repayment rates in the Grameen Bank. An increase in the opportunity cost of a borrower's time is found to have a negative effect on repayment, and variations in opportunity costs have different impacts on the repayment performance of men and women. The results suggest that the success of the Grameen Bank rests partly on its time-intensive procedures for borrowers that screen out those with high opportunity costs. The findings may also explain the higher repayment rates of women who typically face a lower opportunity cost of time in rural Bangladesh.

NOTES

1. The overall loan repayment rate for the Grameen Bank is reported to be over 97%. Repayment rates vary depending on the region and the branch. See Hossain (1988) and

Yunus (1982, 1984, 1986) for detailed descriptions of the Grameen Bank program. For a general overview of the role of groups in rural lending, see Huppi and Feder (1990).

2. On average, repayment rates in the Grameen Bank are higher for loans to women, compared to loans given to men.

3. The Badan Kredit Kecamatan (BKK) in Indonesia makes loans mostly to women in rural areas. It does not require any kind of group involvement. The activities financed are small-scale off-farm activities. The BKK's loan repayment rate is about 80% (Yaron, 1992). While this rate is considerably lower than that of the Grameen Bank, it must be noted that the BKK uses a different definition of overdue loans than does the Grameen Bank. For the BKK, a loan is considered to be overdue if the last installment due has not been paid on time. For the Grameen Bank, however, overdue loans are those that have not been repaid one year after the original due date. Thus, by the Grameen Bank's calculation, the BKK would have a considerably higher repayment rate.

4. As of August 2002, the Grameen Bank served 2,366,488 borrowers in 41,015 villages of Bangladesh. Thus, the bank now has branches in over 60% of Bangladesh's 68,000 villages.

5. Some of the other replications (and their repayment rates in the mid-1990s) are Amanah Ikhtiar Malaysia, Project Dungganon in Philippines (94.21%), Presidential Trust Fund in Tanzania (95%), Foundacion Contigo in Chile (98.8%), Microenterprise Loan Program in North Carolina, USA (86%), Community Credit Service in Sri Lanka (95%). The source for this information is Khandker, Khalily and Khan (1995).

6. All borrowers of the Grameen Bank have to pledge to abide by the so-called "Sixteen Decisions" manifesto. These 16 decisions include social and community-oriented pledges. See http://www.grameen-info.org/bank.

7. Excerpted from "Grameen Bank: As I See it" by Muhammad Yunus, p. 95, in "The Grameen Reader," edited by David Gibbons (1992).

8. Gibbons and Kasim (1990) note the difficulties faced by the Amanah Ikhtiar Malaysia (a replication of the Grameen Bank), in the early stages of their credit program, when exceptions were made to these seemingly unnecessarily stringent rules.

9. Almost all Grameen Bank staff interviewed by the author in 1990 at the Konokdia branch in Patuakhali maintained that women managed the loans better, that they were better organizers, and that they worked much better in groups, compared to their male counterparts.

10. The Grameen bank defines a landless person as one who owns no more than 0.5 acres of land, or assets worth 1.0 acre of medium quality cultivable land.

11. During a visit to the Konokdia branch of the Grameen Bank in Patuakhali, I found several bank staff used part of their weekends to "catch-up" on visits to struggling borrowers. The visits were considered important to "motivate" the borrowers, through both support and pressure. The bank staff themselves seemed under pressure to perform this task.

12. Hossain (1988) found that less than 5% of borrowers have assets of value greater than the amount defined as the maximum amount to be considered functionally landless/assetless by the Grameen Bank. Some anecdotal evidence suggests that in recent years the proportion of non-target group borrowers has grown, due to the inability to perfectly screen out those borrowers.

13. For example, some places as close as five miles from Dhaka, the capital, are accessible only by boat and foot, and may take up to an hour and a half to travel.

14. The word "Krishi," in Bengali, means agricultural or related to agriculture and farming.

15. The most common type of loan advanced is the "general" loan, or the individual loans given to members of a group to be used for any of a wide range of non-farm rural activities. "Collective" loans are given to a group or a center (which is a group of about five or six groups) jointly for some large-scale activity such as a collective farming project where the entire center (about 30 people) might lease in a plot of land for farming. "Technology" loans are relatively new and are also given jointly for projects such as the installation of a lift pump or the purchase or hire of machinery for processing grain, etc. "House-building" loans are given to enable borrowers to set up the basic foundations of a house (wooden pillars and a roof). These loans are to be repaid over a period of seven years. Collective, technology and house-building loans are usually given to borrowers and groups that have demonstrated the ability to use and repay "general" loans for several rounds.

16. A "thana" is a governmental administrative unit comprising of several villages in a region. Literally, in Bengali, a thana is a police station. Each thana has at least one police station, post office, a civil service office, etc.

17. In order to check the validity of using a random effects model, I perform a Breusch and Pagan Lagrange multiplier test (Baltagi & Qi, 1990; Breusch & Pagan, 1980) for random effects. The result supports the contention that these unobserved effects are present. The Hausman specification test (Hausman, 1978), however, indicates that the difference between the FE and RE estimates may be systematic, suggesting that the random effects may be correlated with the other regressors. The FE model may therefore provide more reliable results.

18. The Breusch and Pagan Lagrange multiplier test does not reject the possible existence of branch-specific random effects. However, the Hausman specification test suggests that the FE and RE models have systematically different coefficients. Thus, the results of the RE model should be interpreted with caution.

19. In order to prevent favoritism or patronage of any kind, bank staff are not recruited from the region where a branch is located, implying that bank staff have little prior local information. Exception is made for women bank assistants, as their mobility is constrained due to societal norms. While bank assistants live in dormitories at the branch, women employees are exempted from this requirement. In any case, the percentage of branch-level women employees is typically not very high.

ACKNOWLEDGMENTS

I would like to thank Djavad Salehi-Isfahani for invaluable discussions and critical suggestions throughout the writing of this paper. I also want to thank Iftekhar Hasan and Catherine Eckel for their insightful criticisms and ideas on the empirical analysis. I am grateful to the World Bank for providing the data used in this study, and to Zahed Khan for his encouragement and for many useful discussions. I want to express my gratitude to Muhammad Yunus and various staff members of the Grameen Bank in Bangladesh, and to Sukumar Das and other bank assistants at the Konokdia branch for giving generously of their time and for their hospitality. I would also like to thank Zakia, Anjali Rani, and other Grameen Bank borrowers in Konokdia who took the time to share with me their stories of struggle and success.

REFERENCES

Armendariz de Aghion, B. (1999). On the design of a credit agreement with peer monitoring. *Journal of Development Economics*, *60*, 401–420.

Baltagi, B. H., & Qi, L. (1990). A Lagrange multiplier test for the error components model with incomplete panels. *Econometrics Reviews*, *9*(1), 103–107.

Bernasek, A. (1991). *Endogenous group formation and group lending: The Grameen bank*. University of Michigan.

Besley, T., & Coate, S. (1995). Group lending, repayment incentives and social collateral. *Journal of Development Economics*, *41*(1), 1–18.

Breusch, T., & Pagan, A. (1980). The Lagrange multiplier test and its applications to model specifications in econometrics. *Review of Economic Studies*, *47*, 239–253.

Gibbons, D. S. (1992). *The Grameen reader*. Grameen Bank.

Gibbons, D. S., & Kasim, S. (1990). *Banking on the rural poor*. Center for Policy Research, University Sains Malaysia, and Asian and Pacific Development Center.

Hausman, J. A. (1978). Specification tests in econometrics. *Econometrica*, *46*, 69–85.

Hoff, K., & Stiglitz, J. (1990). Introduction: Imperfect information and rural credit markets – puzzles and policy perspectives. *The World Bank Economic Review*, *4*(3).

Hossain, M. (1986). *The impact of Grameen Bank on women's involvement in productive activities*. Grameen Bank publication 33.

Hossain, M. (1988). Credit for alleviation of rural poverty: The Grameen Bank in Bangladesh, Research Report 65, International Food Policy Research Institute in collaboration with Bangladesh Institute of Development Studies.

Huppi, M., & Feder, G. (1990). The role of groups and credit cooperatives in rural lending. *The World Bank Research Observer*, *5*(2).

Jain, P. S. (1996). Managing credit for rural poor: Lessons from Grameen bank. *World Development*, *24*(1).

Khandker, S. R. (1993). *Grameen bank and its impact on the poor*. World Bank.

Khandker, S. R., Khalily, B., & Khan, Z. (1993). *Grameen bank: What do we know*. World Bank.

Khandker, S. R., Khalily, B., & Khan, Z. (1994). Is Grameen bank sustainable? *HROWP*, *23*. World Bank.

Khandker, S. R., Khalily, B., & Khan, Z. (1995). Grameen bank: Performance and sustainability. World Bank Discussion Paper 306. World Bank.

Paxton, J., Graham, D., & Thraen, C. (2000). Modeling group loan repayment behavior: New insights from Burkina Faso. *Economic Development and Cultural Change*, *48*(3), 639–655.

Pitt, M., & Khandker, S. (1998). The impact of group-based credit programs on poor households in Bangladesh: Does the gender of participants matter? *Journal of Political Economy*, *106*(5), 958–996.

Stiglitz, J. (1990). Peer monitoring and credit markets. *The World Bank Economic Review*, *4*(3).

Varian, H. R. (1990). Monitoring agents with other agents. *Journal of Institutional and Theoretical Economics*, *146*(1).

Yaron, J. (1992). Successful rural finance institutions. World Bank Discussion Paper 150.

Yunus, M. (1982). *Grameen bank project in Bangladesh: A poverty focused rural development programme*. Grameen Bank publication 19.

Yunus, M. (1984). *On reaching the poor*. Grameen Bank publication 24.

Yunus, M. (1986). *Group-based savings and credit for the rural poor*. Grameen Bank publication 23.

BANCASSURANCE AND THE FUTURE OF BANKING

Mohamed Nurullah

ABSTRACT

This paper seeks to provide an analysis of the impact of last two decades process on bancassurance activities. The analysis is set against the background of the broader structural changes that have been taken place in national, regional and global banking markets during the last two decades. There is a discussion on the progress that has been made so far to create a common market for banking and insurance and on what still needs to be achieved. Five particularly important issues are reviewed: effects on different entry modes of bancassurance, risk and return effects of banks as well as insurance companies, benefit of bancassurance with particular reference to economies of scale and economies of scope, shareholders wealth effects, and the effects on regulation and supervision. Finally the paper discuss for the future of banking.

1. INTRODUCTION

This paper seeks to provide an analysis of the impact of last two decades process on bancassurance activities. The analysis is set against the background of the broader structural changes that have been taken place in national, regional and global banking markets during the last two decades. There is a discussion on the progress that has been made so far to create a common market for banking and insurance and on what still needs to be achieved. Five

Bank and Financial Market Efficiency: Global Perspectives
Research in Banking and Finance, Volume 5, 137–156

ISSN: 1567-7915/doi:10.1016/S1567-7915(04)05007-4

particularly important issues are reviewed: effects on different entry modes of bancassurance, risk and return effects of banks as well as insurance companies, benefit of bancassurance with particular reference to economies of scale and economies of scope, shareholders wealth effects, and the effects on regulation and supervision.

The rest of the paper is as follows: Section 2 defines the term of bancassurance and its association with assurancebank and alfinanz; Section 3 provides an analysis as to how bancassurance system works at branch level; Section 4 reviews some important issues on bancassurance, and Section 5 concludes.

2. BANCASSURANCE

The word "*bancassurance*" is a French word. It is a term where insurance products are sold through a bank countrywide branch networks to its existing client base. Though for banks and insurance companies such changing interfaces have become widespread only from the late 1980s (e.g. Dickinson, 1994; Dickinson & Dinenis, 1993; OECD, 1992), such relationships have long been established, especially in the UK. This was found in Crick and Wadsworth (1936). In 1836 a firm of Scottish solicitors was responsible for the formation of both the North of Scotland Bank and the Northern Insurance Company. Through mergers and absorptions, they were later on part of the Midland Bank (now HSBC) and Commercial Union Assurance Company (now CGNU). Some definitions of bancassurance are given below.

2.1. Different Definitions of Bancassurance

Sigma (1992) defined bancassurance as a strategy adopted by banks or insurance companies aiming to operate in the financial services market in a more or less integrated manner. Hielkema (1994) defined bancassurance as, "a marketing strategy aimed at increasing sales for a bank or an insurance company by selling the product of the one through the distribution channels of the other, whereby the benefits also can be extended to various forms of cost sharing." Leach (1996) defined "bancassurance as insurance sales made by insurance companies in which banks have an equal or controlling stake of the equity." Coopers and Lybrand (1993) mentioned bancassurance as "strategies adopted by banks or insurance companies aiming to operate in the personal sector of financial services market in a more or less integrated manner." In the view of Morgan (1994), "bancassurance refers to a financial institution with a branch network, which in addition to its money transmission and lending services also sells its own insurance and investment products to its branch customers."

Pramee and Papasavvas (1992) defined "bancassurance" as the provision of insurance and banking products or services through a common distribution channel or to a common client base . . . The word "provision" embraces both manufacturer and distributor of the products or services.

All the authors, mentioned above, define "*bancassurance*" when banks engage into insurance business or insurance companies engage into banking business. Bancassurance is a situation when financial holding companies major activities are banking business rather than insurance business, and assurancebank is a situation where financial holding companies major activities are insurance business rather than banking business.

Some writers defined "bancassurance" and "*allfinanz*" as having the same meaning. But there are significant differences between "*bancassurance*" and "*allfinanz*." The "*Allfinanz*" is a German word, which includes securities business in addition to banking and insurance. Farny (1990) defined allfinanz in Germany as concerning the integration of the following set of activities in banking and insurance: (a) Production; (b) Distribution; (c) Marketing; (d) Consumer demand; and (e) Consumption. Wager (1990) defined allfinanz as an integration or combination of the supply of services from three groups of financial organisations, namely: (i) commercial banks, savings bank, and credit institutions; (ii) Building societies; (iii) Life and non-life insurance.

3. HOW BANCASSURANCE WORK AT BRANCH LEVEL?

In the bank branch, there are branch staff who do day to day banking activities to meet the customers need. These branch staffs are trained as to how to sell life assurance at least at a basic level. In legal term they can act as agent of banks' own life assurance company or a company with whom the bank is tied up for insurance distribution. In case of long-term insurance distribution process banks do mainly three tasks: (a) create a special database for identifying potential life insurance customer from the bank accounts. They consider various factor to create such database such as age, occupation, income etc.; (b) pass these data bases to the banks insurance sales force as "warm lead" or by making links between sales force and the potential customer; and (c) sell simple life insurance, if this is allowed, or just pass the customer to sales people. Individual branches have certain quota for insurance selling to be filled up by that branch. Banks sometimes employ specialist sales force especially for long-term insurance selling. Such specialists are employed either from amongst the branch staffs or from outside. Such specialists are allocated two to three branches each. They give comprehensive advice to the customers and perform selling if possible. The specialist make appointments at a mutual time and place, mostly at the branch, after the referral by branch staffs, or alternatively branch staff may make the appointment on their behalf.

There is another channel for insurance distribution. This is called Direct Sales Force. They mainly work from home but have a strong link with the allocated branch from where they may acquire their prospective customer or potential customers' information from the branch staffs referral process or warm lead. These sales forces also cover those who do not frequently visit the branch and they try to make contact at the customer's home.

Direct Marketing is another marketing channel where products are distributed directly from the manufacturer to the consumers without any intermediaries. In the U.K., Direct Line Insurance, a subsidiary of Royal Bank of Scotland group started this method in 1984 for motor insurance. This method was later on followed by other insurance companies and banks in the U.K. and abroad. Today Direct Line is one of the top ten motor insurance company in the U.K.

The IFA (Independent Financial Adviser) is a traditional insurance distribution channel. Though the main purpose of the banks' involvement in insurance business was to maximise the use of bank branch net work, banks are using the IFA with traditional insurers. A parent bank can establish an insurance broking subsidiary with a corporate status. This company has separate legal identity. The broking subsidiary then make special strategic alliance with traditional insurance underwriters including its own parent group's insurance underwriting company (if there is any). For an independent and a wide variety of product coverage they keep different types of insurance products from different insurers. They then sell the insurance products like other traditional IFAs. But the special advantage of these broking firms is that they have a very close link with their parent banks. If any bank customer inquires for insurance in the branch he/she is then referred to that broking subsidiary or, in some cases, branch staff can do the job on their behalf. A bancassurance model is shown in the Fig. 1.

3.1. Bancassurance Companies Market Share

Insurance companies' survival or death mainly depends on this premium income. More over, in commercial practice, insurance companies' soundness and efficiency is determined from the premium income. In the Table 1, we have shown European banks insurance distribution performance. We compare the ratio of bancassurance channel with traditional insurance channel.

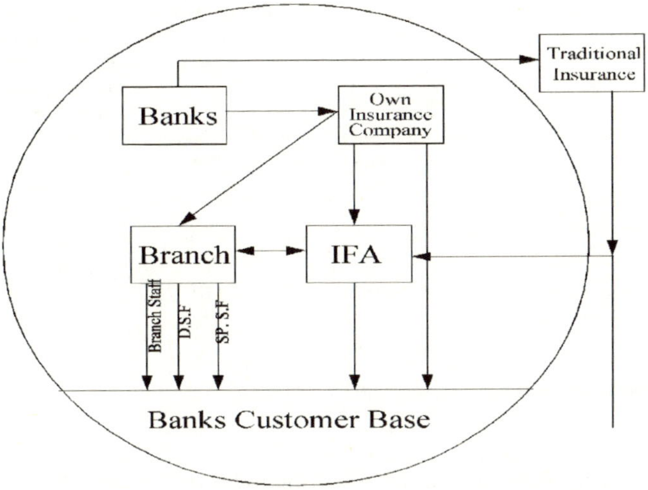

Fig. 1. Bancassurance Model (Nurullah & C. Parsons, 2003).

The Table 1 shows that banks are dominating in life insurance distribution in a number of EU countries. Banks in Portugal, Spain France and Italy account over 60% of life insurance distribution in domestic markets. Only in the U.K. and Netherlands, the banks market shares are 10.2 and 21% respectively. The lower percentage of premium income by these countries banks are because these countries traditional insurance intermediaries are unique in the world that pose a long established skill, knowledge and culture in insurance distribution.

Table 1. Life Insurance Distribution Channels.

Country	Insurance Companies Employees	Agents (Tied and Multiple)	Brokers	Other Networks (Banks, Post Office etc)	Others
Austraia	25.8	4.1	15.7	51.6	2.9
Belgium[a]	3.6	3.4	26.6	50.0	16.4
Spain	0.0	14.2	2.7	72.2	10.9
France	16.0	8.0	9.0	61.0	6.0
U.K.	17.2	4.0	64.9	10.2	3.7
Italy	8.6	27.0	0.9	63.5	0.0
Natherlands	14.0	52.0	0.0	21.0	13.0
Portugal	5.4	10.8	0.7	82.3	0.9
Sweden	28.0	0.0	19.0	45.0	8.0

Source: Comite Europeen des Assurances 2002.
[a] 1999 figure.

Table 2. Non-Life Insurance Distribution Channels.

Country	Insurance Companies Employees	Agents (Tied and Multiple)	Brokers	Other Networks (Banks, Post Office etc)	Others
Austraia	56.6	4.4	30.8	3.1	5.2
Belgium[a]	2.2	8.9	65.9	7.4	15.6
Spain	0.0	48.8	21.6	4.4	25.2
France	37.0	35.0	17.0	8.0	3.0
U.K.[a]	21.0	18.0	47.0	11.0	3.0
Italy	4.7	79.4	15.1	0.8	0.0
Natherlands	32.0	53.0	0.0	11.0	4.0
Portugal	12.4	57.8	15.3	9.6	5.0

Source: Comite Europeen des Assurances 2002.
[a] 1999 figure.

However, from Table 2, it is seen that the traditional distribution channels are still dominant in general insurance distribution. In general insurance business banks market share is still very small from 3% to 11%. This is because the banks have still not entered into the distribution of large risk exposure insurance products such as marine, aviation etc, which require very special technical knowledge and skill and the banks have not acquired such expertise yet.

4. SOME ISSUES ON BANCASSURANCE

4.1. Which Entry Strategies in Bancassurance

Banks use various entry strategies in order to engage in insurance business (Hoschka, 1994; Kane, 1995; OECD, 1992; Parmee & Papasavvas, 1992; Walter & Saunders, 1994). According to the level of integration and the degree of riskiness, all the entry strategies can be classified into five groups. These are: (i) start-up approach; (ii) mergers and acquisitions; (iii) creation of a holding company; (iv) joint venture; and (v) strategic alliance.

4.1.1. Start-up Approach

The start-up approach (some times referred to as "de novo entry") is one of the most important entry tools used by the banks in order to enter into insurance activities. In this approach banks set up their own insurance subsidiary from scratch. All the rights and responsibilities of such a new venture then belong to the parent bank.

The choice of this entry strategy has merits and demerits. As a start up approach into new areas of business, the key demerits are the difficulty of getting the team expertise and adjusting the two separate management bodies and more capital (compared to strategic alliance or joint venture) is required here. Furthermore, to learn the "know how" of business and to get the benefits from this type of entry is lengthy, and a lot of advertisements and time is required for its publicity in order to build up a client base. However, the banks have already a client base in their banking area, which may be a prospective client base for insurance products too. But some customer may not be interested in doing business with such a new unknown insurance company or may not wish to put "all his eggs in one basket."

Empirical results show that such strategy takes at least nine years to become a profitable enterprise (e.g. De Young & Hasan, 1998). Rose and Savage (1984) found that the de novo banks had riskier assets, incurred higher operating expenses. Huyser (1986) found that the failure of de novo banks were more likely than established banks.

The good side of this entry is that a bank can build up a subsidiary according to its own choice and need, and keep match with its banking products. Hoschka (1994) suggested this type of entry strategy for bancassurance companies. The Barclays, the largest U.K. bank, has adopted this strategy. It has set up its own life assurance company, the Barclays Life Assurance Company, in 1965. This life insurance subsidiary is used as workshop of life and pension products, and marketed by the Barclays bank branch network.

Some other big banks in the U.K. and in Europe have also adopted the same strategy. For example, the TSB, the fifth largest U.K. bank, has set up its own life and non-life as well as insurance broking subsidiaries. These are the TSB Life Ltd, the TSB General Insurance Ltd, and the TSB General insurance services Ltd. In France, the Credit Agricole, the country's largest and Europe's number one bank has set up its own life and non-life insurance companies named the Predica and the Pacifica respectively. Predica is now the third largest life assurance company in France. The Deutsche Bank, Germany's largest bank, has set up its own life assurance company, the DB Leben. The DB Leben, later on in 1994, has merged with Deutsche Harold, a general insurance subsidiary.

4.1.2. Mergers and/or Acquisitions

This is another important entry strategy where banks merge with another insurer or acquire an existing insurance company. There may be two ways of doing this. One is cross-section and the other is cross-border. After the take over, the two companies remain in being but the Offeree Company becomes a subsidiary company of the other and controlled and monitored by the acquiring company.

Vander Vennet (1996) found that domestic *mergers* among equal-sized partners significantly increase the performance of the merged banks. Improvement of cost efficiency was also found in cross-boarder *acquisitions*.

In the U.K., the Lloyds bank, the fourth largest commercial bank in the country, has adopted this entry strategy. It has acquired the Abbey Life, which is now the tenth largest U.K. life assurance company in terms of premium income. The Banco Central Hispano of Spain has acquired the Generali of Italy through this entry strategy. Similarly, the Rabobank in the Netherlands has also adopted this strategy to acquire the Interpolis.

4.1.3. Joint Venture

Harrigan (1981) defined joint venture as "business agreements where two or more owners create a separate entity." In this strategy, one bank and one insurance company set up a new insurance company, which is jointly own by them. This may be on a fifty-fifty share holding basis or fifty one forty nine-share bases. The balance of ownership will depend on the strengths of each company and their respective contributions to the new joint venture company. But the insurance companies are likely to be minority shareholders as banks have the upperhand through its ownership of the strong distribution channel. The parent insurance company provides technical support such as underwriting and sales training administration and investment management services while the parent bank provides support of distribution through its countrywide branch network to its banking client base. For example, the Credit Commercial de France (CCF) and the Elysees Sante have created a joint venture insurance company, the ERISA, where the CCF and Elysees both hold 50% equity each. McConnell and Nantell (1985) found significant wealth gain from *joint ventures*.

4.1.4. Equity Holding

While in equity holding banks (or insurance companies in *assurancebank* strategy) do not generally involve themselves in operating business activities directly, they rather simply acquire equity from insurance companies and receive dividends as a shareholder. But some companies acquire a significant share of the equity of insurance companies and use their bank branches for distribution of insurance. For instance, the Bank of Scotland has 34% of equity holding of the Standard life. In the case of the formation of holding companies, a common management body is set up for the holding company to see the overall affairs of the entire holding with separate management for banking and insurance. ING has adopted this type of entry strategy. In a *holding company merger* analysis, Cornett and Tehranian (1992) found that the profitability improved significantly after the merger while in a study by Pilloff (1996) it was found that the mergers were not associated with any significant change in performance.

4.1.5. Strategic Alliance

A strategic alliance is a long-term business agreement between two or more companies to pool exchange and/or integrate specified company resources for achieving some agreed objectives (e.g. Hung, 1992). Dawson and Shaw (1992) described alliance as "co-operation between two or more retail companies whereby each partner seeks to add to its competencies by combining some resources with those of its partners." In case of bancassurance, a bank makes a strategic alliance with an established insurance company to conduct joint sales of business in return for fees or commissions. Through such a strategic alliance, the banks sell insurance products with its banking products to its existing banking customers, and on the other hand, the insurance companies sell banking products with its insurance products to its existing insurance customer base. But they do not bear the underwriting risks for such cross-business distribution activities. In Germany, Dresdner Bank, the country's second largest bank, has such a strategic alliance with the country's largest insurer, Allianz, for joint sales of business. Chan et al. (1997) found significant positive wealth effects on non-equity *strategic alliance* and no evidence of wealth transfers between partners. These results support the conjecture in Jensen and Meckling (1991) that strategic alliances provide a cost effective way to place decision-making authority in the hands of individuals who possess the knowledge to make the best decisions.

All the entry mode studies mentioned above looked at from a bank viewpoint or other financial and non-financial services industries' viewpoint. There is little study on the entry strategies from a bancassurance company perspective. The only study that looked at the different entry mores of bancassurance was by Hoschka (1994). The Hoschka (1994) study conducted a qualitative analysis of different entry modes of bancassurance and suggested for de nov entry mode. Further works is necessary on this issue.

4.2. The Benefits of Bancassurance

The benefits of bancassurance can be analysed from four viewpoints. These are from a bank viewpoint, from a regulator's viewpoint, from an insurance company viewpoint and from a consumer viewpoint. The main emphasises from a bank view is the potential benefits of Economies of scale and economies of scope. Economies of scale exist if average production costs decline as output rises, i.e.

banking products. On the other hand, economies of scope arise if two or more products can be jointly produced at a lower cost than is incurred in their independent production (Panzar & Wiliig, 1981). Specifically, there are economies of scope over the production of goods X and Y if

$$C(x, y) < C(x, 0) + C(0, y)$$

where C(x,y) are the firm's (minimised) costs of producing x units of good X jointly with y units of good Y at a given vector of input prices.

Banks, by using their country wide branch net work with huge number of staffs can offer insurance products with traditional banking products to their vast client base and thus can save unit cost as well as maximise the available utilities. However, there may be diseconomies of scope. This is because to run an insurance agency is much cheaper than to run a bank branch. Further more, insurance agents mainly work from home which means even lower overhead costs.

The main emphasises from a regulator's view to allow bancassurance activities is to have: (a) a wider integration within the EU financial services market, especially in the EU countries where the bancassurance originate from (b) creating competition; and (c) allowing diversification for risk deduction. The integration will fulfil the European Community's single market for a global strategy (e.g. Loheac, 1991), while the competition will make the prices competitive and the consumer will enjoy lower prices and better quality of services. The prime duty of the regulators is to provide safety net to policyholders, depositors and savers, and above all to stabilise the economy as a whole by using different supervisory tools. Allowing diversification is treated as one of risk deduction tools (Boyd & Graham, 1988; Litan, 1987). However, such liberalisation may cause problems for supervision, especially on solvency control and alleged double gearing (e.g. Hesberg & Karten, 1994; Nurullah & Dinenis, 2000).

The main emphasises from an insurance company viewpoint is to access to new channel and new customer base. Diacon (1990) mentioned nine reasons from the insurance companies' viewpoint. These are: (i) access to banks customer base; (ii) lower marginal costs in generating new business; (iii) cost allocation method; (iv) banks better image; (v) easy exploitation of cross-selling; (vi) better post-sales service because of physical presence; (vii) useful distribution medium for insurance; (viii) utilisation of capital-intensive operation; and (ix) downstream vertical integration to secure distribution.

The main emphasis's from a consumer view is that a consumer can get all his/her financial products from a single source. The Swiss Re (1993) conducted a survey about the consumers' attitude towards insurance. The survey shows that 34% prefer to buy life assurance from sales man, 21% from brokers, 18% from building societies, 15% from banks and 3% choose post as their favoured method.

The banks and building societies combined account for (18% + 15%) = 33%, which is one third of the national market. Responding to customers changing habits and attitudes, the banks are now changing their name in the branch offices. For instance, instead of using "Barclays Bank," or "National Westminster Bank," or "Midland Bank" or "Halifax Building Society" as they used to use before, most of the branches are now simply using "Barclays," "Natwest," "Midland"(HSBC), and "Halifax" respectively. This means they are no longer only a bank but a universal financial institutions for all sorts of the financial products. There are a number of studies on the economies of scale and economies of scope that looked at banking industry (e.g. Allen & Rai, 1997; Berger, Hunter & Timme, 1993; Berger et al., 1987; De Young & Hasan, 1998; Hasan et al., 2000). Also, there are a number of studies on the economies of scale and economies of scope that looked at insurance industry (e.g. Cummins & Weiss, 1993; Hardwick, 1997; Kaye, 1991). The only empirical study on the economies of scale and economies of scope that looked at bancassurance industry is the study of Dinenis and Jung (1999). Dinenis and Jung (1999) conducted a study on the existence of economies of scale and economies of scope in the U.K. bancassurance companies over the period of 1988–1996 and found positive scale and scope economies. The study is based on a smaller sample and the study period is early period of bancassurance. A further study on the EU wide bancassurance companies' economies of scale and economies of scope is currently under way by the same author of this paper.

4.3. Bancassurance and Risk Effects

Bancassurance may be potentially beneficial since it allows the commercial banks to diversify into insurance activities as diversification spread risk and thus reduce the risk of failure. On the other hand, insurance activities may be riskier than banking activities when viewed on a stand-alone basis. If so happen then *the "bancassurance"* firms may increase the probability of bank failure. There is little empirical work on this issue. However, as American banks were prohibited form engaging in activities that are out side the traditional concept prior to the Gramm-Leach-Bliley Act, early studies tried to examine the potential effect of American banks expansion into non-banking activities by creating a hypothetical mergers scenarios between actual banks and non-bank firms as if such merger had been permitted. After creating these hypothetical mergers, sample risk and return statistics for the hypothetical industries are calculated and then compared to risk and return statistics for the unmerged industry. Such comparison allows for examining the effects of the merge between banks and non-banks industries. It was a common practice among the different studies that used this approach to use return on equity or assets (ROA and ROE) as a measure of profitability. To measure the risk, volatility of rate of return on equity and the Z-score measure of bankruptcy probability are usually used.

Boyd and Graham (1988) examined the effects of banks holding companies (BHC) expanding into non-banking activities on the profitability and risk of banks by creating a simulation mergers between actual bank holding companies and non-blank firms using both accounting and market data between 1971 and 1984. The results showed slight increase in profitability measure when banks merge with both life insurance and securities firms. However, the volatility of returns was shown to increase when securities firms are presented while decrease when life insurance firms are presented. Therefore, simulation mergers between banks and securities firms (the riskiest firms among other financial firms) substantially increase the risk, where mergers between banks and life insurance firms (the least risky firms among other financial firms) decrease the risk. Taking both results together to assess whether the increase in profitability can offset the increase in their volatility, the paper does not support the view for BHC mergers with securities firms, while it is in favour of expanding into life insurance.

Boyd, Graham and Hewitt (1993) extracted the same results in their study to test the debate over whether bank holding companies should be permitted to enter non-banking activities. Creating simulation mergers between BHCs and securities, real estate, and insurance industries for the period 1971–1987, they found that BHCs are roughly in the middle among the other industries in terms of profitability. The median Z-scores computed with accounting data and the median Z-scores computed with market data suggests that the securities, real estate, and insurance agent/broker industries exhibit the highest risk. In terms of post-merger analysis, Simulations with accounting data indicate that mergers between BHCs and firms in securities, real estate development, other real estate, and insurance agent/brokers increase BHC risk of failure. On the other hand, according to market data, BHC combinations with securities, real estate development, and other real estate firms increase risk. However, BHC mergers with insurance agent/brokers using market data produce slightly more favourable results than those with accounting data. Where, BHC mergers with life insurance and property/casualty insurance firms using market data reinforce the results obtained with accounting data. Therefore, the paper resulted to the conclusion that BHC should be permitted to acquire life and Property/casualty insurance firms, but prohibited from acquiring securities and real estate firms. The tests suggest that BHC mergers with life and property/casualty insurance firms are less risky than BHC mergers with securities firms, insurance agent/brokers, and real estate firms. Similar simulation studies were conducted by Saunders and Walters (1994).

Allen and Jagtiani (2000) examine the potential risk diversification from combining imperfectly correlated banking, securities and insurance activities. The paper considers the impact on total risk as well as systematic risk of such combination in the absence of any synergistic gains (reusability of information). The synthetic approach has carried out using market data between January 1986 and December 1994 to create hypothetical universal banks, consisting of one bank, one securities firm, and one insurance company. Then the risk of the synthetic universal banks is compared with the risk of the undiversified banks.

Unlike other studies, this study examines the full range of activities provided by securities firms and insurance companies. Moreover, instead of focusing only on total risk, this paper examines also systematic risk and the risk premiums demanded by the market as the relevant measure of risk and the risk-adjusted cost of capital. Incorporation systematic risk into the analysis provides an important policy implication for the expanded bank powers. That is, bank holding companies' systematic risk exposure may be considered a proxy for the systemic risk faced by the U.S. banking system. If the expanded bank powers into securities and insurance activities increased bank holding companies' systematic risk, this would suggest that it would be more likely that a common economic shock could lead to massive bank failures across the entire banking system. Moreover, the methodology used in this paper allows isolating the potential risk diversification benefits from any synergistic gains.

Examining the impact of securities and insurance activities on bank holding companies' total risk, the paper found that the new bank powers, which will allow U.S. banking firms to offer securities and insurance underwriting, will likely lower the overall risk of the U.S. banking industry. This is due to the imperfect correlation of the returns between 1986 and 1994, which cause the volatility of returns (total risk) of universal banks, on average, to be lower than that of the bank holding companies. The average monthly returns, however, will also decline slightly.

The only empirical study on the effects of risk and return of the *actual* bancassurance companies was conducted by Dinenis and Nurullah (2001). Dinenis and Nurullah (2001) conducted a study on the risk and return effects of EU bank diversification into life insurance underwriting, general insurance underwriting and insurance broking. They used accounting data for their analysis and found that banks decreased bankruptcy risk in insurance broking but not in underwriting activities. Another study by Nurullah et al. (2003) on EU insurance companies diversification into banking activities found that insurance companies decreased their bankruptcy risk. A further study on the risk and return effects of EU bancassurance companies is under way by the same author which uses market data rather than accounting data.

4.4. Bancassurance and Shareholders Wealth Effects

There are a number of studies on the shareholders wealth effect of banking firms. Some of these studies are Swary (1983), Rhoades (1993), Hannan and Wolken (1989), Baradwaj, Fraser and Furtado (1990), DeLong (2001) and Arnold et al. (2002). Also, there are a number of studies on the shareholders wealth effect of insurance firms. But there is only one study in the U.S. and two studies in the EU on the shareholders wealth effects of bancassurance.

Carow (2001) conducted a study on the wealth effects of allowing U.S. bank entry into the insurance company. The study is based on three Supreme Court Ruling[1] prior to Gramm-Leach-Bliley Act (GLBA) of 1999. The study of Carow (2001) shows that bank stock prices have not changed significantly surrounding these rulings. However, these rulings significantly decreased insurance company stock prices. Life and health insurance companies and insurance agencies have the most negative reactions. Property-liability insurance companies have a less negative response. Insurance companies that sell via a brokerage system have the highest stock returns. The results are consistent with contestable market theory. Decreasing entry barriers reduces the economic rents of insurance companies and changes the competitive structure among insurance companies.

The only two studies on wealth effect of European bank diversification into non-banking activities were by Cybo-Ottone and Murgia (1999) and Beitel and Dchiereck (2001). However, these two studies do not focus on the diversification phenomena it self, but rather they focus on M&A transactions between European banks in general and the studies are restrictive by selected time periods. These limitations affect the credibility of the findings as the wealth effect of banks entry into non-banks line of businesses is studied as sub-sample and in time-limited period.

Cybo-Ottone and Murgia (1999) provide the first analysis of the stock market evaluation of the largest mergers and acquisitions between banks and financial institutions that have been announced form 1988 to 1997 in 14 European markets; the 13 European Union banking markets and the Swiss market. To test the scope prospective, the paper compares mergers and acquisitions between commercial banks against cross-product deals, mainly mergers and acquisitions between banks and insurance companies and banks and security firms. The imperial results in terms of scope prospective show that the market reaction on the value-weighted returns level were positive and statistically significant in the selected event window. This positive reaction was mainly driven by deals involving banks and non-banks firms. Bidding banks show a negative market reaction in case of M&A between banks, while reach a positive results when it involved a cross-products deal. On the cross product deals level, further examining of this positive result shows that deals involve banks and insurance firms has been the driven force for such result since they show a positive and significant market reaction, whereas, deals involving banks and security firms show non-significant positive market reaction.

In a similar approach to Cybo-Ottone and Mugia, Beitel and Schiereck (2001) also suggest that European M&A are not just a transfer in value from the shareholders of the bidders to the shareholders of the targets as their results show significant positive cumulated abnormal returns for the combined entity. On the separate entities level, the paper has found that the shareholders of targets earn significant positive abnormal returns, where there was no evidence of significant abnormal returns for the bidders' shareholders. Therefore, these results suggest that although the M&A transactions of European banks are overall not a clear success from the shareholder point of view, it cannot be considered as a significant value-destroying event.

Beitel and Dirk Schiereck's study in many aspects can be considered as almost an updated version of Cybo-Ottone and Mugia study. Both studies examine the European Banking mergers and acquisitions deals using event study methodology to assess the value implication of these transactions, also they both take into consideration the M&A transactions that involve insurance and securities firms. However, Beitel and Dirk paper examines merger and acquisition transactions that occurred between 1985 and 2000. This counts for more completed large mergers and acquisition in comparison to the 1985–1997 period used by Cybo-Ottone and Mugia. This time period includes 98 completed transactions, where both the bidder and the target are listed, which doubles the amount of transactions used by Cybo-Ottone and Mugia. The inclusion of the 1997–2000 period accounts for all the difference between the two data. During this period the European M&A have witnessed a profound increase in volume and number comparing to the previous 14 years, especially in 1999 (the year in which the second phase of the European monetary union has been implemented) where the M&A transactions in Europe reached its peak with approximately USD 125bn. This circumstance makes the used time period more representing.

4.5. Bancassurance and its Impact to Bank Regulation/Supervision

Although the banks and insurance companies cross-business activities are allowed, the regulators and supervisors of these businesses mostly remain traditional, i.e. different regulators for banking, insurance and securities industries. This different regulatory/supervisory system for the bancassurance and financial conglomerate firms has created a number of problems such as double gearing, contagion risk to the regulatory and supervisory authorities (Nurullah & Dinenis, 2000). One may argue that there is no need to have an integrated regulator/supervisor because the banking supervisor will supervise the banking part of a financial conglomerate and, similarly, the insurance supervisor will supervise the insurance part, and the securities supervisor will supervise the securities part. But it is very important for the supervisors to understand material risk concentrations as part of their efforts to identify the overall risk profile of financial conglomerates, because losses may arise from the correlation or interaction of risk across sectors within the conglomerate. Therefore, in such cases, a single/integrated supervisor would be in a better position for overall risk assessment and thus able to minimise these risks (Nurullah & Nakajima, 2003).

In order to minimise such problems, the U.K. in 1997 decided to adopt a single regulatory system (which gave birth to the Financial Services Authority) for all financial services, and the Financial Services and Markets Act 2000 was enacted in this regard. Other countries such as Australia, Canada, Denmark, Iceland, Japan, Korea, Norway, Singapore, Sweden have adopted similar approach. But the U.S. government in 2000 introduced the Financial Services and Markets Act which now permits cross-industry activities in financial services, and a number of financial conglomerates have already been emerged in the U.S. financial market. However, there are still a number of regulators to oversee the U.S. financial system, such as the Federal Reserve System, the Office of the Comptroller of the Currency, the National Association of Insurance Commissioners, the Securities and Exchange Commission, the Office of Thrift Supervision, etc. The U.S. believes that different regulators have expertise at supervising different activities, and that it is inefficient and impractical to expect a regulator to have or develop expertise in the regulation of all aspects of financial services. Therefore, as an alternative to a single regulator, the U.S. has come up with a new approach. In keeping with the Federal Reserve Board's role as an umbrella supervisor, the new legislation intends to ensure that banking activities are regulated by banking regulators, securities activities are regulated by securities regulators, and insurance activities are regulated by insurance regulators. As an umbrella supervisor, the Board is authorised to examine each holding company and its subsidiaries subject to certain restrictions.

A further work is necessary in the area of regulation and supervision of bancassurance and financial conglomerate firms. The European Commission is working on this issue. One of the provisions is to put insurance regulation/supervision within the Basle II accord of banking. The work will be completed by 2007.

Single regulatory system may be a better option but more works needed to be done on commonality achievements, especially in the accounting of banking, insurance and securities since the regulatory and supervisory annual returns are provided by accounting data.

5. FUTURE

The banks will continue to engage in insurance activities because of its success on cost and profit dynamics. Vennet (1998) conducted a study on cost and profit dynamics in financial conglomerates and universal banks in Europe and found that financial conglomerates were more revenue efficient than their more specialized competitors and indicated that the current trend towards further despecialisation might lead to a more efficient banking system. Cavallo and Rossi (2001) also reached a similar conclusion.

The trend will continue, especially because of the development of e-business and a bank will no longer be a bank. It will rather be a "onestop" shopping centre for all financial services products. But this will put heavy load to the regulators and supervisors in order to maintain a sound and healthy financial system.

NOTE

1. For several years before the passage of the GLBA, banks were allowed to sell insurance products. The Office of the Comptroller of the Currency (OCC) granted national banks the right to sell fixed-rate annuities in 1985 and variable-rate annuities in 1990. The 1995 and 1996 Supreme Court cases upholding the OCC rulings have brought this segment of regulatory change to completion.

REFERENCES

Allen, L., & Jagtiani, J. (2000). The risk effects of combining banking, securities, and insurance activities. *Journal of Economics and Business*, *52*, 485–497.

Allen, L., & Rai, A. (1997). Operational efficiency in banking: An international perspective, reply to the comment. *Journal of Banking and Finance*, *21*, 1451–1455.

Arnold, R. C., Howell, J. C., & Power, M. L. (2002). Wealth effects of banks' rights to market and originate annuities. *The Quarterly Review of Economics and Finance*, *42*(3), 487–503.

Beitel, P., & Dchiereck, D. (2001). Value creation at the ongoing consolidation of the european banking market. Institute for Mergers and Acquisitions (IMA), Working Paper No. 05/01.

Berger, A. N., Hanweck, G. A., & Humphrey, D. B. (1987). Competitive viability in banking: Scale, scope, and product mix economies. *Journal of Monetary Economics*, *20*, 501–520.

Berger, A., Hunter, W., & Timme, S. (1993). The efficiency of financial institutions: A review and preview of research past, present and future. *Journal of Banking and Finance*, *17*, 221–250.

Boyd, J. H., & Graham, S. L. (1988). The profitability and risk effects of allowing bank holding companies to merge with other financial firms: A simulation study. *Federal Reserve Bank of Minneapolis Review* (Spring), 3–21.

Boyd, J. H., Graham, S. L., & Hewitt, R. S. (1993). Bank holding company mergers with nonbabk financial firms: Effects on the risk of failure. *Journal of Banking and Finance*, *17*, 43–63.

Carow, K. A. (2001). The wealth effects of allowing bank entry into the insurance industry. *Journal of Risk and Insurance*, *68*(1), 129–150.

Cavallo, L., & Rossi, S. P. S. (2001). Scale and scope economies in the European banking systems. *Journal of Multinational Financial Management*, *11*(4), 515–531.

Chan, S. H., Kensinger, J. W., Keown, A. J., & Martin, J. D. (1997). Do strategic alliances create value? *Journal of Financial Economics*, *46*, 199–221.

Coopers & Lybrand (1993). *Making bancassurance work: Survey of European financial institutions policies and practice*. European Financial Services Group, Coopers and Lybrand, Amsterdam, The Netherlands.

Cornett, M. M., & Tehranian, H. (1992). Changes in corporate performance associated with bank acquisitions. *Journal of Financial Economics*, *31*, 211–234.

Crick, W. F., & Wadsworth, J. E. (1936). *A hundred years of joint stock banking*. Hodder & Stoughton.

Cummins, J. D., & Weiss, M. A. (1993). Measuring cost efficiency in the property-liability insurance industry. *Journal of Banking and Finance*, *17*, 463–481.

Cybo-Ottone, A., & Murgia, M. (1999). Mergers and shareholder wealth in European banking. *Journal of Banking and Finance*, *24*(6), 831–859.

Dawson, J., & Shaw, S. A. (1992). Interfirm alliances in the retail sector: Evolutionary, strategic, and tactical issues in their creation and management. University of Edinburgh Working Paper Series, no. 92/7.

DeLong, G. (2001). Stockholder gain from focusing vs. diversifying bank mergers. *Journal of Financial Economics*, *59*, 221–252.

De Young, R., & Hasan, I. (1998). The performance of de novo commercial banks: A profit efficiency approach. *Journal of Banking and Finance*, *22*, 565–587.

Diacon, S. (1990). European integration: Strategic implications for the marketing of long-term insurance. *International Journal of Bank Marketing*, *8*(3).

Dickinson, G., & Dinenis, E. (1993). The changing interfaces between insurance companies and banks. Paper presented at the 20th meeting of European Risk and Insurance Economists, Rotterdam, September.

Dinenis, E., & Jung, S. J. (1999). Scale and scope economies in the U.K. life assurance industry. Ph.D. thesis, City University Business School, London.

Dinenis, E., & Nurullah, M. (2001). Testing return and risk effects of european bank diversification into different insurance activities. In: Alen, Gersbach, Krahnen & Santomero (Eds), *Refereed Proceedings of the Conference on Competition among Banks: Good or Bad?* April 7–8, 2000, Frankfurt/Main, Germany.

Farny, D. (1990). Allfinanz – Das betriebswirtschaftliche Konzept. In: Krummel, H.-J., Rehn, H. & Simmert, D. B. (Eds), *Allfinanz – Strukturwandel an den Markten fur Finanzdienstleistungen*. Berlin: Duncker & Humblot.

Hardwick, P. (1997). Measuring cost inefficiency in the U.K. life insurance industry. *Applied Financial Economics*, *7*, 37–44.

Harrigan, K. R. (1981). Barriers to entry and competitive strategies. *Strategic Management Journal*, *2*, 395–412.

Hasan, I., Vivas, A. L., & Pastor, J. T. (2000). *Cross-border performance in European banking*. Bank of Finland Discussion Paper, 24/2000.

Hesberg, D., & Karten, W. (1994). *Supervision of financial conglomerates-remarks on solvency control and alleged double gearing*. The Geneva Papers on Risk and Insurance, 19(70) January 1–21.

Hielkema, H. J. (1994). A decade of change in financial services: The winners, the losers and the future. Paper presented at a Conference of the International Insurance Institute, June 19–23, Madrid, Spain.

Hoschka, T. C. (1994). *Bancassurance in Europe*. Houndsmills, Basingstoke, Hamshire and London: Macmillan Press Ltd.

Hung, C. L. (1992). Strategic business alliance between Canada and the newly industrialised countries of Pacific Asia. *Management International Review*, *32*, 345–361.

Jensen, M. C., & Meckling, W. H. (1991). Theory of the firm: Managerial behavior, agency costs and ownership structure. *Journal of Financial Economics*, *3*.

Kane, E. (1995). The increasing futility of restricting bank participation in insurance activities. Paper presented at Universal Banking conference, New York University.

Kaye, G. (1991). Economies of scale in U.K. life insurance companies: An empirical analysis. *The Geneva Papers on Risk and Insurance Issues and Practice*, *60*, 302–314.

Leach, A. (1996). *New initiatives in European bancassurance: Innovation and diversification*. London: Financial Times Publishing.

Litan, R. E. (1987). *What should banks do?* The Brookings Institution, USA.

Loheac, F. (1991). Deregulation of financial services and liberalisation of international trade in services. *The Geneva Papers on Risk and Insurance*, *16*(October).

McConnell, J., & Nantell, T. (1985). Common stock returns and corporate combinations: The case of joint ventures. *Journal of Finance*, *40*, 519–536.

Morgan, G. (1994). Problems of integration and differentiation in the management of bancassurance. *The Services Industries Journal*, *14*(2), 153–169.

Nurullah, M., & Dinenis, E. (2000). Changing interfaces between European banks and insurance companies and the regulatory/supervisory response. *Journal of Insurance Regulation*, *18*(3), 551–584.

Nurullah, M., & Nakajima, C. (2003). Towards a single regulatory system for the financial services: Evidence from ten countries. *International Review of Law and Economics* (under review).

Nurullah, M., Nakajima, C., & Parsons, C. (2003). Diversification strategies of EU insurance companies into banking: An analysis of potential benefits. *Journal of Risk and Financial Services* (under review).

Nurullah, M., & Parsons, C. (2003). Insurance activities via banks: The European perspective. *Journal of Insurance Research and Practices* (forthcoming).

OECD (1992). *Insurance and other financial services – structural trends*. OECD, Paris.

Panzar, J., & Wiliig, R. D. (1981). Economies of scope. *American Economic Review, Papers and Proceedings*, *71*, 268–272.

Parmee, D., & Papasavvas, D. (1992). *Banks, building societies and insurers: The whole greater than the parts?* Staple Inn Actuarial Society, UK.

Pilloff, S. J. (1996). Performance changes and shareholder wealth creation associated with mergers of publicly traded banking institutions. *Journal of Money, Credit and Banking*, *28*, 294–310.

Rhoades, S. A. (1993). Efficiency effects of horizontal (In-market) bank mergers. *Journal of Banking and Finance*, *17*, 411–422.

Rose, J., & Savage, D. (1984). De novo entry and performance: Bank Holding companies vs. independent banks. *Journal of Bank Research*, 95–106.

Sigma (1992). *Bancassurance: A survey of competition between banking and insurance*. Economic Studies Section, Swiss Reinsurance Company, Zurich.

Swary, I. (1983). Bank acquisition of non-bank firms: An empirical analysis of administrative decisions. *Journal of Banking and Finance*, *7*, 213–230.

Swiss Re (1993). *Consumers attitudes towards life insurance*. Swiss Re, UK.

Vennet, R. V. (1996). The effect of mergers and acquisitions on the efficiency and profitability of EC credit institutions. *Journal of Banking and Finance*, *20*, 1531–1558.

Vennet, R. V. (1998). *Cost and profit dynamics in financial conglomerates and universal banks in Europe*. University of Ghent, Belgium.

Wager, P. (1990). *Die Bildung von Allfinanzkonzernen*. Doctoral dissertation, Bern: Peter Lang.

Walter, I., & Saunders, A. (1994). *Universal banking in the United States, what could we win, what could we lose?* New York: Oxford University Press.

STATE OF INFORMATIONAL EFFICIENCY OF THE SOUTH AFRICAN EQUITY MARKET DURING THE APARTHEID, TRANSITION AND THE POST-APARTHEID PERIODS

Tanweer Hasan and Wares Karim

ABSTRACT

The present study investigates whether the removal of apartheid have had any impact on the state of informational efficiency of the South African equity market. The impact is empirically verified by segmenting the sample period into three subperiods – apartheid period, transition period, and the post-apartheid period and conducting the variance-ratio test (Lo & MacKinlay, 1988) on the monthly closing index values in each subperiod. Overall, the results indicate that the state of informational efficiency of the South African equity market has substantially improved during the transition and post-apartheid period compared to the apartheid period. Furthermore, the index return series is reported to be mean-reverting in the post-apartheid period.

Bank and Financial Market Efficiency: Global Perspectives
Research in Banking and Finance, Volume 5, 157–168

ISSN: 1567-7915/doi:10.1016/S1567-7915(04)05008-6

1. INTRODUCTION

The equity market in South Africa is the largest and most developed market in the African region. Since the creation of the Union of South Africa in 1910 the political control of the country was in the hands of whites. The new government formed, in 1948, by the Afrikaner National Party specifically excluded non-whites from the political and economic systems. This policy of exclusion, known as apartheid, was opposed domestically by the African National Congress (ANC) and later, by the international community. Consequently, South Africa had to endure relative isolation from the global political and economic systems until F. W. de Klerk's election in 1989 as the new president of the Union. President F. W. de Klerk initiated sweeping reforms aimed at dismantling apartheid and introducing democracy. In 1991, the three most vital legal supports for apartheid were eliminated – the Land Acts of 1913 and 1936, the Group Areas Act of 1966, and the Population Registration Act of 1950. With the inauguration of Nelson Mandela as the President on May 10, 1994 the era of a free and democratic South Africa began. Against this backdrop of sea changes it would be interesting to investigate the different dimensions in which the equity market in South Africa was impacted by the removal of apartheid. A recent study by Lamba and Otchere (2001) analyzed the dynamic relationships between the South African and major equity markets in the world and report that South Africa has become much more integrated, economically and financially, with the major developed markets during the post apartheid period. The present study, on the other hand, investigates what role the removal of apartheid played on the state of informational efficiency of the South African equity market using variance-ratio test as developed by Lo and MacKinlay (1988).

If stock prices can be predicted using only historical price information that means the stock market is not efficiently incorporating available information. Such a situation does not foster confidence among new investors in the market who may be interested in diverting some of their savings into stocks rather than more traditional channels. Informational inefficiency of stock prices also distorts resource allocation in an economy. These distortions as well as fostering investors' confidence in the fairness of market prices are serious concerns for stock market regulators as they ensure the transition of their economies to a market based system. Random walk properties of stock returns are seen as an outcome of the efficient market hypothesis i.e. stock prices exhibit unpredictable behavior as they respond to emerging developments rather than historical price information. The presence or absence of random walks in security returns is critical to the formulation of rational expectation models (Liu & Maddala, 1992). Variance-ratio test, as developed by Lo and MacKinlay (1988), provide powerful tests of whether stock returns follow a random walk. These tests use the fact that the variance of the increments of a random walk is linear in the sampling interval. Thus, the variance of two-month returns should be twice as large as that of monthly returns, if the returns follow a random walk. The observed index in a thinly-traded market, like South Africa, may not represent the true underlying index value and consequently, the presence of thin-trading may prompt a systematic bias on the results from the tests used to investigate the state of informational efficiency of a market. Therefore, a modified version of Stoll and Whaley's (1990) approach to correct for infrequent trading (as suggested in Jokivuolle, 1995) is applied to estimate the true unobservable index from the history of the observed index of South Africa. The correction consists of decomposing the log of the observed index into its random and stationary components using the Beveridge and Nelson (1981) methodology.

The results reported in the present study indicate that the state of informational efficiency of the South African equity market has substantially improved during the transition and post-apartheid period compared to the apartheid period. Furthermore, the index return series is reported to be mean-reverting in the post-apartheid period, irrespective of the whether the tests were performed on the observed index or the true index, corrected for infrequent trading.

The remainder of the paper is organized as follows. The detailed steps in the variance-ratio test (Lo & MacKinlay, 1988) and the analytical details of the Beveridge and Nelson (1981) decomposition to estimate the true index are described in Section 2. Data and the reasoning behind subperiod classification are contained in Section 3. Index correction for infrequent trading and empirical results are discussed in Section 4. Section 5 concludes the paper.

2. METHODOLOGY

2.1. Variance-ratio Test

Variance-ratio test compares the ratio of the variances of the stock returns over different holding periods. Under the null hypothesis of a random walk, the variance-ratios are expected to be one. The variance-ratio test allows for the use of overlapping stock return data and thus increases the number of observations used to construct the test statistic. The methodology also includes a correction of the test-statistic for the heteroscedasticity of stock returns. These features increase the efficiency and the power of the tests compared to standard serial correlation tests. In fact, Lo and MacKinlay (1989) show that the variance-ratio test is more powerful than either the Box-Pierce or the Dickey Fuller test for several common time-series processes such as an AR (1) process.

Variance-ratio test uses the fact that the variance of the increments of a random walk is linear in the sampling interval. The variance-ratio, VR(q), is defined as:

$$\frac{\sigma_a^2(q)}{\sigma_b^2(1)}$$

where, $\sigma_a^2(q)$ is an unbiased estimator of $1/q$ times the variance of the qth difference of the series x_t, and $\sigma_b^2(q)$ is an unbiased estimator of the first difference of x_t. These variances are computed as follows:

$$\sigma^2(q) = \frac{1}{m}\sum_{t=q}^{nq}(x_t - x_{t-q} - q\hat{\mu})^2$$

where $m = q\ (nq - q + 1)\ (1 - q/nq)$, $\hat{\mu} = (x_{nq} - x_0)/nq$ and

$$\sigma_b^2(q) = \frac{1}{nq - 1}\sum_{t=1}^{nq}(x_t - x_{t-1} - \hat{\mu})^2$$

where x_0 and x_{nq} are the first and last observations of x_t.

Under homoscedasticity, the asymptotic variance of the variance-ratio is given by, $\phi(q)$:

$$\phi(q) = \frac{2(2q - 1)(q - 1)}{3q(nq)}$$

The standard normal test statistic under homoscedasticity, $Z(q)$, is then given by:

$$Z(q) = \frac{\mathrm{VR}(q) - 1}{[\phi(q)]^{1/2}} \overset{a}{\sim} N(0, 1)$$

where $\overset{a}{\sim}$ indicates that the distributional equivalence is asymptotic.

The heteroscedasticity-consistent asymptotic variance of the variance-ratio, $\phi^*(q)$ is given by:

$$\phi^*(q) = \sum_{j=1}^{q-1}\left[\frac{2(q - j)}{q}\right]^2 \hat{\delta}(j)$$

where

$$\hat{\delta}(j) = \frac{\sum_{t=j+1}^{nq}(x_t - x_{t-1} - \hat{\mu})^2(x_{t-j} - x_{t-j} - x_{t-j-1} - \hat{\mu})^2}{\left[\sum_{k=1}^{nq}(x_t - x_{t-1} - \hat{\mu})^2\right]^2}$$

The standard normal test statistic under heteroscedasticity $Z^*(q)$, is given by

$$Z^*(q) = \frac{\mathrm{VR}(q) - 1}{[\phi^*(q)]^{1/2}} \overset{a}{\sim} N(0, 1)$$

2.2. *Estimating the True Index-Correcting for Infrequent Trading*

Using the Beveridge and Nelson (1981) methodology the observed index is decomposed into its permanent and cyclical component. If we assume that $\tilde{Y}_t^0$ as the log of the true unobservable index corresponding to Y_t^0, the log of the observed index, it can be shown that the permanent component of the log of the observed index equals the log of the true unobserved index (Jokivuolle, 1995). The permanent component of the decomposition of an infinite order MA process can be written as:

$$\tilde{Y}_t^0 = Y_t^0 + \lim_{T\to\infty}\left[\sum_{j=1}^{T-t} R_t^0(j) - (T - t)\mu\right]$$

Where $R_t^0(j)$ is the optimal forecast of R_{t+j}^0 made at time t, and μ is the slope of the ARMA process. It is important to note here that it is well established that any ARMA(p, q) process can be represented as an infinite order MA process. Again following the notation in Jokivuolle (1995), assuming $y_t^0 = R_t^0 - \mu$, the permanent component can be written as:

$$\tilde{Y}_t^0 = Y_t^0 + \lim_{T\to\infty}\left[\sum_{j=1}^{T-t} \hat{y}_t^0(j)\right]$$

An algorithm developed by Newbold (1990) is used to evaluate the second term on the right-hand side.

$$\lim_{T\to\infty}\left[\sum_{j=1}^{T-t} \hat{y}_t^0(j)\right] = \sum_{j=1}^{q} \hat{y}_t^0(j) + (1 - \phi_1 - \cdots - \phi_p)^{-1} \sum_{j=1}^{p}\sum_{i=j}^{p} \phi_1 \hat{y}_t^0(q - j + 1)$$

$$\hat{y}_t^0(i) = \hat{y}_{t+1}^0 \quad \forall i \leq 0$$

where p and q represent the order of the ARMA(p, q) process followed by the log of the observed index.

3. DATA AND CLASSIFICATION OF SUBPERIODS

3.1. Data

The data correspond to monthly JSE All Share Index expressed in local currency. The data obtained from the Meridian Securities (Round Rock, Texas) covers the period January 1975 to May 2003. The JSE All Share Index is an arithmetic average of the prices of their constituent securities, weighted by their market capitalization. This means that for a larger company, its share price movement would have greater effect on the index than that of a smaller company.

A summary of the basic statistics of monthly returns, for both the observed and estimated true index returns, is provided in Table 1. The returns exhibit large standard deviations, negative skewness and positive kurtosis. Negative skewness implies that the return series is more flattened to the left compared to the normal distribution. The kurtosis reported indicates that the stock return distributions have sharper peaks compared to the normal distribution. Furthermore, studentized

Table 1. Descriptive Statistics for the Observed and True Index Returns, Corrected for Infrequent Trading, for the South African Equity Market, Local Currency: January 1975 to May 2003.

Variables	Observed Index Return	True Index Return, Corrected for Infrequent Trading
Mean	1.02	1.07
Median	1.74	1.50
Maximum	16.13	17.17
Minimum	−35.48	−33.88
Std. Dev.	6.61	6.74
Skewness	−0.99	−0.90
Kurtosis	3.18	2.87
Studentized range	7.81	7.57
Observations	340	336

Notes:

(1) Monthly Returns are Computed as $R_t = 100 \times \ln(P_t/P_{t-1})$.

(2) Number of observations in the full sample period differs because the observed index return is corrected for infrequent trading using an ARMA[1, (1, 4)] process.

(3) The studentized range is computed as:

$$\text{Studentized range} = \frac{\text{Max}(R) - \text{Min}(R)}{\sigma_R}$$

where Max(R) is the maximum return, Min(R) is the minimum return, and σ_R is the standard deviation of returns.

ranges, reported in Table 1, are all larger than six suggesting a departure from normality.

3.2. Classification of Subperiods

In order to investigate what role the removal of apartheid played on the state of informational efficiency of the South African equity market the sample period was divided into apartheid, transition and post-apartheid periods. The era of apartheid formally started in 1948 with the government formed by the Afrikaner National Party. The first set reforms aimed at dismantling the apartheid was initiated by President F. W. de Klerk after being elected to the office on September 15, 1989. President de Klerk successfully instituted major reforms that took way some of the apartheid's most vital legal support during his tenure as Presidency which ended with the election of Nelson Mandela as President in April 1994. The new era of a free South African republic began under the leadership of Nelson Mandela. Given this political history, the present study designates the time period from January 1975 through September 1989 as the apartheid period, October 1989 through April 1994 as the transition period (de Klerk's tenure of Presidency), and May 1994 through May 2003 (Mandela and post-Mandela period) as the post-apartheid period. Table 2 reports some basic statistics on the South African equity market during these three periods. Average market capitalization, number of shares traded,

Table 2. Summary Statistics of the South African Equity Market.

Period	Average Market Capitalization (Rand, Million)	Average Market Capitalization (US$, Million)	Average No. of Shares Traded (Million)	Liquidity [(Trading Value × 100)/Average Market Capitalization] in US$
Apartheid Period[a] (1975:01–1989:09)	131,476	68,656	1,045	4.28
Transition Period[b] (1989:10–1994:04)	611,012	115,599	3,270	5.39
Post Apartheid Period[c] (1994:05–2003:05)	1,295,346	152,944	31,232	23.81

Source: 2002 World Stock Exchange Fact Book I, Meridian Securities Markets, LLC, Texas.
[a]Yearly data was used from 1975 through 1989 due to lack of availability of monthly data.
[b]Yearly data was used from 1990 through 1994 due to lack of availability of monthly data.
[c]Yearly data was used from 1995 through 2001 due to lack of availability of monthly data as well yearly data for 2002 and 2003.

and liquidity increased substantially in each successive period. Average market capitalization increased by about 10 times, the average number of shares traded increased by about 30 times, and the liquidity increased by about 6 times during the post-apartheid period compared to the apartheid period. This gives us a clear idea of the strong positive impact the gradual easing and then the formal removal of apartheid did to the South African equity market.

4. INDEX CORRECTION FOR INFREQUENT TRADING AND EMPIRICAL RESULTS

4.1. Index Correction for Infrequent Trading

ARMA[1, (1, 4)] specification is taken as an economically meaningful representation for South African data. The observed index returns are represented as

$$R_t^0 = \mu + \varphi R_{t-1}^0 + \theta_{t-1}^0 + \lambda \varepsilon_{t-4}^0 + \varepsilon_t^0$$

where R_t^0 is the log relative of the observed index levels and μ the slope of the ARMA process. Estimated ARMA coefficients are reported in Table 3 and are highly significant.

4.2. Empirical Results

The empirical results are reported in two parts. First, the results from the variance-ratio test applied on the observed index return series is reported in Table 4. Then the results from the same test on the corrected index return series are reported in

Table 3. Estimated ARMA[1, (1, 4)] Coefficients for the South African Index Returns, Local Currency: January 1975 to May 2003.

	Coefficient (Standard Error)			
	μ	ω	θ	λ
AR	0.01195*	0.8966*	−0.8705*	−0.0735**
	(0.0022)	(0.0556)	(0.0651)	(0.0380)

Notes: The South African Index is modeled as $R_t^0 = \mu + \varphi R_{t-1}^0 + \theta \varepsilon_{t-1}^0 + \lambda \varepsilon_{t-4}^0 + \varepsilon_t^0$ where R_t^0 is the log relative of the observed index levels.

*Indicates statistical significance at the 0.01 level.

**Indicates statistical significance at the 0.05 level.

Table 4. Variance-Ratio Estimates and Variance-Ratio Test Statistics on the Observed Index of the South African Equity Market, Local Currency: January 1975 to May 2003.

	Number of Base Observations Aggregated to Form Variance-Ratios			
	$q = 2$	$q = 4$	$q = 8$	$q = 16$
Panel A: Variance-ratios assuming homoskedasticity				
Full sample period (1975:01 to 2003:05)	1.09 (1.68)	1.16 (1.54)	1.12 (0.73)	1.03 (0.11)
Apartheid period (1975:01 to 1989:09)	1.16* (2.17)	1.29* (2.09)	1.37 (1.67)	1.39 (1.17)
Transition period (1989:10 to 1994:04)	1.02 (0.12)	1.15 (0.58)	1.25 (0.63)	0.92 (−0.13)
Post apartheid period (1994:05 to 2003:05)	1.00 (−0.04)	0.96 (−0.24)	0.69 (−1.07)	0.51 (−1.16)
Panel B: Heteroskedaticity-consistent variance-ratios				
Full sample period (1975:01 to 2003:05)	1.09 (1.79)	1.16 (1.46)	1.12 (0.67)	1.03 (0.10)
Apartheid period (1975:01 to 1989:09)	1.16* (2.17)	1.29* (2.03)	1.37 (1.60)	1.39 (1.15)
Transition period (1989:10 to 1994:04)	1.02 (0.12)	1.15 (0.62)	1.25 (0.67)	0.92 (−0.15)
Post apartheid period (1994:05 to 2003:05)	1.00 (−0.05)	0.96 (−0.22)	0.69 (−0.96)	0.51 (−1.07)

Notes:

(1) The variance-ratios are defined as the ratio of $(1/q)\sigma_q^2$ to σ_1^2 for values of $q = 2$, 4, 8, and 16, where σ_i^2 is the variance of the observed index return defined as $\ln(P_t/P_{t-i})$. The value estimates of VR(q) and $Z(q)$ under the assumption of homoskedasticity are presented in Panel A. Panel B contains the estimates of VR(q) and the heteroskedasticity-consistent $Z^*(q)$.

(2) An asterisk (*) indicates statistical significance at the 0.05 level.

Table 5. The base observation interval is one month. The variance-ratio is computed for each of the intervals $q = 2, 4, 8$, and 16. That means, variance-ratio is calculated for each q by comparing the variance of the one-month base interval with that of two-month, four-month, eight-month and sixteen-month observation intervals.

The estimated variance-ratios for the monthly index return series, and the corresponding test statistics, Z and Z^* (in parentheses) under conditions of homoskedasticity and heteroskedasticity respectively, are reported in Panels A and Panels B of both Tables 4 and 5. Qualitatively, the results reported in both tables are similar which indicates that infrequent trading does not have a whole lot of impact on the observed index in the South African equity market. Four

Table 5. Variance-Ratio Estimates and Variance-Ratio Test Statistics on the True Index, Corrected for Infrequent Trading, of the South African Equity Market, Local Currency: January 1975 to May 2003.

	Number of Base Observations Aggregated to Form Variance-Ratios			
	$q = 2$	$q = 4$	$q = 8$	$q = 16$
Panel A: Variance-ratios assuming homoskedasticity				
Full sample period (1975:01 to 2003:05)	1.14 (2.65)*	1.13 (1.27)	0.94 (−0.40)	0.81 (0.78)
Apartheid period (1975:01 to 1989:09)	1.20* (2.68)	1.25 (1.73)	1.09 (0.51)	1.05 (0.16)
Transition period (1989:10 to 1994:04)	1.12 (0.85)	1.15 (0.59)	1.12 (0.30)	0.81 (−0.31)
Post apartheid period (1994:05 to 2003:05)	1.07 (0.68)	0.97 (−0.17)	0.61 (−1.37)	0.44 (−1.31)
Panel B: Heteroskedaticity-consistent variance-ratios				
Full sample period (1975:01 to 2003:05)	1.14 (2.78)*	1.13 (1.18)	0.94 (−0.37)	0.81 (−0.74)
Apartheid period (1975:01 to 1989:09)	1.20* (2.60)	1.25 (1.69)	1.09 (0.51)	1.05 (0.16)
Transition period (1989:10 to 1994:04)	1.12 (0.85)	1.15 (0.62)	1.12 (0.32)	0.81 (−0.35)
Post apartheid period (1994:05 to 2003:05)	1.07 (0.93)	0.97 (−0.15)	0.61 (−1.17)	0.44 (−1.18)

Notes:

(1) The variance-ratios are defined as the ratio of $(1/q)\sigma_q^2$ to σ_1^2 for values of $q = 2, 4, 8$, and 16, where σ_i^2 is the variance of the index return, corrected for infrequent trading, defined as $\ln(P_t/P_{t-i})$. The value estimates of VR(q) and $Z(q)$ under the assumption of homoskedasticity are presented in Panel A. Panel B contains the estimates of VR(q) and the heteroskedasticity-consistent $Z^*(q)$.
(2) An asterisk (*) indicates statistical significance at the 0.05 level.

clear patterns can be detected in the results reported in Tables 4 and 5. First, the estimated variance-ratios are significantly larger than unity, in shorter intervals, during the apartheid period. Second, the variance-ratios are not significantly different from one in any interval during the transition and post apartheid period. This indicates that the stock prices seem to follow random walk during the transition and post-apartheid period only. As random walk properties of stock returns are seen as an outcome of the efficient market hypothesis we can infer that the state of informational efficiency of the South Africa has improved significantly with the gradual easing and then the formal removal of apartheid. These results reported in the present study compliment the Lamba and Otchere (2001) study that reports that South Africa has become much more integrated, economically and financially, with the major developed markets during the post apartheid period. Third, the estimated variance-ratios at all the intervals are larger than one during the apartheid and transition periods.[1] Finally, the estimated variance-ratios during the post-apartheid period are all less than one (except at interval $q = 2$) and gradually decline. Since the variance-ratio minus one, [VR $(q) - 1$], is approximately a weighted sum of the first $q - 1$ autocorrelation coefficients (Lo & MacKinlay, 1988) we can infer from the last two points that the index return series exhibits positive serial correlation during both the apartheid and transition periods and negative serial correlation during the post-apartheid period. The presence of negative serial correlation during the post-apartheid period, in turn, implies that the index return series is mean-reverting during the post-apartheid period.[2]

5. CONCLUDING REMARKS

The present study investigates the impact of gradual easing and then the formal removal of apartheid on the informational efficiency of the South African equity market. Monthly closing index data in local currency is used over the period January 1975 to May 2003. The entire sample period is then divided into apartheid (1975:01–1989:09), transition (1989:10) and post-apartheid (1994:05 through 2003:05) periods. Variance-ratio estimates (Lo & MacKinlay, 1988) obtained during the apartheid, transition and post-apartheid periods clearly indicate that the state of informational efficiency of the South African equity market has substantially improved during the transition and post-apartheid periods as compared to the apartheid period. This suggests that domestic investors might not be able to detect patterns in stock prices and develop strategies to earn abnormal returns during the transition and post-apartheid period. Furthermore, the index return series is mean-reverting in the post-apartheid period. This indicates that investors, on the average, would get some average reward for bearing the risk of the market during the post-apartheid period which, in turn, can be expected to retain and increase investors' continued participation in the market place.

NOTES

1. Except at $q = 16$ during the transition period.
2. Bradfield and Ardington (1997) report similar mean-reverting behavior for the annual index return series over the period 1980 through 1996 in South Africa. However, at a later date, when the authors extend the sample period to cover index returns from 1960 through 1999 this phenomenon of annual mean-reversion turns out to be insignificant.

REFERENCES

Beveridge, S., & Nelson, C. R. (1981). A new approach to decomposition of economic time series into permanent and transitory components with particular attention to measurement of business cycle. *Journal of Monetary Economics*, *7*, 151–174.

Jokivuolle, E. (1995). Measuring true stock index value in the presence of infrequent trading. *Journal of Financial and Quantitative Analysis*, *30*, 455–464.

Lamba, A., & Otchere, I. (2001). An analysis of the dynamic relationships between the South African equity market and major world equity markets. *Multinational Finance Journal*, *5*, 201–224.

Lo, A., & MacKinlay, C. (1988). Stock market prices do not follow random walks: Evidence from a simple specification test. *Review of Financial Studies*, *1*, 41–66.

Lo, A., & MacKinlay, C. (1989). The size and power of variance ratio test in finite samples: A Monte Carlo investigation. *Journal of Econometrics*, *40*, 203–238.

Newbold, P. (1990). Precise and efficient contribution of the Beveridge Nelson decomposition of economic time series. *Journal of Monetary Economics*, *26*, 453–457.

Stoll, H. R., & Whaley, R. E. (1990). The dynamics of stock index and stock index futures returns. *Journal of Financial and Quantitative Analysis*, *25*, 441–468.

World Stock Exchange Fact Book I (2002). Meridian Securities Markets, LLC, Texas.

BANK MERGERS IN SOUTH KOREA: DOES GOVERNMENT INTERVENTION ADD VALUE?

Sungho Choi and James P. Murtagh

ABSTRACT

This paper examines the effects of mergers and acquisitions among South Korean commercial banks from 1998 to 2002. We investigate the market reaction to merger announcements and the potential impact associated with government intervention in the M&A process. In particular, we examine the value of "government seal of approval" (Gupta, 1997) in the purchase and assumption of five failed Korean banks in 1998. The results indicate significant negative abnormal returns to acquirer banks as well as target banks in the entire sample, ranging from −3.41 to −9.96%. Contrary to Gupta's (1997) claim about the value addition of government seal of approval, we do not find any value of the government seal of approval in South Korean failed bank mergers. Results of solvent bank mergers reveal that bidders and targets exhibit positive announcement date abnormal returns, consistent with Cornett and De (1991a, b), while targets experience large negative abnormal returns afterward. Finally, 1998 mergers exhibit negative abnormal returns for both bidders and targets, while the result is somewhat different for the post 1998 mergers. The results appear sensitive to the level of government involvement and the financial health of the participants.

Bank and Financial Market Efficiency: Global Perspectives
Research in Banking and Finance, Volume 5, 169–193

ISSN: 1567-7915/doi:10.1016/S1567-7915(04)05009-8

1. INTRODUCTION

The South Korean economy was so devastated by the financial crisis starting late 1997 that the country required a $58 billion bailout from the IMF to recover. Joh (2003) argues that a weak legal environment and poor governance system made many countries suffer during the crisis in Asia. The financial crisis and conditions imposed by the IMF forced the South Korean government to improve the country's corporate governance as well as reducing debt and reliance on loans. The financial crisis also changed financial regulation and the banking system of South Korea in many different ways. At the time of the crisis, twelve Korean banks had capital adequacy ratios lower than the 8% BIS threshold. The government forced these banks to submit rehabilitation plans. Five other commercial banks were in such deep trouble that they were ordered by the government to close their doors on June 29, 1998. These failed banks were merged with relatively solvent banks through a purchase and assumptions (P&As) method. In this type of merger, the acquiring banks assumed the liabilities and purchased only the good assets. This was the first incidence of bank closure in Korean banking history.

In addition to the closure of five poorly performing commercial banks in June of 1998, there has been considerable merger activity among South Korean commercial banks. Korean banks have been seeking to become larger through mergers and acquisitions in order to survive under intensifying competition from domestic banks as well as foreign banks. The belief is that only large and diversified banks can compete and survive in the global competition. Size has taken on greater importance following the birth of a mega-bank through the marriage announcement between Kook Min Bank and Housing and Commercial Bank (H&C) in December, 2000.

Previous research on South Korean commercial banks has focused on bank efficiency using balance sheet and income statement variables. One important contribution of this paper is to investigate the market reaction to merger and acquisition announcements among Korean commercial banks, under varying conditions of solvency and government intervention. Earlier studies of mergers of financial firms report that bidders experience positive abnormal returns (Bertin et al., 1989; Cornett & De, 1991a, b; James & Weir, 1987a, b). Accordingly, we investigate whether the market reaction to mergers and acquisitions announcement among South Korean commercial banks is consistent with this result.

While many studies on bank mergers and acquisitions test the market valuation of solvent bank mergers, few have investigated the failed bank cases. Gupta (1997) investigated the value effect of a firm receiving a regulatory seal of approval when a bank acquires a failed bank. He claimed that since a regulatory seal of approval reduces market uncertainty about the financial health of the bidding bank, obtaining a regulatory seal of approval adds firm value. Another contribution of this paper is the investigation of the value of the regulatory seal of approval on South Korean banks by studying the purchase and assumption of the five failed banks in 1998. We examine bidder bank gains and test whether a government seal of approval added any value to an acquirer.

Pettway and Trifts (1995), James and Weir (1987b) and Bertin et al. (1989) investigated FDIC-assisted acquisitions of failed banks. They found positive abnormal returns to winning bidders. James and Weir (1987b) claimed that this positive return was the evidence of wealth transfers from the FDIC to the bidder bank. Since the South Korean Government was deeply involved in many merger cases, we examine the effect of the government involvement in merger and acquisition activities. Specifically, we investigate the market reaction to the government-assisted mergers with and without failed bank mergers of 1998.

Neely (1987) and Sushka and Bendeck (1988) study solvent bank acquisitions arranged without FDIC assistance in the 1980s. Neely (1987) finds a significant abnormal return for the target banks during the announcement period while the bidder banks experience an insignificant positive return for the same period. In this respect, we investigate how the market reacts to bank mergers between solvent banks in which there was no government involvement. Finally, if we include failed bank mergers in the sample, ten mergers occurred in 1998 and six more occurred in 1999–2002. We examine whether there is a difference between mergers occurred in 1998 and post-1998 mergers.

Our study shows there is a significant negative announcement period abnormal return to acquirer banks as well as target banks on average for all merger announcements. The abnormal return ranges from −3.41 to −9.96% depending on the event windows. In addition, there is an evidence of speculation on target banks being acquired, possible evidence of leakage of news prior to the official merger announcement. However, we do not have any significant return to bidders prior to announcement date. Unlike Gupta's (1997) finding, our study does not find any value addition of obtaining a government seal of approval for South Korean failed bank cases. Our failed bank mergers reveal that the market penalizes a bidder that acquires a failed bank. In this case, the market does not recognize the vale of governmental subsidies to the bidder bank. The market reacts to the failed bank mergers negatively but not in a significant way that it does not believe in the wealth transfer from the government to the bidder banks.

The result is relatively consistent with our prediction when we examine the effect of the government involvement in merger activities. If the government is involved in mergers, the market reacts negatively regardless of whether we consider bidders or targets. Bidder and target banks experience a small return before the public announcement date. Bidder banks are penalized heavily after the announcement, having a statistically significant negative abnormal return, while the return to target banks is not significant. Using solvent bank mergers, our result reveals that a bidder and a target exhibit a positive announcement date abnormal return and this result is somewhat consistent with Cornett and De (1991a, b), while a target experiences a large negative abnormal return afterward. Finally, the result of year 1998 mergers exhibits a negative abnormal return regardless whether it is a bidder or a target while the result is somewhat different for the post 1998 mergers. The result is mixed depending on the government involvement and the bank's financial health.

The rest of the paper is organized as follows: Section 2 presents a brief review of the literature related to the effects of bank mergers and acquisitions. Section 3 presents the brief history of the South Korean banking system and summarizes the relevant events to this study. Section 4 describes the data, presents summary statistics and gives an explanation of methodology that is employed in this study. Section 5 presents the results of the analysis on the effects of mergers and acquisitions among Korean commercial banks. Concluding remarks are presented in Section 6.

2. LITERATURE REVIEW

Many researchers have investigated bank mergers and acquisitions in the U.S. and the world. James and Weir (1987a) examine 60 bank mergers and acquisitions and find statistically significant small positive abnormal returns to the bidder bank. They investigate the effect of competition in the market for bank acquisitions on the bidder's stock returns. They find that gains to bidders are positively related to the number of alternative target firms available and negatively related to the number of other potential bidders in the market.

Neely (1987) studies the effects on shareholders' returns of merger and acquisition announcements for individual banks and bank holding companies. He examines 26 solvent bank mergers that are without FDIC involvement for the period of 1979–1985 and finds that small abnormal returns for both acquirers and targets occur as early as 10 weeks and 7 weeks before public announcement of bank acquisitions. Very large significant abnormal returns occurred for target banks during the announcement period while the bidders experienced insignificant positive returns for the same period.

James and Weir (1987b) investigate whether the FDIC failed bank auctions transfer wealth to the acquiring banks using a sample of 19 purchase and assumptions during 1973–1982. They find that winning bidder banks experience significant positive abnormal returns from the FDIC auctions. Therefore, they claim that this is the evidence for wealth transfers from the FDIC to winning bidders.

Sushka and Bendeck (1998) analyze the effect of bank mergers on the market value of acquiring firms during the period surrounding the approval of mergers by the Federal Reserve. Using a sample of 41 solvent bank mergers over the period 1972–1985, they find that acquirer banks realized negative returns for external mergers indicating that the market views the acquisition of target banks as negative net present investment while there were positive abnormal returns to bidder banks for internal mergers.

Bertin et al. (1989) study the returns to acquiring banks involved in FDIC-assisted mergers for the period of 1982–1987. Using a sample of 33 banks acquiring failed banks under the assistance from the FDIC, they examine whether acquiring banks overbid when engage in an FDIC arranged merger. They find that acquiring banks gain significant positive abnormal returns over the period just prior to and on the announcement date. However, unlike some previous studies, they find that successful acquirers underbid failed targets.

Cornett and De (1991a, b) investigate stock market reactions to the announcements of interstate bank mergers following the Douglas Amendment to the Bank Holding Company Act of 1956. Using 152 interstate bank acquisition bids, they find that there are significant positive announcement period abnormal returns for target banks that are the consistent result with the non-banking industry merger results. They report, however, that unlike the result of non-banking mergers, the bidder banks experience significant positive abnormal returns as well.

Gupta (1997) examines whether obtaining a regulatory seal of approval adds value to a bidder bank that acquires the insured deposit of a failed bank from the FDIC. Using 37 winning bidders in insured deposit transfers, he finds that a bidder realizes a small significant positive abnormal return by the announcement. He concludes that the evidence supports the proposition that observed value gains to winning bidders are driven by removing uncertainty about health of bidder banks through a regulatory seal of approval.

Gupta et al. (1997a) examine the wealth effects of acquisitions of solvent stock-held thrift institutions and investigate the underlying possible motivations for mergers. Using a sample of 138 acquisitions for the period of 1979–1992, they find that firms acquiring solvent stock held thrifts realized statistically significant negative announcement date abnormal returns. They report that the motives of bidding firm provide evidence indicating the presence of synergy, agency, and hubris motivations for both pre and post FIRREA periods.

Gupta et al. (1997b) investigate the market reaction to acquisitions of failed thrifts before and after the passage of FIRREA. They find that unlike pre-FIRREA deals the acquirers do not realize significant abnormal returns in RTC assisted transactions. The evidence suggests that regulatory and institutional changes instituted by FIRREA resulted in an improvement in the resolution process for failed thrifts.

Berger et al. (2000) review research studies on the causes and consequences of consolidation and analyze cross-border banking efficiency in five home countries. They study the home field advantage and the global field advantage hypotheses on cross-boarder financial institutions mergers. They find that in some countries the aggregate domestic banks hold an advantage over foreign banks. Foreign banks from some countries have a competitive advantage in some other countries.

Gupta and Misra (2002) investigate the gains to bidders of failed thrifts in auctions conducted by the FSLIC-assisted acquisitions during the 1980s and the RTC-assisted acquisitions in the early 1990s. They examined whether the earlier experience of failed thrift transactions helped regulators to improve the auction process. They find that earlier failed thrifts resolution does not lead to improved regulatory performance. They report that regulatory learning works only to repeated acquirers, eliminating abnormal returns to the bidders and reducing taxpayer costs of failure resolution.

Bessler and Murtagh (2002) investigate the stock market reactions to Canadian banks' merger announcements of cross-border acquisitions of financial services firms. They find that foreign acquisitions in the wealth management and retail banking sectors create value, while foreign acquisitions in the insurance sector do not create value. The opposite is true for Canadian domestic acquisitions.

3. BRIEF HISTORY OF THE KOREAN BANKING SYSTEM

The Bank of Korea (BOK) is the central bank of Korea and it provides a precise and specific historical overview of the Korean banking system as well as the Korean financial system. We adapt much of the historical information on the Korean banking system from the Bank of Korea (2002).

The Korean banking system has been transformed many times since its beginning. Until 1945, the Japanese banks dominated the Korean banking system because of Japanese colonialism. The National Assembly of the Republic of Korea passed a series of central and general banking statutes, and created a new central bank, the Bank of Korea, on June 12, 1950. However, the banking system did not work properly during the 1950s because all banks were essentially government controlled and failed to exercise their roles.

During the 1960s and 1970s, major components of the Korean financial system were nationalized after the short period of privatization in the late 1950s. The government used its control of banks to mobilize financial resources and pursue its export-oriented industrialization policy (Bank of Korea, 2002). Hao, Hunter and Yang (2001) report that in the late 70s, policy loans, which support government programs, account for nearly 80% of domestic credit.

Although the economy was growing under the nationalized banking system, some policymakers recognized that privatization and deregulation of the banking sector was necessary. The General Banking Act was revised in 1982 and again in 1991, 1993 and 1994. These revisions gave commercial banks more autonomy in their business activities and management. By the early 1980s, the government tried to reduce the extent of its control on credit allocation. The government bank, Sang Up Bank, was privatized in 1972, followed by Hanil Bank in 1981. The privatization of national banks continued so that Korea First Bank and Bank of Seoul were privatized in 1982 followed by Cho Hung Bank in 1983. These five national banks dominated the Korean commercial banking industry in the early 1980s. Kook Min Bank was privatized in January 1995 and Housing & Commercial (H&C) Bank was privatized in August 1997.

While there was a series of bank privatizations, the establishment of several new banks created more competition among Korean commercial banks during this same time period. Shin Han Bank was the first one opened in 1982 and Hanmi Bank began operation in 1983. Korea Exchange Bank converted to a commercial bank in 1989. Dongwhoa, Dongnam, and Daedong all opened their doors in 1989. Finally, Hana and Boram began operation in 1992 and Pyongwha (Peace Bank) opened in 1993.

Although the number of banks increased over the last two decades, their profitability did not. Gilbert and Wilson (1998) argue that because of deregulation and influencing bank lending decisions through more informal means called "window guidance," the Korean commercial banking system was in a critical condition in the mid-1980s. Bad loans rose to over 7%, however, none of the Korean commercial banks were closed in this period.

Bank of Seoul and Korea First Bank became the first insolvent commercial banks during the Korean financial crisis. Apparently they were too big to fail. The government nationalized and recapitalized both banks in January 1998. In February 1998, the Monetary Board of the Bank of Korea identified 12 of the remaining 24 Korean banks as falling below the BIS capital adequacy standard of 8%. They were Cho Hung, Hanil, Korea Exchange, Sang Up, Dongwhoa, Dongnam, Daedong, Pyongwha, Chung Cheong, Kyong Gi, Chung Buk, and Kang Won.

The Financial Supervisory Commission (FSC) examined the financial conditions of those twelve banks after the management improvement orders or recommendations of the Monetary Board, it ordered the five banks to close: Daedong, Dongnam, Dongwha, Kyong Gi, and Chung Cheong. Those five banks closed and their assets were added to solvent banks through purchase and assumptions (P&As) by five relatively sound commercial banks on June 29, 1998. Specifically, Kook Min acquired Daedong, Housing & Commercial acquired Dongnam, Shinhan acquired Dongwha, Hanmi acquired Kyong Gi, and Hana acquired Chung Cheong.

Consolidation among banks started after the closure of five commercial banks and has continued to 2002, a complete timeline is in Appendix. The first merger between commercial banks occurred in July 31, 1998 when Sang Up bank and Hanil bank announced their merger creating the new Hanvit starting operation in January 1999. Hana bank and Boram bank announced their merger on September 7, 1998 and became Hana starting operation in January 1999. Kook Min bank announced its acquisition of Korea Long-Term Credit bank in September 11, 1998. Cho Hung bank announced to acquire Kang Won, and Hyundai investment trust company in December 17, 1998.

Korea First bank became the first Korean commercial bank to be sold to a foreign firm on December 31, 1998. Newbridge Capital acquired 51% of Korea First ownership by purchasing its shares from the Korean Government. In February 11, 1999, Cho Hung bank acquired Chung Buk bank. Shin Han bank announced its merger with Cheju bank in December 8, 2000. Hanvit, Kwang Ju, Kyong Nam, and Hanaro merchant bank merged together and created Woori Financial Holding company on December 13, 2000 to become the first financial holding company in South Korea. Kook Min and Housing & Commercial merged together and became Kook Min in December 22, 2000. Shinhan became Shinhan Financial Group Company in 2001. Peace bank was acquired by Hanvit in November 14, 2001 and became a member of the Woori Financial Holding company. On September 13, 2002, the Korean government approved the purchase of Bank of Seoul by Hana bank. This merger was completed by November 2002. On October 2002, the Korean government announced that it plans to sell its 80% ownership of Cho Hung bank to the public.

As there have been many changes in the number of banks as well as the changes in name and ownership, some of its major banking regulations have also been changed. The General Banking Act was revised on December 1982 to give banks more discretion and to set limits on the amount of bank stocks that could be held by a single shareholder. The purpose of this limitation on ownership is to prevent the large business groups in South Korea, Chaebols, from controlling a bank and using a bank as its private bank. The ownership restriction in 1982 was 8% and was decreased to 4% under the revision of the General

Banking Act of December 1994. The exception of this limitation was possible up until 12% but it was abolished by the revision of the General Banking Act of January 1998.

Under the revision of 2002, the current ownership limitation is 10%, but it is required to notify to FSC if the ownership exceeds 4%. There are also a few exceptions allowed: the ownership by the government and the Korean Deposit Insurance Corporation (KDIC), regional banks (15%). The ownership restriction was applied differently for the foreigners and foreign financial institutions under the revision of 1998. However, the limitation is applied in a same way to Korean firms. Foreign firms can own up to 10% (15% for regional banks) and need to be approved if their ownership exceeds 10, 25, and 33% which is the same regulation for Korean firms.

In order to strengthen the corporate governance structure of financial institutions, a number of related acts were revised. Under the revision of the General Banking Act of 2000, banks are required to change the title of their non-executive directors to outside directors and establish an audit committee two-thirds of whose members should be outside directors. Under the revision of 2000, the bank has to have at least 3 outside board members, and the number of outside board member should be at least 50% of the total board members.

4. DATA AND METHODOLOGY

In order to study the stock market reaction to the series of mergers and acquisitions, we need stock market information so that the sample data is taken from the Korean Stock Exchange (KSE). The data set is obtained from the KSE and contains date, securities code, opening/high/low/closing price, trading volume, trading value, company name, standard price, number of listed shares, PER, dividend yield, market value and industry code. We carefully sort out all Korean commercial banks from the original data set for the period of 1998 to 2002. By using a closing price and dividends, we calculate individual bank's returns.

The total number of commercial banks varies in each year due to the several mergers and acquisitions over the same period. We exclude banks when they are nationalized and de-listed. We investigate the abnormal return (AR) of South Korean commercial banks for all events that occurred over the period from 1998 to 2002. Among the sample banks, national banks are headquartered in the main financial district in Seoul with branch networks across the nation. The main business focus of national banks are short-term loans and their primary sources of funding are customer deposits and borrowing from the central bank. The average borrowing from the central bank is very small compared to customer deposits. The rest of them are regional banks that are headquartered in major cities and mainly operated locally.

The measurement of abnormal return generated from particular stock in response to certain event is known as event study. In this paper, we use standard event study methodology to test for abnormal stock returns surrounding the specific company events. The event date is defined as the official announcement date in which banks announce in public. We determine these event dates by comparing two Korean leading newspapers, Chosun Ilbo and Maeil KyungJae ShinMoon (MaeKyung). Chosun Ilbo is the leading daily new paper in South Korea, similar to the *New York Times* in the U.S. and MaeKyung is the leading business newspaper, similar to the *Wall Street Journal* in the US. The official announcement dates can be found in the Table 1.

We use a common event study methodology and assume security returns are driven by a single-index market model, given by

$$R_{i,t} = \alpha_i + \beta_i R_{m,t} + \varepsilon_{i,t} \tag{1}$$

where $R_{i,t}$ is the return of security i on day t, $R_{m,t}$ is the return on a market index that is KOSPI on day t, and α and β are market model coefficients. Deviations from the expected return for security i on day t, given by the market model, are termed abnormal returns.

Table 1. Summary for Mergers and Acquisitions During the Period 1998–2002: Bidder, Target and Resulting Bank.

Announcement	Bidder Bank	Target Bank	Result
6/29/1998	5 Banks[a]	5 Failed Bank Closure[a]	Bidder Name
7/31/1998	Sang Up	Hanil	Hanvit
9/07/1998	Hana	Boram	Hana
9/11/1998	Kook Min	Long Term Capital	Kook Min
12/17/1998	Cho Hung	Kang Won	Cho Hung
12/31/1998	Newbridge Capital	Korea First	Korea First
2/11/1999	Cho Hung	Chung Buk	Cho Hung
12/08/2000	Shin Han	Che Ju	Shin Han Financial
12/13/2000	Hanvit	Kwangju, Kyung Nam	Woori Financial
12/22/2000	Kookmin	Housing & Commercial	Kookmin
11/14/2001	Hanvit	Peace	Hanvit
9/13/2002	Hana	Seoul	Hana

[a]Kook Min acquired Daedong, Housing & Commercial acquired Dongnam, Shin Han acquired Dongwhoa, Hanmi acquired Kyong Gi, and Hana acquired Chung Cheong.

Daily abnormal returns for each firm between $t = -10$ and $t = 10$ in event time are computed as

$$\mathrm{AR}_{i,t} = R_{i,t} - (\hat{\alpha}_i + \hat{\beta}_i R_{m,t}) \tag{2}$$

where $\mathrm{AR}_{i,t}$ is the abnormal return for firm i on day t, and the other variables are as defined above. For each firm i, we estimate the market model coefficients by ordinary least square (OLS) using daily returns for the 200-day period $t = (-110, -11{:}\ 11, 110)$, then compute the cumulative abnormal return (CAR) by summing the AR over various intervals. In the absence of abnormal performance, the expected values of AR and CAR are zero.

For each day $t = (-10, 10)$, we obtain the portfolio average returns as:

$$\mathrm{AAR}_t = \frac{1}{N}\sum_{t=1}^{N} \mathrm{AR}_{i,t} \tag{3}$$

where N is the number of firms. We then compute the cumulative average abnormal return (CAAR) by summing the AAR over various intervals. In the absence of abnormal performance, the expected values of AAR and CAAR are zero. Test statistics for AAR and CAAR are based on the average standardized abnormal return (ASAR_t) and the average standardized cumulative abnormal return (ASCAR_t) and their descriptions and derivations are well explained by Gupta (1997).

Table 2 presents the summary characteristics of the 16 mergers and acquisitions included in the sample. It presents the summary statistics (mean, standard deviation, and median) for the value of total asset of participating banks, the value of total deposit as well as the 200-day average daily stock return. We separate the sample into each sub-category based on whether they are a bidder or a target. We examine the values of asset and deposit in a group: total sample mergers, failed banks mergers, government assisted mergers, no government involved mergers (solvent bank mergers), year-1998 mergers and post-1998 mergers. Table 2 presents the descriptive statistics of the mergers based on the above category. For all mergers, the average asset size of bidder is about 56 trillion Won and its standard deviation is about 24 trillion Won which indicates that the size of mergers varies widely. The value of the total deposit is also very similar to the value of asset. On average, the target firms are relatively small compared to the bidders. Their average asset size is about 15 trillion Won which is 29% of the average asset size of the bidders. The average deposit of target banks is about 32% of the average deposit of the bidder banks.

There are five failed banks in our sample. In these transactions, bidders on average have 42 trillion Won in assets and the value of their deposits is about

Table 2. Summary Statistics for Mergers and Acquisitions During the Period 1998–2002 (Billion Won).

	Mean	S.D.	Median
Value of asset			
Bidder	56,003	24,809	47,416
Target	15,551	17,438	7,403
Value of deposit			
Bidder deposit	31,375	15,347	30,334
Target deposit	10,759	13,455	4,629
Failed bank mergers			
Bidder asset	42,525	24,305	42,560
Target asset	6,029	1,004	5,884
Bidder deposit	20,812	10,607	20,448
Target deposit	4,159	455	4,337
Government assisted mergers			
Bidder asset	61,761	18,497	49,568
Target asset	16,489	15,586	10,796
Bidder deposit	37,397	11,921	35,553
Target deposit	11,517	13,354	6,709
No government involved			
Bidder asset	65,033	37,524	81,975
Target asset	32,417	26,188	23,552
Bidder deposit	34,927	23,927	36,591
Target deposit	21,660	22,752	10,667
1998 mergers and acquisitions			
Bidder asset	50,489	27,738	43,188
Target asset	15,216	15,388	6,903
Bidder deposit	23,590	9,767	21,431
Target deposit	11,787	11,711	4,493
Post-1998 mergers			
Bidder asset	64,275	18,853	61,175
Target asset	16,029	21,336	7,447
Bidder deposit	43,051	12,826	42,008
Target deposit	12,177	16,524	4,988
200-day average return			
Bidder	0.11%	0.46%	0.19%
Target	−0.10%	0.68%	−0.17%
KOSPI (market index)	0.14%	0.24%	0.14%

20 trillion Won. In comparison, the target banks have assets valued at 6 trillion Won, which is about 14% of the value of the acquirers. Their standard deviation is relatively low indicating that the targets are about the same size and are very small compared to the bidders. Therefore, we assume that the Korean government allows only small banks to fail, which is very common practice in the rest of the world. The government-assisted mergers are mergers in which the government was involved either as a bidder or as a target. In these merger cases, the government usually provided some kind of subsidy, in the form of tax benefits, lower interest borrowings or both. The descriptive statistics indicate that these mergers were very close to all merger cases which is somewhat consistent with our expectation. Since 13 mergers out of 16 are government assisted mergers, the resulting statistics from this case would be very close to overall merger statistics. However, the values of asset and deposit are little smaller that those of all mergers. The average asset size is about 43 trillion Won while the deposit is about 12 trillion Won.

When two solvent banks merge together, the government is only involved as a regulator. Therefore, the government is not actually involved in merger proposal. The average bidder asset value for transactions between solvent banks is about 65 trillion Won which is the highest value in any category. The average deposits are valued at 35 trillion Won. The target banks' assets are 37 trillion Won on average while the deposits are about 21 trillion Won. The average bidder asset value of 1998 mergers and acquisitions is 50 trillion Won while the average bidder asset value of post-1998 merger is 64 trillion Won about 28% increase in value. Their deposits, however, increased merely 79%. On the other hand, the value of the target banks did not vary much between two groups, assets increased 6% and deposits increased 9%.

5. EMPIRICAL RESULTS

We first analyze the stock market reaction to all merger announcements among South Korean commercial banks for the period of 1998–2002. We also examine the failed bank mergers of June 29, 1998. Next, we analyze the effect of government involvement to the proposed mergers by separating the events into two: one is with government involvement and the other is without. We also separate all merger events into two groups depending upon its financial condition and examine the effect of the financial condition to the proposed mergers. Finally, we investigate whether there is any difference in the market reaction for two different event groups: events in 1998 vs. post-1998 mergers.

5.1. All Proposed Mergers

There are total 16 mergers and acquisitions among Korean commercial banks for the period of 1998–2002. Table 1 lists the announcement dates as well as the name of bidder and target banks. There were total 16 merger events for the period and 10 of which were announced in 1998 including 5 failed banks mergers of June 29, 1998. We calculate abnormal returns (AR) using a single index market model, average abnormal returns, average cumulative abnormal return (CAAR) and average standardized cumulative abnormal return (ASCAR) for all 16 merger events.

Table 3 presents CAAR values and associated significance statistics for various event windows for the entire sample of 16 bank mergers. Even though it is not reported in the table, for the nine days preceding the announcement, the AAR for bidders is positive on 6 days and negative on 3 days and for target it is positive on seven days and negative on two days. The CAAR for bidders for period $t = (-10,-2)$ is 3.59% which is not significant (Z-value = 0.44) while the CAAR for target for the same window is −4.10% which is not significant (Z-value = −0.21). For the ten days following the announcement, the AAR (not reported here) for bidders is positive on two days and negative on 8 days while the AAR for targets is positive on four days and negative on six days. The CAAR of bidders for the window $t = (1,10)$ is –9.03% which is significant (Z-value = −2.18) while the CAAR of targets for the same window is −8.17% which is also significant (Z-value = −1.62) at 10% level.

The CAAR of bidders for the two-day announcement period $t = (-1,0)$ is 0.18% which is not significant while the CAAR of target for the same window is

Table 3. All Bank Mergers ($N = 16$).

Window	Bidders		Targets	
	CAAR (%)	Z-Statistic	CAAR (%)	Z-Statistic
(−10,10)	−5.26	−1.186	−11.70	−1.145
(−10,−2)	3.59	0.444	−4.10	−0.214
(−5,−2)	2.27	0.351	−14.53***	−3.979
(−1,0)	0.18	0.209	0.57	0.128
(−1,1)	−3.41	−1.221	−4.87	−1.245
(−3,3)	−3.23	−0.747	−9.96*	−1.891
(1,5)	−7.68**	−2.371	−7.83*	−1.743
(1,10)	−9.03**	−2.181	−8.17*	−1.616

*10% level.
**5% level.
***1% level.

0.57% which is not significant. For bidders, the CAAR for the $t = (1,5)$ window is −7.68% which is significant at 5% level. For target banks, the CAAR for the $t = (-5,-2)$ window is −14.53% and it is significant at the any level while the CAAR for the $t = (-3,3)$ window is −9.96% and it is significant at the 10% level.

Overall, target banks as well as bidder banks experienced negative abnormal returns in general. This result is not consistent with those of many other bank merger papers (Cornett & De, 1991a, b; James & Weir, 1987). Unlike the past researches, South Korean bank mergers reveal that both bidders and targets are penalized by the market.

5.2. Failed Bank Mergers

Gupta (1997) argues that obtaining a regulatory seal of approval adds to firm value. His study finds significant announcement abnormal returns for firms acquiring the assets of a failed bank. He then argues that this significant abnormal return is evidence of the increase in firm value by obtaining a regulatory seal of approval. This seal of approval results in the transfer of wealth from the government to the acquirer. We apply his approach on the South Korean failed bank mergers.

Table 4 presents CAAR values and associated significance statistics for various event windows for the sample of failed bank mergers. For the nine days preceding the announcement, the AAR for bidder banks is positive on three days and negative on six days. The CAAR for the period $t = (-10,-2)$ is −5.97% which is not significant (Z-value = −1.13). For the ten days following the announcement, the AAR is positive on three days and negative on seven days. The CAAR of bidders for the window $t = (1,10)$ is −6.43% which is not significant (Z-value = −1.20).

Table 4. Failed Bank Mergers of June 29, 1998 ($N = 5$).

Window	Bidders	
	CAAR (%)	Z-Statistic
(−10,10)	−13.41*	−1.772
(−10,−2)	−5.97	−1.128
(−5,−2)	0.88	0.185
(−1,0)	−1.00	−0.331
(−1,1)	−3.94	−1.326
(−3,3)	−1.73	−0.366
(1,5)	−4.48	−1.129
(1,10)	−6.43	−1.203

*10% level.

The CAAR for the two-day announcement period $t = (-1,0)$ is -1% which is not significant (Z-value $= -0.33$) while the CAAR for the $t = (-1,1)$ window is -3.94% which is not significant (Z-value $= -1.33$). The CAAR for the $t = (1,5)$ window is -4.48% which is not significant at any level (Z-value $= -1.13$).

Even though we have tried many different set of windows and estimated abnormal returns by varying the length of the estimation period for market model parameters, we get a very similar result. In most cases, we observe the negative CAAR and it is not significant in any level. Unlike Gupta (1997), the evidence from the Korean failed bank mergers indicates that a regulatory seal of approval does not add value to bidder banks. While our study does not find any value of obtaining a government seal of approval, our results indicate that the market penalizes a bidder that acquires a failed bank even though the abnormal return is not statistically significant. We interpret this result as the evidence that, in the case of these government-directed mergers, any positive value from a regulatory seal of approval is more than offset by the poor financial condition of the acquired banks.

5.3. Government Assisted Mergers

The effect of the government involvement among the Korean commercial bank mergers is one of interest in our study. Prior to our study on these bank mergers, we predicted that the involvement of the government in merger events would have a positive effect as well as a negative effect. One positive effect of the government assisted merger may come from the fact that the government would provide subsidies to banks, both bidder and target, in a many different forms. In particular, the government may provide big tax benefits to a bidder bank as well as a special lower rate for its borrowing from the central bank. The direct and indirect subsidies from the government give a comparative advantage to a bidder bank over its competitors. This may lead to a positive market reaction to the bidder as well as a target bank.

In contrast, government involvement may cause a negative effect to a bidder bank. Historically, government involvement in bank operations in South Korea has been deeply related to the government policy that a bank was directed to support a government-lead industry as a policy loan (Hao et al., 2001). In other words, as soon as the government becomes involved in bank operations, banks lose some of their autonomy in bank lending. One of the causes of the Korean financial crisis of the late 1997 was the non-performing bad loans of the banking industry. Many of these bad loans were originated under the prior system of government directed loan approvals.

Table 5. Government Assisted Mergers With and Without (W/O) Failed Mergers.

Window	Bidders		Targets		Bidders (W/O)	
	CAAR (%)	*Z*-Statistic	CAAR (%)	*Z*-Statistic	CAAR (%)	*Z*-Statistic
(−10,10)	−8.65*	−1.743	−5.26%	−0.603	−4.69	−0.743
(−10,−2)	2.11	−0.211	3.59	−0.741	8.85	1.008
(−5,−2)	2.92	0.411	2.27***	−5.241	4.63	0.524
(−1,0)	−0.10	0.076	0.18	−0.368	0.66	0.717
(−1,1)	−4.54	−1.483	−3.41	−1.152	−5.04	−1.258
(−3,3)	−5.25	−1.240	−3.23**	−2.054	−8.17*	−1.820
(1,5)	−10.13***	−2.927	−7.68	−0.835	−14.85***	−3.971
(1,10)	−10.67**	−2.107	−9.03	0.062	−14.20**	−2.375

*10% level.
**5% level.
***1% level.

Table 5 presents CAAR values and associated significance statistics for various event time windows for the sample of government assisted bank mergers. Bidder bank results are shown in total and without including failed mergers. The result including failed bank mergers for bidder banks is somewhat different from the result excluding failed bank mergers. For the nine days preceding the announcement including five failed bank mergers, the AAR for bidder banks is positive on six days and negative on three days while the AAR for target banks is positive on four days and negative on 5 days. The CAAR of bidder banks for the period $t = (-10,-2)$ is 2.11% which is not significant (*Z*-value = −0.21) while the target banks experience positive 3.59% for the same window but it is not significant.

For the ten days following the announcement including failed bank mergers, the AAR for bidder banks is positive on three days and negative on seven days while the targets have a positive AAR on five days and a negative AAR on five days as well. The CAAR of bidders including failed mergers for the window $t = (1,10)$ is −10.67% which is significant (*Z*-value = −2.11). The target banks experience a negative CAAR for the same period but it is not significant. The CAAR of bidder banks for the two-day announcement period $t = (-1,0)$ is −0.1% which is not significant (*Z*-value = 0.08) while the CAAR for the $t = (-1,1)$ window is −4.54% which is not significant (*Z*-value = −1.48). The target banks experience 0.18 and −3.41% CAAR respectively for the same windows but they are not significant. The CAAR of bidder banks for the $t = (1,5)$ window is −10.13% which is significant at any level (*Z*-value = −2.93) while the CAAR for target banks is −7.68% which is not significant.

The result for bidder banks excluding failed bank mergers has similar signs but the result is slightly different. For the nine days preceding the announcement, the AAR is positive on seven days and negative on two days. The CAAR for the period $t = (-10,-2)$ is 8.85% which is not significant (Z-value = 1.01) while the including result is 2.11% but it is not significant.

For the ten days following the announcement, the AAR is positive on four days and negative on six days. The CAAR for the period $t = (1,10)$ window is −14.20% which is significant (Z-value = −2.38). The CAAR is much lower than the result including failed mergers. The CAAR for the two-day announcement period $t = (-1,0)$ is 0.66% which is not significant (Z-value = 0.72) while the CAAR for the $t = (-1,1)$ window is −5.04% which is not significant (Z-value = −1.26). The CAAR for the $t = (1,5)$ window is −14.85% which is significant at any level (Z-value = −3.97) while the result from including failed mergers is −10.13% which is significant at any level.

Overall, the result is relatively consistent with our prediction. If the government is involved in mergers, the market reacts negatively to the public announcement regardless of whether it is a bidder or a target. Bidder and target banks experience a small positive abnormal return before the public announcement date. However, a bidder bank is penalized heavily after their public announcement date and its CAAR is significantly negative while a return to target banks is not significant. It is obvious from the table that once the government becomes involved in mergers, the market becomes worried about government interruption in bank operations and penalizes an acquirer accordingly.

5.4. No Government Involvement (Solvent Bank Mergers)

We now shift the focus of our analysis to the effect of the financial health or solvency of the banks that are engaged in merger activities. Since size has become a great issue for the Korean commercial banks in this period, we expect that the merger between solvent banks should create a positive merger synergy and the market will react accordingly. We expect that the increased size of a healthy bank will create a positive reaction to the proposed merger. Therefore, we predict that there should be a positive reaction to the merger between solvent banks.

Table 6 presents CAAR values and associated significance statistics for various event windows for the sample of mergers among solvent banks. For the nine days preceding the announcement, the AAR for bidder banks is positive on six days and negative on three days while the AAR for target banks is positive on five days and negative on four days. The CAAR of bidder banks for the period

Table 6. Mergers Between Solvent Banks ($N = 3$).

Window	Bidders		Targets	
	CAAR (%)	Z-Statistic	CAAR (%)	Z-Statistic
(−10,10)	7.16	0.777	−15.46	−1.170
(−10,−2)	8.99	1.362	4.57	0.768
(−5,−2)	−0.14	0.053	2.84	0.710
(−1,0)	1.22	0.348	3.06	0.796
(−1,1)	0.76	0.202	−4.03	−0.513
(−3,3)	4.15	0.760	−3.13	−0.315
(1,5)	1.34	0.483	−11.88*	−1.907
(1,10)	−3.04	−0.454	−23.08***	−2.855

*10% level.
***1% level.

$t = (-10,-2)$ is 8.99% which is not significant (Z-value = 1.36) while the target banks experience positive 4.57% but it is not significant (Z-value = 0.77).

For the ten days following the announcement, the AAR for bidder banks is positive on five days and negative on five days while the targets have a positive AAR on two days and a negative AAR on eight days. The CAAR of bidders for this period $t = (1,10)$ is −3.04% which is not significant (Z-value = −0.45). The target banks experience a negative CAAR (−23.08%) as well for the same period but it is significant at any level (Z-value = −2.86). The CAAR of bidder banks for the two-day announcement period $t = (-1,0)$ is 1.22% which is not significant (Z-value = 0.35) while the CAAR for the $t = (-1,1)$ window is 0.76% which is not significant (Z-value = 0.20). The target banks experience 3.06 and −4.03% CAAR respectively for the same windows but they are not significant. The CAAR of bidder banks for the $t = (1,5)$ window is 1.34% which is not significant (Z-value = 0.48) while the CAAR for target banks is −11.88% which is significant (Z-value = −1.907).

Even though we do not observe a statistical significance due to the small sample, it is clearly shown in Table 6 that the market reacts positively to a bidder and has a mixed reaction to the target. The general result is somewhat consistent with our prediction regarding to the financial health of the bank. The bidder banks experience positive returns around the public announcement as we expected under the conjecture about increasing the size of a healthy bank. However, the target banks have a positive return on the announcement day and experience a negative gain after that time. This result is somewhat consistent with Cornett and De's results (1991a, b).

Table 7. 1998 Mergers vs. Post-1998 Mergers.

Window	Bidders		Targets		Bidders (W/O)	
	CAAR (%)	Z-Statistic	CAAR (%)	Z-Statistic	CAAR (%)	Z-Statistic
Panel A: Year 1998 mergers						
(−10,10)	−5.04	−0.965	−27.40**	−2.059	2.41	0.533
(−10,−2)	6.98	1.052	−10.17	−0.619	10.30***	2.838
(−5,−2)	5.60	1.280	−4.11	−0.306	5.12*	1.713
(−1,0)	0.00	−0.061	3.63	0.815	0.56	0.279
(−1,1)	−4.45	−1.408	−9.02*	−1.681	−2.26	−0.790
(−3,3)	−6.21	−1.234	−16.34**	−2.106	−5.25	−1.441
(1,5)	−10.34**	−2.533	−21.03***	−3.499	−7.85**	−2.538
(1,10)	−12.02**	−2.310	−20.86***	−2.829	−8.45**	−2.120
Panel B: Post-1998 mergers						
(−10,10)	−5.66	−0.689	4.00	0.440		
(−10,−2)	−2.52	−0.668	1.97	0.316		
(−5,−2)	−3.74	−1.130	−24.95***	−5.321		
(−1,0)	0.51	0.430	−2.49	−0.634		
(−1,1)	−1.52	−0.155	−0.72	−0.080		
(−3,3)	2.13	0.405	−3.59	−0.568		
(1,5)	−2.89	−0.569	5.36	1.033		
(1,10)	−3.66	−0.550	4.53	0.545		

*10% level.
**5% level.
***1% level.

5.5. Year 1998 Mergers and Post-1998 Mergers

Finally, we compare the year-1998 mergers and post-1998 mergers. Ten of sixteen bank merger announcements, including failed bank mergers, occur in 1998, we investigate whether there is any difference between 1998 mergers and post-1998 mergers. Table 7 shows CAAR values and associated significance statistics for various event windows for the sample of all merger events. The merger between Hanvit bank and Peace bank is excluded due to the lack of price information.

Panel A in Table 7 contains year-1998 mergers results including failed bank mergers as well as excluding failed mergers. The result including failed bank mergers for bidder banks is somewhat different from the result excluding failed bank mergers. For the nine days preceding the announcement including five failed bank mergers, the AAR for bidder banks is positive on seven days and negative on two days while the AAR for target banks is positive on two days and negative on seven days. The CAAR of bidder banks for the period $t = (-10, -2)$ is

6.98% which is not significant (Z-value = 1.05) while the target banks experience −10.17% but it is not significant (Z-value = −0.62).

For the ten days following the announcement including failed bank mergers, the AAR for bidder banks is positive on three days and negative on seven days while the targets have a positive AAR on four days and a negative AAR on six days. The CAAR of bidders including failed mergers for this period $t = (1,10)$ is −12.02% which is significant (Z-value = −2.31). The target banks experience a negative CAAR (−20.86%) for the same period and it is highly significant (Z-value = −2.83). The CAAR of bidder banks for the two-day announcement period $t = (-1,0)$ is 0% which is not significant (Z-value = −0.06) while the CAAR for the $t = (-1,1)$ window is −4.54% which is significant (Z-value = −1.41). The target banks experience 3.63% and statistically significant −9.02% CAAR respectively for the same windows. The CAAR of bidder banks for the $t = (1,5)$ window is −10.34% which is significant at any level (Z-value = −2.53) while the CAAR for target banks is −21.03% which is highly significant.

The result for bidder banks excluding failed bank mergers has a different result compared to including failed bank mergers while the result for target banks remains the same. For the nine days preceding the announcement, the AAR is positive on eight days and negative on one day. The CAAR for the period $t = (-10,-2)$ is 10.30% which is significant (Z-value = 2.84) while the including result is 6.98% but it is not significant (Z-value = 1.05). The result indicates that a merger announcement is speculated in this period without failed ones so that bidders experience a significant positive abnormal return.

For the ten days following the announcement, the AAR is positive on three days and negative on six days. The CAAR for the period $t = (1,10)$ window is −8.45% which is significant (Z-value = −2.12). The negative CAAR is much greater than the result including failed mergers. The CAAR for the two-day announcement period $t = (-1,0)$ is 0.56% which is not significant (Z-value = 0.28) while the CAAR for the $t = (-1,1)$ window is −2.26% which is not significant (Z-value = −0.79). The CAAR for the $t = (1,5)$ window is −7.85% which is significant at 5% level (Z-value = −2.54) while the result from including failed mergers is −10.34% which is significant at 5% level.

Panel B in Table 7 contains the result of the post-1998 mergers. It presents CAAR values and associated significance statistics for various windows for the sample of five bank mergers. We exclude one merger because of the lack of the price information. For the nine days preceding the announcement, the AAR for bidders is positive on four days and negative on five days and for target banks it is positive on five days and negative on four days. The CAAR for bidders for period $t = (-10,-2)$ is −2.52% which is not significant (Z-value = −0.67) while the CAAR for target for the same window is 1.97% which is not significant (Z-value = 0.32).

For the ten days following the announcement, the AAR for bidders is positive on four days and negative on six days while the AAR for targets is positive on five days and negative on five days as well. The CAAR of bidders for this period $t =$ (1,10) is −3.66% which is not significant (Z-value = −0.55) while the CAAR of targets for the same period is 4.53% which is not significant (Z-value = 0.55).

The CAAR of bidders for the two-day announcement period $t =$ (−1,0) is 0.51% which is not significant while the CAAR of target for the same window is −2.49% which is not significant (Z-value = −0.63). For bidders, the CAAR for the $t =$ (1,5) window is −2.89% which is not significant and for target banks the CAAR for the $t =$ (−5,−2) window is −24.95% and it is highly significant at the any level (Z-value = −5.321) while the CAAR for the $t =$ (−3,3) window is −3.59% and it is not significant.

As it can be seen in Table 7, most of the year-1998 mergers exhibit negative returns by a target bank except the announcement day which shows a 3.63% gain. A bidder bank, however, experiences a positive abnormal return prior to the public announcement date and exhibits a negative gain afterward. This is consistent between with failed bank merger group and without failed merger group, but the without group results shoes statistically more significance. On the other hand, post-1998 mergers tell a different story on the bidder gains. Except the announcement date and the (−3,3) window returns, bidders experienced negative, but not significant, abnormal returns. Target banks, however, experience significantly large negative abnormal returns (−24.95%) and this window result is very different from year-1998 mergers. Therefore, we observe the difference between year-1998 mergers and post-1998 mergers for bidder banks as well as target banks.

6. CONCLUSION

Our study investigates the effects of mergers and acquisitions among South Korean commercial banks for the period of 1998–2002. We analyze the merger announcements as a whole and examine them in several groups: failed mergers, government assisted mergers, year-1998 mergers and post-1998 mergers. In generally, we do not find significant abnormal returns for the bidders in the pre-announcement period. We do find significantly negative returns after its public announcement, for example in the (1,5) and (1,10) windows. In contrast, we find a significantly negative abnormal returns for the target banks for the (−5,−2) window. The result indicates that there is evidence of speculation on target banks being acquired. Evidence of leakage of news prior to the official merger announcement is unlikely since we do not show any significant returns to bidders prior to announcement date. In addition, there were negative returns for a target as well as a bidder which is somewhat unusual compared to the general merger and acquisition result.

Unlike Gupta's (1997) results, our study does not find any value of obtaining a government seal of approval. In our failed bank mergers reveal that the market penalizes a bidder that acquires a failed bank. The market reacts to the failed bank merger so negatively that it does not believe in the wealth transfer from the government to the bidder banks. Gupta's (1997) claim on the government seal of approval is not consistent with the evidence from the South Korean failed banks mergers.

With regard to government assisted bank mergers, the result is consistent with our expectation. If the government is involved in mergers, the market reacts negatively regardless of whether it is a bidder or a target. Bidder and target banks experience a small return before the public announcement. Bidder banks are penalized heavily after the announcement, having a statistically significant negative abnormal return, while a return to target banks is not significant.

Using three mergers among solvent banks, we investigate the market reaction to those mergers and analyze and compare the result with the result from the government assisted mergers. We draw a somewhat consistent result with our prior prediction. The result using three healthy bank mergers reveals that a bidder and a target exhibit a positive announcement date abnormal return, consistent with Cornett and De (1991a, b), while a target experiences a large negative abnormal return afterward.

Finally, we examined whether there is any difference between mergers in year-1998 and post-1998 mergers. The result of year-1998 mergers exhibits a negative abnormal return regardless whether it is a bidder or a target while the result is somewhat different for the post 1998 mergers. The result is mixed depending on the government involvement and its financial condition. There is a clear difference between year-1998 mergers and post-1998 mergers.

1998–2002 was a period of crisis and transition in the Korean banking system. There were sixteen merger events in this time, including mergers of failed banks and government-directed mergers. A major contribution of this paper is the systematic investigation of this important time in Korean banking. This study does not find evidence of positive valuations in government-directed mergers. Apparently, the markets did not value the seal of government approval in the merger of failed Korean banks. An interesting continuation of this study will be to evaluate Korean bank performance in the post-merger era.

ACKNOWLEDGMENTS

The authors wish to thank Prof. Iftekhar Hasan for helpful comments and advice in improving this study.

REFERENCES

Bank of Korea (2002). *Financial system in Korea*. Seoul: Bank of Korea.

Berger, A. N., DeYoung, R., Genay, H., & Udell, G. (2000). Globalization of financial institutions: Evidence from cross-border banking performance. *Brookings-Wharton Papers on Financial Services*, 23–158.

Bertin, W. J., Ghazanfari, F., & Torabzadeh, K. M. (1989). Failed bank acquisitions and successful bidders' returns. *Financial Management* (Summer), 93–100.

Bessler, W., & Murtagh, J. P. (2002). The stock market reaction to cross-border acquisitions of financial services firms: An analysis of Canadian banks. *Journal of International Financial Markets, Institutions and Money*, *12*, 419–440.

Cornett, M., & De, S. (1991a). Common stock returns in corporate takeover bids: Evidence from interstate bank mergers. *Journal of Banking and Finance*, *15*, 273–295.

Cornett, M., & De, S. (1991b). Note: Medium of payment in corporate acquisitions: Evidence from interstate bank mergers. *Journal of Money, Credit and Banking*, *23*, 767–776.

Gilbert, R. A., & Wilson, P. W. (1998). Effects of regulation on the productivity of Korean banks. *Journal of Economics and Business*, *50*, 133–155.

Gupta, A. (1997). The value of a regulatory seal of approval. *Journal of Financial Research*, *20*, 111–128.

Gupta, A., & Misra, L. (2002). Regulatory learning in failed thrift auctions. *Journal of Banking & Finance*, *26*, 651–669.

Hao, J., Hunter, W. C., & Yang, W. (2001). Deregulation and efficiency: The case of private Korean banks. *Journal of Economics & Business*, *53*(2/3), 237, 18p.

James, C., & Weir, P. (1987a). Returns to acquirers and competition in the acquisition market: The case of banking. *Journal of Political Economy*, *95*, 355–370.

James, C., & Weir, P. (1987b). An analysis of FDIC bank auctions. *Journal of Monetary Economic*, *20*, 141–153.

Joh, S. W. (2003). Corporate governance and firm profitability: Evidence from Korea before the economic crisis. *Journal of Financial Economics*, *68*, 287–322.

Neely, W. P. (1987). Banking acquisitions: Acquirer and target shareholder returns. *Financial Management*, *16*(Winter), 66–74.

Sushka, M. E., & Bendeck, Y. (1998). Bank acquisitions and stockholders' wealth. *Journal of Banking & Finance*, *12*, 551–562.

APPENDIX

Major Bank History in South Korea-Time Table

Year	Bank Name	Event
1972	Sang Up	Privatized
1981	Hanil	Privatized
1982	Korea First	Privatized
1982	Seoul	Privatized
1982	Shinhan	Open
1983	Hanmi	Open
1983	Cho Hung	Privatized
1989	Korea Exchange	Commercial Bank
1989	Dongwha, Dongnam, Daedong	Open
1992	Hana, Boram	Open
1993	Pyongwha	Open
1995	Kookmin	Privatized
1997	Housing & Commercial	Privatized
1998	5 Banks[a]	Closed
1998	Kookm & Korea Long-Term Credit	Merger
1999	Sang Up & Hanil	Merge to new Hanvit
1999	Hana & Boram	Merger
1999	Cho Hung, Chung Buk, Kangwon	Merger
1999	Korea First	Sold to New bridge
2000	Kookmin, Housing & Commercial	Merger
2001	Hanvit, Kwangju, KyongNan, Hanaro Merchant	Merged to New Woori Financial Holding
2001	Shinhan	Financial Holding
2002	Hana & Seoul	Sold to Hana
2002	Cho Hung	Expected to sold

[a]5 Banks are Daedong, Dongnam, Dongwha, Kyong Gi, and Chung Cheong.

STOCK MARKET AND ECONOMIC FORCES DURING LIBERALIZATION: KOREAN EXPERIENCE

Gautam Goswami, Sung-Chang Jung and S. Young Chung

ABSTRACT

This paper studies the short-run dynamics as well as the long-run relationships between stock prices and six macroeconomic variables of the Korean economy, using a vector error correction model. The long-term relationships between stock prices and the macroeconomic factors in Korea are similar to that of USA and Japan as shown in earlier research. The Korean economy had undergone dramatic financial liberalization since the second half of the 1980s and this liberalization process may have altered the economic structure of Korea. We conduct a structural break test to investigate that whether there exists a regime shift within last two decades. We conclude that the liberalization caused a structural break in the Korean economy around 1990. We divide the whole sample into two sub-sample periods and investigate the long-term relationship in two sub-sample periods. We find that the liberalization of the Korean economy have altered the long-term relationship between stock prices and some macroeconomic variables. We also show that the forecasting ability of a VECM is better than a VAR estimating procedure.

Bank and Financial Market Efficiency: Global Perspectives
Research in Banking and Finance, Volume 5, 195–216

ISSN: 1567-7915/doi:10.1016/S1567-7915(04)05010-4

1. INTRODUCTION

The Korean economy began a period of rapid economic progress by transforming the manufacturing sector in the early 1960s. At the same time the government nationalized the banking industry to provide stability in the financial sector. The Korean stock exchange, after opening in 1956, became very active during the 1980s and provided an alternative source for financing the manufacturing sector. In 1990, the Korean stock market peaked with a market capitalization of $140 billion and became the eighth largest financial market in the world. At the beginning of the 1980s government policymakers realized that a highly regulated financial system had become a hindrance to continued economic development. In the mid-1980s, the Korean government planned to gradually liberalize its financial sector by partly transferring control of the banks to the private sector and also allowing foreign participation in the Korean stock market. To boost the economy further during early 1990s, the financial sector was further deregulated by removing control on interest rates and exchange rates. The success of such a policy is evident from the growth rate in the Korean stock market (11.75% per year) and of its industrial production (10.7% per year) over the last twenty years. However, there are hardly any studies on the changing relationship between stock prices and economic activities in Korea.

There are several compelling reasons for undertaking this investigation. To our knowledge there is no paper that investigated the changing relationship between stock prices and the macroeconomic variables due to the recent financial market deregulation. Also, the nature of the relationships between stock prices and macroeconomic variables in developed economies like Japan and U.S. may not be the same in a less developed economy like Korea.

In this paper, we investigate the long-term relationship between stock prices and macroeconomic variables in the Korean economy using Johansen's (1991) co-integration analysis. Conventional tests for co-integration are conducted under the assumption that the long run equilibrium between the variables is stable over the entire sample period. This may be a misleading assumption especially if there were significant changes in the economic environment over the sample period. Korea has experienced dramatic changes in its financial markets and economic environments from late 1980s to early 1990s due to the liberalization of its economy.[1] Therefore, we conduct dynamic econometric specification analysis following Hansen and Johansen (1993) to investigate the existence of a structural break in the sample period. We then re-estimate the long-term relationships between stock prices and the economic variables in both sub-samples.

We find that the Korean stock market is co-integrated with six macroeconomic variables. Korean stock prices are negatively related with the long-term interest rate and the oil price and positively related to inflation and the real money stock. Devaluation of the Korean won against the U.S. dollar is negatively related to stock price changes. The effect of industrial production on stock prices is weak and ambiguous in the full sample. In addition, using normalized recursive likelihood ratio test of constant co-integration space, we find a structural break point within the sample period. This regime shift in the Korean economy took place some time in 1990. We investigate the co-integration relationship in the two sub-sample periods and find that the second sub-sample generally supports the hypothesized long-term relationship in terms of industrial production and the long-term interest rate. We also show that the forecasting ability of a VECM is generally better than a VAR estimating procedure both in the full sample and sub-sample periods.

During the last three decades, numerous studies investigated both theoretically and empirically the relationship between asset prices and economic activities. Real economic activities are commonly believed to affect stock prices. Fama (1981, 1990), Chen, Roll and Ross (CRR) (1986) and Chen (1991) empirically investigated the relationships between stock prices and macroeconomic variables with U.S. economic data.[2] Hamao (1988) carried out the earliest study on the Japanese stock market. Elton and Gruber (1988), Brown and Otsuki (1990) conducted arbitrage pricing theory (APT) tests on Japanese stock returns and several macroeconomic variables such as, industrial production, the money supply, the crude oil price, short-term interest rates, etc. Mukherjee and Naka (1995) employed a vector error correction model (VECM) and find that the Japanese stock market is cointegrated with a group of six macroeconomic variables.

Several papers have examined the relationship between stock returns and macroeconomic factors in the Korean economy in an APT framework. Bark (1991) and Kwon and Shin (1997) investigated the relationship in a CAPM and multifactor CAPM framework respectively. Mukherji, Dhatt and Kim (1997) and Chung and Lee (1998) analyzed the effect of fundamental factors on stock prices. Chung and Lee (1998) concluded that nonfundamental factors affect the Korean economy more than the fundamental factors. Titman and Wei (1999) compared the Korean and Taiwanese stock markets based on volatility. Kwon and Shin (1999) analyzed the relationship between stock returns and economic variables in an Engle and Granger (1987) framework.[3]

The remainder of the paper is divided in four sections. Section 2 develops the hypotheses to be tested and explains the Korean economic data. Section 3 explains the methodology used in this paper. Section 4 presents the empirical results including the structural break test and comments on efficiency and predictability of a VECM. The concluding remarks are presented in Section 5.

2. DATA

We obtain data on the stock market and on each of the macroeconomic variables from various issues of the *Monthly Bulletin* published by the Bank of Korea. The sample period spans from February 1980 to November 1999, consisting of 238 monthly observations for each variable. The Stock prices in Korean market are represented by Korea Composite Stock Price Index. The Korean stock price index is a value-weighted average of all stocks traded in Korean Stock Exchange. We chose the monthly average as our stock price variable and denote it by (KOSPI).

We consider three sectors of the Korean economy: the financial sector, the manufacturing sector and the foreign sector. We then use macroeconomic factors to represent each sector of the economy. Korea being a small open and oil importing economy, the foreign sector as well as the oil price may considerably affect stock prices. The long-term interest rate (CBY), inflation rate (INF) and the money supply (RM2) represent the financial sector. Industrial production (IP) and the oil price (OIL) represent the manufacturing sector and the exchange rate (WS) represents foreign sector.

In the financial sector, we should include the interest rate for short-term and long-term government bonds as well as risky corporate bonds. Typically, most researchers following CRR (1986) have used the default risk premium and the maturity risk premium as factors, which affect the stock market. But long term government bonds (comparable to 10–30 years T-bond) and short-term government notes (comparable to 3 month T-bill) are not popular in Korea. Also, the Korean economy does not have a well-developed speculative grade bond (junk bond) market. The long-term interest rate (CBY), calculated as the monthly average of the yield to maturity for three-year corporate bonds, is widely believed to be the most representative interest rate in the Korean economy. We hypothesize that stock prices will be negatively related with long-term interest rates.[4]

We choose two variables to measure inflation, one is the money supply and the other is the annualized inflation rate. The annualized inflation (INF) is calculated from the consumer price index, with the index equal to 100 in 1990. The variable (RM2) is the average balance of the real money supply measured in billions of Won. Since an increase in inflation increases the discount rate, it should affect stock prices negatively. However, an increase in inflation also increases expected future cashflows, thus having a positive effect on stock prices. In most developing economies, a steady and low inflation rate helps the growth in the real sector, and have a positive effect on stock prices. Most previous studies, e.g. Fama and Schwert (1977), Geske and Roll (1980), CRR (1986), and Chen (1991) document a negative relationship between stock returns and inflation in a developed economy.

The effect of the money supply on stock price is an empirical question. In the short run, an increase in the money supply reduces the interest rate and thus increases the discount rate in the valuation model. An increase in the money supply also increases investment in the production sector, which may increase expected future cashflows, thus increasing stock prices. Mandelker and Tandon (1985) show that the rate of growth of the money supply has a positive impact on real stock returns in six major industrialized countries. Asprem (1989) finds that expectation about future real activity and measures of money supply are positively related to stock prices in ten European countries.

Industrial production or the gross national product measures economic activity in the manufacturing sector. The variable (IP) represents the end of the month industrial production figure from the Bank of Korea. Fama (1990), CRR (1986) and Geske and Roll (1983) found a positive relationship between stock prices and the real economic activity. Economic activities as measured by stock prices often depend on oil prices, particularly in small oil importing economies. Since Korea is a net crude oil importer, the performance of the economy is expected to be negatively related to oil prices.[5] The variable (OIL) represents the U.S. composite

Table 1A. Summary Statistics of All Variables from February 1980 to November 1999.

	KOSPI	CBY	INF	IP	RM2	OIL	WS
Panel A: Data in level form							
Mean	515.87	15.44	6.147	66.65	668.6	21.15	825.1
Median	588.85	14.03	5.263	63.50	575.1	18.60	789.0
Std. Dev.	315.50	4.749	8.761	32.55	438.2	6.729	177.3
Max.	1110.5	32.20	49.80	152.4	2235	37.48	1640
Min.	103.10	7.560	−12.54	20.00	185.8	9.810	580.7
Panel B: Data in natural logarithm							
Mean	5.969	n.a.	n.a.	4.064	6.316	3.003	6.697
Median	6.378	n.a.	n.a.	4.151	6.355	2.923	6.671
Std. Dev.	0.824	n.a.	n.a.	0.544	0.615	0.312	0.184
Max.	7.013	n.a.	n.a.	5.027	7.712	3.624	7.403
Min.	4.636	n.a.	n.a.	2.996	5.225	2.283	6.364
Panel C: Data in first difference							
Mean	0.009	−0.091	−0.219	0.009	0.010	−0.001	0.003
Median	0.005	0.000	−0.156	0.008	0.009	0.000	0.002
Std. Dev.	0.067	1.020	9.187	0.0582	0.026	0.067	0.027
Max.	0.207	10.23	32.56	0.1876	0.096	0.375	0.196
Min.	−0.236	−4.10	−35.32	−0.1551	−0.076	−0.289	−0.174

Note: Interest rates and annualized inflation rates are not presented in natural logarithm.

crude oil prices and is collected from the monthly energy review published by Energy Information Administration. This composite price is very similar to both WTI and North Sea oil prices.

As in most other small countries, the foreign sector in Korea also plays a major role in its economic growth. Since the U.S. is a major trade partner of Korea, we use the Won per U.S. Dollar exchange rate to represent the foreign sector. Appreciation of the Korean Won against the U.S. Dollar negatively affects exports to U.S. and increases import from the U.S. An appreciation of the Won will cause a decrease in stock prices for the export sector and an increase in stock prices for the import sector of the economy. Therefore, the relationship between the exchange rate and stock prices is positive because Korea is a net exporting country to the USA.

Table 1A shows the descriptive statistics of all these variables for the sample period. The variables are presented in levels in panel A, natural logarithms in panel B and first difference form in panel C. The data show that the Korean stock market grew approximately at a rate of 11.74% per year (0.93% per month) over last twenty years. Industrial production grew at the rate of 0.857% per month and the Korean won has depreciated against the U.S. dollar at an average rate of 0.29% per month. Though the real money supply M2 grew at a rate of 1.03% per month, inflation grew at a lower rate. The interest rate change is negative but small. The oil price has decreased over twenty years but at a very low rate.

The data are divided into two periods based on the test for a structural break. A structural break is obtained around 1990, based on the recursive procedure used to test the stability of the cointegration parameter developed by Hansen and Johansen (1993).[6] The first sub-sample period spans from February 1980 to

Table 1B. Summary Statistics of All Variables from February 1980 to December 1989.

	KOSPI	CBY	INF	IP	RM2	OIL	WS
Panel A: Data in level form							
Mean	302.34	16.85	6.803	39.153	350.69	24.49	759.9
Median	136.30	14.40	5.361	36.300	333.06	27.02	760.8
Std. Dev.	276.28	5.511	10.42	13.856	112.21	7.353	84.71
Max.	965.90	32.20	49.80	64.700	613.19	37.48	892.2
Min.	103.10	12.40	−12.54	20.00	185.8	11.26	580.7
Panel B: Data in first difference							
Mean	0.018	−0.135	−0.437	0.010	0.0098	−0.002	0.0013
Median	0.008	0.000	−0.002	0.012	0.0093	−0.001	0.0017
Std. Dev.	0.049	0.790	10.75	0.056	0.0233	0.054	0.0091
Max.	0.170	3.000	32.56	0.175	0.096	0.153	0.0417
Min.	−0.075	−4.10	−35.32	−0.1551	−0.052	−0.289	−0.0270

Table 1C. Summary Statistics of All Variables from January 1990 to November 1999.

	KOSPI	CBY	INF	IP	RM2	OIL	WS
Panel A: Data in level form							
Mean	729.39	14.04	5.491	94.140	986.45	17.81	890.36
Median	713.10	13.31	5.087	95.500	864.80	17.69	796.90
Std. Dev.	177.87	3.308	5.685	20.285	411.36	3.759	217.64
Max.	1110.5	24.31	29.97	152.40	2235.7	33.14	1640.1
Min.	312.20	7.560	−7.098	58.400	572.95	9.810	686.30
Panel B: Data in first difference							
Mean	0.0004	−0.476	−0.0023	0.007	0.0109	−0.0014	0.0045
Median	−0.0061	0.010	−0.0270	0.0045	0.0086	−0.0055	0.0016
Std. Dev.	0.0809	1.209	7.357	0.060	0.0280	0.0778	0.0371
Max.	0.2071	10.230	29.04	0.188	0.0954	0.3747	0.1956
Min.	−0.236	−3.580	−22.51	−0.1549	−0.076	−0.8565	−0.1735

December 1989, which is characterized by Government regulation of the capital market, thus creating a segmented capital market.[7] The second sub-sample period is from January 1990 to November 1999 when the Korean Government made an effort to liberalize the financial market. Tables 1B and 1C present the descriptive statistics for all variables for the sub-sample periods. It is interesting to note that the standard deviation of growth rate of each variable for the second period is greater than that of the first period. This higher volatility may also result from Asian financial crisis during 1997.

3. METHODOLOGY

3.1. Unit Root Test

In order to check the stationarity of the macroeconomic variables, we use a Dickey and Pantula (1987) unit root test and a Kwiatkowski, Phillips, Schmidt and Shin (KPSS) (1992) test for all the variables in this study. Dickey and Pantula (1987) extend the Augmented Dickey-Fuller test (1979, 1981) to determine the order of differencing in autoregressive processes. To test the unit root hypothesis, the following form of the Dickey-Pantula test equation is used on each of the variables.

$$\Delta^2 x_t = \alpha + \rho_1 x_{t-1} + \rho_2 \Delta x_{t-1} + \sum_{j=1}^{k} \xi_j \Delta^2 x_{t-j} + \varepsilon_t \tag{1}$$

where k is the number of lags that is sufficient to remove any serial correlations as measured by Ljung-Box Q-statistic. In a unit root test the null hypothesis to be tested for level stationarity and the first differenced stationarity are $\rho_i = 0$, where $i = 1$ and 2, respectively. The critical values for the Dickey-Pantula test are same as the critical values calculated by Dickey and Fuller (1981).

It is well known that ADF types of unit root tests including Dickey and Pantula (1987) have low power against local alternatives. Another method to test the unit root is proposed by KPSS (1992) which takes stationarity as the null hypothesis (H_0: $I(0)$) against the non-stationarity alternatives (H_1: $I(1)$). The KPSS test is based on the LM score principal as follows:

$$\eta_\mu = \frac{\sum_{t=1}^{T} S_t^2}{T^2 s^2(k)} \tag{2}$$

where S_t is the partial sum of the residuals from a regression of the time series on a constant. T is the sample size, and $s^2(k)$ is a consistent estimate of the long-run variance obtained by the Newey-West (1987) procedure.

3.2. Cointegration and Structural Break Test

We use a cointegration analysis, which is more appropriate than a VAR because it can investigate the long-term as well as short-term dynamic comovements among macroeconomic variables. A number of studies e.g. Mukherjee and Naka (1995), Mookerjee and Yu (1997) and Cheung and Ng (1998) used Johansen (1991) cointegration analysis to find the long-term relationship between stock prices and economic factors.

Johansen's (1991) multivariate estimation of a VECM allows testing for cointegration in a system of equations. This method does not require a specific variable to be normalized and gives more efficient estimators of the cointegrating vectors (Phillips, 1991). A VECM is a better method because it can use all variables as endogenous. The VECM can be written as follows:

$$\Delta X_t = \mu - \Pi X_{t-k} + \sum_{j=1}^{k-1} \Gamma_j \Delta X_{t-j} + \varepsilon_t \tag{3}$$

where $\Gamma_j = -I + \Pi_1 + \Pi_2 + \cdots + \Pi_j,\ j = 1, 2, \ldots k,$ and $\Pi = -I + \Pi_1 + \Pi_2 + \cdots + \Pi_k$.

The coefficient matrix Π contains information about the long-run relationship between the seven variables in the data vector. If the matrix Π has full rank, it implies that the vector process $\boldsymbol{X}_t$ is stationary and a VAR model with no difference can be used. If the rank of matrix Π is zero i.e. a null matrix, it also implies that there is no long-term relationship between level variables and a first difference VAR model is appropriate. If the rank of matrix Π is r and lies between one and seven, it implies that there exist $(7 \times r)$ matrices of α and β such that $\prod = \alpha\beta'$ where α denotes the adjustment coefficient and β denotes the cointegrating vector. In this case the vector $\beta' \boldsymbol{X}_t$ is stationary, even though $\boldsymbol{X}_t$ is nonstationary. Since the error correction term is stationary, Eq. (3) can be interpreted as a vector error correction model (VECM).

To test for the order of co-integration, Johansen (1991) provides trace and maximum eigenvalue tests. The Johansen procedure outlined above assumes that the long-term relationship and its cointegration vectors are constant over the sample period. This assumption may not be correct if some exogenous events affect the variables during the sample period. To test the stability of the co-integration vectors we use the recursive LR test of constant cointegration space proposed by Hansen and Johansen (1993). They fix the short-run dynamics at the full sample values and recursively estimate and test the long-run parameters. The suggested test statistic is as follows:

$$t\sum_{i=1}^{p} \frac{\ln(1-\lambda_i^*)}{\ln(1-\lambda_i)}, \qquad t = T_0, \ldots, T. \tag{4}$$

λ_i^* are the eigenvalues from the restricted MLE. This statistic follows a $\chi^2(r(p-r))$ distribution where p and r represent the number of variables and the number of cointegration vectors, respectively.

4. EMPIRICAL RESULTS

4.1. Unit Root Test Results

Before testing for the relationship between the seven variables in the system of equations, we first test for the stationarity of each variable by employing a unit root test. Table 2 shows the results of the Dickey-Pantula unit root tests for the full sample.[8] In Table 2, $I(i)$ represents the null hypothesis of $\rho_i = 0$, where $i = 1$ and 2, respectively. The lag lengths are added until the residuals become white noise. According to the results presented in Table 2, all the variables are non-stationary except inflation and the interest rate. Considering the fact that unit root tests like ADF have lower power against local alternatives, we also conduct a KPSS test. The results are presented in Table 3. KPSS (1992) caution that a high lag truncations result in significant loss of power in the KPSS test and therefore, they recommend

Table 2. Dickey Pantular Unit Root Tests from February 1980 to November 1999.

Series	Lags	$I(1)$	$I(2)$
KOSPI	1	−1.126	−9.147*
CBY	1	−3.590*	−10.21*
INF	10	−4.394*	−5.162*
IP	11	−1.230	−4.530*
RM2	8	1.317	−4.810*
OIL	1	−2.540	−8.670*
WS	1	−1.433	−9.370*

Note: An asterisk (*) indicates significance level at the 5% confidence interval.

at most 8 lag truncations. Table 3 shows that all the variables used in this study are nonstationary at the 10% level of significance. Mukherjee and Naka (1995) used an ADF test and found that all seven macroeconomic time series in Japan are integrated of order one. Cheung and Ng (1998) found that four real macroeconomic variables in five different industrialized countries are also $I(1)$ using both KPSS and ADF. Mookerjee and Yu (1997) found a similar result using both KPSS and ADF tests with Singapore data.

4.2. Johansen's Multivariate Cointegration Test and Structural Break Test

The results of Johansen's cointegration test in terms of Trace and λ_{max} for the full sample period are reported in Table 4A. The constant term is allowed in the cointegration vector, to generalize the form of cointegration specification. In order to find the appropriate time lags, we use the Akaike Information Criterion (AIC) and the Schwartz Bayesian Criterion (SBC). The AIC indicates 4 lags and the SBC indicates 2 lags.[9] Because of the conflicting results from these two tests, we use the more powerful likelihood ratio (LR) test. Based on the result of the LR test,[10]

Table 3. KPSS Tests in Level from February 1980 to November 1999.

Lags	KOSPI	CBY	INF	IP	RM2	OIL	WS
4	3.662*	1.568*	0.622*	4.774*	4.680*	2.467*	1.867*
8	2.073*	0.960*	0.449**	2.702*	2.666*	1.471*	1.091*
12	1.463*	0.732*	0.356**	1.906*	1.892*	1.084*	0.795*

Note: 5 and 10% critical values of 0.463 and 0.347 are taken from KPSS (1989). The asterisks (*) denotes significant at the 5% level and (**) denotes significant at the 10% level.

Table 4A. Cointegration Test for the Full Sample.

Null Hypothesis	Maximum Eigenvalue Test			Trace Test		
	λ_{max}	1%	5%	Trace	1%	5%
$r = 0$	84.05	51.91	46.45	264.06	143.09	131.70
$r \leq 1$	60.42	46.82	40.30	180.01	111.01	102.14
$r \leq 2$	45.73	39.79	34.40	119.60	84.45	76.07
$r \leq 3$	38.91	33.24	28.14	73.87	60.16	53.12
$r \leq 4$	17.38	26.81	22.00	34.95	41.07	34.91
$r \leq 5$	13.15	20.20	15.67	17.57	24.60	19.96
$r \leq 6$	4.419	12.97	9.24	4.419	12.97	9.24

Note: The critical values are from Osterwald-Lenum (1992).

we conclude that 4 time lags are the most appropriate one. The LR test provides us with an additional insight into the selection of lag length. Since both the LR test and the AIC test select the same number of lags, we choose 4 lags for our cointegration analysis. Most other papers selected the 12 lags for cointegration analysis (see e.g. Mookerjee & Yu, 1997; Mukherjee & Naka, 1995). Chung and Lee (1998) used the Schwartz Bayesian Criterion (SBC) for selecting the lag length.

Table 4A presents the results of a multivariate co-integration test for the full sample. The maximum eigenvalue test indicates 4 cointegration vectors, while the trace test indicates 5 cointegration vectors at the 5% level of significance. Following Johansen and Juselius (1990) who favors the maximum eigenvalue test, we conclude that $r = 4$ i.e. four co-integration vectors. Engle and Yoo (1987) and Clements and Hendry (1995) suggest that the larger the number of cointegration vectors, the higher the predictability of the endogenous variables. This implies that the stock price (KOSPI) is well explained by the macroeconomic variables in Korea. However, the existence of a larger number of cointegrating vectors gives rise to the serious problem of how to explain the nature of relationship between the macroeconomic variables and stock prices.[11] Mukherjee and Naka found two (three) cointegrating vectors with λ_{max} (Trace) statistics and chose two cointegrating vectors. Cheung and Ng (1998) found two cointegrating vectors for Germany and Italy and one cointegrating vector for all other countries. We also use an exclusion test for the constant term. The LR test statistic for the exclusion of the constant term is 33.74, and it follows a χ^2 distribution with 4 degrees of freedom. By rejecting the null hypothesis, we allow the constant term in cointegration vectors.

Cointegration vectors normalized by KOSPI are in Table 4B. In the presence of more than one cointegrating vector, we consider the cointegrating factor represented by largest eigenvalue for the purpose of interpretation following

Table 4B. Cointegration Vectors for the Full Sample.

Variable	Vector 1	Vector 2	Vector 3	Vector 4
KOSPI	1.0000	1.0000	1.0000	1.0000
CBY	0.1553	−2.7950	0.1043	−0.0317
INF	−0.1327	1.3970	0.0468	0.0005
IP	0.0157	60.5700	3.3299	−0.8699
RM2	−0.8848	−53.8987	−3.9913	−0.6329
OIL	0.9318	20.8562	2.6426	0.6596
WS	2.6608	−11.8723	7.0848	2.9137
Constant	−22.7070	121.9554	−51.5458	−19.3699

Mukherjee and Naka (1995). The first vector in Table 4B is the long-term elasticity measures of each economic variable with respect to stock price. In the full sample period, Korean stock prices are negatively related to the long-term interest rate, and the oil price and positively related to inflation and the real money stock. These relationships are similar to the earlier results explained in Section 2. The coefficient of the variable IP is close to zero but has opposite of the predicted sign. Also, devaluation of the Korean Won against the U.S. Dollar is negatively related to stock price changes.[12]

The results of Johansen's test assume that the cointegration vectors are constant over the whole sample period. Considering the recent trend of financial market liberalization, cointegration vectors may not be constant over the full sample period. The sub-sample periods, if any structural break exists, may have a different number of cointegration vectors with different signs. That implies that the economic structure may be altered after the structural break point.

Figure 1 presents the structural break test. We use the normalized recursive likelihood ratio test of constant cointegration space, proposed by Hansen and Johansen (1993) for the whole sample period. Since the LR statistics are normalized by the critical value of 5% level of significance, normalized recursive LR statistics that are greater than one imply that the hypothesis of a constant co-integration vector is rejected. According to Fig. 1 there exists a structural break around early 1990, which may reflect the current trend of financial market liberalization in Korea. To check the robustness of the structural break point, we examine whether the 1997 Korean financial crisis affects the structural break test. We, therefore, conduct the normalized recursive likelihood ratio test of constant cointegration space for the period between February 1980 and May 1997, which is shown in Fig. 2. This excludes the period of the Asian financial crisis. Figure 2 also indicates a structural break around 1990, which implies that the structural break point is robust to changes in sample period.

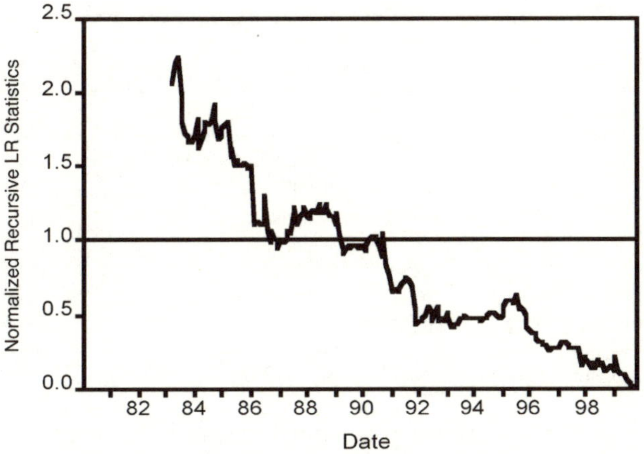

Fig. 1. Normalized Recursive Tests of Constant Cointegration Vector (February 1980 to November 1999).

Based on the test of the structural break we divide the whole sample into two sub-samples – before and after 1990 and re-estimate the number of cointegration vector.[13] Results of the pre-1990 period from February 1980 to December 1989 and the post-1990 period from January 1990 to November 1999 are presented

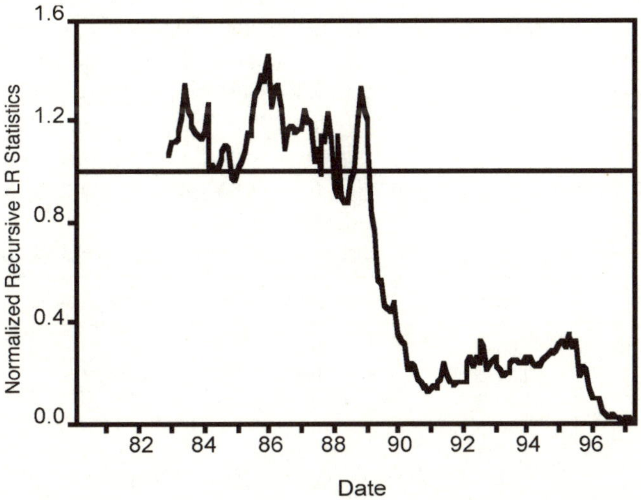

Fig. 2. Normalized Recursive Tests of Constant Cointegration Vector (February 1980 to May 1997).

Table 5A. Cointegration Test Between February 1980 and December 1989.

Null Hypothesis	Maximum Eigenvalue Test			Trace Test		
	λ_{max}	1%	5%	Trace	1%	5%
$r = 0$	58.22	51.91	46.45	181.23	143.09	131.70
$r \leq 1$	37.00	46.82	40.30	123.01	111.01	102.14
$r \leq 2$	32.82	39.79	34.40	86.02	84.45	76.07
$r \leq 3$	20.24	33.24	28.14	53.20	60.16	53.12
$r \leq 4$	15.28	26.81	22.00	32.96	41.07	34.91
$r \leq 5$	10.10	20.20	15.67	17.68	24.60	19.96
$r \leq 6$	7.58	12.97	9.24	7.58	12.97	9.24

Note: The critical values are from Osterwald-Lenum (1992).

in Tables 5A and 5B and Tables 6A and 6B, respectively. There exist 1 (4) and 3 (3) cointegration vector(s) using λ_{max} (trace) statistics for the first and second sub-sample periods at the 5% level of significance, respectively. We use the first cointegration vector for each period for the purpose of identifying the relationship between KOSPI and the other variables. The signs of coefficients of some variables are different in two sub-periods. The interest rates are negatively related to stock prices in the full sample as well as in the second subperiod. We argue that since the interest rates are more managed by the Korean government during the 80s their relation to stock prices is incorrectly predicted by a VECM. The inflation rate, just like interest rates, is correctly predicted in the full sample and in the second sub-period. Among other variables, the sign on industrial production becomes negative only in the second sub-sample, which supports the hypothesized relationship described earlier. The exchange rate variable is negatively (positively) related to stock prices in the first (second) sub-period. The interpretation is that during the first period Korea was a net importing country and after the liberalization in the second sub-period Korea has changed to a net exporting country. To examine

Table 5B. Cointegration Vectors Between February 1980 and December 1989.

Variable	Vector 1	Vector 2	Vector 3	Vector 4
KOSPI	1.0000	1.0000	1.0000	1.0000
CBY	−0.2335	0.0904	−0.0727	−0.0417
INF	0.1475	−0.0254	−0.0439	0.0217
IP	0.5465	−3.6525	1.4910	−3.0639
RM2	−4.8333	2.3078	−4.5193	0.9129
OIL	−1.4825	0.4399	−0.7880	0.0549
WS	4.0988	3.8996	0.5110	2.3268
Constant	2.0843	−33.9737	16.1765	−14.8135

Table 6A. Cointegration Test Between January 1990 and November 1999.

Null Hypothesis	Maximum Eigenvalue Test			Trace Test		
	λ_{max}	1%	5%	Trace	1%	5%
$r = 0$	77.79	51.91	46.45	231.96	143.09	131.70
$r \leq 1$	57.85	46.82	40.30	154.17	111.01	102.14
$r \leq 2$	44.86	39.79	34.40	96.32	84.45	76.07
$r \leq 3$	24.23	33.24	28.14	51.46	60.16	53.12
$r \leq 4$	10.56	26.81	22.00	27.22	41.07	34.91
$r \leq 5$	10.08	20.20	15.67	16.66	24.60	19.96
$r \leq 6$	6.58	12.97	9.24	6.58	12.97	9.24

Note: The critical values are from Osterwald-Lenum (1992).

the validity of this interpretation we collected the trade balance data for Korea and found that Korea was a net importing country up to 1985, a net exporting country up to 1993 and again changed to a net importing country till 1997. Therefore, the result generally validates the hypothesis.

4.3. Efficiency and Predictability in Korean Stock Market

The existence of cointegrating vectors in full sample as well as both sub-periods implies that there exists a long-term relationship between Korean stock prices and other macroeconomic variables. However, such a long-term relationship has been interpreted as potential market inefficiency. In the context of the stock market, efficiency implies the absence of predictability and therefore, many researchers argue that stock prices cannot be cointergrated with macroeconomic variables in an efficient market. However, Dwyer and Wallace (1992) have argued that the cointegration does not necessarily violate the concept of informational efficiency.

Table 6B. Cointegration Vectors Between January 1990 and November 1999.

Variable	Vector 1	Vector 2	Vector 3
KOSPI	1.0000	1.0000	1.0000
CBY	0.1149	0.0785	0.0068
INF	−0.3389	−0.2104	−0.0363
IP	−11.1088	3.6764	−0.7536
RM2	10.1242	−6.8548	0.0260
OIL	−1.0856	1.3331	1.1221
WS	−6.3665	10.4069	0.4052
Constant	21.6717	−50.3024	−9.5275

Following Dwyer and Wallace (1992), Mukherjee and Naka (1995) concluded that such predictability of Japanese stock market might not necessarily provide arbitrage profit opportunities. Chung and Lee (1998) analyzed four Pacific-Rim countries and concluded that both Korean and Japanese stock prices are strongly influenced by nonfundamental factors. Even if we are unable to comment on Korean stock market efficiency, we can surely use this long-term relationship to predict the future stock prices.

We chose a VECM over a VAR because a VECM can investigate the long-term relationship between stock prices and macroeconomic variables. The VAR approach has a potential problem in predicting the short-term dynamics in the presence of cointegrating vectors. To show that a VECM performs better than a VAR we present the short-term adjustment process in Tables 7 and 8. Please note that though the long-term relation of industrial production to stock prices was not correctly predicted by VECM, inductrial production plays a significant

Table 7. Vector Error Correction Model (VECM) Results for First Difference Variables with 4 Lags (Standard Errors) and [*t*-Statistics] are in First and Third Parenthesis.

Variable	Time Lag 1	Time Lag 2	Time Lag 3	Time Lag 4
KOSPI	0.2495***	0.0153	−0.1405*	−0.0507
	(0.0771)	(0.0807)	(0.079)	(0.0761)
	[3.237]	[0.191]	[−1.76]	[−0.6663]
CBY	0.00299	0.00398	−0.00464	−0.00343
	(0.00514)	(0.00538)	(0.00498)	(0.00513)
	[0.58188]	[0.7399]	[−0.9302]	[−0.6699]
INF	0.000425	0.00092	0.000847	0.000398
	(0.00061)	(0.00072)	(0.00074)	(0.000596)
	[0.6939]	[1.2706]	[1.1467]	[0.6677]
IP	0.2614***	0.1198	0.2117***	0.17195**
	(0.088)	(0.088)	(0.0877)	(0.0842)
	[2.958]	[1.359]	[2.414]	[2.0434]
RM2	−0.09386	−0.06355	−0.00635	−0.06204
	(0.1771)	(0.1904)	(0.186)	(0.195)
	[−0.52999]	[−0.3338]	[−0.0342]	[−0.318]
OIL	−0.1125	0.1486	0.0168	-0.6352
	(0.0799)	(0.0943)	(0.942)	(0.0810)
	[−1.408]	[1.576]	[0.178]	[−0.7928]
WS	−0.1822	0.5171***	−0.2942	−0.11303
	(0.2223)	(0.2198)	(0.21395)	(0.206)
	[−0.819]	[2.353]	[−1.375]	[−0.5487]

Note: The asterisks (*), (**) and (***) indicates significance level at 10%, 5% and 1%, respectively.

Table 8. Vector Auto Regression (VAR) Results for First Difference Variables with 4 Lags (Standard Errors) and [*t*-Statistics] in First and Third Parenthesis.

Variable	Time Lag 1	Time Lag 2	Time Lag 3	Time Lag 4
KOSPI	0.3133***	0.0754	−0.1198	−0.01176
	(0.0752)	(0.0817)	(0.080)	(0.0756)
	[4.164]	[0.9403]	[−1.489]	[−0.1557]
CBY	0.00439	0.00609	−0.00396	−0.00388
	(0.00508)	(0.00516)	(0.00495)	(0.00526)
	[0.865]	[1.179]	[−0.79915]	[−0.757]
INF	0.000656	0.001255*	0.0011	0.000655
	(0.0006)	(0.000699)	(0.00071)	(0.000587)
	[1.09]	[1.794]	[1.537]	[1.115]
IP	0.2495***	0.1419	0.23457***	0.1829**
	(0.089)	(0.0892)	(0.0884)	(0.0854)
	[2.793]	[1.591]	[2.653]	[2.1413]
RM2	0.02057	0.1527	0.1571	0.0698
	(0.1745)	(0.17413)	(0.17553)	(0.1897)
	[0.1178]	[0.8769]	[0.8951]	[0.3684]
OIL	−0.1054	0.12104	0.0281	−0.0855
	(0.0789)	(0.0935)	(0.0955)	(0.0794)
	[−1.336]	[1.294]	[0.2944]	[−1.077]
WS	−0.2882	0.5217***	−0.3937*	−0.1393
	(0.2058)	(0.2114)	(0.2088)	(0.1923)
	[−1.4001]	[2.468]	[−1.885]	[−0.7241]

Note: The asterisks (*), (**) and (***) indicates significance level at 10%, 5% and 1%, respectively.

role in short-term dynamic relation between stock prices and the macroeconomic variables as predicted by both a VAR and a VECM analysis. We compare both models by their forecasting accuracy measured by three different criteria, e.g. root mean square error (RMSQE), mean absolute error (MAE) and Theil's inequality coefficient (Theil). The results for the whole sample period and two sub-sample periods are presented in Table 9. From Table 9 panel A, the RMSQE's of VAR and VECM are 0.05974 and 0.05677, MAE's are 0.046778 and 0.044536, and the Theil's U coefficients for VAR and VECM are 0.58362 and 0.532842, respectively. We conclude that the VECM's forecasting accuracy is superior to that of the VAR's. These numbers are calculated by using a dynamic simulation procedure, which gives true multiperiod forecasting.

Table 9 panels B and C present the forecasting ability of the VAR and the VECM for the two sub-sample periods. In the first sub-sample period, the VECM seem to increase the forecasting ability a little (about 5–8%), while VECM in the second sub-sample period increases the forecasting accuracy considerably (about 11–16%). This implies that the short-term adjustment process using the VECM

Table 9. Forecasting Accuracy of the VECM Over the VAR Method.

	VAR	VECM	% Increase in Forecasting Accuracy
Panel A: Whole sample period from Feb. 1980 to 1999 (5 vectors)			
RMSQE	0.05974	0.056770	4.97
MAE	0.046778	0.044536	4.79
Theil	0.585362	0.532842	8.97
Panel B: Sample period 1 from Feb. 1980 to Dec. 1989 (4 vectors)			
RMSQE	0.03883	0.037089	4.48
MAE	0.03042	0.028955	4.81
Theil	0.438897	0.401859	8.43
Panel C: Sample period 2 from Jan. 1990 to Nov. 1999 (3 vectors)			
RMSQE	0.069450	0.061884	10.89
MAE	0.056681	0.050057	11.68
Theil	0.546781	0.456881	16.44

Note: RMSQE and MAE represent a value of root mean squared error and mean absolute error, respectively.

is superior to that of the VAR after the liberalization of Korean economy. Based on the above results, we conclude that the VECM's forecasting accuracy is better than that of the VAR's in all sample periods.

5. CONCLUSION

Following Fama (1981, 1990) and CRR (1986), we expect to find an equilibrium relationship between stock prices and six macroeconomic variables in Korea. Since most of the time series of macroeconomic variables are non-stationary, a vector error correction model (VECM) enables us to study the equilibrium relationship within a system of equations. Moreover, we can investigate the long-term relationship as well as the nature of the short-term adjustment process between the Korean stock price index and other macroeconomic variables. We find that the Korean stock price index is co-intergrated with six macroeconomic variables. The Korean stock prices are negatively related to the long-term interest rate, industrial production, and the oil price and positively related to inflation and the real money stock. Devaluation of the Korean won against the U.S. dollar is negatively related to stock price changes.

Cointegration analysis assumes that the long-run equilibrium between the variables is stable over the entire sample period. However, the Korean financial market has experienced dramatic changes during the early 90s. The change started with the creation of the Korea fund in 1984, and the Korean government allowed foreign investors to participate in the Korean stock market in the early 90s. Furthermore, the Korean government allowed the interest rates to move freely since the mid 80s. So we test for a structural break in our full sample period and find that the Korean economy has undergone a regime shift in 1990. Therefore, we divide the entire sample into two sub-periods and investigate the long-term relationship in both sub-periods. The second sub-sample generally supports the hypothesized long-term relationship in terms of industrial production, inflation, long-term interest rates and exchange rates.

We also show that the forecasting ability of a VECM is generally better than a VAR estimating procedure both in the full sample as well as sub-sample periods. The volatility for all variables for the second sample period is higher than that for the first sample period. The higher values of the variance of all factors in the second sub-sample period may reflect the unusually uncertain circumstances during the period of Asian financial crisis or may be due to the process of liberalization of the capital market in Korea. It is true that the Korean Government accelerated the liberalization of the capital market after the financial crisis to make the market more efficient as well as more integrated with the international capital market. Whether the Korean government is successful in increasing market efficiency and integration is left for further research.

NOTES

1. Foreign participation in the stock market started with the formation of Korea Fund in 1984. In January 1992, non-Koreans were first allowed to invest directly in Korean stock market with some limitations, which was further deregulated in 1994 and 1996. Interest rates in Korea were deregulated in four phases starting from November 1991.
2. Fama (1981) documents a strong positive correlation between common stock returns and real economic variables like capital expenditures, industrial production, real GNP, money supply, lagged inflation and interest rates. CRR (1986) find that the economic factors such as the changes in aggregate production, inflation, short-term interest rates, maturity risk and default risk premia explain the changes in stock prices.
3. Other related papers include Lee and Yoo (1992), which used factor analysis using Korean stock market data, and Silvapulle and Choi (1999) analyzed daily stock price and trading volume in Korea.
4. See James, Koreisha and Partch (1985) for a time series causal analysis of stock prices and nominal interest rate with U.S. data.
5. See Jones and Kaul (1996) for effect of oil prices on different stock markets.
6. The structural break test is formally presented in the empirical result section.
7. For segmentation argument in Korean economy, see Cheung and Lee (1993).
8. The results are similar to those of the Augmented Dickey Fuller (ADF). The results of ADF tests are available upon request. In addition, the results of unit root

tests for the sub-samples are not reported. These results are very similar to those of the full sample.

9. Calculated AICs are −8.04 for one lag, −8.85 for two lags, −9.19 for three lags, −9.30 for four lags, −9.16 for five lags, and so on. Calculated SBCs are −7.189 for one lag, −7.31 for two lags, −6.927 for three lags, −6.30 for four lags, and −5.43 for five lags.

10. Calculated LR statistic is 298 which leads to reject the null hypothesis based on the critical value of 122 ($\chi^2(98)$) at the 5% level of significance.

11. We tried to identify all cointegration relationship based on the LR test. However, the large number of variables makes it hard to extract the implications of each vector. We decide to use all vectors in Vector Error Correction Model (VECM) for the purpose of forecasting ability.

12. These ambiguous results are not unique to our study and are common in several other studies (see e.g. Cheung & Ng, 1998).

13. We follow the same procedures to select the lags for the cointegration analysis for both periods, which result in the 4 lags for both sub-samples.

ACKNOWLEDGMENTS

We wish to thank two anonymous referees, Sris Chatterjee, Iftekhar Hasan, Jim Lothian, Cornelia McCurthey, Thomas Noe and Liuren Wu for their helpful comments. Goswami gratefully acknowledges research support from Forham University. The usual disclaimer applies.

REFERENCES

Asprem, M. (1989). Stock prices, asset portfolios and macroeconomic variables in ten European countries. *Journal of Banking and Finance*, *13*, 589–612.

Bark, H.-K. (1991). Risk, return, and equilibrium in the emerging markets: Evidence from the Korean stock market. *Journal of Economics and Business*, *43*, 353–362.

Brown, S. J., & Otsuki, T. (1990). Macroeconomic factors and the Japanese equity market: The CAPMD project. In: E. J. Elton & M. Gruber (Eds), *Japanese Capital Markets*. New York: Haper & Row.

Chen, N. (1991). Financial opportunity and the macroeconomy. *Journal of Finance*, *46*, 529–554.

Chen, N., Roll, R., & Ross, S. (1986). Economic forces and the stock market. *Journal of Business*, *59*, 383–403.

Cheung, C. S., & Lee, J. (1993). Integration vs. segmentation in the Korean stock market. *Journal of Business Finance and Accounting*, *20*, 267–273.

Cheung, Y.-W., & Ng, L. K. (1998). International evidence on the stock market and aggregate economic activity. *Journal of Empirical Finance*, *5*, 281–296.

Chung, H., & Lee, B.-S. (1998). Fundamental and nonfundamental components in stock prices of Pacific-Rim countries. *Pacific-Basin Finance Journal*, *6*, 321–346.

Clements, M. P., & Hendry, D. F. (1995). Forecasting in cointegrated systems. *Journal of Applied Econometrics*, *10*, 127–146.

Dickey, D. A., & Fuller, W. A. (1979). Distribution of the estimators for autoregressive time series with a unit root. *Journal of the American Statistical Association*, *74*, 421–427.

Dickey, D. A., & Fuller, W. A. (1981). Likelihood ratio statistics of autoregressive time series with a unit root. *Econometrica*, 1057–1072.

Dickey, D. A., & Pantula, S. G. (1987). Determining the order if differencing in autoregressive processes. *Journal of Business & Economic Statistics*, *5*, 455–461.

Elton, E. J., & Gruber, M. (1988). A multi-index risk model of the Japanese stock market. *Japan and the World Economy*, 21–44.

Engle, R. F., & Granger, C. W. J. (1987). Co-integration and error correction: Representation, estimation, and testing. *Econometrica*, *55*, 251–276.

Engle, R. F., & Yoo, B. S. (1987). Forecasting and testing in co-integrated system. *Journal of Econometrics*, *35*, 143–159.

Fama, E., & Schwert, W. (1977). Asset returns and inflation. *Journal of Financial Economics*, *5*, 115–146.

Fama, E. (1981). Stock returns, real activity, inflation and money. *American Economic Review*, *71*, 545–565.

Fama, E. (1990). Stock returns, expected returns, and real activity. *Journal of Finance*, *45*, 1089–1108.

Geske, R., & Roll, R. (1983). The monetary and fiscal linkage between stock return and inflation. *Journal of Finance*, *38*, 1–33.

Hamao, Y. (1988). An empirical investigation of the arbitrage pricing theory. *Japan and the World Economy*, 45–61.

Hansen, H., & Johansen, S. (1993). Recursive estimation in cointegrated VAR-models. Working Paper, Institute of Mathematical Statistics, University of Copenhagen.

James, C., Koreisha, S., & Partch, M. (1985). A VARMA analysis of the causal relations among stock returns, real output, and nominal interest rates. *Journal of Finance*, 1375–1384.

Johansen, S., & Juselius, K. (1990). Maximum likelihood estimation and inference on co-integration – with applications to the demand for money. *Oxford Bulletin of Economics and Statistics*, *52*, 169–210.

Johansen, S. (1991). Estimation and hypothesis testing of cointegration vectors in Gaussian vector autoregressive models. *Econometrica*, *59*, 1551–1580.

Jones, C. M., & Kaul, G. (1996). Oil and the stock market. *Journal of Finance*, 463–491.

Kwiatkowski, D., Phillips, P. C. B., Schmidt, P., & Shin, Y. (1992). Testing the null hypothesis of stationary against the alternative of a unit root. *Journal of Econometrics*, *54*, 159–178.

Kwon, C. S., & Shin, T. S. (1997). The effect of macroeconomic variables on stock market returns in developing markets. *Multinational Business Review/Fall*, 63–70.

Kwon, C. S., & Shin, T. S. (1999). Cointegration and causality between macroeconomic variables and stock market returns. *Global Finance Journal*, *10*(1), 71–81.

Lee, S. B., & Yoo, T. Y. (1992). On the robustness of goodness-of-fit criteria for factor identification: Simulation and some Korean evidence. *Quarterly Journal of Business and Economics*, *31*(4), 18–40.

Mandelker, G., & Tandon, K. (1985). Common stock returns, real activity, money, and inflation: Some international evidence. *Journal of International Money and Finance*, *4*, 267–286.

Mookerjee, R., & Yu, Q. (1997). Macroeconomic variables and stock prices in a small open economy: The case of Singapore. *Pacific-Basin Finance Journal*, *5*, 377–388.

Mukherji, S., Dhatt, M. S., & Kim, Y. H. (1997). A fundamental analysis of Korean stock returns. *Financial Analysts Journal* (May/June), 75–80.

Mukherjee, T. K., & Naka, A. (1995). Dynamic relations between macroeconomic variables and the Japanese stock market: An application of a vector error correction model. *The Journal of Financial Research*, 223–237.

Newey, W. K., & West, K. D. (1987). A simple, positive semi-definite, heteroskedasticity and autoregression consistent covariance matrix. *Econometrica*, *55*, 703–705.

Osterwald-Lenum (1992). A note with quantiles of the asymptotic distribution of the maximum likelihood cointegration rank test statistics. *Oxford Bulletin of Economics and Statistics*, *54*, 461–471.

Phillips, P. C. B. (1991). Optimal inference in cointegrated systems. *Econometrica*, *59*, 283–306.

Silvapulle, P., & Choi, J.-S. (1999). Testing for linear and nonlinear granger causality in the stock price-volume relation: Korean evidence. *The Quarterly Review of Economics and Finance*, *39*(1), 59–76.

Titman, S., & Wei, K. C. J. (1999). Understanding stock market volatility: The case of Korea and Taiwan. *Pacific-Basin Finance Journal*, *7*, 41–66.

BIDDER GAINS: THE UNDERVALUATION HYPOTHESIS

Mahendra Raj

ABSTRACT

Empirical evidence has shown bidder returns to be negative in the period surrounding a takeover announcement. This paper analyses the relation between bidder returns and the acquisition of undervalued targets. Unlike other studies this paper measures undervaluation by using valuation ratios: price-earnings ratio and market-to-book ratio. The results show the bidding-firm stock returns are significantly positive in the period around the announcement of acquiring an undervalued firm. The paper also finds that the bid premium in these deals is lower than the control sample and a relatively large number of these bidders pay for the deal with their own shares.

1. INTRODUCTION

Corporate control literature abounds with many individual theories explaining the rationale behind mergers and acquisitions. One theory is that a target firm maybe undervalued by the market and so forms the basis of a takeover.

Empirical evidence has shown that bidder shareholders, on average, suffer from acquisitions and encounter negative returns over the announcement period (Morck, Shleifer & Vishny, 1990; Travlos, 1987). Travlos (1987) explains that bidder returns are negative due to the information effect that arises from the chosen

Bank and Financial Market Efficiency: Global Perspectives
Research in Banking and Finance, Volume 5, 217–234

ISSN: 1567-7915/doi:10.1016/S1567-7915(04)05011-6

method of payment. In that if the bidder prefers to pay by cash (stock) it is felt the market is currently undervaluing (overvaluing) the stock. As a result the market perceives a cash-financed (stock-financed) bid positively (negatively). However, Morck, Shleifer and Vishny (1990) state that the reasoning behind negative bidder returns is due to the explanation provided by the overpayment hypothesis, where the bidder pays too much for the target. The basis of this hypothesis is that for a bid to succeed a sufficiently high offer must be tabled. Another reason that supplements the overpayment hypothesis is where bidding firm management suffer from hubris and overestimate their own abilities in gleaning value from the deal and subsequently overpay (Roll, 1986). In terms of the valuation approach the ratios used in this paper combine accounting and stock market data. Basu (1983) has shown that the price-earnings ratio helps to explain the cross-section of average stock returns. Price-earning ratios are likely to be lower for stocks with lower risks and expected returns. As a result, firms with low (high) price-earnings ratios are likely to be undervalued (overvalued). Similarly firms with low (high) market-to-book ratios are considered to be undervalued (overvalued). Beaver and Ryan (1993) show that the market-to-book ratios along with cash-flow yield have a positive effect on stock returns. Fama and French (1995) also find that firms with low market-to-book ratios find it increasingly difficult to perform. Alternatively, firms with high market-to-book ratios usually enjoy sustained profitability and so have high average returns. Empirically it seems that firms with low price-earnings ratios and low market-to-book ratios are likely to be undervalued or distressed and are therefore strong candidates for value-enhancing takeovers. As a result, bidding firms acquiring undervalued targets will not necessarily overpay, and if so, will achieve greater announcement-period returns than what is usually found. Since the valuation ratios used are specific to the industry it is necessary to judge the ratios of the target firms to their respective industry averages.

1.1. Takeover Performance

There has been a host of studies that have researched the area of mergers and acquisitions. Many hypotheses exist on why acquisitions transpire (see Berkovitch & Narayanan, 1993). One generally accepted theory is that of removing inefficient management from power. As Damodaran (1997) states "...in which poorly managed firms are taken over and restructured by the new owners, who lay claim to the additional value." It is standard to note that many firms can improve with better management, however there is more scope for improvement in firms that are already performing poorly. If this were a key motive of bidding firms there would be an expectation of target firms performing poorly in the pre-bid period. This hypothesis is usually referred to as the inefficient management hypothesis. Most of the research in this area has basically examined stock returns in a period of one or two years before takeover initiation. Martin and McConnell (1991) study 253 tender offers over the period 1958–1984, and measure abnormal performance by using the market model and also make an adjustment for industry. They examine the existence of abnormalities in stock returns from −48 to −3 months before the announcement and find no indication of the inefficient management hypothesis. The study by Kini, Kracaw and Mian (1995) even find positive returns for targets in the period of −48 through to −3 months before a takeover approach. Martin and McConnell (1991) also find no difference in pre-bid abnormal return performance between friendly and hostile takeover targets. Lang, Stulz and Walking (1989) show that the q-ratio of hostile targets in the pre-bid period is not significantly different to that of targets subject to friendly offers. Nonetheless, Barber, Palmer and Wallace (1995) examine 71 acquisitions over the period 1963–1968 and find a negative relationship between disciplinary takeovers and the target q-ratio, while this was not found in friendly takeovers. Mitchell and Lehn (1990) also show that bad bidders are more likely to be subsequently acquired than good bidders. However, Agrawal and Walking (1994) and Denis and Denis (1995) provide strong support for takeovers being of a disciplinary nature. These studies report poor pre-bid performance in addition to high top management turnover.

1.2. Method of Payment and Bid Premiums

Bidders purchasing poor performing targets may benefit from replacing the existing management. Perhaps, bidder firms are taking over underperforming target firms in the expectation that the superior management skills present in the former can be put to good use in managing the latter. Nevertheless, the bidder may not be able to capitalise on private information about the inefficiency of the target; the bid may reveal this information to the market and invite competing bids. Thus, others could free ride on this information. However, the bidder may have valuable information about potential compatible users for the target's assets.

The issue when recognising undervalued targets is that due to the opportunities that exist within the target to create added value it is more than likely to attract multiple bidders. Bradley, Desai and Kim (1988) also find that in turn multiple-bidder competition results in higher takeover premia as compared to single bids. However, Fishman (1989) finds that bidders offer initially high premiums to protect themselves from other bidders entering into the deal. He also states that a rational bidder will offer a high premium to signal its high valuation. As per this study, an undervalued firm would then be subject to a lower bid premium.

Also amongst previous literature, several studies investigate the payment methods in M&A deals. Many different theories exist explaining the payment options in M&As. According to these theories the chosen method of payment is an important feature in the deal and many implications have been advanced and tested. Myers and Majluf (1984) find that in a world of asymmetric information the method of financing preferred by the bidding firm provides specific information about that firm. Theory suggests that when a bidder pays by shares it signals that that the existing assets of the bidder is overvalued and opposite when the payment method is cash. As a result, the market participants look at a cash offer encouragingly, while a share-exchange is considered as damaging news relating to the asset value of the bidder.

It is also reasonable to link the method of payment with taxation implications. Clearly capital gains must be measured for taxation purposes and so theoretically it can be assumed that cash offers in M&A could result in higher premiums as compared to share-exchanges. Accordingly the acquirer needs to pay a higher takeover premia when paying by cash so as to offset the tax burden borne by the target shareholders (Huang & Walking, 1987).

A number of hypotheses are present in M&A literature to explain the choice of payment methods to finance these deals. One hypothesis that has been tested is where the larger the target it is more likely that share financing is used (Ghosh & Ruland, 1998; Grullon, Michaely & Swary, 1997; Martin, 1996). The closer in size the target is to the acquirer, the more power the target management has in the negotiation process and therefore more chance of being an influence in the combined firm as so a share-exchange would be preferred. Furthermore, the larger the target firm the more cash the acquirer would need to fund the bid and so this will also influence the chosen method of payment. Martin (1996) also shows that a firm with greater growth potential is more likely to use their own shares to finance the bid. Another factor that may come into the selection of funding the bid is the performance of the acquirer before the bid approach. If the bidder has enjoyed a successful period leading up to the bid the most preferred method would be a share-exchange. In addition the target shareholders will be more receptive to a share exchange in this instance, especially if the target firm is poorly run and has endured a period of suffering in the pre-bid period.

Overall it seems that although the inefficient management hypothesis is generally regarded as a major theoretical reasoning behind takeovers the empirical evidence does not provide strong support for this hypothesis. However, it must be noted that underperformance is not expected in all cases of acquisition as other motives are present. It is felt that previous research examines targets as a group and does not analyse specific sub-samples where the scope for management improvement in the target is more likely and constitutes the logic of the bid.

This paper examines whether the undervaluation phenomena as a motive for takeovers contribute to value creation for the shareholders of the acquiring firms. This study concentrates on identifying target companies that are undervalued and analysing the returns to both bidders and targets. Very few studies, if any, have examined bidder gains from acquiring an undervalued target. This is probably the first study that specifically identifies undervalued target firms using a valuation ratio approach. Acquisitions that occurred in the U.K. between the period 1992 and 1998 are examined. A control sample of bidders from the same period is examined to compare and highlight the gains enjoyed by bidders that acquire undervalued targets. The paper also examines the method of payment characteristics and the bid premiums paid by bidders in undervalued acquisitions.

The next section presents the undervaluation model used in the paper. The data and methodology are then described. The results of the study are then presented. The final section concludes the paper.

2. UNDERVALUATION MODEL (U-V MODEL)

This study is distinct in identifying undervalued targets from a larger sample of completed takeovers that have already occurred. The market-to-book and price-to-earnings ratios are used to identify the undervalued targets. The study specifically tests the undervaluation hypothesis by means of a thorough screening process to single out undervalued targets. Therefore, by undertaking a detailed procedure, we specifically examine one major motivation behind the market for corporate control and the resulting effects on the identified targets and bidders.

One simple measure of how the market evaluates the firm is the market-to-book ratio, which is simply the ratio of the stock market value of the firm's outstanding common shares to the book value of this equity. To the extent that the stock market evaluates incumbent management highly, the market-to-book ratio should be high and the threat of takeover correspondingly low. Such firms offer little incentive to outsiders seeking a quick capital gain from ousting inefficient management. It is important to stress that no ratio is good or bad in itself, only relative to the company's industry. The price/earnings ratio is a significant investment concept. A low P/E ratio can sometimes be a quick and easy way to identify cheap stock. High valuation ratios indicate management is quite competent and successful. In contrast, low valuation ratios perhaps indicate management's ineffective use of assets to maximise corporate wealth.

The following screens were applied to an initial data set of target firms to identify undervaluation:

(i) The price/earnings ratio and market-to-book ratio of each target firm within the sample was collected in the year the first bid announcement occurred.
(ii) The average price/earnings ratio and market-to-book ratio of the industry the target firm belonged to was obtained.
(iii) Further screening took place to identify target firms that possessed both ratios below the industry average.

Since acquisitions affect the shareholders of both bidders and targets, it is necessary to examine the extent of the share price changes experienced by bidder shareholders when its management pursue undervalued target firms. This one motivation is tested in this paper. The hypotheses are:

H1. Bidder shareholders experience significant wealth gains around the announcement of acquiring an undervalued firm.

H2. The pre-bid performance of bidders acquiring undervalued targets is strong.

The remaining target firms left from the screening process were matched to the bidding company to form a control sample, (referred to as bidder^{general}). Previous literature has reported that bidders earn approximately zero returns around the announcement of a takeover. If this is the case, the returns from the control sample used should report similar results. This leads onto the third hypotheses:

H3. Bidders shareholders in general experience no excess returns on the announcement of a takeover.

It has been shown that a firm with greater growth potential is more likely to use their own shares to finance the bid. Another factor that may come into the selection of funding the bid is the performance of the acquirer before the bid approach. If the bidder has enjoyed a successful period leading up to the bid the most preferred method would be a share-exchange. It is felt that a bidder acquiring an undervalued target is more likely to meet this criteria and leads onto the fourth hypothesis:

H4. Share-exchange offers will be more common in undervalued acquisitions.

It has been stated that a rational bidder will offer a high premium to signal its high valuation. In the case of this study, an undervalued firm would then be subject to a lower bid premium. Furthermore, as it is felt that there will be more share-exchange offers in undervalued acquisitions this will also contribute to a lower premium being offered.

H5. The bid premium in an undervalued target acquisition will be lower than what is a usually paid in a general acquisition.

3. SAMPLE SELECTION, DATA AND METHODOLOGY

3.1. Sample

For the period 1992–1998 we obtained a sample of 228 successful takeovers by U.K. public firms for which we were able to retrieve the necessary financial data for the target firms, and share price data for bidder and target firms. The model employed by this study found 25 of these 228 target firms to be undervalued. Thereafter, the control sample was constructed as follows. Data was available for 90 takeover deals in terms of bid price, method of payment, bidder and target share prices. From the 90, targets that were subject to multiple bids and hostile bids were removed. Related takeovers, where the bidder and target are from the same industry were also removed from the control sample. In addition, we also removed bidders that were very successful pre-bid and paid excessive premiums for a target. This resulted in a final control sample of 30 bidders and the respective targets.

3.2. Data Collection

The daily share price data was collected from Extel's Equity Research. The dates and information content of the first bid announcement was gathered from a news search using McCarthy CD-ROM. The financial ratios were collected from Extel and Sequencer.

3.3. Methodology

The Market-Index Adjusted Model is employed to measure any abnormal returns surrounding the bid announcement of a bidder acquiring an undervalued target. Daily stock returns are defined as:

$$R_{it} = \frac{P_{it} - P_{it-1}}{P_{it-1}}$$

(P_{it} is the closing price on stock i at time t.)

The next step is to calculate the predicted or normal return (ER_{it}), this is the return that would be observed if no event occurred. In this case, ER_{it}, is represented by the return on the FT-SE 100 Index for each day in the event period.

Each bidder's abnormal return is calculated over each day of the event period as:

$$\mathrm{AR}_{it} = R_{it} - \mathrm{ER}_{it}$$

The abnormal returns of the n bidder in each group (u-v/control) are collected to determine the average abnormal return for each day:

$$\mathrm{AAR}_t = \frac{\sum_{i=1}^{n} \mathrm{AR}_{it}}{n}$$

The final step is to calculate the cumulative average abnormal return for each day over the entire event window:

$$\mathrm{CAAR} = \sum_{-60}^{+10} \mathrm{AAR}_t$$

To test AAR_t for significance the following t-stat is applied:

$$t = \frac{\mathrm{AAR}_t}{S(\mathrm{AAR}_t)} \quad \text{where } S(\mathrm{AAR}_t) = \left[\frac{1}{60} \sum_{-30}^{+30} (\mathrm{AAR}_t - \overline{\mathrm{AAR}_t})^2 \right]^{1/2}$$

Following Boehmer, Musumeci and Poulsen (1991), we use the test statistic for the cumulative daily average abnormal return (CAAR), cumulating over the period specified and is computed as follows:

$$t = \frac{\mathrm{CAAR}}{S(\mathrm{CAAR})} = \frac{\sum_{-10}^{+10} \mathrm{AAR}_t}{\sum_{-10}^{+10} S(\mathrm{AAR})} = \frac{\sum_{-10}^{+10} \mathrm{AAR}_t}{\sqrt{21} S(\mathrm{AAR})}$$

This study also employs two non-parametric tests. Non-parametric tests used in event studies do not require the stringent assumptions concerning return distributions as does parametric tests. The generalised sign test compares the proportion of positive cumulative abnormal returns around an event to the proportion from a period not affected by the event. The number expected is from the abnormal returns seen in a 100-day estimation period before the event-window (−160 to −61) and the 21-day event period studied (−10 to +10).

$$p = \frac{1}{n} \sum_{j=1}^{n} \frac{1}{100} \sum_{t=E1}^{E100} S_{it}, \quad \text{where } S_{it} = \begin{cases} 1 & \text{if } \mathrm{AR}_{it} > 0 \\ 0 & \text{otherwise} \end{cases}$$

Define w as the number of stocks in the event-window for which the cumulative abnormal return $\mathrm{CAR}_{i,(\mathrm{D1},\mathrm{Dd})}$ is positive. The generalised sign test statistic is:

$$Z_G = \frac{w - \mathrm{np}}{[\mathrm{np}(1 - p)]^{1/2}}$$

The Wilcoxon Signed Ranks Test is also employed to examine whether the returns of the undervaluation sample and the control sample are close in location, if so the ranks should be randomly mixed between the two samples, and the null hypothesis cannot be rejected. This test is done to determine whether a significant difference exists between the two samples in terms of the abnormal returns found in the announcement period.

4. RESULTS

This section reports the results of the hypotheses tested. The results for all the announcements appear in Tables 1–6. Table 7 details the bid premiums and method of payment of the undervalued acquisitions studied as compared to a general control sample.

4.1. Target Results: Announcement Returns

Studies that have examined acquisitions have found target shareholders to benefit significantly. Datta et al. (1992) finds target shareholders to gain around 22% in

Table 1. Performance Surrounding the Ann. Bid (Target-UV Sample).

Days	AAR	CAAR	Std. Dev.
−10	−0.0004	−0.0004	0.0156
−9	0.0006	0.0002	0.0181
−8	0.0002	0.0004	0.0154
−7	−0.0023	−0.0019	0.0341
−6	−0.0045	−0.0064	0.0160
−5	−0.0069	−0.0133	0.0267
−4	0.0128	−0.0005	0.0323
−3	0.0043	0.0038	0.0415
−2	0.0217	0.0255	0.0679
−1	0.0256	0.0511	0.0522
0	0.0774	0.1285	0.1309
1	0.0144	0.1430	0.0623
2	0.0107	0.1537	0.0510
3	−0.0021	0.1516	0.0077
4	0.0074	0.1590	0.0235
5	0.0028	0.1618	0.0140
6	0.0046	0.1664	0.0689
7	0.0025	0.1689	0.0121
8	0.0051	0.1740	0.0161
9	−0.0007	0.1733	0.0364
10	−0.0035	0.1697	0.0198

Note: t-test on cumulative abnormal returns. CAAR −10 days to +10 days = 0.1697 (significant at the 1% level).

Table 2. Performance Surrounding the Ann. Bid (Target Control Sample).

Days	AAR	CAAR	Std. Dev.
−10	−0.0041	−0.0041	0.0208
−9	0.0006	−0.0034	0.0226
−8	−0.0018	−0.0052	0.0176
−7	−0.0011	−0.0063	0.0219
−6	−0.0032	−0.0095	0.0173
−5	−0.0018	−0.0113	0.0165
−4	−0.0023	−0.0136	0.0230
−3	0.0026	−0.0110	0.0385
−2	0.0124	0.0014	0.0257
−1	0.0279	0.0293	0.0550
0	0.2472	0.2765	0.1982
1	0.0126	0.2891	0.0417
2	−0.0041	0.2851	0.0478
3	−0.0021	0.2830	0.0191
4	0.0005	0.2881	0.0351
5	0.0010	0.2892	0.0162
6	0.0143	0.3035	0.0365
7	0.0046	0.3081	0.0223
8	0.0025	0.3106	0.0213
9	0.0040	0.3146	0.0291
10	0.0002	0.3148	0.0155

Note: t-test on cumulative abnormal returns. CAAR −10 days to +10 days = 0.3148 (significant at the 1% level).

the month of the announcement. The result of this study is no different in that target shareholders do benefit significantly as Tables 1 and 2 show. However, as can be seen from Table 1, the target^{control} sample gains notably more in the period of ten days before and ten days after the first public announcement bid. The target$^{\text{u-valuation}}$ sample also gains significantly with a CAAR of 0.1697 over the event period as compared to 0.3148 for the target^{control} sample. One explanation is the payment method used and also the subsequent bid premium offered to the target$^{\text{u-valuation}}$ sample. This will be addressed in the latter part of this study.

4.2. Bidder Results: Announcement Returns

Table 3 presents the abnormal returns for the sample of bidding firms that have acquired undervalued targets (bidder$^{\text{u-valuation}}$). Table 3 shows that bidder$^{\text{u-valuation}}$ shareholders will experience positive gains from the event of acquiring an

Table 3. Performance Surrounding the Ann. Bid (Bidder-UV Sample).

Days	AAR	CAAR	Std. Dev.
−10	−0.0025	−0.0025	0.0151
−9	0.0054	0.0028	0.0130
−8	0.0025	0.0054	0.0240
−7	0.0040	0.0094	0.0146
−6	−0.0015	0.0079	0.0100
−5	−0.0029	0.0050	0.0123
−4	−0.0010	0.0040	0.0124
−3	0.0046	0.0086	0.0170
−2	0.0074	0.0160	0.0193
−1	0.0001	0.0161	0.0115
0	−0.0003	0.0158	0.0355
1	0.0035	0.0193	0.0223
2	0.0013	0.0206	0.0224
3	0.0061	0.0267	0.0241
4	0.0017	0.0284	0.0129
5	0.0033	0.0317	0.0218
6	0.0009	0.0325	0.0253
7	−0.0049	0.0276	0.0238
8	0.0030	0.0306	0.0127
9	0.0035	0.0341	0.0273
10	−0.0021	0.0320	0.0123

Note: *t*-test on cumulative abnormal returns. CAAR −10 days to +10 days = 0.0320 (significant at the 1% level).

undervalued firm. In the 20-day period surrounding the takeover announcement, the gains reported are significantly positive, with shareholders benefiting by over 3%, thus supporting H1. This is significantly higher than has been noticed in past studies. Sudarsanam et al. (1996) find bidders generally lose by around 5%, while Barnes (1998) reports positive bidder returns of 1% surrounding the bid announcement. However, prior studies have not separated under-valuation motivated takeovers from that of general takeovers. The returns for the bidder^{control} sample (Table 4) are found to be small and insignificant. As the bidder$^{\text{uv target}}$ sample consists of 25 companies it was felt non-parametric tests such as the Generalised Sign Rank Test and Wilcoxon Signed Ranks Test would be appropriate. The results of the Generalised Sign Rank Test indicate the cumulative abnormal returns in the event period are significantly positive as compared to the non-event period studied for the bidder$^{\text{uv target}}$ sample. The Wilcoxon Signed Ranks Test illustrates that the bidder$^{\text{uv target}}$ abnormal returns found in the event-window differ significantly from the bidder^{general} sample returns.

Table 4. Performance Surrounding the Ann. Bid (Bidder Control Sample).

Days	AAR	CAAR	Std. Dev.
−10	0.0039	0.0039	0.0151
−9	−0.0029	0.0010	0.0130
−8	−0.0005	0.0005	0.0240
−7	−0.0009	−0.0004	0.0146
−6	0.0001	−0.0004	0.0100
−5	0.0009	0.0005	0.0123
−4	−0.0085	−0.0080	0.0124
−3	0.0063	−0.0016	0.0170
−2	0.0038	0.0021	0.0193
−1	−0.0003	0.0018	0.0115
0	0.0007	0.0088	0.0335
1	0.0063	0.0152	0.0223
2	−0.0006	0.0146	0.0224
3	−0.0001	0.0144	0.0241
4	0.0012	0.0157	0.0129
5	−0.0052	0.0104	0.0128
6	0.0044	0.0148	0.0253
7	0.0050	0.0198	0.0238
8	−0.0035	0.0163	0.0127
9	−0.0060	0.0103	0.0273
10	0.0049	0.0153	0.0123

Note: t-test on cumulative abnormal returns. CAAR −10 days to +10 days = 0.0153 (significant at the 1% level).

4.3. Pre-Bid Target Performance

This section examines the performance of the U-V targets one-year before the first public bid announcement is made. The stock prices are examined because poor valuation ratios are likely to be associated with poor market performance also. Table 5 presents the pre-bid abnormal returns for the 25 target firms found to be undervalued by applying a valuation ratio approach. Table 5 also details the pre-bid performance of the target^{control} sample. As Table 5 indicates the pre-bid period is measured from 12 months before the bid to three months before the takeover announcement. This period is sufficient to measure pre-bid performance, the period ends three months before the bid as some studies have found abnormal returns concerning the bid approach up to 2 months before the takeover bid announcement. The results here make interesting reading in that the target^{control} sample loses significantly over this period. The CAAR is significantly negative at around −19% and supports the disciplinary hypothesis in that bidders are acquiring inefficiently run companies and also supports the findings of Agrawal

Table 5. The Pre-Bid Performance (a) Target-UV Sample and (b) Target Control Sample.

Months	AAR	CAAR	Std. Dev.
(a) Target-UV sample[a]			
−12	−0.0035	−0.0035	0.0134
−11	−0.0039	−0.0052	0.0092
−10	−0.0037	−0.0254	0.0142
−9	−0.0026	−0.0360	0.0166
−8	−0.0009	−0.0136	0.0221
−7	0.0066	−0.0396	0.0239
−6	−0.0049	−0.0380	0.0198
−5	−0.0010	−0.0229	0.0134
−4	−0.0027	−0.0321	0.0414
−3	−0.0037	−0.0798	0.0165
(b) Target control sample[b]			
−12	−0.0039	−0.0039	0.0139
−11	0.0028	−0.0394	0.0100
−10	0.0003	−0.0824	0.0286
−9	0.0014	−0.1031	0.0219
−8	−0.0030	−0.1349	0.0126
−7	−0.0020	−0.1337	0.0153
−6	−0.0004	−0.1690	0.0164
−5	0.0005	−0.1835	0.0159
−4	0.0073	−0.1858	0.0302
−3	0.0370	−0.1907	0.1850

[a] *t*-test on cumulative abnormal returns. CAAR −12 months to −3 months = −0.0798 (not statistically significant).

[b] *t*-test on cumulative abnormal returns. CAAR −12 months to −3 months = −0.1907 (significant at the 1% level).

and Walking (1994) and Denis and Denis (1995). The target$^{\text{uv target}}$ sample also reports losses of around 7% in this period, but this is not found to be significant. This may be expected as the market has mispriced the company and does not necessarily reflect the hypothesis of the firm being poorly run, but simply that the firm has been valued incorrectly and the bidder has tried to capitalise on this.

4.4. Pre-Bid Bidder Performance

Table 6 presents the pre-bid performance of the bidder$^{\text{uv target}}$ sample and bidder^{control} sample. The pre-bid performance of bidders that acquire undervalued

Table 6. The Pre-Bid Performance (a) Bidder-UV Sample and (b) Bidder Control Sample.

Months	AAR	CAAR	Std. Dev.
(a) Bidder-UV sample[a]			
−12	0.0055	0.0055	0.0338
−11	−0.0036	0.0062	0.0123
−10	0.0008	0.0006	0.0144
−9	0.0013	0.0318	0.0167
−8	0.0009	0.0281	0.0087
−7	0.0010	0.0416	0.0158
−6	0.0000	0.0561	0.0103
−5	−0.0017	0.0725	0.0270
−4	0.0005	0.0842	0.0128
−3	0.0064	0.0924	0.0152
(b) Bidder control sample[b]			
−12	0.0012	0.0012	0.0153
−11	−0.0021	−0.0055	0.0198
−10	−0.0021	−0.0486	0.0169
−9	−0.0027	−0.0501	0.0152
−8	−0.0041	−0.0801	0.0191
−7	−0.0008	−0.0954	0.0176
−6	0.0030	−0.0913	0.0226
−5	0.0002	−0.0892	0.0157
−4	0.0015	−0.0861	0.0106
−3	0.0043	−0.0736	0.0214

[a] *t*-test on cumulative abnormal returns. CAAR −12 months to −3 months = 0.0924 (significant at the 5% level).

[b] *t*-test on cumulative abnormal returns. CAAR −12 months to −3 months = −0.0736 (significant at the 10% level).

targets is significantly strong in this period, showing gains of around 9%. In contrast, the control sample of bidders significantly underperforms in this period, losing significantly by approximately 7%. A *t*-test for independent samples shows a significant difference exists between these two samples. Studies by Lang, Stulz and Walking (1989) and Servaes (1991) find that in both tender offers and mergers

Table 7. Payment Method.

	Cash (%)	Share (%)	Mixed (%)	Average Bid Premium (%)
$Sample^{U\text{-}V}$	56	24	20	34
$Sample^{Control}$	53	20	27	45

efficient bidders with a Tobin's q value greater than one gain substantially when acquiring a target with a Tobin's q value less than one. This implies that high performing bidders taking over low performing targets are able to gain as the market perceives them to be capable of turning around underperforming target firms. In this study, we do not differentiate between bidders in terms of their q value, but in terms of pre-bid stock performance. The results do not necessarily support the findings of Lang, Stulz and Walking. From the control sample used in the study, the findings are that bidders that are underperforming also acquire underperforming targets. In the case of high performing bidders, the targets are not necessarily underperforming, simply undervalued.

To shed further light on these results it is necessary to look at the subsequent payment methods chosen by these samples and also the bid premium that was offered. In line with the hypothesis, it is expected that a lower premium is associated with the bidder$^{\text{uv target}}$ sample in addition to higher degree of share-exchange offers.

In order to examine this concept we looked at the bid premium paid for the undervalued targets studied in the paper. Bid premiums were calculated as:

$$\frac{\text{BidOffer} - \text{Target}_{\text{price}-20}}{\text{Target}_{\text{price}-20}}$$

Where BidOffer is the final price paid per target share by the bidder and $\text{Target}_{\text{price}-20}$ is the value of the target shares twenty days prior to the first bid announcement.

Jensen (1993) reports that bid premiums averaged 41%, but some were over 100% during the period 1976–1990. In the U.K., Barnes (1998) states that bid premiums need to be in excess of 30% before the market accepts the bid as serious and has the possibility of a positive response.

It is found that the bid premium paid by the bidder$^{\text{uv target}}$ sample is on average 34%. We also examine a general control sample of 30 firms to determine the average bid premiums paid in the U.K. during a similar time period and find this to be 45%. This implies that when the bidder identifies an undervalued target it is not willing to pay a higher premium for the company. Competitors would not have this information unless they incur similar costs in identifying an undervalued target. Hence, it is possible that competitors see the acquisition as signalling the firm does not require a high premium due to its value, yet it is possible other prospective bidders do not know the target is indeed undervalued.

We also examined the method of payment in undervalued acquisitions to determine any systematic pattern. Table 7 also displays the chosen method of payment with regard to the undervaluation sample and the control sample.

It is found that a share offer is the preferred method of payment (24% against 20%) in undervalued acquisitions. This could imply that the target shareholders would find it more attractive to dispose of their undervalued shares in return for bidder shares. Previous literature has shown the market to react adversely to bidders approaching target firms with share-offer bids as compared to all-cash bids, reinforcing the positive gains found in this study. However, this evidence is not conclusive and more studies need to be done to shed further light on this aspect. The main conclusion that can be taken from examining the chosen method of payment and the bid premium details is that bidders acquiring undervalued target pay a lower premium as compared to the control group studied. The findings of the control sample support the overpayment hypothesis, where bidders tend to increase the takeover premia to ensure success. However, in the case of undervalued targets it allows the bidder to offer a lower premium and therefore enjoy higher gains over the announcement period.

5. CONCLUSION

This study set out to examine the announcement period performance of bidding firms wherein the takeover is driven by the motivation of acquiring undervalued firms. A novel process of identifying undervalued firms was used in this study based on valuation ratios. Prior studies are ambiguous concerning bidder gains. As the takeovers in this study are primarily motivated by undervaluation it is expected that bidders gain significantly more. The results of the study endorses this hypothesis as the cumulative abnormal return from day -10 to $+10$ is in excess of 3%, which is notably more than what previous studies have found. The results from the non-parametric tests reveal that the abnormal returns to bidders involved in undervalued acquisitions is significantly different when compared to a null period and also to a control sample.

The result of this study sheds some distinctive insights into the market for corporate control. The market is able to identify takeovers driven by the undervaluation phenomenon and accordingly impounds this into the bidders stock price. The study also finds that in the case of undervalued acquisitions the bidder may have a dominant position as evidenced by the greater use of share payments. It is also seen that the bidder offers a lower bid premium for the target. This has valuable strategic implications for existing management in that it tells them that they can increase the value of their company by identifying and acquiring undervalued firms. As a result, it is in the interest of the management and shareholders to ensure that any merger or takeover they enter into takes these aspects into consideration.

ACKNOWLEDGMENT

The author wishes to acknowledge the excellent research assistance provided by Michael Forsyth, doctoral student at the Robert Gordon University.

REFERENCES

Agrawal, A., & Walking, R. A. (1994). Executive careers and compensation surrounding takeover bids. *Journal of Finance*, *49*, 985–1014.

Barber, B. M., Palmer, D., & Wallace, J. (1995). Determinants of conglomerate and predatory acquisitions: Evidence from the 1960s. *Journal of Corporate Finance*, *1*, 283–318.

Barnes, P. (1998). Why do bidders do badly out of mergers? Some U.K. evidence. *Journal of Business Finance and Accounting*, *25*(5–6), 571–595.

Basu, S. (1983). 'The relationship between earnings' yield, market value and return for NYSE common stocks: Further evidence. *Journal of Financial Economics*, *12*, 129–156.

Beaver, W. H., & Ryan, S. H. (1993). Accounting fundamentals of the book-to-market ratio. *Financial Analysts Journal*, *49*(6), 50–56.

Berkovitch, E., & Narayanan, M. P. (1993). Motives for takeovers: An empirical investigation. *Journal of Financial and Quantitative Analysis*, *28*, 347–362.

Boehmer, E., Musumeci, M. P., & Poulsen, A. B. (1991). Event-study methodology under conditions of event-induced variance. *Journal of Financial Economics*, *30*, 253–272.

Bradley, M., Desai, A., & Kim, E. H. (1988). Synergistic gains from corporate acquisitions and their division between the stockholders of target and acquiring firms. *Journal of Financial Economics*, *21*, 3–40.

Damodaran, A. (1997). *Corporate finance: Theory and practice*. Wiley.

Datta, D. K., Pinches, G. E., & Narayanan, V. K. (1992). Factors influencing wealth acquisitions: A meta analysis. *Strategic Management Journal*, *13*, 67–84.

Denis, D., & Denis, D. (1995). Performance changes following top management dismissals. *Journal of Finance*, *50*, 1029–1057.

Fama, E. F., & French, K. R. (1995). Size and book-to-market factors in earnings and returns. *Journal of Finance*, *50*, 131–156.

Fishman, M. J. (1989). Pre-emptive bidding and the role of medium of exchange in acquisitions. *Journal of Finance*, *44*, 41–57.

Ghosh, A., & Ruland, K. R. (1998). Managerial ownership, the method of payment for acquisitions, and executive job retention. *Journal of Finance*, *53*, 785–798.

Grullon, G., Michaely, R., & Swary, I. (1997). Capital adequacy, bank mergers, and the medium of payment. *Journal of Business Finance and Accounting*, *24*(1), 97–124.

Huang, Y., & Walking, R. (1987). Target abnormal returns associated with acquisition announcements – payment, acquisition form and managerial resistance. *Journal of Financial Economics*, *19*, 329–349.

Jensen, M. C. (1993). The modern industrial revolution, exit and failure of internal control systems. *Journal of Finance*, *48*, 53–80.

Kini, O., Kracaw, R., & Mian, S. (1995). Corporate takeovers, firm performance and board composition. *Journal of Corporate Finance*, *1*, 383–412.

Lang, L. H. P., Stulz, R. M., & Walking, R. A. (1989). Managerial performance, Tobin's q and the gains from successful tender offers. *Journal of Financial Economics*, *24*, 137–154.

Martin, K. J. (1996). The method of payment in corporate acquisitions, investment opportunities, and management ownership. *Journal of Finance*, *51*(4), 1227–1246.

Martin, K. J., & McConnell, J. J. (1991). Corporate performance, corporate takeovers, and management turnover. *Journal of Finance*, *46*, 671–688.

Mitchell, M., & Lehn, K. (1990). Do bad bidders make good targets? *Journal of Political Economy*, *98*, 372–398.

Morck, R., Shleifer, A., & Vishny, R. W. (1990). Do managerial objectives drive bad acquisitions? *Journal of Finance*, *45*, 31–48.

Myers, S. C., & Majluf, N. S. (1984). Corporate financing and investment decisions when firms have information that investors do not have. *Journal of Financial Economics*, *13*(2), 184–221.

Roll, R. (1986). The hubris hypothesis of corporate takeovers. *Journal of Business*, *59*, 197–216.

Servaes, H. (1991). Tobin's Q and the gains from takeovers. *Journal of Finance*, *46*(1), 409–419.

Sudarsanam, S., Holl, P., & Salami, A. (1996). Shareholder wealth gains in mergers: Effect of synergy and ownership structure. *Journal of Business Finance and Accounting*, *23*(5–6), 673–698.

Travlos, N. (1987). Corporate takeover bids, methods of payment, and bidding firms' stock returns. *Journal of Finance*, *42*(4), 943–963.

REPLICATING PATTERNS IN AUTOCORRELATED FINANCIAL TIME SERIES

Rifat Gorener, Omer Demirel and John R. Norsworthy

ABSTRACT

Bootstrap replications of financial time series are used to test the efficacy of portfolio selection algorithms, arbitrage strategies, and other risk management techniques. This paper shows several methods for bootstrapping financial time series with the objective of preserving autocorrelation structure and allowing time-varying variance in the replicated series. The replicated series are tested against the original distributions by two criteria: comparison of the distributions' moments, and of their autocorrelation coefficients. Our modification of the moving block bootstrap substantially out-performs the conventional bootstrap.

1. BOOTSTRAPPING FINANCIAL TIME SERIES

Important reasons for bootstrapping or otherwise replicating the distributions of financial time series include the use of the resulting data to test the efficacy of portfolio selection algorithms, arbitrage strategies, and other risk management techniques. Data from macroeconomic forecasts, which are comparatively very low frequency, are generally not helpful when the decision model is to be applied to distributions of weekly or higher frequency financial data.

Bank and Financial Market Efficiency: Global Perspectives
Research in Banking and Finance, Volume 5, 235–250

ISSN: 1567-7915/doi:10.1016/S1567-7915(04)05012-8

Broadly, there are two conventional ways to replicate the properties of a distribution: bootstrapping from the (discrete) empirical distribution itself,[1] and sampling randomly from a (possibly continuous) fitted distribution. Where the investigator wishes to preserve properties of the distribution beyond the mean and variance, a moment-based approach may be taken. Families of distributions, such as the Pearson or Johnson curves, offer the possibility of fitting or selecting the target distribution in terms of its moments – or other calculated characteristics – and then sampling from the fitted distribution to replicate the target distribution.

Simple bootstrapping or moment-based re-sampling techniques do not take into account the autocorrelation aspects of time series structure. Moreover, the tests for the quality of replication of an empirical distribution often are limited to the means and variances of the new distributions, omitting autocorrelation and higher moments.[2] There is ample evidence that asset prices are sensitive to properties of returns distributions beyond the first two moments.[3] Yet, as argued below, it is the occasional "spikes" in autocorrelation that it may be most important to replicate for testing asset selection models, because – in actual trading data – asset prices do not change instantaneously, but rather they "ramp up" to the new level.

In this paper, we show moving block bootstrapping techniques can be applied in a few simple ways to generate replicates of target financial time series, and demonstrate several methods for quantitatively comparing the replicate series to the target. The approach, we believe, can also be applied to sets of cointegrated series, but in this paper, we do not "go there."

2. MOVING BLOCKS BOOTSTRAP (MBB)

The moving blocks bootstrap technique, which we use in this paper, was introduced independently by Kunsch (1989), and Liu and Singh (1992). Let $X_1, X_2 \ldots X_n$ be a stationary time series and B_i be the block of b consecutive observations starting from the ith observation. The $B_i = (X_i \ \ldots \ X_{i+b-1})$, $i = 1, 2 \ldots n - b + 1$, form $n - b + 1$ overlapping blocks from the original sample. Sampling with replacement and concatenating n/b blocks from the set $\{B_1, B_2 \ldots B_{n-b+1}\}$ produces the bootstrap sample. In the MBB, the reason for blocking the series is to preserve the serial dependence structure within blocks. The assumption is that, for block size b, observations more than b time units apart are essentially independent. The MBB becomes the conventional bootstrap when $b = 1$.

One must carefully select the block size for the MBB. If the block size is too big, the bootstrap samples will simply be reproductions of the original series, so there will be too little variety in the bootstrap samples. On the other hand, if the block length is too small, the dependence structure will not be preserved, so there will be too little fidelity in the bootstrap samples.

3. FINDING THE OPTIMAL BLOCK SIZE

We used the procedure for generating time series scenarios introduced by Demirel and Willemain (2002). This approach follows Kedem (1993) in characterizing a time series by its higher order crossing counts (HOC), i.e. the counts of zero crossings made by the series and its successive differences. Kedem showed that this characterization is equivalent to the classical characterizations provided by the autocorrelation function and spectral density function. Demirel and Willemain (2002) developed an index Δ that measures the distance between two time series based on differences in their higher order crossing counts. Δ is the sum of squared standardized differences between the coordinates of the two series in normalized HOC space. Given a series of length n and maximum order of difference $K-1$, the largest possible number of sign changes is $n-K$. Let D_{ki} and D_{kj} be the kth HOC for the ith and jth series. To standardize across series lengths, define the normalized HOC

$$d_{ki} = \frac{D_{ki}}{n-K}$$

$$d_{kj} = \frac{D_{kj}}{n-K}$$

then Δ is computed by,

$$\Delta = \sum Z_k^2, \quad k = 1, \ldots, K$$

where

$$Z_k = \frac{d_{ki} - d_{kj}}{\mathrm{SE}\{d_{ki} - d_{kj}\}}$$

and

$$\mathrm{SE}\{d_{ki} - d_{kj}\} = \left\{ \frac{d_{ki}(1-d_{ki}) + d_{kj}(1-d_{kj})}{n-K} \right\}^{1/2}.$$ We used $K = 10$

The steps of finding optimal block size can be summarized as follows:

(1) Divide the original series of 1240 observations into 10 subseries with 124 observations each.

(2) Compute $\binom{10}{2} = 45$ values of Δ using all pairs of subseries.

(3) Create $r = 50$ bootstrap samples of each subseries, beginning with a block size of one and incrementing by one.

(4) For each block size, compute the 50 values of Δ^* between each of the subseries and its bootstrap samples.

(5) Compare the sample distributions of 45 sample values of Δ and $45 \times 50 = 2250$ sample values of Δ^* using the K-S two sample test.
(6) The block size, which gives the minimum K-S statistic value D, is the best block size for subseries, $\hat{b}_m$.
(7) Estimate the optimal block size for the whole series by using the square root rule relation established by Demirel and Willemain (2002), $\hat{b}_{1240}=10^{1/2}\hat{b}_{124}$.

The optimal block sizes computed for each stock prices are given in Table 1.

The objective for this paper is to compare conventional bootstrapping of several distributions of prices and returns for stocks of several large companies with the autocorrelation-based approach that we have developed. The stock prices will generally be strongly autocorrelated, the returns weakly autocorrelated. Testing both provides an idea of the relative importance of the new approach for the two categories of series.

The comparisons between sets of replicated distributions are based on inspection of the first four moments of the distributions and on the frequency breakdowns of the distributions based on wavelet analysis. Such comparisons will of course favor the bootstrap techniques that seek explicitly to capture autocorrelation structure; conventional replication is expected to duplicate the distribution of observations, but of course, when based on independent trials, is very unlikely to approximate the autocorrelation structure. Consequently, three approaches to identifying and replicating first order autocorrelation are also assessed against each other. These are described below as Model A, the linear model; Model B, the ratio model; and Model C, the log linear model.

Assume that $y = \{y_i\}, i = 1 \ldots T$, is the empirical time series with sample mean

$$\bar{x} = \frac{1}{T}\sum_{i=1}^{T} y_i \tag{1}$$

and sample variance

$$s^2 = \frac{1}{T-1}\sum_{i=1}^{T}(y_i - \bar{x})^2 = \frac{1}{T-1}\sum_{i=1}^{T} e_i^2 \tag{2}$$

Table 1. The Optimal Block Size of Normalized Price Data Residuals for the Job of Scenario Generation.

Stock symbol	CSCO	GE	JPM	XOM	SP500
Optimal block size	9	22	16	19	12

4. DATA SOURCES AND TRANSFORMATIONS

The data set used in this research, contains 5-year, 1996–2000, daily stock prices for 4 large cap companies from various industries and S&P500 index. The data were obtained from The Center for Research in Security Prices (CRSP). In this initial effort, price series from various industries, such as energy, technology and banking & financial services in the sample, give us a range of characteristics of

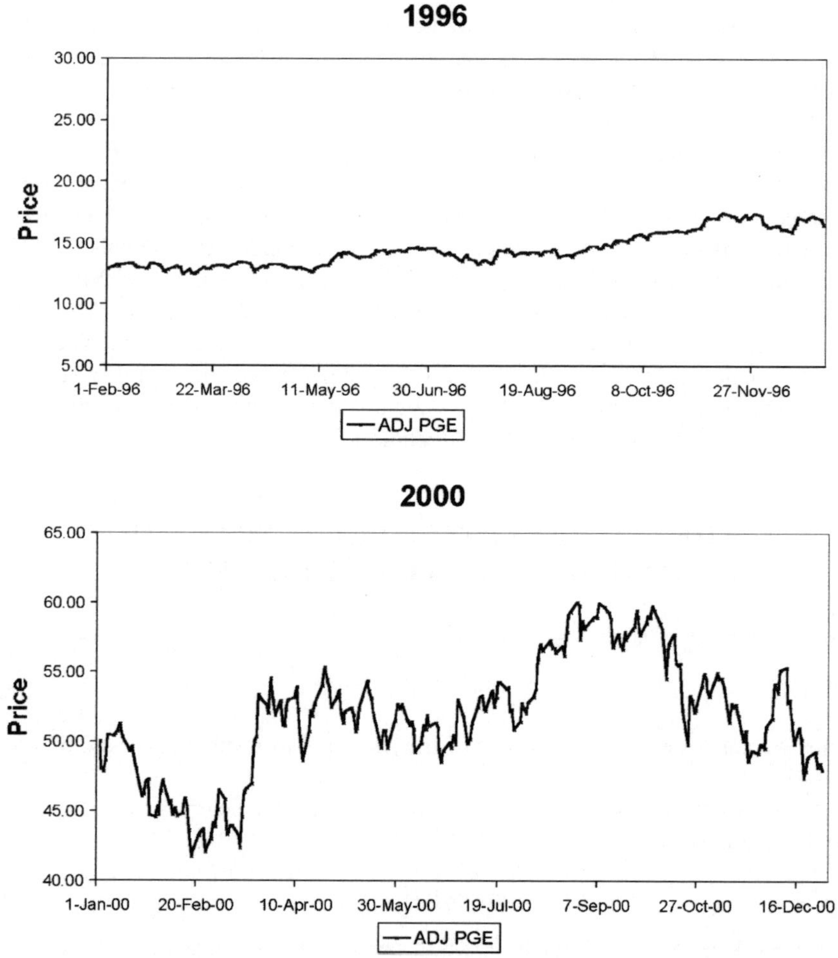

Fig. 1. The Split Adjusted Price Data of GE for the Years 1996 and 2000.

the time series such as volatility, and provides differing optimal block sizes for the moving block bootstrap technique. Companies studied are General Electric (GE), Cisco Systems (CSCO), J. P. Morgan & Chase (JPM), and Exxon-Mobile (XOM).

Stock prices are, in general, non-stationary time series, while returns are often stationary. It is common that stock *price* data have substantial autocorrelation, and that this autocorrelation must be preserved to test investment strategies. However, bootstrap technique requires that we have stationary series. Therefore, two data transformations were applied to the stock price series. The first transformation performed is 10-period moving average to smooth out trends and high frequency cycles. 10-period moving average transformed series are stationary in the first order, however non-stationarity of the series remains in the second moment due to unstable variance. The second transformation used to obtain constant variance is a 10-period rolling standard deviation.

Before applying the bootstrap technique to the sample, it is important to explain data transformation further. In the first data transformation, a 10-period moving average smoothing is calculated from the original series. In the second data transformation, 10-period rolling standard deviation is applied to residuals obtained by subtracting 10-period moving average series from original series. Without the second data transformation, residual series are non-stationary, with substantially increasing variance through time, as Fig. 1 shows clearly: the variance is considerably greater in 2000 than in 1996 for GE (shown) and for the other series as well. After the data transformations, we obtained constant variance residuals that conform to requirements of the MBB technique.

5. THE CONVENTIONAL BOOTSTRAP MODEL (WITHOUT AUTOCORRELATION)

The target model may be described as

$$y_t = \mu + e_t \tag{3}$$

Thus we can view the construction of the Model A as estimating μ and σ^2 from Eq. (3).

The conventional bootstrap model expresses the ith element $\tilde{y}_i$, $i = 1 \ldots I$, of the bootstrap series as

$$\tilde{y}_i = \mu + r\{e_t\} \tag{4}$$

where $r\{\cdot\}$ denotes an element drawn at random (with replacement) – i.e. independently – from the distribution in brackets, the error terms from the base model.

6. TRANSFORMATION OF THE STOCK PRICE SERIES

An important characteristic of many financial time series, even in relatively short periods of time, is that the variance of the series changes in time. The bootstrap technique is most conveniently applied to a homoskedastic series, however. To adjust for the changing variance, we transform the series by dividing by a ten-period rolling standard deviation.[4] Then define e_t as

$$e_t = \frac{\eta_t}{s_t}$$

so that $\{e_t\}$ is the set of variance-stable residuals to be used in bootstrapping.

The bootstrapping procedure then proceeds sequentially for each element of the replicate series $\tilde{y}_t$. Consider initially the first P elements, where $P = \max(M, k)$. These elements may be omitted entirely, or replicated as

$$\tilde{y}_t = y_t^0 + r\{e_t\} \quad t = 1 \ldots P - 1$$

For elements of the series $t \geq P$,

$$\tilde{y}_t = \sum_{m=1}^{M} (\tilde{y}_{t-1}) + \alpha t + s_t r\{e_t\}$$

and the replicate of the original series is

$$\tilde{Y}_t = e^{\tilde{y}_i}$$

7. RESULTS OF EMPIRICAL STUDY

Table 1 shows the optimal block size for the five price series studied. The range is substantial: from 9 observations for Cisco to 22 observations for GE. In general, the greater the optimal block size, the greater the autocorrelation in the price series.

Table 2 reports the results of the MBB bootstrap procedure for the five stock price series. Clearly, the procedure reasonably well replicates the first four moments of the distributions rather well. There is some tendency for the maxima of the replicated series to be somewhat higher on average, particularly for the S&P500 and for Cisco. This tendency, however, is less serious than would be the case if the range (maximum minus minimum) were reduced: damping the range could make the resulting scenarios less satisfactory for testing investment strategies. To the extent that other properties are preserved, the slightly larger range would tend to make the tests of investment strategies more robust. The conventional

Table 2. Descriptive Statistics: Original Series and 200 Bootstrap Replications.

Series	Mean	Std. Dev.	Kurt	Skew	Min	Max
CSCO stock price series, 1996–2000						
Original price	24.5215	21.0735	−0.5190	0.9470	4.6944	80.0630
200-MBB replication average	24.7637	21.5087	−0.4336	0.9774	4.4929	85.3632
GE stock price series, 1996–2000						
Original price	31.0196	13.6025	−0.9759	0.4497	12.4375	60.0000
200-MBB replication average	31.1312	13.7812	−0.9366	0.4721	12.3161	62.5452
XON stock price series, 1996–2000						
Original price	66.4805	14.5790	−0.9716	−0.3991	39.1250	94.4380
200-MBB replication average	66.5483	14.7390	−0.9819	−0.3795	38.6778	95.9080
JPM stock price series, 1996–2000						
Original price	114.9120	20.8647	−0.2930	0.2980	74.5000	181.5000
200-MBB replication average	114.8836	21.0473	−0.2417	0.3065	73.3403	184.4209
S&P500 stock price series, 1996–2000						
Real index level	1084.5171	282.3209	−1.3677	−0.1541	626.6386	1527.4388
200-MBB replication average	1087.1149	285.8023	−1.3604	−0.1335	617.9685	1597.9052
Conventional bootstrap replications of SP500 stock price series, 1996–2000						
50-replication average	1087.1718	285.8702	−1.3596	−0.1334	612.5892	1621.5249

Table 3. K-S Tests for Normality of Moments of Distributions.

	Kolmogorov-Smirnov		
	Test-Stat	df	Sig.
CSCO			
Mean	0.03498	200	0.200[a]
Variance	0.04075	200	0.200[a]
Skew	0.03462	200	0.200[a]
Kurtosis	0.05398	200	0.200[a]
GE			
Mean	0.02663	200	0.200[a]
Variance	0.04223	200	0.200[a]
Skew	0.06138	200	0.06417
Kurtosis	0.03461	200	0.200[a]
JPM			
Mean	0.03573	200	0.200[a]
Variance	0.04875	200	0.200[a]
Skew	0.05279	200	0.200[a]
Kurtosis	0.06151	200	0.06307
XOM			
Mean	0.03589	200	0.200[a]
Variance	0.04792	200	0.200[a]
Skew	0.04687	200	0.200[a]
Kurtosis	0.04877	200	0.200[a]
SP500			
Mean	0.05501	200	0.200[a]
Variance	0.05804	200	0.09817
Skew	0.02717	200	0.200[a]
Kurtosis	0.04911	200	0.200[a]

[a]Lilliefors significance correction.

bootstrap is shown for 50 replications of the S&P500 Index for comparison with the MBB. The reproduction of the four moments of the original series is quite good; the increase in the range is larger for the conventional bootstrap than for the MBB.

Table 3 reports the results of the normality tests on the distribution properties of MBB replication series. We use Kolmogorov-Smirnov (K-S) test to determine whether the first four moments of the replicated distributions are normally distributed. As shown in the table, distributions of GE, J. P. Morgan and Exxon-Mobil replications are normal according to both K-S and JB tests at significance level of $\alpha = 0.05$.[5] Kurtosis of J. P. Morgan and skew of GE are close

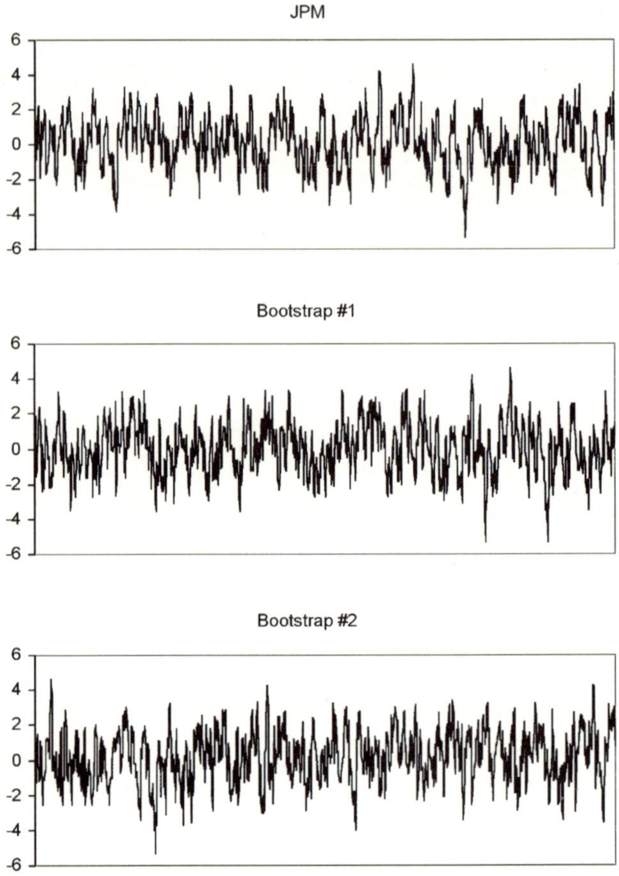

Fig. 2. The Normalized Residuals from the Stock Prices of J. P. Morgan and Chase and Two Bootstrap Replications. The MBB is Used with Optimal Block Size of 16.

calls as normal distributions by the K-S test, but normality is not rejected at the 0.05 level.

Figures 2 and 3 show the original JPM price series and two MBB replicates (Fig. 2), and the original and two conventional bootstrap replicates (Fig. 3). The MBB replicates are by no means identical, but the serial dependence structure is much better preserved than by the conventional bootstrap. It is clear that the number of zero crossings is much greater in the conventional case. Thus despite the finding that the conventional bootstrap preserves the moments of the distributions of prices

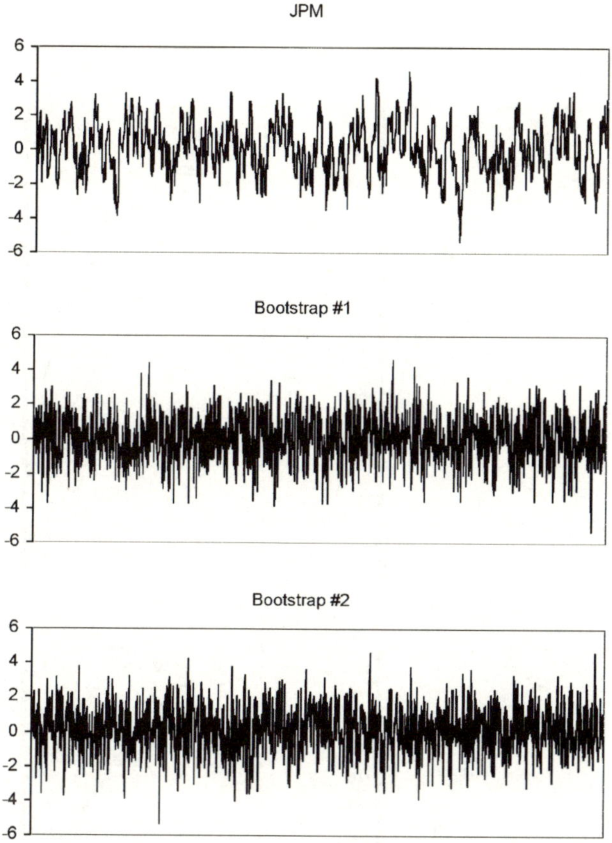

Fig. 3. Normalized Residuals from the Stock Prices of J. P. Morgan and Chase and Two Bootstrap Replications. The Conventional Bootstrap is Used.

quite well, it is inferior to the MBB concerning the intertemporal structure of the series.

Figure 4 shows the original Cisco stock price series and three MBB replicates. Cisco is the most volatile of the price series studied (as measured by the standard deviation or the range relative to the mean), and it also displays the strongest low frequency movement. It is thus the best choice of the stocks we examine to appraise the MBB's ability to capture the coarse features of a series. Figure 4 shows that these features are captured quite well in individual replicates, and gives strong visual evidence that the coarse time series structure is preserved.

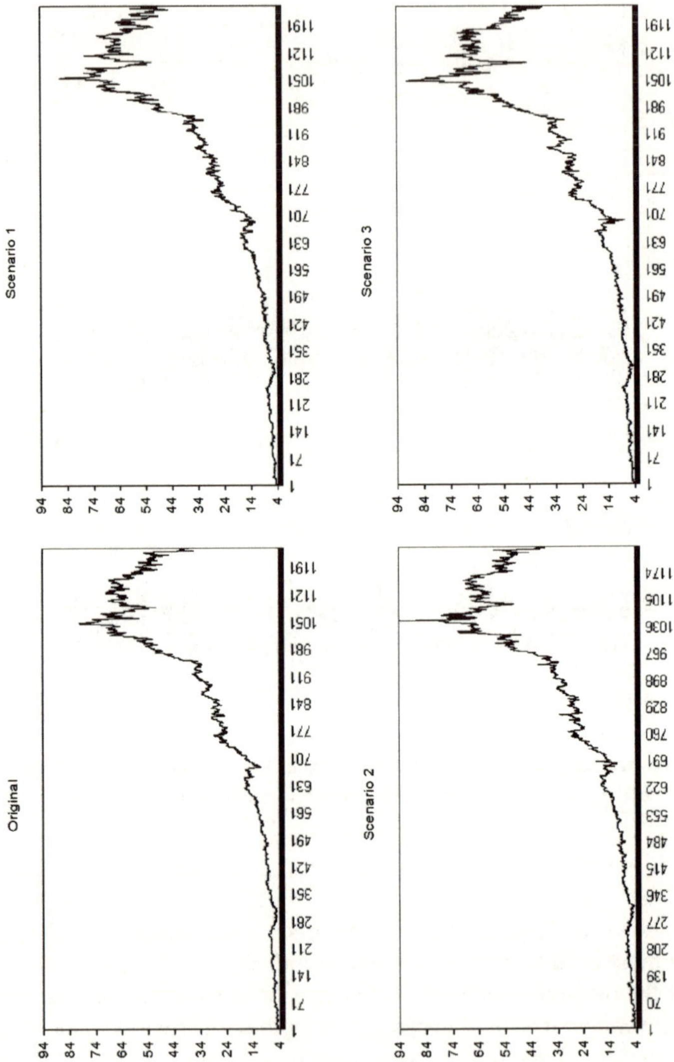

Fig. 4. The Split Adjusted Price Data of Cisco and 3 Scenarios Generated by Optimally Tuned MBB for Five Years.

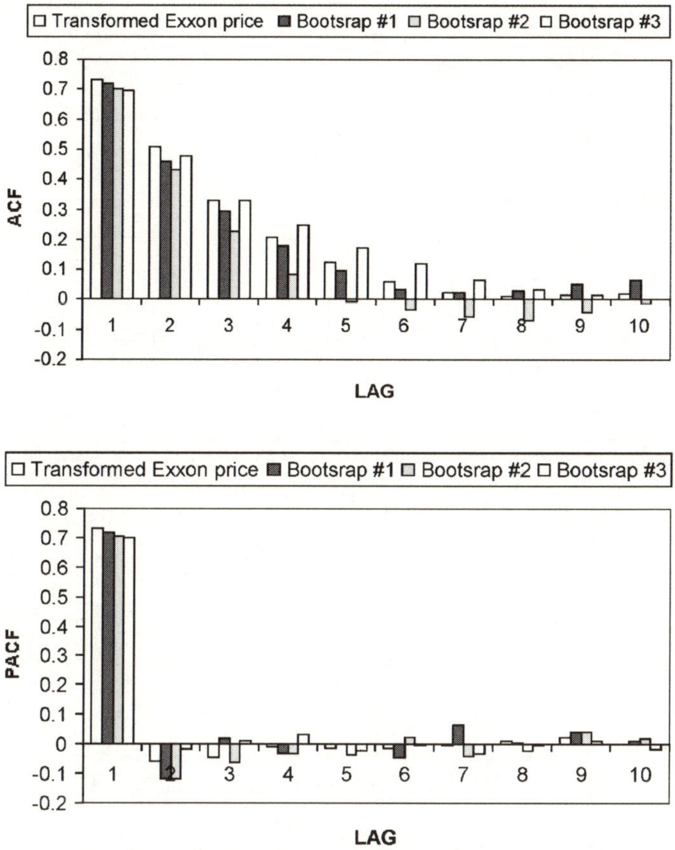

Fig. 5. Autocorrelations and Partial Autocorrelations of Exxon Price Data and Three Optimally Tuned MBB Replications.

Figures 5 and 6 display plots of the first ten coefficients of the full and partial autocorrelation functions for Exxon-Mobil for the five-year period for the MBB (Fig. 5) and the conventional bootstrap (Fig. 6). The upper panel in each figure shows the full autocorrelation coefficients for the original series (in the left-moat position) followed by the corresponding coefficients for three randomly chosen replicate scenarios. The lower panels show the same ordering of information for the partial autocorrelation coefficients. These figures depict starkly the advantage of the MBB over the conventional bootstrap. The MBB replicates quite closely the full autocorrelation structure as well as the partial structure (which largely determines the former, of course).

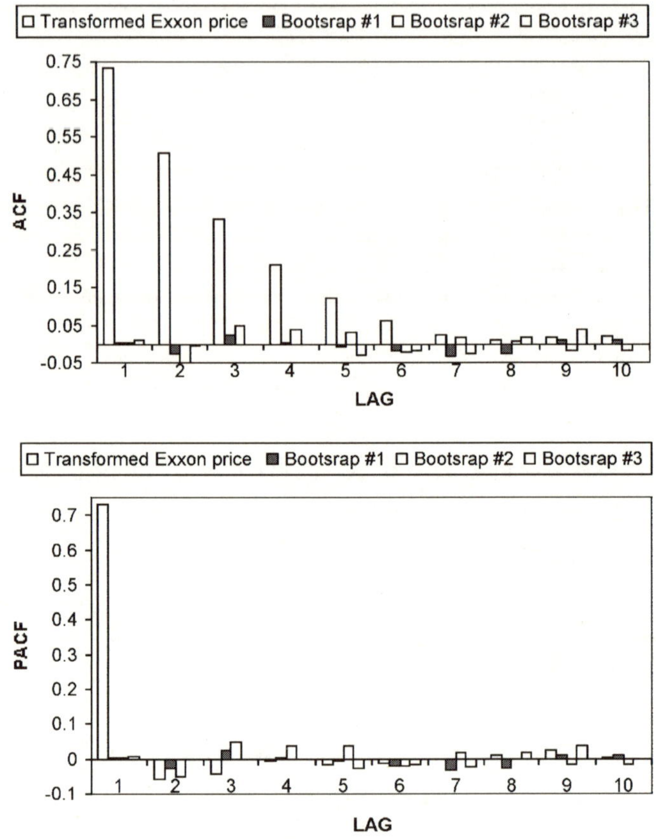

Fig. 6. Autocorrelations and Partial Autocorrelations of Exxon Price Data and Three Conventional Bootstrap Replications.

8. CONCLUSIONS

The moving block bootstrap (MBB) with the optimal block size chosen by the Demirel-Willemain (2002) criterion, replicates the features of non-stationary time series, including especially the autocorrelation structure. In this regard, it outperforms the conventional bootstrap by a wide (if herein unquantified) margin. The MBB therefore offers a basis for replicating a historical time series for testing various investment strategies for portfolio selection and turnover, arbitrage techniques, and risk management techniques generally. The conventional bootstrap misses the autocorrelation structure (essentially by design – the iid property of the conventional bootstrap replicates is the principle reason for the failure).

We note that all of the normality tests show that the replicated moments are somewhat larger than the moments of the original series, except in the case of the means. This systematic tendency requires further investigation; the slight increase in the variance is faintly detectable in Fig. 4.

On balance, however, the statistical and visual results of the replications suggest that the MBB method applied to these stock price series are sufficient to justify their use in simulation tests of strategic investment algorithms for single assets. The reproduction of the properties of the original series is generally quite good. The fact that the replicated series deviate slightly more from normality than the original series is at least better that if the bias were *toward* the normal distribution, in the sense that the tests will be slightly more robust.

There are several additional ways that we may extend the analysis. Formal hypothesis tests of the MBB against the alternative(s) are one way; use of wavelets analysis to appraise and compare the autocorrelation structures of the original and replicate distributions is another.[6] Application to intraday data may prove useful, especially in detecting periods of price changes in (almost) real time.

NOTES

1. Definitive work on the bootstrap is that of Efron. See, e.g. his 1979 paper. Application to economic series is reviewed by Vinod (1992).
2. For example, Norsworthy et al. (1998) reject the normal distribution for all Dow-Jones Industrials for 1984–1998 and three sub-periods. They also reject symmetric valuation of gains and losses.
3. For examples, see Fang and Lai (1997), Arditti (1971), and Barone-Adesi (1985). Their results are confirmed by Norsworthy et al. (1998).
4. The 10-period window is arbitrary. In subsequent work, it may be optimized for particular situations, possibly the optimal block size.
5. For samples with $n > 35$, the critical value at the 0.05 level is approximately 1.36/SQRT(n), where n is the sample size.
6. Wavelet analysis is a frequency-based technique beginning to penetrate the finance literature. See, e.g. Norsworthy et al. (2000) for a demonstration of the use of wavelets in asset pricing.

REFERENCES

Arditti, F. D. (1971). Another look at mutual fund performance. *Journal of Financial and Quantitative Analysis*, *6*(June), 909–912.

Barone-Adesi, G. (1985). Arbitrage equilibrium with skewed asset returns. *Journal of Financial and Quantitative Analysis*, *20*(September), 299–313.

Demirel, O. F., & Willemain, T. R. (2002). Generation of simulation input scenarios using bootstrap methods. *Journal of the Operational Research Society*, *53*, 69–78.

Efron, B. (1979). Bootstrapping methods: Another look at the jackknife. *Annals of Statistics*, *7*, 1–26.

Fang, H., & Lai, T.-Y. (1997). Co-Kurtosis and capital asset pricing. *The Financial Review* (May), 293–307.

Kedem, B. (1993). *Time series analysis by higher order crossings*. Piscataway, NJ: IEEE Press.

Kunsch, H. (1989). The jackknife and the bootstrap for general stationary observations. *The Annals of Statistics*, *17*, 1217–1241.

Norsworthy, J. R., Bessler, W., Schuler, R. E., Jr., Morgan, I. W., Gorener, R., & Li, D. (1998). Risk and return in asset pricing models: Conditional expectations and asymmetric risk aversion. Presented at the conference of the Financial Management Association, Chicago, IL (October).

Norsworthy, J. R., Li, D., & Gorener, R. (2000). Wavelet-based analysis of time series: An export from engineering to finance, leading technology change: Management issues and challenges. Proceedings of the IEEE Engineering Management Society, Albuquerque, NM, pp. 126–132.

Vinod, H. (1992). Bootstrap, jackknife, resampling and simulation methods: Applications in econometrics. In: G. Maddala, C. Rao & H. Vinod (Eds), *Handbook of Statistics: Econometrics* (Chap. 11, p. 11). Amsterdam: North-Holland.

FOREIGN PORTFOLIO INVESTMENTS AND STOCK PRICES: AN APPLICATION TO AN EMERGING MARKET

Halil Kiymaz and Uygar Urganci

ABSTRACT

This study investigates the impact of foreign direct investment on Turkish stocks. Findings show that there is a strong relationship between net foreign purchases of Turkish stocks and ISE Index returns. Net purchases of foreign investors have statistically highly significant positive impact on returns with much of the effect coming from the unexpected component of foreign purchases. Our results, further, demonstrate that net foreign purchases influence each industry portfolios differently. While three portfolios show a negative relation with foreign purchases, the remaining twelve portfolios exhibit a positive relationship between industry returns and foreign purchases.

1. INTRODUCTION

In the last two decades many so called "emerging" markets have liberalized and opened their capital markets to foreign investors, creating inflows of portfolio capital from mutual funds, institutional, and other investors. Stock market liberalization may lower the liberalizing country's cost of capital, which in turn can cause an increase in stock prices.

Bank and Financial Market Efficiency: Global Perspectives
Research in Banking and Finance, Volume 5, 251–268

ISSN: 1567-7915/doi:10.1016/S1567-7915(04)05013-X

The impact of foreign portfolio investments on equity market prices has been investigated from various perspectives. Bohn and Tesar (1996), Clark and Berko (1997), Brennan and Cao (1997) and Henry (2000) investigate the impacts of foreign purchases on market equity prices and report that U.S. purchases of equities in developed and emerging markets are positively associated with foreign market returns. For example, Henry (2000) reports that emerging markets experience average abnormal returns of 4.7% per month in real dollar terms during the implementation of a country's initial market liberalization. Clark and Berko (1997) report a statistically significant correlation between foreign purchases and stock returns in the Mexican stock market.

Literature also expands the impacts of foreign portfolio investments on the stability of foreign markets. By increasing the liquidity in foreign markets, portfolio investments were expected to bring stock price stability but the series of collapses observed in emerging markets (i.e. Mexican and East Asian crises) have questioned the benefits of these portfolio investments to local markets. Choe, Kho and Shulz (1999) find no evidence that foreign investors play a destabilizing role. Similarly, Bekaert and Harvey (2000) report insignificant increases in volatility of stock returns following capital market liberalization. Aitken (1998), on the other hand, reports the destabilizing influence of institutional investors in emerging markets.

How do international portfolio flows influence asset returns? Are stock prices vulnerable to such flows? What is the magnitude of those impacts? These questions have been of considerable interest to investors, economists, and policy makers in Turkey, and were posed with greater urgency during the times of financial turbulence during the last decade. Turkey liberalized its financial markets in August 1989 when the government issued Decree No. 32 for the capital account transactions. With this development, foreign investors were permitted to trade in listed securities without any restriction and the Turkish securities market became fully open to foreign institutional and individual investors.

This study examines the impact of net purchases of foreign investors on stock returns in Turkey over the period of January 1997 and December 2000 to provide evidence from a highly inflationary emerging market. Additionally, the study examines the impact of foreign portfolio investments on various industries. While other studies use market indices to investigate the impact of foreign purchases on stock prices, this study uses both market index and individual stock prices.

The study proceeds as follows: Section 2 provides a review of the literature. Section 3 gives a brief history of major events and developments in the Turkish economy and securities market with its characteristics during the last decade. Section 4 outlines our data and methodology. Section 5 reports empirical findings pertaining to the impact of monthly capital flows on equity returns in the ISE. Finally, Section 6 concludes the paper.

2. LITERATURE REVIEW

Foreign portfolio investments to emerging economies increased substantially during the 1990s following financial liberalization taking place during the 1980s and 1990s. The impact of these investments on equity market prices has been widely investigated. While the majority of studies report several potential benefits associated with financial market liberalization, some studies question the instability created in financial markets by foreign portfolio investments. The benefits of the financial market liberalization include lowering cost of capital, increasing liquidity and stock prices, and providing an important opportunity to attract foreign capital to finance growth in the economy in general. There are, however, various costs associated with financial market liberalization including financial markets becoming more destabilized as a result of sudden inflows and outflow of funds. Furthermore, market liberalization would expose domestic markets to foreign influence so that domestic markets may become more volatile if volatility is relatively higher in foreign markets.

Among the first group of studies, Brennan and Cao (1997) develop a model of international equity portfolio investment flows based on differences in information endowments between foreign and domestic investors. They analyze U.S. portfolio flows to 16 emerging markets, including Turkey, by assuming that in the case of a domestic cumulative information advantage, foreign investors would tend to behave as trend followers in a given period, buying in periods when the index rises and selling when the index falls. Their overall findings indicate that U.S. securities purchases in emerging markets are positively associated with local market returns of several countries.

Henry (2000) demonstrates that a government decision to let foreigners purchase securities in that country's stock market increases equity stock prices and reduces cost of equity capital. Kim and Singal (2000) also provide evidence that stock prices increase following liberalization of financial markets with no accompanying increase in the volatility of stock returns. Moreover the findings indicate that stock markets tend to become more efficient. Froot, O'Connell and Seasholes (2001) use daily international portfolio flows into 44 countries, including Turkey, to analyze the behavior of portfolio flows and their relationship with equity returns. Findings show that flows are strongly influenced by past returns, consistent with positive feedback trading views. They also note that inflows have statistically significant positive forecasting power for equity returns. In addition, they report a positive and large sensitivity of local stock prices to foreign inflows.

Clark and Berko (1997) find an economically and statistically significant positive correlation between monthly foreign purchases of Mexican stocks and Mexican stock returns. Their findings indicate that foreign purchases of 1% of market capitalization are associated with a 6% rise in market index. They do not find any evidence that foreign investors are positive feedback traders since the lagged monthly returns do not help forecast unpublicized flows.

Another stream of studies focuses on the destabilizing effects of foreign portfolio investments. Bohn and Tesar (1996) argue that U.S. investments in foreign markets are driven by the changing investment opportunities. Investors move into markets where returns are expected to be high and retreat from markets where predicted returns are low.

Choe, Kho and Stulz (1999) analysis how foreign investors trade and how they impact stock prices in Korea. They classify each transaction based on the type of investors and analyze the behavior of purchases by foreign investors during the trading day as well as across days. The results show clear evidence of positive feedback trading and herd behavior by foreign investors before the crisis. For example, foreign investors buy (sell) more Korean stocks on days following an increase (decrease) in the market as a whole and they buy (sell) Korean shares that outperformed (under performed) the market on the previous day. However, during the crisis period the evidence of positive feedback trading becomes much weaker. The study further concludes that foreign investors do not stabilize the market. Similar findings are reported by Wang and Shen (1999) who investigate whether portfolio investment has any influence on volatility of stock and foreign exchange market in Taiwan. Findings show that foreign portfolio investment increases the volatility of exchange rate but it has less influence on volatility of the stock market. This influence only accounts for a small fraction of stock market volatility.

There are two studies reporting an increase in volatility in domestic markets as a result of foreign capital flows. Aitken (1998) argues that the trend-chasing behavior of institutional investors has its destabilizing effect by resulting in asset price overshooting and bubble-like booms and busts. Bekaert and Harvey (2000) and Bekaert et al. (2003) investigate the impact of market liberalization in emerging equity markets on the cost of capital, volatility, and beta. Findings indicate that cost of capital declines and a small but insignificant increase in volatility is observed.

This study contributes literature in the following ways: First, it provides evidence from a highly inflationary emerging market. Second, it analyzes and reports the impact of foreign purchases not only on market indices but also on various sector portfolios. Third, unlike other studies this study uses individual firm data to measure the impact of foreign purchases on stock prices.

3. EVENTS AND CHARACTERISTICS OF TURKISH ECONOMY IN THE LAST DECADE AND THE TURKISH SECURITIES MARKET

Turkey liberalized its capital account in August 1989 when the government issued Decree No. 32 for the capital account transactions. With this development, the securities market in Turkey became fully open to foreign institutional and individual investors.

After the liberalization steps, capital flows increased significantly and the financial system became increasingly linked with external markets. While in most emerging market economies (specifically East Asia and Latin America) financial liberalization was accompanied or preceded by fiscal and structural reforms, this was not the case in Turkey. The new regime began under conditions of chronic and high inflation that averaged about 70% in the late 1980s. Due to persistently poor public finances, this situation continued throughout the 1990s and achieving stabilization still remains a challenge. Panel A of Table 1 outlines main economic indicators and capital flows to Turkey during the 1990s. Inflation has ranged between 38% and 60% annually while the average growth rate of GNP has been about 4% annually. Capital flows to Turkey have been associated with large public sector borrowing requirements and over time external flows have become increasingly important in financing the deficits that distorted the flow of funds in the domestic financial system in favor of the public sector. The large borrowing requirements have also been associated with growing a share of interest payments, and a large turnover of domestic debt. While a significant portion of capital accounts have been short-term borrowing and short-term portfolio flows, a predominant share of domestic public debt has been of short-term maturity. This problem has been the major limiting factor for the supply of loanable funds available for the private sector and the capital markets. Panel A of Table 1 further shows that portfolio investment constitutes a large percentage of net flows to Turkey. Portfolio investment ranges from 5% in 1995 to 73% in 1999.

During the 1990s, Turkey faced two major economic crises. First, the inconsistent mix of government policies in 1993 triggered devaluation expectations, a domestic demand led boom, and worsened export performance and trade deficit. When the crisis erupted in the first quarter of 1994, there was a massive outflow of capital, and the Turkish Lira depreciated by almost half in nominal terms.

Another critical event was the loss of the control in the measures of the Staff Monitored Program[1] in 1998 that was developed to stabilize the chronic inflation, this time because of an external factor that affected almost all of the emerging markets. The economic crisis in Russia in 1998 that was triggered by the Southeast

Table 1. Economic Indicators and Istanbul Stock Exchange.

Panel A: Main Economic Indicators and Capital Flows[a]

Years	GNP Growth	Inflation	Debt/GNP	Capital Account[b]	Portfolio Investment[b]	% of Flow	FDI[b]	% of Flow
1992	6.4	63.5	38.9	3,648	2,411	66.1	779	21.4
1993	8.1	67.4	38.8	8,963	3,917	43.7	622	6.9
1994	−6.1	107.3	51.2	−4,194	1,158	n.a.	559	n.a.
1995	8.0	87.2	44.1	4,643	237	5.1	772	16.6
1996	7.1	78.0	47.1	5,555	570	10.3	612	11.0
1997	8.3	81.2	46.6	7,053	1,634	23.1	554	7.9
1998	3.9	75.3	47.9	−755	−6,711	n.a.	573	n.a.
1999	−6.1	55.8	58.7	4,671	3,429	73.4	138	3.0
2000	6.1	51.6	59.9	9,445	1,022	10.8	112	1.2

Panel B: Istanbul Stock Exchange[c]

Years	Number of Firms	Number of Shares Traded (Millions)	Traded Value (Million USD)	Market Value of Firms (Million USD)
1992	145	10,285.6	8,567	9,992
1993	160	35,249.0	21,771	37,824
1994	176	100,062.0	23,203	21,785
1995	205	306,253.7	52,357	20,782
1996	228	390,917.2	37,737	30,797
1997	258	919,783.7	58,104	61,879
1998	277	2,242,531.2	70,396	33,975
1999	285	5,823,858.2	84,034	114,271
2000	315	11,075,684.2	181,937	69,507

a: Sources: Central Bank of the Republic of Turkey and Turkish Treasury.
[b] In million USD.
[c] *Source:* Istanbul Stock Exchange.

Asian crisis in 1997 resulted in a massive capital flight (over $6 billion) from Turkey. The capital outflow resulted in liquidity squeeze with a rise in the level and the volatility of interest rates. With the rise in interest rates and the liquidity problem the Treasury's debt program was detrimentally affected by the increased cost of debt financing and decreased maturity of the debt.

The Turkish banking system had become vulnerable to shifts in market confidence with its integration in international financial markets in the last decade. The banks borrowed abroad in response to macroeconomic imbalances to benefit from high interest rates on domestic loans and government securities. During this process banks exposed themselves to interest rate risk, to foreign exchange risk, and to large credit risk. For example, the trigger for the November 2000 crisis was the emergence of financial problems in mid-sized banks that had positioned themselves aggressively for continuing decline in interest rates via longer-term investments that were highly leveraged by short-term funds.

The Istanbul Stock Exchange (ISE) is the only stock exchange in Turkey, and began operations in 1986 following the setting up of the Capital Market Board in 1982. The ISE has shown tremendous growth since its establishment. Panel B of Table 1 reports the development of the ISE during the 1990s. The number of companies traded on the exchange climbed from 145 at the end of 1992 to 315 at the end of 2000. There are currently four different markets: National Market, Regional Market, New Companies Market, and Watch-List Companies Market. However, most of the firms (93.4%) are traded at National Market. The total market capitalization of the firms traded has increased from $938 million at the end of 1986 to $114.2 billion at the end of 1999. A similar trend is observed in trading value over the years. It has sharply increased from $13 million in 1986 to over $181 billion in 2000.

The major milestone in the Turkish financial liberalization process was the government's issuance of Decree No. 32 in 1989 regarding capital account transactions. With the declaration of Decree No. 32 in the Official Gazette, the securities market in Turkey became fully open to foreign institutional and individual investors. Under the decree, nonresidents were allowed to buy and sell Turkish securities through intermediary institutions operating in Turkey. They were also permitted to transfer income and the sales proceeds of these securities abroad through banks and other authorized financial institutions. With Decree No. 32 Turkish citizens were allowed to purchase securities issued by foreign countries through authorized financial institutions. They were also permitted to transfer the foreign exchange required to purchase such securities abroad.

There has been a considerable increase in the proportion of shares held by foreign residents in ISE, which creates the proper laboratory for our analysis to examine their effects on the equity returns. Foreign holdings of the market capitalization reached more than 10% in 2000, as compared to less than 5% in 1990. At the end of April 2000, the highest level in net equity investments by foreign investors reached approximately $15 billion with the positive prospects of the stabilization program supported by the IMF.

4. DATA AND METHODOLOGY

4.1. Data

We investigate the relationship between foreign capital flows and the ISE equity prices using monthly data. We normalize the net foreign purchases data by rationing the net foreign purchases to the market capitalization of individual equities in percentages. The sample period spans from January 1997 to December 2000 and covers the entire period from when ISE started to collect the foreign transactions data from its member brokerage houses. We further classify the entire sample of firms into various subgroups by using their industry classification. Accordingly, we form 15 portfolios and investigate the impact of foreign purchases on each portfolio in addition to the overall analysis of the ISE Index. Furthermore, we separate the foreign capital flow data to the Turkish equities into expected and unexpected net foreign purchases as a percentage of market capitalization.

Our additional variables in the sector analysis include the ISE Index returns and the percentage changes in the Turkish Lira/U.S. Dollar exchange rate.[2] The individual stock price returns and market capitalization statistics were collected from Istanbul Stock Exchange. The individual stock returns were measured using the percentage change in the end-of-month stock prices in nominal Turkish Lira and the U.S. Dollar.

4.2. Methodology

Our study analyzes the impact of net foreign purchases on Turkish stocks. Following Clark and Berko (1997), our first regression has the following form:

$$\text{Return}_t = \beta_0 + \beta_1 \times \left(\frac{\text{NP}_t}{\text{MCAP}_{t-1}}\right) + \varepsilon_t \tag{1}$$

Where; Return_t is the return on stocks in the sector being analyzed during month t, NP_t is the net foreign purchase of Turkish equity at time t, MCAP_{t-1} is the

Turkish market capitalization in previous period. We would expect to reject the null that the coefficient on net purchases, β_1, equals zero in favor of the one sided alternative: $\beta_1 > 0$.

4.2.1. Expected Versus Unexpected Inflows

According to the efficient market hypothesis, relevant information available at the start of the period should already be reflected in the price of assets at the start of the period. In this case, the β_1 coefficient would understate the impact of foreign inflows on the equities traded at the ISE, since foreign demand that is expected pushes prices to a higher equilibrium level ahead of those inflows. In addition, it is the arrival of new information that causes investors to raise their estimate of total foreign inflows, which should push prices to a higher level.

Accordingly, we decomposed capital flows into expected and unexpected components and then regressed returns on both expected and unexpected foreign capital flows separately and together in different regression equations. In order to segregate the capital flows into expected and unexpected components we assumed that investors forecast the future evolution of the investor base by studying realized flows with a time series for net purchases:

$$\mathrm{NP}_t = \mathrm{A(L)NP}_{t-1} + \mathrm{B(L)}\Omega_{t-1} +_t \tag{2}$$

Where Ω_{t-1} is a vector of other variables useful for forecasting net purchases. Then, observations in this time series of net purchases can serve as a proxy measure for expectational revisions to the time path of investor inflows.

We define unexpected net purchases, $\mathrm{U}_t(\mathrm{NP}_t/\mathrm{MCAP}_{t-1})$, as being equal to observed purchases minus investor's expectation of net purchases, $\mathrm{E}_t(\mathrm{NP}_t/\mathrm{MCAP}_{t-1})$, i.e. $\mathrm{U}_t(\mathrm{NP}_t/\mathrm{MCAP}_{t-1}) \equiv \mathrm{NP}_t/\mathrm{MCAP}_{t-1} - \mathrm{E}_t(\mathrm{NP}_t/\mathrm{MCAP}_{t-1})$. We further test the following regression for each of the 15 sub-sectors and in the ISE Index.

$$\mathrm{Return}_t = \beta_0 + \beta_1 \mathrm{E}_t\left(\frac{\mathrm{NP}_t}{\mathrm{MCAP}_{t-1}}\right) + \beta_2 \mathrm{U}_t\left(\frac{\mathrm{NP}_t}{\mathrm{MCAP}_{t-1}}\right) + \varepsilon_t \tag{3}$$

In this regression we would expect to find that returns would show significant co-variance with unexpected inflows, but less co-variance with expected inflows:

$$\mathrm{B}_2 > \beta_1 \geq 0$$

4.2.2. The Additional Variables

There might be some variables that are correlated with foreign capital inflows to ISE and that also cause prices of the equities to move simultaneously. In this case, the correlation between foreign capital inflows and equity prices may reflect the influence of these third factors, and not the independent effect of foreign capital moves. To measure the possible bias caused by these third factors, we added two additional control variables to our regression analysis: the ISE Index returns and the percentage changes in the Turkish Lira/U.S. Dollar exchange rate.

$$\text{Return}_t = \beta_0 + \beta_1 \text{E}_t \left(\frac{\text{NP}_t}{\text{MCAP}_{t-1}}\right) + \beta_2 \text{U}_t \left(\frac{\text{NP}_t}{\text{MCAP}_{t-1}}\right) + \beta_3 \text{ISEINDEX}_{t-1} + \varepsilon_t \quad (4)$$

$$\text{Return}_t = \beta_0 + \beta_1 \text{E}_t \left(\frac{\text{NP}_t}{\text{MCAP}_{t-1}}\right) + \beta_2 \text{U}_t \left(\frac{\text{NP}_t}{\text{MCAP}_{t-1}}\right) + \beta_3 \text{FXRATE}_{t-1} + \varepsilon_t \quad (5)$$

5. EMPIRICAL RESULTS

5.1. Returns and Total Foreign Capital Flows

The relationship between the foreign purchases of Turkish stocks and the ISE index returns are reported in Table 2. Both U.S. dollars and Turkish Lira based index returns are used. Each panel in Table 2 outlines four different regression results. The first one relates the index returns to net foreign purchases. The second and third regression use the unexpected and expected net foreign purchases respectively. Finally, fourth regression employs both expected and unexpected net foreign purchases components of foreign purchases.

Panel A of Table 2 reports Turkish Lira (TL) based analysis. Net purchases of foreign investors have statistically highly significant positive impact on the index returns with a coefficient of 0.026. When we decompose purchases expected and unexpected components and analyze the impact of each on index return, we notice that only the unexpected component has a statistically significant impact on index returns. U.S. dollars based analysis is also reported in Panel B of Table 2. The findings are similar to those of Panel A even though the magnitude of coefficients is slightly different. The regression coefficient, foreign net purchases of 1% of market capitalization are associated with about 2.4% rise in the ISE Index. This value is also much smaller also when compared with the study of Clark and Berko (1997) where they obtained a 6% figure for the same regression equation in the Bolsa index in Mexico during the period from January 1989 to March 1996. However, as can be seen from Table 2, the regression coefficient on capital inflows did not rise with this replacement, and the regression R square decreased slightly

Table 2. The Impact of Foreign Purchases on ISE Index.

	1	2	3	4
Panel A: The impact of foreign purchases on the Turkish Lira denominated ISE Index				
CONSTANT	0.067	0.056	0.054	0.054
	(2.31)**	(2.06)**	(1.87)*	(1.99)*
NETFPTL	0.026			
	(2.76)***			
UNETFPTL		0.024		0.024
		(2.66)***		(2.65)***
ENETFPTL			0.055	0.055
			(0.89)	(0.95)
R^2	0.142	0.135	0.017	0.153
Adj. R^2	0.123	0.116	−0.004	0.114
F-value	6.594	5.642	2.260	4.055
Panel A: The impact of foreign purchases on the US Dollar denominated ISE Index				
CONSTANT	0.021	0.016	0.007	0.007
	(0.72)	(0.62)	(0.12)	(0.12)
NETFPUS	0.024			
	(0.09)			
UNETFPUS		0.023		0.023
		(2.50)**		(2.47)**
ENETFPUS			0.033	0.032
			(0.16)	(0.19)
R^2	0.118	0.122	0.001	0.123
Adj. R^2	0.099	0.102	−0.022	0.083
F-value	3.574	3.327	0.184	2.180

*, **, and *** indicate statistical significance at 10%, 5%, and 1%, level, respectively.

in Turkish Lira ISE Index. These results are also contrary to our expectations. In a similar study where Clark and Berko (1997) replaced total equity inflows with surprise unpublicized inflows in their Bolsa Index study in Mexico, both their regression coefficient and the regression R square rose. Overall, we conclude that there is a statistically significant relationship between the net purchases of foreign investors and the ISE market index return.

Table 3 reports the impact of net foreign purchases on returns of various industries. The findings indicate that there are differences among industries with respect to sensitivity to foreign purchases. The only industries that show a insignificant negative relation between net foreign purchases as a percentage of market capitalization and industry monthly returns, which are contrary to our expectations, are Metal, Insurance, and Investment Trust industries. The remaining 12 industries experience a positive correlation between industry returns and foreign purchases. Four of these twelve industries (Chemical, Tourism,

Table 3. The Impact of Net Foreign Purchases on Various Sectors.

$$\text{Return}_t = \beta_0 + \beta_1 \times \left(\frac{\text{NP}_t}{\text{MCAP}_{t-1}}\right)$$

Sectors	β_0	β_1	R^2	F-value
Manufacturing				
Food/beverage	0.007	9.397	0.034	3.54
	(2.59)**	(1.28)		
Textile	0.049	4.387	0.001	1.58
	(1.68)*	(0.19)		
Chemical	0.089	57.690	0.036	4.51
	(2.89)***	(1.66)*		
Paper products	0.071	2.974	0.002	3.34
	(2.57)**	(0.31)		
Metal	7.539	138.830	0.001	2.73
	(2.30)**	(0.050)		
Cement	0.072	13.328	0.016	3.50
	(2.65)**	(0.86)		
Basic metal	0.054	−0.823	0.017	2.33
	(1.81)*	(−0.88)		
Other manufacturing	0.091	10.798	0.007	4.24
	(2.91)***	(0.54)		
Service/retail				
Tourism	0.071	19.787	0.082	3.96
	(2.27) **	(2.02) **		
Wholesale/retail	0.091	65.428	0.053	5.24
	(2.96)***	(1.91)*		
Financials				
Banks	0.072	5.236	0.001	2.95
	(2.43)**	(0.11)		
Holding	0.089	125.050	0.093	6.22
	(2.72)***	(2.41)**		
Insurance	0.083	−3.999	0.007	2.63
	(2.28)**	(−0.73)		
Leasing	0.052	3.547	0.006	2.08
	(1.61)	(1.14)		
Investment trusts	0.078	−72.315	0.009	2.99
	(2.22)**	(−0.65)		

*, **, and *** indicate statistical significance at 10%, 5%, and 1% level, respectively.

Wholesale/Retail, and Holding) show statistically significant positive relations to net purchases of foreign investors.

According to the efficient market hypothesis, the impact of expected inflows might already be reflected in the prices of the equities at the start of the period. Hence, in order to perceive the sole impact of unexpected inflows on equity returns and test for this hypothesis we decompose the net purchases of equity into expected and unexpected components. The results for industry analysis are reported in Table 4.

Tourism and Wholesale/Retail industry returns are influenced by both expected and unexpected components of foreign purchases. The metal industry is only influenced by expected purchases of foreign investors while the holding sector is mostly influenced by unexpected purchases of foreign investors.

To control for market movement and exchange rate movements, we added two additional variables in our analysis. Tables 5 and 6 report the impact of these variables along with expected and unexpected components of foreign purchases. The additional variables employed explain a significant share of equity returns in all sectors. Table 5 includes the return on the ISE composite index as an explanatory variable in addition to the expected and unexpected purchases of foreign investors. The explanatory power of the model increases drastically for each of the sectors. The coefficient of the ISE index return is statistically highly significant for each of the sectors. There are statistically significant inverse relationships between the expected purchases and industry returns for Chemical, Holding, and Insurance groups. Tourism and Wholesale/Retail sectors, on the other hand, experience positive significant relationships between industry returns and the expected and unexpected purchases of foreign investors respectively.[3]

In Table 6 we take into account the impact of depreciation/appreciation of Turkish Lira against U.S. dollars. The returns in each sector are highly sensitive to the changes in exchange rates as well. Some of the industry returns are explained by both expected/unexpected purchases of foreigners while controlling for the foreign exchange movements. For example, while the Metal industry returns are influenced by the expected purchases of foreign investors, Tourism, Wholesale/Retail, and Holding industry returns are influenced by the unexpected component of the purchases of foreign investors.

Overall, the analysis of industry based returns and the foreign capital flow show that there are substantial differences among industries with respect to the flow of foreign capital. Returns in Chemical, Tourism, Wholesale/Retail, Holding, Metal, and Insurance are influenced significantly by the purchases of foreign investors while other industries are not very sensitive to the purchases of foreign investors.

Table 4. The Impact of Expected and Unexpected Foreign Purchases on Various Sectors.

$$\text{Return}_t = \beta_0 + \beta_1 \text{E}_t\left(\frac{\text{NP}_t}{\text{MCAP}_{t-1}}\right) + \beta_2 \text{U}_t\left(\frac{\text{NP}_t}{\text{MCAP}_{t-1}}\right)$$

Sectors	β_0	β_1	β_2	R^2	F-value
Manufacturing					
Food/beverage	0.040	−11.052	7.781	0.024	1.81
	(0.29)	(−0.08)	(1.03)		
Textile	0.066	45.546	5.976	0.004	0.86
	(0.79)	(0.31)	(0.26)		
Chemical	0.065	2.627	51.828	0.046	2.34
	(1.37)	(0.02)	(1.46)		
Paper products	0.028	−48.717	−0.370	0.003	1.82
	(0.28)	(−0.36)	(−0.04)		
Metal	44.580	199.682	517.310	0.060	2.50
	(1.94)*	(1.66)*	(0.21)		
Cement	0.091	72.662	14.561	0.033	2.18
	(1.69)*	(0.74)	(0.98)		
Basic metal	−0.159	−512.351	−2.933	0.033	1.43
	(−0.89)	(−1.18)	(−0.32)		
Other manufacturing	0.098	88.011	5.569	0.053	3.18
	(3.05)***	(1.54)	(0.28)		
Service/retail					
Tourism	0.146	149.771	16.314	0.121	3.05
	(2.40)**	(1.80)*	(1.67)*		
Wholesale/retail	−0.030	−506.660	68.332	0.150	4.60
	(−0.49)	(−1.84)*	(2.08)**		
Financials					
Banks	0.069	150.300	−13.633	0.002	2.43
	(2.27)**	(0.73)	(−0.28)		
Holding	0.041	−736.820	124.950	0.138	4.17
	(0.85)	(−0.95)	(2.47)**		
Insurance	0.065	1.397	−4.423	0.008	1.36
	(1.81)*	(0.08)	(−0.58)		
Leasing	0.048	−8.824	1.864	0.008	0.79
	(1.43)	(−0.23)	(0.57)		
Investment trusts	0.061	−268.590	−74.716	0.011	1.71
	(0.75)	(−0.19)	(−0.66)		

*, **, and *** indicate statistical significance at 10%, 5%, and 1% level, respectively.

Table 5. The Impact of Foreign Purchases and the ISE Market Index on Various Sectors.

$$\text{Return}_t = \beta_0 + \beta_1 \text{E}_t\left(\frac{\text{NP}_t}{\text{MCAP}_{t-1}}\right) + \beta_2 \text{U}_t\left(\frac{\text{NP}_t}{\text{MCAP}_{t-1}}\right) + \beta_3 \text{ISEINDEX}_{t-1}$$

Sectors	β_0	β_1	β_2	β_3	R^2	F-value
Manufacturing						
Food/beverage	0.020	7.691	1.254	0.719	0.712	30.23
	(0.27)	(0.11)	(0.30)	(10.14)***		
Textile	0.016	30.176	−20.206	0.742	0.649	21.57
	(0.32)	(0.34)	(−1.45)	(8.89)***		
Chemical	−0.013	−90.240	11.259	0.926	0.854	70.73
	(−0.66)	(−1.72)*	(0.78)	(15.43)***		
Paper products	0.028	−47.765	−0.588	0.775	0.739	35.44
	(0.28)	(−0.67)	(−0.12)	(11.02)***		
Metal	12.008	577.230	−662.810	0.958	0.841	63.87
	(1.94)*	(1.11)	(−0.65)	(14.56)***		
Cement	0.019	10.101	−0.730	0.737	0.744	35.82
	(0.67)	(0.19)	(−0.09)	(10.92)***		
Basic metal	−0.026	−67.953	−2.916	0.837	0.774	39.78
	(−0.31)	(−0.31)	(−0.66)	(11.88)**		
Other manufacturing	0.024	−15.230	11.935	0.899	0.755	39.58
	(1.37)	(−0.49)	(1.18)	(11.10)***		
Service/retail						
Tourism	0.068	101.240	3.039	0.870	0.690	26.09
	(1.84)*	(2.01)**	(0.50)	(8.888)***		
Wholesale/retail	−0.016	−182.200	36.861	0.907	0.844	66.56
	(−0.61)	(−1.50)	(2.57)**	(13.87) ***		
Financials						
Banks	0.013	−3.615	1.606	0.892	0.817	54.09
	(0.97)	(−0.04)	(0.08)	(13.72)***		
Holding	−0.008	−465.950	−15.243	1.113	0.901	109.55
	(−0.51)	(−1.77)*	(−0.80)	(18.21)***		
Insurance	0.021	−14.921	−2.015	1.004	0.719	30.75
	(1.07)	(−1.72)*	(−0.48)	(10.44) ***		
Leasing	−0.010	19.424	2.786	0.939	0.699	26.62
	(−0.52)	(0.91)	(1.51)	(9.94)***		
Investment trusts	0.023	−36.235	−8.732	0.897	0.568	16.74
	(0.43)	(−0.03)	(−0.11)	(7.45)***		

*, **, and *** indicate statistical significance at 10%, 5%, and 1% level, respectively.

Table 6. The Impact of Foreign Purchases and Foreign Exchange Rate on Sectors.

$$\text{Return}_t = \beta_0 + \beta_1 \text{E}_t\left(\frac{\text{NP}_t}{\text{MCAP}_{t-1}}\right) + \beta_2 \text{U}_t\left(\frac{\text{NP}_t}{\text{MCAP}_{t-1}}\right) + \beta_3 \text{FXRATE}_{t-1} + \varepsilon_t$$

Sectors	β_0	β_1	β_2	β_3	R^2	F-value
Manufacturing						
Food/beverage	−0.091	9.346	7.584	3.912	0.206	4.11
	(−0.69)	(0.08)	(1.11)	(3.14)***		
Textile	−0.034	77.214	7.818	2.971	0.097	1.82
	(−0.37)	(0.54)	(0.36)	(2.11)**		
Chemical	−0.124	18.360	44.684	4.944	0.256	5.24
	(−1.80)*	(0.16)	(1.40)	(3.48)***		
Paper products	−0.151	−15.154	−5.805	5.156	0.279	5.98
	(−1.58)	(−0.13)	(−0.69)	(4.06)***		
Metal	22.372	184.080	423.120	491.230	0.236	4.74
	(1.01)	(1.68)*	(0.19)	(3.15)***		
Cement	−0.073	43.427	8.292	3.822	0.202	4.22
	(−0.99)	(0.48)	(0.59)	(3.02)***		
Basic metal	−0.314	−506.080	−0.209	4.231	0.202	3.56
	(−1.89)*	(−1.25)	(−0.03)	(3.02)***		
Other manufacturing	−0.089	75.131	6.654	4.713	0.239	5.53
	(−1.38)	(1.45)	(0.37)	(3.23)***		
Service/retail						
Tourism	0.053	117.450	15.624	4.587	0.267	4.83
	(−0.60)	(1.51)	(1.73)*	(2.93)***		
Wholesale/retail	−0.178	−402.980	65.219	4.294	0.292	6.21
	(−2.34)**	(−1.56)	(2.16)**	(2.04)**		
Financials						
Banks	−0.157	101.290	−36.774	5.668	0.296	6.15
	(−2.64)**	(0.54)	(−0.89)	(4.15)***		
Holding	−0.110	−39.102	86.848	4.681	0.253	5.18
	(−1.49)	(−0.05)	(1.74)*	(2.57)**		
Insurance	−0.158	4.927	−8.492	5.628	0.203	3.88
	(−2.07)**	(0.34)	(−1.20)	(3.25)***		
Leasing	−0.188	−12.236	0.051	6.057	0.259	4.40
	(−2.73)***	(−0.36)	(0.01)	(3.81)***		
Investment trusts	−0.103	928.600	−76.040	5.812	0.202	4.13
	(−1.14)	(0.70)	(−0.74)	(3.21)***		

*, **, and *** indicate statistical significance at 10%, 5%, and 1% level, respectively.

6. CONCLUSION

This study investigates the impact of foreign direct investment on the stocks of a highly inflationary emerging market, the Istanbul Stock Exchange. The data includes monthly returns of firms traded at ISE along with the monthly foreign purchases/sales of stocks, the ISE index returns, and Turkish Lira/U.S. Dollar exchange rates during the period of January 1997 thorough December 2000.

Our findings show that there is a strong relationship between the foreign purchases of Turkish stocks and the ISE index returns. Net purchases of foreign investors have a statistically highly significant positive impact on index returns with much of the effect being from the unexpected component of the purchases of foreign investors. Clark and Berko (1997) report similar results in their study of the Mexican stock market.

We further analyze the impact of net foreign purchases on returns of various sectors. The magnitude of impact by net foreign purchases differs for each sector portfolio. While three industries show an insignificant negative relation with foreign purchases, the remaining twelve industries exhibit a positive relationship between industry returns and foreign purchases. When we control for the existence of other variables (i.e. the ISE Index return and Turkish Lira/U.S dollar exchange rates), we note that the purchases by foreign investors continues to be an important factor influencing stock return for certain industries. Particularly, returns in Chemical, Tourism, Wholesale/Retail, Holding, Metal and Insurance are influenced significantly by the purchases of foreign investors.

The results from our study of the foreign purchases and equity return linkage are in conformity with the belief that foreign capital inflows to emerging equity markets have an important impact on emerging market equity returns. In the Turkish market on average foreign net purchases of 1% of market capitalization are associated with 2.6% rise in the ISE Index.

NOTES

1. With the Staff Monitored Program, the Central Bank had announced a new monetary program in July 1998 that was aimed at targeting a new monetary aggregate on the Central Bank's balance sheet that was the net domestic debt.

2. We also use various exchange rates (i.e. Turkish Lira/German Mark exchange rate, Turkish Lira/Euro exchange rate, and Turkish Lira/Basket (Euro and US Dollar) exchange rate. The results are similar to TL/US Dollar exchange rates and hence are not reported.

3. We also take into account the fact that industry returns and the ISE index returns may be highly correlated and hence the unexpected returns portion of the ISE index return is used as an additional explanatory variable. The results are similar to previous findings that

the unexpected ISE returns explain the greatest portion of the variations in industry returns, and these results hold across all industries.

REFERENCES

Aitken, B. (1998). Have institutional investors destabilized emerging markets? *Contemporary Economic Policy*, *16*, 173–184.

Bekaert, G., & Harvey, C. R. (2000). Foreign speculators and emerging equity markets. *Journal of Finance*, *55*, 565–611.

Bekaert, G., Harvey, C. R., & Lundblad, C. T. (2003). Equity market liberalization in emerging markets. *Journal of Financial Research*, *26*, 275–299.

Bohn, H., & Tesar, L. L. (1996). U.S. equity investment in foreign markets: Portfolio rebalancing or return chasing? *The American Economic Review*, *86*, 77–81.

Brennan, M. J., & Cao, H. H. (1997). International portfolio investment flows. *Journal of Finance*, *52*, 1851–1880.

Choe, H., Kho, B. C., & Stulz, R. M. (1999). Do foreign investors destabilize stock markets? The Korean experience in 1997. *Journal of Financial Economics*, *54*, 227–264.

Clark, J., & Berko, E. (1997). Foreign Investment fluctuations and emerging market stock returns: The Case of Mexico. *Reserve Bank of New York Staff Reports 24*.

Froot, K. A., O'Connell, P., & Seasholes, M. (2001). The portfolio flows of international investors. *Journal of Financial Economics*, *59*, 151–194.

Henry, P. B. (2000). Stock market liberalization, economic reform, and emerging market equity prices. *Journal of Finance*, *55*, 529–564.

Kim, E. H., & Singal, V. (2000). Stock market openings: Experience of emerging economies. *Journal of Business*, *73*, 25–66.

Wang, L., & Shen, C. (1999). Do foreign investments affect foreign exchange and stock markets – the case of Taiwan. *Applied Economics*, *31*, 1303–1314.